THE I TATTI
RENAISSANCE LIBRARY

James Hankins, General Editor

PIUS II
COMMENTARIES

VOLUME I

ITRL 12

PIUS II

COMMENTARIES

VOLUME I • BOOKS I–II

EDITED BY

MARGARET MESERVE

AND

MARCELLO SIMONETTA

THE I TATTI RENAISSANCE LIBRARY
HARVARD UNIVERSITY PRESS
CAMBRIDGE, MASSACHUSETTS
LONDON, ENGLAND
2003

Printed in the United States of America

Series design by Dean Bornstein

Library of Congress Cataloging-in-Publication Data

Pius II, Pope, 1405–1464.
[Commentarii rerum memorabilium. English & Latin]
Commentaries / Pius II ; edited by Margaret Meserve and Marcello Simonetta.
p. cm — (The I Tatti Renaissance library)
Includes bibliographical references and index.
ISBN 0-674-01164-3 (v. 1 : cloth : alk. paper)
1. Pius II, Pope, 1405–1464. 2. Church history — Middle Ages, 600 — 1500.
3. Popes — Biography. I. Meserve, Margaret.
II. Simonetta, Marcello, 1968– III. Title. IV. Series.
BX1308.P5813 2003
282′.092 — dc22
[B] 2003056659

Contents

Introduction

> We have not cheated the people of the time that is owed them, for we have never missed a mass nor a private nor public consistory, and we have denied no supplicant a hearing. Rather, in our old age we have deprived ourselves of rest . . . These are labors of the night, for we have borrowed the hours owed to sleep and spent the better part of them on our writing. Another man, it is true, might have used his watch better, but I felt an obligation to my mind, which took such delight in the task.[1]

So wrote Pope Pius II in 1462, during one of the busiest and tensest periods of his six-year tenure of the papal throne. The task he referred to was the encyclopedic treatise on the history and geography of Asia that he had just completed, part of a projected *Cosmographia*, or universal history of the world. In taking on this ambitious venture, the pope continued a long habit of balancing the duties of a political career with the calling of his literary muse. As a young law student, later as a secretary, ambassador, bishop, cardinal and finally pope, Aeneas Silvius Piccolomini always thought of himself, and often signed himself, as a man of letters, *orator* and *poeta*, proud bearer of a laurel crown. In his youth he wrote love poems and classical comedy; during his long years of imperial and papal service he turned out a steady stream of histories, dialogues, didactic treatises, biographies, orations and letters. Nor was the *Asia* the only work he composed while pope. Between 1458 and his death in 1464, he completed a *History of Bohemia* (begun the summer before his election), an epitome of Flavio Biondo's *Decades* of Roman history, several ringing orations invoking a crusade against the Turks, his famous letter to Sultan

Mehmed II and — his longest, most engaging and most enduring monument — the *Commentaries*, the story of his life. Written in spare hours, sometimes in his own hand and sometimes by dictation to secretaries, in the dead of night, at odd moments between meetings or in the course of his long peregrinations through Italy, even when arthritis and gout confined him to his bed, the *Commentaries* are a unique document in the history of Renaissance literature. The only autobiography ever written by a reigning pope, they offer a vivid portrait of a Renaissance man and a very typically Renaissance career, set against the background of a continent in turmoil, and an age of conflict and dispute.

Aeneas Silvius Piccolomini was born in the Tuscan village of Corsignano on October 18, 1405.[2] His mother and father were both of noble Sienese birth, though from families that had seen more prosperous days. Aeneas grew up in conditions of near-poverty on the family's one remaining farm. After learning the rudiments of grammar from the local parish priest, he went up to the city at age eighteen to study literature and law at the University of Siena. There followed a period of travel in 1429–31, about which little is known save that Aeneas made a tour of northern Italian schools and universities and spent some time in Florence studying with the humanist scholar Francesco Filelfo.[3]

By 1431 he was back in Siena, unemployed and apparently uninspired by the prospect of the legal career for which his education had prepared him. Though the preaching of San Bernardino, the great Sienese reformer, affected him deeply and he briefly considered joining the Franciscans, in the end he found his calling in a different sort of service, in the retinue of Cardinal Domenico Capranica, a wealthy prelate who passed through Siena in the autumn of 1431 on his way to the Council of Basel. Capranica offered Aeneas a post in his household as his secretary, responsible for composing his letters, writing his speeches and performing similar administrative duties. For the young student, it was a welcome op-

portunity—to get out of Siena, to start earning money and, not least, to attend and participate in the most momentous political assembly of his day. The Council of Basel had recently convened to consider questions of church reform and to try to impose certain limits on papal authority; powerful cardinals and prominent representatives of most European states frequented its deliberations.[4] At the Council, Aeneas soon found new employment, moving nimbly from the service of one prelate to another as opportunities arose. Notoriously, he undertook a covert diplomatic mission to Scotland on behalf of Niccolò Albergati, the powerful cardinal of Santa Croce, a journey which not only provided him with some of the most entertaining anecdotes he would later recount in the *Commentaries*, but also irreparably damaged his feet, leaving him nearly lame for much of his later life.

Back in Basel, Aeneas adopted the prevailing anti-papal stance of the Council and soon obtained a prominent post in the Council's bureaucracy, chairing committees, leading embassies and composing important communiqués. In 1439, when the assembled delegates deposed Eugenius IV and hailed the reclusive Duke Amadeus VIII of Savoy as their new pope, it was Aeneas who was dispatched to serve as his personal secretary. But life at the court of Felix V (as the antipope styled himself) was tedious by comparison to the intrigues and frequent opportunities for oratorical display that the Council had provided, and by 1440 Aeneas had managed a transfer to the imperial chancery of Frederick III.

His position in Austria had its disadvantages, too—the weather was cold, the work dull, and his German colleagues unfriendly—but the move was politic. The Council of Basel had come under the sway of an intransigent French faction and was fast losing the support of moderates in the Church. The Savoyard Felix V had failed to win a following; Aeneas could see that his fortunes lay elsewhere. His enthusiasm for the conciliar position fading, he took orders in 1446, received profitable benefices from

both Eugenius and Frederick, and led a series of imperial embassies to Italy where he did much to effect a reconciliation between the emperor and pope. As a reward for his services, Eugenius made him an apostolic secretary, a position he held both during this pontificate and that of Eugenius's successor, Nicholas v. (He did not know, he later noted, "whether anyone else has ever had the good luck . . . to serve as secretary to two popes, an emperor and an antipope.")[5] His ascent through the ecclesiastical ranks was astonishingly quick: he was made a bishop, first of Trieste in 1447, and then of his native Siena in 1451; was created cardinal of Santa Sabina by Pope Calixtus III in 1456; and just two years later was elected by his fellow cardinals Pope Pius II.

From his initial position as a leading conciliar theorist, dedicated to imposing firm limits on papal power, Aeneas had come to embrace, and in the end himself embody, the supremacy of Rome. Now he saw little reason why pontifical authority should be restrained. In the six years of his reign he tried everywhere to extend and secure the pope's right to command: in matters of church governance, including the appointment of bishops and the collection of tithes; in the Papal States, where the Roman barons continually challenged the temporal lordship of the pope; in international relations, especially on the troublesome issues of ecclesiastical sovereignty in France, heresy in Bohemia and the Neapolitan succession; and above all in the defense of Christian Europe against the Ottoman Empire, where the mercantile and political interests of competing Western states threatened fatally to undermine papal efforts to lead a new crusade against the Turks.

The political crises which demanded the pope's attention were, many of them, the same as had shaped and directed the course of his earlier career; many would continue to vex Europe for the rest of the fifteenth century. One of the great attractions of Aeneas' autobiography is the vivid insight he offers into these contemporary

problems, often from the standpoint of an eyewitness observer of the main characters and events. At the Council of Basel, where Aeneas launched his career, two of the era's most bitter contemporary conflicts approached—but did not reach—resolution. These were, first, the contest between the pope and the universal church "in council" for supreme ecclesiastical authority; and, second, the papacy's (and by extension, Italy's) continuing effort to extract itself from the political grasp of the kingdom of France. The popes had spent the better part of the fourteenth century in residence in Avignon, and Gregory XI's attempt to restore the Holy See to Rome in 1378 had resulted in chaotic failure. The Great Schism that ensued saw antipopes excommunicating one another from rival courts in France and Italy, a woeful state of affairs which only a general synod of the church, the Council of Constance (1414–1417), was able to settle. The council's choice fell on Oddone Colonna, a Roman who, as Pope Martin V, made a triumphant return to the Vatican in 1420, and thereupon promptly disavowed the declaration of conciliar supremacy that had been the price of his election. His successor Eugenius IV proved even bolder an autocrat, and soon found himself called to account by a new generation of conciliarists at Basel.

The Basel coalition of prelates and theologians challenged Eugenius's claims to *plenitudo potestatis,* insisting instead on the need for consensus or at least consultation between the pope and other members of the Church in matters of ecclesiastical governance. The conciliarists derived their intellectual leadership, as well as many of their best arguments, from the theology faculty of the University of Paris. It was the intransigence of the French representatives that eventually drove Aeneas away from Basel altogether; and years later, in the conclave of 1458, a French cardinal, Guillaume d'Estouteville, would fiercely oppose Aeneas's election to the papal throne. The new pope's decision to acknowledge Ferrante, the bastard son of Alfonso of Aragon, as legitimate heir

to the crown of Naples over the claims of René of Anjou only worsened the tensions between France and Rome. Throughout the pope's reign, Louis XI would throw up obstacles to his policies, often through the intervention of his creature Cardinal Jean Jouffroy, who is cast, alongside d'Estouteville, as one of the chief villains of the *Commentaries*. Louis also exerted constant and frequently dangerous pressure on Milan (which, like Naples, had attracted French claims to its succession); he also undermined the pope's efforts to raise funds and political support for his projected crusade.

Relations among the rest of the European powers were as fraught as those between France and Rome, and likewise proved detrimental to the policies Pope Pius hoped to pursue. England, Scotland, Burgundy and France remained locked in wary stalemate even after the conclusion of the Hundred Years' War in 1453. Although Philip of Burgundy made frequent chivalrous gestures in support of the crusade, continuing troubles on his own borders kept him from offering as much tangible support as he—and the pope—would have liked. The crowns of central Europe carried their own share of tarnish. The Habsburg Frederick III managed only sporadic attempts to impose his rule over the Holy Roman Empire. Frederick faced constant challenges from his electors (most notoriously from Diether von Isenberg, archbishop of Mainz, a headstrong prelate who would resist papal authority with equal resolve, as the new pope was to discover) and from nationalist movements in Hungary and especially Bohemia, where the popularity of the Hussite and Taborite heresies further diluted the force of imperial authority. Tense relations among various Habsburg brothers and cousins in Austria, most of them involved in hopelessly complicated succession disputes, also inhibited Frederick's ability to exert any real control over territories which he ruled at best in name. The emperor took a special interest in the proceedings at Basel, and some of his own diets addressed the ques-

tion of ultramontane sovereignty. Though he was reconciled with Eugenius IV in 1447 (largely through Aeneas's own diplomacy), Frederick remained at best a cautious ally of Rome. His irresolution with regard to the Turkish problem, and his failure to appear either at the diets he had himself convened to discuss the question or at the Congress of Mantua, left Aeneas both shocked and deeply disappointed.

The question of political leadership within Italy was similarly unclear. In the kingdom of Naples, violent conflicts between the forces of Anjou and Aragon repeatedly flared in the decades after the death of the childless Queen Giovanna II in 1435. Alfonso and his son Ferrante frequently emerged the victors in these skirmishes, but victory came at a cost both to themselves and to the popes who chose to support them. Instability seemed to radiate out from the southern kingdom across the rest of the peninsula: within the Papal States, rival *condottieri* and local barons took advantage of the almost constant state of crisis to stake claims of their own to disputed territories and titles. Throughout the *Commentaries* Aeneas darkly condemns the disruptions these ambitious soldiers-of-fortune caused, among them the Piccinino family, Count Everso of Anguillara and, above all, the "prince of all wickedness," Sigismondo Malatesta, the sinister lord of Rimini. In reality, these petty barons were simply watching out for their own interests, seeking to turn the chaotic course of events to their best advantage, but they made the mistake, from posterity's point of view, of trying to disadvantage the papacy during the reign of an able propagandist. Aeneas's scorn was matched only by his determination to stamp out their insurrection.

Elsewhere in Italy, however, he openly admired the resourcefulness and grit of self-made soldier princes. Federico da Montefeltro, count of Urbino, the accomplished *condottiere* and patron of arts and letters, earned Aeneas's respect and valuable favors from his regime. Above all, Aeneas admired Francesco Sforza, the Mila-

nese captain-general who in the midst of civil war rose to seize the dukedom for himself after the death of Filippo Maria Visconti. Sforza, in Aeneas's view, embodied an ideal combination of prudence, fortitude and statesmanlike resolve, a man whose bold actions and remarkable strength of character had earned him not only the opportunity but also the right to be a leader of men. The pope's diplomatic relations with Milan did not always run smoothly, but there is no doubt he entertained the greatest respect for Sforza, valued his friendship enormously, and had high hopes of seeing him lead the papal armies to victory against the Turks.

The Ottoman capture of Constantinople in 1453 had shaken Europe to its foundations. At a stroke, Sultan Mehmed II destroyed the last vestiges of the Byzantine Empire and established the supremacy of Islam in the eastern Mediterranean. Little stood between his armies and the Christian kingdoms of the Balkans; the rich Italian colonies dotted around Greece and the Adriatic depended totally on his mercy, and the southern coasts of Italy itself were said to lie within his sights. As news of the catastrophe spread, the princes and republics of Europe attempted, momentarily, to cease their usual squabbling. In the spring of 1454 the Italian states formed a pact of mutual nonaggression at Lodi, hoping to present a united front against the infidel foe; in the same year, Duke Philip of Burgundy took the crusader's vow, and Frederick III convened a series of diets to discuss an imperial offensive. But no action was taken, for as Aeneas himself often observed, a wary self-interest seemed to have paralyzed the best intentions of every Western prince. No one wanted to be the first to commit men and resources to a new crusade; no one wanted to leave his own borders exposed, his own lands and treasure at risk, unless he knew his neighbors had already signed on. For five years Aeneas watched the princes of Christendom stand by in futile stalemate as the sultan's forces advanced. It seemed that nothing — not the impassioned propaganda of Calixtus III, nor the astute diplomacy of

the Greek Cardinal Bessarion, nor the rousing sermons of the mendicant preacher Fra Giovanni Capistrano—could stir an indifferent and war-weary Europe to the cause of a new crusade. Yet it was this cause which Aeneas adopted as his own at the very moment of his coronation; resolving, in the face of Ottoman aggression, "to stake not just the city and the patrimony of Peter, but his own health, indeed his very life."[6]

The sincerity of Aeneas's commitment to the crusade has sometimes been called into doubt. His adoption of the cause in the mid-1450s could be seen as a cynical ploy, the former conciliarist leaping adroitly to the defense of a quintessentially papal project. Even his activities on behalf of the crusade after his election have been questioned: was the Congress at Mantua no more than a ruse (and a failed one, at that) to command the submission and allegiance of the secular powers? But the opposite could just as easily be true: the urgent threat of Ottoman expansionism may have directly prompted Aeneas to embrace the doctrine of papal supremacy, and disappointment with Frederick's vacillation at the diets of 1454–1455 could well have driven him to seek a career in the Church under the militant Calixtus. As the inaction of the secular princes repeatedly showed, no one in Europe but the pope seemed to possess the moral authority and strength of purpose to confront the Turkish problem. The portrait Aeneas develops of himself in the *Commentaries* as a crusader pope thus serves to illustrate—and plead—the central position of papal authority in the fifteenth-century world.

Aeneas's secretarial career had prepared him well to negotiate the complexities of the international situation. It could be said, in fact, that the role of the humanist secretary in which Aeneas so excelled was itself a product of the general crisis of political, religious and moral authority that gripped Europe in the first half of the fifteenth century. In an age of seemingly incessant disputation, with

the dynastic and legal status of so many crowns — not least that of the papacy — subject to ferocious contest, rhetorical skill had come to be seen as a necessary weapon in the armory of any reigning or aspiring prince. As Aeneas's own career so amply demonstrates, a talented secretary could provide his master with valuable help in a variety of tight situations, diplomatic, legal or military. By arguing points of law, leading embassies, negotiating among various parties, drafting agreements and composing persuasive orations, letters and other, more subtle forms of propaganda, the humanist secretary served his employer alternately as advocate, counselor, ambassador and spy. Both in person and on paper, the secretary could pose a dangerous threat to any who challenged his employer's interests, while at the same time winning hearts and minds in the increasingly important court of international public opinion.

Most Quattrocento secretaries had a background in the liberal arts, and some of them were humanist scholars of considerable standing. The revival of classical literature and culture which characterized the Renaissance humanist movement was thus much more than a matter of aesthetics or style. By studying and adopting ancient techniques of rhetorical argumentation, the humanists developed a potent weapon for use in contemporary struggles for political survival. "Coluccio's pen could do more harm than thirty troops of Florentine cavalry,"[7] remarked the duke of Milan during his war against Florence at the end of the fourteenth century — a war fought with words as well as weaponry, and one that the duke ultimately lost on both fronts. Salutati, classical scholar, historian and chancellor of Florence, was one of the towering figures of the early humanist movement, perhaps the first to achieve what would become the paradigmatic humanist synthesis of literary achievement and service to the state. He and the Florentine humanists of his circle, brilliant writers all of them, who by their hard work and rhetorical skill made good careers for themselves and brought

honor to the government they served, were important role models for Aeneas. The biographical sketches of Salutati and his circle that he offers in chapter 2.30 of the *Commentaries* reveal the extent of his admiration: it is here that Aeneas repeats the duke of Milan's rueful assessment of Salutati's powers. Although he never served his own city-state in the same capacity (for republican Siena remained forever suspicious of Aeneas's noble birth and international ambitions), he nevertheless embraced the activist ideals of the Florentine humanists and attempted in his own peripatetic career to emulate their accomplishments.

He believed he had succeeded: as he tells it in Book 1 of the *Commentaries*, which treats his life and career up to his election as pope, it is oratorical skill alone which raises the young secretary up through the ranks of the various European diplomatic corps in which he serves. His life (or rather, as we must keep in mind, his *Life*) unfolds in a series of astonishing verbal triumphs: everywhere Aeneas goes, he has only to speak or put pen to paper and victory is his. At several critical junctures in his career, in Milan or at Basel, in the papal conclave or during tense negotiations at Mantua, Aeneas will save the day—and his own or his master's political skin—by means of an oratorical *tour de force*. The speech is invariably one of monumental length and complicated structure, but miraculously, we are told, no one fidgets or falls asleep ("or even spits"); rather, all sit transfixed, unless moved to tears, as Aeneas's words command unanimous assent and confound all possible objections.

In his youth, Aeneas had found ways to express his subtle command of language in poetry and fiction; but as his career progressed he concentrated more and more on applying his skills to the achievement of practical, political goals—whether composing diplomatic briefs and political orations, or writing accounts of contemporary history (often boldly tendentious and closely linked to his political designs), or burnishing his own image as a states-

man by collecting, editing and publishing his personal correspondence. Although once elected to the papacy he implored the world to "reject Aeneas and embrace Pius"[8] (in other words, to trust that the worldly man of affairs had fully embraced his life in the Church), in intellectual and political matters he remained ever faithful to the humanist ideal of engagement. His goal was to restore the papacy to a position of leadership in Europe, and he intended to use all his skills — literary and rhetorical as well as diplomatic and political — to do so.

It is a curious fact that, despite the decades Aeneas spent offering his pen for hire, exchanging his literary services for patronage and employment, as pope he was notoriously ungenerous to men of letters; Filelfo would complain bitterly of his former pupil's ingratitude. But the pope preferred to write his own speeches and conduct his own correspondence — in short, to fight his own oratorical battles, as his training and career had prepared him to do. This is precisely the spirit in which the *Commentaries* themselves are written, and in which they should be read. While there are, here and there, a few passages of candid introspection, as a whole the work is unabashedly apologetic; it is, in fact, a supremely accomplished example of humanist secretarial rhetoric, written not only to justify Aeneas's conversion to the papal cause and, then, his ascent to the papal throne, but also to assert the authority of the papacy itself in the face of violent challenges from both within and without the Church.

The Renaissance humanists had little doubt that history-writing was a form of rhetoric, and that the historian's job was to narrate the record of political events in such a way as to inspire admiration or outrage or otherwise convince readers of a particular point of view. The first generation of Italian humanists had certainly done much to clarify the practice of writing about the past, eschewing traditional notions of fortune, chance or providence as an invisible

force determining the course of human events, in favor of more rational, secular models of causation, often based on careful and critical study of the original sources. Nonetheless, even the pioneering monuments of early humanist historiography, Leonardo Bruni's *History of the Florentine People* and Lorenzo Valla's treatise on the Donation of Constantine, were written in a partisan spirit, the one glorifying Florence's traditions of political liberty, the other demolishing the papacy's claims to temporal dominion. The tendency to view history as yet another rhetorical arena in which a writer might promote his own or his employer's political interests, rebut the challenges of rivals or raise popular morale, spread rapidly through the princely courts of Italy in the middle years of the fifteenth century. At Naples, where Alfonso of Aragon had fought a bloody war to seize the crown and defend it against a series of Angevin pretenders, court humanists composed partisan accounts of his victories that insisted on Alfonso as the only candidate worthy of the prize. Bartolomeo Facio's encomiastic *Commentaries on the Deeds of Alphonso* (1455), in particular, provided a model for humanists in the pay of image-conscious princes (Antonio Panormita and Lorenzo Valla also wrote commentaries on Alfonso). The *condottiere* princes Braccio da Montone, Federico da Montefeltro and Francesco Sforza also commissioned humanists to write commentaries on their careers, often in order to justify similar legally dubious acts of conquest and usurpation, in the late 1450s and 1460s.[9]

Humanist *commentarii* owed a great debt, as their titles imply, to the *Commentaries* of Julius Caesar. Not quite biography, nor on the other hand a purely narrative account of contemporary affairs, these historical works focused rather on the interaction between a great man and the larger forces of history which had directed his career and which he in turn had done much to shape. The point was to demonstrate the superior character, abilities and *virtù* of the man, and then show how, thanks to these traits, he had mastered

the challenges thrown up by contemporary events. As in so many other areas of the humanist secretary's remit, the task of writing historical commentaries drew on rhetorical art to settle questions of political legitimacy. The humanist commentator's task was to identify those personal attributes—whether wealth, military skill, political shrewdness or sheer good fortune—which constituted the new prince's *de facto* right to rule and which must trump the bids of weaker parties who might yet assert a *de jure* claim.

This is clearly the tradition in which Aeneas was writing; what sets his *Commentaries* apart from their contemporaries is the fact that in his case the rhetorical argument is made not on behalf of a forceful condottiere or affluent Maecenas, but rather for the sake of the rhetorician himself. What is more, the rhetorician constructing this argument is none other the prince in question, performing the task of his own literary aggrandizement. Writing the commentaries of his own career, Aeneas Silvius, politician and scribe, becomes a secretary to himself, raising oratorical skill to the level of brute force or fabulous wealth. Eloquence thus becomes not only a means of acquiring power, but also a justification for holding it.

The method usually employed by writers of humanist *commentarii* was to gather and collate primary documents (often supplied by the chancery of the prince who commissioned the work) and then construct out of these a polished, literary account of the people and events concerned.[10] Aeneas, too, resorts quite frequently in the *Commentaries* to documents from his own archives, quoting or paraphrasing the texts of treaties, memoranda, orations and the like, many of them in fact his own compositions. In places, though, the final process of editing and polishing remained unfinished, for he was still at work on the book at the time of his death: Book XIII treats events in the spring of 1464 and ends abruptly. Some sections of the *Commentaries* thus read like rough notes,

while elsewhere the narrative can become repetitive or even confused, as anecdotes and descriptive passages are interrupted and then either forgotten or only much later resumed. It should be recalled, though, that Aeneas composed much of the work orally, by dictating to his secretaries, often in short interludes snatched from more pressing curial business. Given the circumstances of its composition, the structural coherence of the work is in fact remarkably strong; the author's control of his narrative and the artistry with which he modulates its diverse themes is only confirmed by the few occasions where that control and artistry break down.

In matters of style, his generic debt to Caesar notwithstanding, Aeneas strives to imitate the rhetorical fullness of Ciceronian prose. In those passages where he was able to edit the *Commentaries* to his satisfaction, his periods are long, heavily subordinated—and occasionally unwieldy. One sometimes senses the author struggling to marshal the many details of time, place, personality, motivation, cause and effect which his remarkable memory had stored up over the long decades of an eventful career. His closeness to his subject matter becomes, in this sense, the greatest weakness of the work. And yet it is also its greatest strength. For if Aeneas never quite achieves the distinction of writing history in the grand style (to which he clearly seems to have aspired), what he does possess—and frequently displays to thrilling effect—is an extraordinary talent for reportage. His true gift lies in his eye for detail, his unerring sense of what scrap of dialogue or passage of scenery, diverting anecdote or historical tale will most precisely capture the essence of a moment, a place or a personality. At his best, Aeneas can explore the hidden motivations of his contemporaries, and delineate their complex characters, with an elegant economy that transcends the preoccupations of mere stylistic correctness. And the literary brilliance of the work does more than simply enliven the historical narrative of Aeneas's life; it also does much to soften the polemical agenda he

sought to pursue by telling it. The nail-biting account of the conclave of 1458 with which Book I concludes, for example, was clearly composed to establish Aeneas's triumphant, unassailable right to occupy the throne of Peter. But it is also one of the great setpieces of Renaissance prose, a classic essay in dramatic suspense and resolution.

By contrast, the long account of the journey to Mantua, which occupies the second half of Book II, portrays a slow and steady progress through the Papal State and its neighbors — a ponderous tour, in fact, of the territories and troubles with which the new pope must contend. Throughout these chapters of the *Commentaries*, the oligarchical sympathies of the author are never hidden. Surveying the treacherous political landscape of central Italy in the first year of his reign, Aeneas finds an unstable terrain of republics and despotisms and — all too few — good lords, those enlightened princes like Federico Montefeltro and Lodovico Gonzaga whose greatest virtue, in Aeneas's eyes, is their loyalty to Rome. Yet even as it offers a sort of *tableau vivant* of the pope's political philosophy, the account of the journey to Mantua also stands as an inspired passage of travel narrative, a marvelous panoply of vivid impressions and striking detail, possessed of its own momentum. It also — and perhaps most importantly — contributes much to the dramatic characterization of Aeneas himself as a man on a quest, steadily progressing through triumphs and trials, on the track of a momentous destiny that seems always to lie just beyond his grasp.

The *Commentaries* are, above all, an epic work, the heroic dramatization of a life and a career. The opening chapters skip lightly over Aeneas's early life and education in Corsignano, Siena and Florence.[11] In the author's view, it seems, "real life" began with rhetoric, with the start of a secretarial career. And it is no accident that, almost immediately after Domenico Capranica takes him into his service, we find Aeneas literally swept away from his home and the familiar shores of Tuscany. The epic storm that drives

him, like his hero and namesake Aeneas of Troy, far from his Italian *patria* to within sight of Africa itself, initiates a series of diverting and challenging adventures which will, ultimately, be the making of the man. It is at the moments of highest drama — whether on the storm-racked coast of Elba, or up a Scottish hayloft, or (more usually) at a lamplit desk in Basel or Rome — that the echoes of Vergil begin to sound with frequency in the text. The life of this *pius Aeneas,* too, is one of shipwrecks and sleepless nights, the recurring motif of the *nox insomnis* being especially appropriate for a hero wielding a pen and not a sword, the vigil kept not in anticipation of the heat of battle, but rather in an effort to polish off the perfect speech. Our Aeneas will likewise endure decades of wandering before he can at last, by his wit and force of will, make his way to Italy. Following the path of divinely sanctioned duty, through sea-wanderings, fierce combats and tremendous suffering, his story tends inexorably toward a sacred Italian destiny and (as the author of the *Commentaries* so clearly hoped) a legacy of triumph and renown.

In the present volume, Marcello Simonetta established the Latin text and compiled the index; Margaret Meserve undertook the revision of the English translation and supplied the notes and introduction. This volume contains Books I–II of the *Commentaries* and is the first of a projected five. The remaining eleven books being much shorter than the first two, it is anticipated that Volume 2 will contain Books III–V; Volume 3, Books VI–VIII; Volume 4, Books IX–XI; and Volume 5, Books XII–XIII and a cumulative index.

We wish to thank the General Editor of the series, James Hankins, for entrusting us with this task in the first place, and for the generous support, expert advice, gentle pressure and unfailing patience with which he has kept us at it in the ensuing years.

We owe a great debt, as well, to the scholars in whose footsteps

we follow.[12] In preparing both the edition and the translation, we have made constant reference to the previous editions of Totaro, van Heck, and Bellus and Boronkai; their labors have made our work considerably lighter than it would otherwise have been. We have also relied on the historical notes to the *Commentaries* composed by Leona C. Gabel for the first English translation of the work, and we have endeavored to record our debts to her in the Notes to the Translation.

The translation itself is a thorough revision of Florence Alden Gragg's monumental English version, first published in five volumes of the *Smith College Studies in History* over two decades, from 1936 to 1957, and subsequently reprinted in several abridged editions. For nearly half a century, Gragg's translation has stood as the definitive—indeed, the only—complete English edition of the work. Although much of her text has here been either altered to agree with recent editorial work on the *Commentaries* or updated to suit twenty-first-century tastes, readers will recognize the traces of her elegant and judicious prose, and her innate sympathy for the character and perspective of Aeneas Silvius Piccolomini, on every one of the following pages. We dedicate this work to her memory.

NOTES

1. Aeneas Silvius Piccolomini, *Historia rerum ubique gestarum,* sometimes entitled *Asia* or *Cosmographia,* in *Opera,* 281–282: "Nec nos plebem suo tempore fraudavimus, qui nec rem divinam negleximus, nec consistoria seu publica seu secreta praetermisimus, nec supplices audire contempsimus. Sed nostrum senium sua quiete privavimus . . . Nocturni sunt hi labores, nam quae somno debebantur horarum maximam partem scribendo consumpsimus. Fatemur, melius suas vigilias expendisset alius, sed dandum fuit aliquid menti, quae his lucubrationibus oblectata est."

2. The *Commentaries* themselves remain the fullest account of Aeneas Silvius' life. For modern biographies see Voigt, Paparelli, Mitchell, listed

in the Bibliography; the sketch by Iris Origo, "Pope Pius II," in *The Italian Renaissance,* ed. J. H. Plumb (Boston, 1961), 238–253; and Pastor, III, *passim.*

3. Mitchell, 39–46 and 56–59, gathers the scattered sources for this period in Aeneas's life, which he treats in the *Commentaries* only briefly.

4. One of the best accounts of the Council of Basel and the conciliar movement may be found in the translators' introduction to Aeneas's own treatise on the topic, *De gestis Concilii Basiliensis commentariorum libri II,* ed. D. Hay and W. K. Smith (Oxford, 1967), ix–xxx.

5. *Commentaries,* 1.14.1.

6. *Commentaries,* 2.2.5. The definitive account of Aeneas's crusading ideology is J. Helmrath, "Pius II und die Türken" in *Europa und die Türken in der Renaissance,* ed B. Guthmüller and W. Kühlmann (Tübingen, 2000), 79–138, with an exhaustive survey of the previous literature.

7. *Commentaries,* 2.30.2

8. "Aeneam reiicite, Pium suscipite," *Opera,* 870.

9. See G. Ianziti, "Storiografia come propaganda: Il caso dei 'commentarii' rinascimentali," *Società e storia* 22 (1983): 909–918; and his *Humanistic Historiography under the Sforzas* (Oxford, 1988).

10. See the works of Ianziti listed in the previous note.

11. He makes no mention, for instance, of his devotion to his law professor Mariano Sozzini, nor of the exhilarating influence of S. Bernardino, nor does he mention his early efforts at erotic poetry (i.e., his *Nymphilexis* and the *Cynthia* collection), drama (*Chrysis*) or romance (*The Tale of Two Lovers*). He likewise draws a judicious veil over the lives and early deaths of his bastard sons, born from two separate brief encounters on secretarial missions to Scotland (1436) and Germany (1442).

12. See also the Note on the Text and Translation.

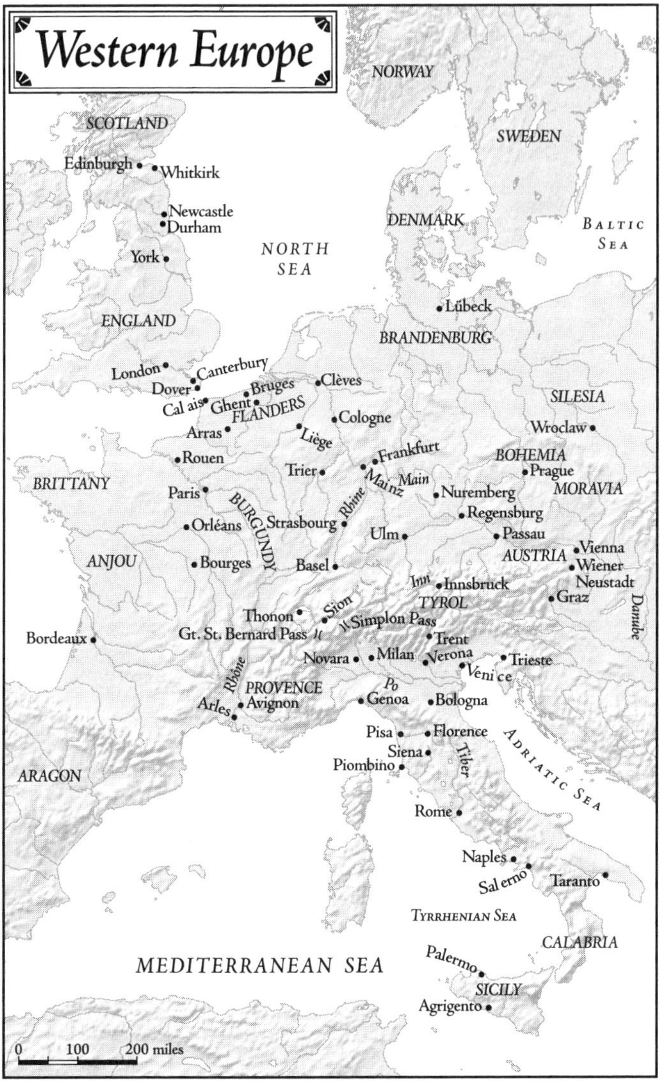
Western Europe
NORWAY
SWEDEN
SCOTLAND
Edinburgh
Whitkirk
Newcastle
Durham
York
DENMARK
BALTIC SEA
NORTH SEA
Lübeck
ENGLAND
BRANDENBURG
London
Canterbury
Dover
Calais
Bruges
Ghent
FLANDERS
Clèves
Cologne
SILESIA
Wroclaw
Arras
Liège
Rouen
Frankfurt
BOHEMIA
Prague
Trier
Mainz
Main
MORAVIA
BRITTANY
Paris
Rhine
Nuremberg
BURGUNDY
Regensburg
Orléans
Strasbourg
Ulm
Passau
AUSTRIA
Vienna
Wiener Neustadt
ANJOU
Bourges
Basel
Inn
Innsbruck
Graz
TYROL
Danube
Thonon
Sion
Simplon Pass
Bordeaux
Gt. St. Bernard Pass
Trent
Novara
Milan
Verona
Trieste
Venice
Rhône
PROVENCE
Po
Avignon
Arles
Genoa
Bologna
Pisa
Florence
ADRIATIC SEA
Siena
Tiber
Piombino
ARAGON
Rome
Naples
Salerno
Taranto
TYRRHENIAN SEA
CALABRIA
Palermo
MEDITERRANEAN SEA
SICILY
Agrigento
0
100
200 miles

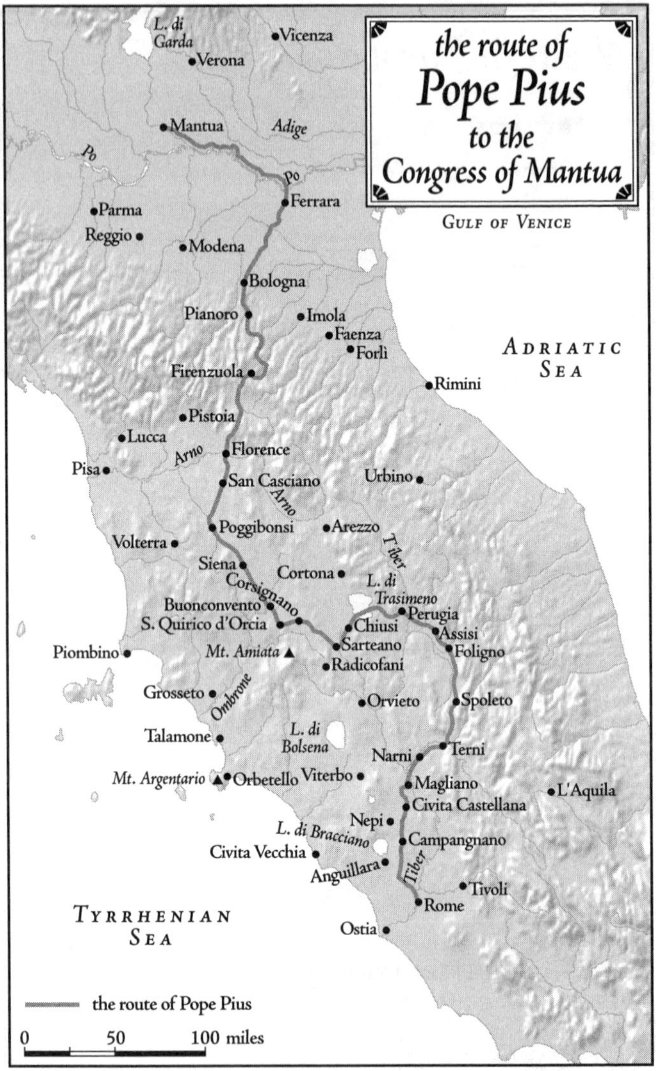

the route of
Pope Pius
to the
Congress of Mantua
L. di Garda
Vicenza
Verona
Mantua
Adige
Po
Po
Ferrara
Parma
Reggio
Modena
Gulf of Venice
Bologna
Pianoro
Imola
Faenza
Forlì
Adriatic Sea
Firenzuola
Rimini
Pistoia
Lucca
Arno
Florence
Pisa
San Casciano
Arno
Urbino
Poggibonsi
Arezzo
Tiber
Volterra
Siena
Cortona
Corsignano
L. di Trasimeno
Buonconvento
Perugia
S. Quirico d'Orcia
Chiusi
Assisi
Sarteano
Foligno
Piombino
Mt. Amiata
Radicofani
Grosseto
Ombrone
Orvieto
Spoleto
Talamone
L. di Bolsena
Terni
Narni
Mt. Argentario
Orbetello
Viterbo
Magliano
L'Aquila
Civita Castellana
Nepi
L. di Bracciano
Campangnano
Civita Vecchia
Anguillara
Tiber
Tivoli
Rome
Tyrrhenian Sea
Ostia
the route of Pope Pius
0
50
100 miles

COMMENTARIORUM PII SECUNDI PONTIFICIS MAXIMI LIBRI XIII

THE COMMENTARIES OF PIUS II PONTIFEX MAXIMUS IN THIRTEEN BOOKS

PRAEFATIO

1 Si perit morte animus, ut falso censuit Epicurus, nihil habet fama quod ei conferat. Sin vivit corporea mole dimissa,[1] aut miseram accipit sortem aut felicibus admiscetur spiritibus. Miseriae nulla inest voluptas, vel famae quidem; beatorum plena felicitas nec laude mortalium augetur, nec vituperio comminuitur. Quid est igitur, quod tantopere boni nominis gloriam quaerimus? Fortasse qui purgantur animi dulcedinem aliquam hauriunt relictae in terris famae? At sentiant contentiosi de mortuis quicquid libuerit, dum viventes oblectari gloria quae adest, et quae post obitum futura speratur, minime negent! Haec est enim quae clarissimas alit mentes et ultra spem vitae caelestis, quae cum advenerit numquam finietur, humanum fovet ac recreat animum, praecipue vero pontificis Romani, quem[2] in terra viventem omnium fere linguae vituperant, mortuum laudant. Martinum Quintum vidimus et Eugenium Quartum et Nicolaum item Quintum et Callistum Tertium, quos dum vixere damnavit populus, fato defunctos magnis extulit praeconiis. Sequuntur vicarii suum dominum: salvatorem Christum, dum vixit inter homines, daemonium habere dixerunt, pendentem in cruce mortuum, Filium Dei recognoverunt. Non est servus maior domino suo. Non parcet Pio Secundo pontifici maximo lingua dolosa quae tot Christi vicariis et ipsi Christo non pepercit. Accusatur, reprobatur dum vivit inter nos Pius Secundus; extinctus laudabitur et desiderabitur cum haberi non poterit. Cessabit invidia post obitum et, sublatis qui iudicia pervertunt privatis affectibus, vera resurget fama Piumque inter claros pontifices collocabit.

PREFACE

1 If the soul dies with the body, as Epicurus wrongly supposed, fame can do it no good. But if it lives on after its release from the bodily frame, it either suffers a wretched fate or joins the company of happy souls. In wretchedness there is no pleasure, not even from renown; and the perfect happiness of the blessed is neither increased by the praise of mortals nor diminished by their scorn. Why then do we strive so hard to achieve the glory of a good name? Do souls in Purgatory perhaps taste some sweetness from the reputation they left on earth? Argumentative types can debate all they like about the state of the dead, but there can be no doubt that the living take pleasure in the glory that is theirs today, and hope it will continue after death. It is this which sustains the most brilliant intellects and (even more than the hope of a celestial life, which once begun will never end) encourages and invigorates the human spirit. This is especially true of the pope of Rome, whom almost all men abuse while he lives among them but praise once he is dead. We ourselves have seen Martin V, Eugenius IV, Nicholas V and Calixtus III condemned by the public while they lived and extolled to the skies after their deaths. The vicars follow in the footsteps of their Lord. Christ our Savior, while He lived, was thought to have a demon;[1] but once He hung upon the cross, He was acknowledged to be the son of God. The servant is no greater than his master:[2] the treacherous tongue that has not spared so many of Christ's vicars, nor Christ himself, will not spare Pope Pius II. He is accused and condemned while he lives among us. At his death, he will be praised; he will be missed when he is no longer here. Envy will fade once he is gone, and when men's judgments are no longer clouded by personal interests, the truth will out, and Pius will be numbered among the illustrious popes.

2 Interea nos de pontificatu suo historiam scribemus. In cuius fronte non ab re fuerit pauca de origine suae familiae atque de his quae ante apostolatum ab eo gesta fuerint quam brevissime praemittere, ut intellegant posteri quomodo Aeneas Silvius antea dictus ad Beati Petri cathedram pervenerit et Pii Secundi nomen assumpserit. Tu, qui haec aliquando legeris, ita demum boni consule ut mentienti nihil ignoscas!

In the meantime we intend to write the history of his pontificate. By way of introduction, it will not be out of place to set down very briefly a few facts about the origin of his family and his career before he became pope, so that later generations may understand how he who was called Aeneas Silvius came to sit on the throne of Peter and to assume the name of Pius II. You who may someday read these pages, show them as much respect as you would deny to one who tells a lie. 2

INCIPIT LIBER PRIMUS

: I :

De origine Picolominaeae domus et Pii maioribus.

1 Familia Picolominaeorum ex Roma in Senas translata, inter vetustiores et nobiliores civitatis habita, dum optimates rei publicae praefuerant[1] et litteris et armis claruit, pluresque arces et castella obtinuit.[2] Sed a nobilibus in plebem derivato regimine, sicut et caeterae nobilium, sic et Picolominaea[3] domus humiliata est.

2 Superfuit tamen avo Aeneae Silvio non tenue patrimonium, ex quo potuit vitam honestam ducere. Sed iuvenis immatura morte decessit, relicta Montanina uxore pregnante, ex qua natus est Silvius postumus, quo pupillo bona eius sub tutoribus et actoribus dissipata sunt. Hic tamen educatus ingenue litteris ediscendis traditus est; qui liberalibus artibus eruditus ubi adolevit, in militiam profectus variisque casibus actus tandem domum rediit, vendicataque patrimonii tenui portione, Victoriam ex domo Forteguerrarum, qui patroni sunt ecclesiae Senensis, quamvis nobilem virginem tamen pauperem duxit uxorem; quae adeo fecunda fuit, ut saepe gemellos pepererit. Ex ea Silvius duodeviginti liberos sustulit, non tamen ultra decem simul aggregavit, quos urgente inopia Corsiniani (quod est oppidum vallis Urciae) nutrivit. Sed omnes tandem iniqua lues extinxit, duabus tantum sororibus, Laudomia et Catherina, cum Aenea superstitibus.

BOOK I

: I :

The origin of the Piccolomini family. Pius's forebears.

The Piccolomini came to Siena from Rome and were counted among the oldest and noblest families of the city. As long as the nobility remained in power, the family was renowned for its scholars and soldiers and possessed many fortresses and castles; but when the government passed from the nobles to the people, the Piccolomini were humbled along with the rest.[1] 1

Grandfather Enea Silvio nevertheless retained a considerable fortune which allowed him to live in dignified fashion. He died while still a young man, leaving his pregnant wife Montanina, who gave birth to a son called Silvio. As a boy, his property was squandered by his guardians and agents, though he was still brought up like a gentleman and sent to school. After a thorough training in the liberal arts, he became a soldier and, after various adventures,[2] at last came home to recover a small part of his patrimony and marry a poor but noble girl, Vittoria, of the family of the Forteguerri, who are the patrons of the cathedral of Siena. She was so fertile that she often gave birth to twins, and with her he had eighteen children, though there were never more than ten living at once. He brought his family up in poverty in Corsignano, a town in the Val d'Orcia, but in the end the cruel plague killed them all except Aeneas and his sisters Laodamia and Caterina. 2

: 2 :

Aeneae ortus et puerilia discrimina ac rudimenta et progressus aetatis.

1 Aeneas etiam patris Silvii nomen accepit et, ob reverentiam apostoli quem Indorum barbari decoriarunt, Bartholomei. Trinomius enim fuit, Aeneas Silvius Bartholomeus appellatus. Editus autem est in lucem ipsa luce Sancti evangelistae Lucae, XIIII Kalendas Novembris anno salutis quinto supra millesimum et quadringentesimum.

2 Hic in pueritia trium annorum, dum ludit inter aequales, muro lapsus alto et in saxum allisus ingens capitis vulnus accepit, quod praeter spem et opinionem parentum Nicolaus Monticulanus, qui eum de sacro fonte levaverat, sine litteris medicus — ut dicunt, empericus — brevi curavit. Annum agens octavum in bovem cornupetam cum incidisset, percussus et in altum iactus, divino magis auxilio quam ope humana mortis periculum evasit.

3 Exinde cum diu apud patrem quaevis officia ruris obisset, annos iam duodeviginti natus in urbem migravit exceptusque apud necessarios qui bonae frugis adolescentem minime relinquendum existimabant. Audire grammaticos coepit, deinde poetas et oratores avide sectatus,[4] postremo ad ius civile se contulit, cuius professores cum aliquot annos audivisset, exorto inter Senenses ac Florentinos gravi bello, et litterarum studia intermittere[5] et patriae dulce solum relinquere coactus est.

: 2 :

Aeneas's birth, his boyhood scrapes and progress toward maturity.

Aeneas received both his father's name, Silvio, and a third name, 1
Bartolomeo, in honor of the apostle who was flayed by the barbarous Indians. Thus he was known as Aeneas Silvius Bartolomaeus. He was born at dawn on St. Luke's day, October 18, 1405.

When he was three years old, he was playing with some friends 2
when he fell off a high wall onto a rock and was badly injured in the head. His parents hardly dared hope for his recovery, but the wound was soon healed by his godfather Niccolò Monticuli, an untrained physician, one of the so-called "empirics." When he was eight, he was tossed by a charging bull and escaped death more by the help of heaven than by any human effort.

Thereafter he stayed at home for several years working on the 3
family farm until, at the age of eighteen, he went up to the city. He was supported by his relations, who thought that so promising a youth ought to have his chance. At first he studied grammar, then eagerly pursued poetry and rhetoric, and at last applied himself to civil law.[3] He had been attending lectures on this subject for several years when a serious war broke out between Siena and Florence,[4] forcing him to interrupt his studies and leave the soil of his beloved native city.

: 3 :

Aeneas Firmani secretarius. Profectus cum eo in Basileam, et reditus in Italiam cum Bartholomeo episcopo Novariensi, eiusque oratio in schola Papiensi.

1 Forte fortuna tunc adfuit Dominicus Capranicus, vir et animi et sensus altioris, quem Martinus papa Quintus ad cardinalatus honorem vocaverat, successor Eugenius Quartus repudiaverat. Concilium eo tempore apud Basileam, Helvetiae urbem Rheno adiacentem indictum coeptumque fuit. Dominico, qui Romae contemnebatur, Basileae suam dignitatem vendicare propositum erat. Ab hoc Aeneas in secretarium receptus Plumbinum—quod Populinum alii vocant ex Populoniae ruinis aedificatum[6]—cum eo venit.

2 Ibi cum Dominicus, quia terra non patebat iter, per mare Ligusticum Genuam petere instituisset, iamque navis in conspectu esset qua traiicere animus erat, Iacobus Appianus tyrannus loci, quamvis amicum se fingeret, Dominicum ne quod veheret navigium inhibuit. At ille, ubi dolos sensit, egressus oppidum uno tantum comite ad litus profugit atque ibi lembum nactus ad navim, quae in alto pelago vagabatur, excurrit. Quo intellecto, ceteris qui de familia Dominici fuerunt data est navigandi facultas; nec enim plumas tyrannus insequendas putavit, qui carnes amisisset. Sequenti die Aeneas et Petrus Noxetanus, qui etiam Dominici secretarius fuit, omnesque domestici, qui noctem in Ilva insula sub divo pergelidam duxerant, in navim ad Dominicum pervenerunt.

3 At cum Genuam tenderent, ingentibus iactati procellis in conspectum Libyae delati sunt, timentibus admodum nautis ne barbaris portubus redderentur. Quamvis mirabile dictu et auditu prope[7]

: 3 :

Aeneas made secretary to the bishop of Fermo. He departs with him to Basel and returns to Italy with Bartolomeo, bishop of Novara. His oration on the University of Pavia.

Now it happened that Domenico Capranica was then at Siena,[5] a man of noble character and intellect who had been made a cardinal by Martin v and then repudiated by his successor, Eugenius iv. At the time, a council had been called at Basel, a city of Switzerland on the Rhine.[6] The council was already in session and Domenico, who was in disgrace at Rome, resolved to defend his claims at Basel. He appointed Aeneas his secretary and took him with him to Piombino, a town built on the ruins of the ancient Populonia, which some call Populino. 1

There he decided to go to Genoa by way of the Ligurian Gulf, because the route by land was blocked. The ship in which he meant to sail hove into view when suddenly the lord of the place, Jacopo Appiani, who had up to this point pretended to be friendly, forbade any boat to give him passage. On learning of this treachery, Domenico left town with a single companion and fled to the coast, where he procured a light skiff and rowed out to the ship as it sailed about on the open sea. When the tyrant heard of this, he let the rest of Domenico's party embark, thinking there was no point in chasing the feathers when he had lost the meat. The next day, after a very chilly night in the open air on the island of Elba, Aeneas, Piero da Noceto (another of Domenico's secretaries)[7] and the rest of the cardinal's retinue joined Domenico aboard his ship. 2

As they were making for Genoa, however, violent gales blew up and drove them off their course to within sight of the African coast. The sailors were terrified, sure they would end up in a barbarian port. Marvelous and almost incredible as it sounds, it is 3

incredibile, certum[8] tamen est eos una die ac nocte, ab Italia solventes, inter Ilvam et Corsicam in Africam propulsos, rursus mutatis ventis retrovectos inter Corsicam et Sardiniam, fluctuantes magis quam navigantes, ad Italiam reversos Portum Veneris appulisse, ubi recepta triremi felici navigatione Genuam, atque inde Mediolanum terrestri itinere petiverunt. Ibi magnum illum ducem et fama clarum Philippum Mariam viderunt, nec diu morati per Alpes quas Sancti Gothardi appellant, nive glacieque rigentes ac praeruptos et caelo vicinos montes, Basileam venere. Sigismundus imperator per id temporis Parmae hiemabat, Romam aestate sequenti concessurus.[9]

4 In Basilea Dominicus apud synodum cardinalatus causam movit, atque Aenea procuratore restitutus est dignitati. At cum Dominicum paupertas premeret — quia prohibente Eugenio nil ei propinqui ministrabant — Aeneas ad Nicodemum Scaligerum episcopum Frizingensem, cuius pater apud Veronam tyrannidem obtinuerat, et illo ex Basilea recedente ad Bartholomeum Vicecomitem episcopum Novariensem sese recepit, ab utroque dictandi atque signandi epistolas officio praepositus. Cum Nicodemo ad principes electores qui Francfordiae convenerant profectus est; cum Bartholomeo in Italiam rediit diuque apud Philippum ducem Mediolani, cui Bartholomeus serviebat, versatus est.

5 In eius senatu cum duo de rectoratu scholae Papiensis contenderent — alter Mediolanensis genere clarus, ex[10] domo Crottiadum, alter Novariensis, humili familia natus — et Mediolanensi pars maior universitatis faveret, qui iam magistratus insignia assumpserat ac duos patruos in consilio principis admodum potentes habebat, Aloysium et Lanzelottum, Aeneas Novariensis partes accepit tantumque sua oratione contendit ut erepta Mediolanensi dignitas Novariensi traderetur.

nonetheless true that after leaving Italy, in a single day and night they were driven between Elba and Corsica to Africa and then, when the wind changed, drifted rather than sailed back again between Corsica and Sardinia, to put in at Porto Venere. Here they procured a galley and had a successful voyage to Genoa, and went from there overland to Milan, where they saw the great and illustrious Duke Filippo Maria.[8] After a brief stay they continued their journey, arriving at Basel by way of the St. Gotthard Alps, where the steep mountains, covered in snow and ice, tower to the skies. The emperor Sigismund was then wintering at Parma and planning to go on the next summer to Rome.[9]

In Basel Domenico appeared before the Council to press for recognition of his appointment as cardinal. Through the advocacy of Aeneas, he was restored to high office. But Domenico was in financial difficulties (for Eugenius had forbidden his relations to give him any aid), and so Aeneas transferred his services to Nicodemo della Scala, the bishop of Freising, whose father had been lord of Verona. Then, when Nicodemo left Basel, he served Bartolomeo Visconti, the bishop of Novara. Both men put him in charge of composing and signing their letters. With Nicodemo he went to a meeting of the electors assembled at Frankfurt; with Bartolomeo he returned to Italy and stayed for a while at the court of Duke Filippo of Milan, whom Bartolomeo served. 4

Here two men were competing for the rectorship of the University of Pavia. One was a Milanese of the noble house of the Crotti, the other a man of humble birth from Novara. Most of the university were in favor of the Milanese, who had two very influential uncles, Luigi and Lancellotto, on the duke's council and had already assumed the insignia of office; but Aeneas took up the cause of the Novarese and made so powerful a speech before the ducal senate that the post was taken away from the Milanese and given to the man from Novara. 5

: 4 :

Fit Aeneas secretarius cardinalis Sanctae Crucis, cum quo in Franciam proficiscitur, ab eodemque postea in Scotiam mittitur.

1 Interiecto deinde tempore ad Eugenium, qui Florentiae sedebat, cum Bartholomeo perrexit. Inde ad Nicolaum Picininum, clarum illius aetatis et praecipuum belli ducem, apud balneas Senenses lavantem, non parvis de causis divertit; ac tum primum suos necessarios et amicos revisit veteres, dies quinque apud eos manens. At cum redisset Florentiam, comperit Bartholomeum apud Eugenium magnis de rebus accusatum,[11] capitali iudicio laborantem, ob quam causam ad Nicolaum cardinalem Sanctae Crucis probatissimum et laudatissimum patrem confugit, qui et ipsum in secretarium accepit[12] et Bartholomeum e manibus Eugenii liberavit, Thoma Sarezano magistro domus — qui postea summi pontificis cathedram ascendit Nicolaus papa Quintus appellatus — ac Petro Noxetano, cuius supra mentio facta est, faventibus atque optantibus.

2 Cardinalis Sanctae Crucis eo tempore legatus in Franciam designatus erat, inter Carolum Francorum et Henricum Anglorum reges pacem compositurus. Cum eo Aeneas tertio Mediolanum et urbis ducem vidit atque inde montem Iovis, quem Sancti Bernardi melius hodie vocitant, ad Amedeum Sabaudiae ducem pervenit; qui tunc spreto saeculo in heremo apud Thononium supra lacum Lemannum magis voluptuosam quam poenitentialem cum sex viris equestris ordinis (qui secum penulam et baculum assumpserant, ut mos est heremitis) vitam degebat — credo, quod post annis octo secutum est, expectans ad summi pontificatus cathedram per patres qui Basileae convenerant evocari. Nam et tunc rumor incre-

: 4 :

Aeneas made secretary to the cardinal of Santa Croce, who takes him to France and later sends him to Scotland.

1 Some time after this Aeneas went with Bartolomeo to Pope Eugenius, who was then holding court at Florence.[10] From there he went to discuss some important business with Niccolò Piccinino, the most celebrated general of the age, who was taking the waters at Siena.[11] Then he revisited his old friends and relations for the first time, remaining some five days among them. When he returned to Florence he found that Bartolomeo had been accused of grave offenses before Eugenius and was on trial for his life. Aeneas therefore took refuge with Niccolò,[12] the cardinal of Santa Croce, a most eminent and highly esteemed member of the college, who appointed him his secretary and rescued Bartolomeo from Eugenius. This he did at the urging and pleading of his major-domo, Tommaso of Sarzana—who afterward ascended the papal throne as Nicholas v[13]—and of Piero da Noceto, whom we have already mentioned.

2 At that time, the cardinal of Santa Croce had been appointed ambassador to France with instructions to arrange a peace between Charles of France and Henry of England. In his company, Aeneas visited Milan and saw the duke for the third time; from there he visited Monte Giove, today better known as Monte San Bernardo, to see Duke Amedeo of Savoy. The duke had renounced the world and was living a life of pleasure rather than penitence in a hermitage at Thonon above Lake Geneva, attended by six knights who had assumed the hermit's cloak and staff with him. He was waiting, I suppose, for the event which occurred eight years later, his summons to the papal throne by the cardinals assembled at Basel.[14] For even then there was a rumor that

bruerat Amedeum papam futurum, quem nonnulli a sortilegis Pythonicum habentibus spiritum feminis, quibus Sabaudiae montes abundant, ortum asserebant.

3 Eo salutato cardinalis Basileam venit atque inde per Rhenum Coloniam Agrippinam navigavit, ubi rursus equis conscensis per Aquas Grani Leodiumque atque Lovanium, Duacum et Tornachum in Atrebates descendit, ubi conventus totius Galliae et Angliae cardinalem morabatur. Dux Burgundorum Philippus per id temporis adversus regem Franciae, qui patrem eius[13] occiderat, Anglicorum parti favebat. Cardinalis primum pacem universalem componere studuit; id ubi non successit, Philippum, qui regi Angliae tamquam regnum Franciae ad eum pertineret fidem dederat, iuramento[14] absolutum regi Franciae reconciliavit. Tum quoque de bono pacis Aeneas ad Philippum epistolam versu conscripsit. Prius autem quam Philippus Bartolomeo ab Anglicis deficeret, cardinalis Aeneam in Scotiam misit qui praelatum quendam in regis gratiam reduceret.

: 5 :

Alfonsi captivitas, et Aeneae in itineribus gravia pericula, marisque procellae et Angliae mirabilia.

1 Per id temporis rex Aragonum Alfonsus cum fratribus et omni nobilitate regnorum suorum per Genuenses sub auspiciis Philippi ducis Mediolani maritimo bello victus et captus est.

2 Aeneas, ut Calesium venit, quod est oppidum continentis in Oceani ripa obiectum Anglis, mox quasi suspectus apud hospitem

Amedeo would be pope—a rumor some said had been started by certain fortune-tellers endowed with the gift of prophecy. There are a great many such women in the mountains of Savoy.

After paying his respects to the duke, the cardinal went on to Basel and then sailed down the Rhine to Cologne. Here he again took horse and proceeded by way of Aix, Liège, Louvain, Douai and Tournai to Arras, where a meeting of all the French and English cardinals was in session.[15] At the time, Duke Philip of Burgundy was supporting the English against the king of France, who had put his father to death. At first, the cardinal tried to bring about a general truce. When this failed, he reconciled Philip to the French king by absolving him of the oath he had sworn to the king of England as the rightful ruler (as he then supposed) of France. At this point Aeneas also sent Philip a letter in verse on the blessings of peace. Before Philip broke with the English, however, the cardinal sent Aeneas to Scotland to restore a certain prelate to the king's favor.[16] 3

: 5 :

Captivity of Alfonso. Aeneas exposed to grave perils on his journeys. Storms at sea and the marvels of England.

About this time the Genoese, backed by Duke Filippo of Milan, defeated King Alfonso of Aragon in a naval battle and took him prisoner together with his brothers and all the nobles of his realm.[17] 1

When Aeneas arrived at Calais, a town on the coast opposite England, he found himself at once an object of suspicion to the English. He was put into the custody of his host and forbidden either to carry on or to return until the cardinal of Winchester,[18] on 2

commendatus, neque progredi neque regredi permissus. Auxilio fuit cardinalis Vintoniensis, qui ex Atrebato rediens dimitti eum iussit. At cum venisset Aeneas ad regem Angliae litterasque peteret quibus in Scotiam tutus[15] iret, retrocedere iussus est, timentibus Anglicis ne apud regem Scotiae hostem suum contra se aliquid moliretur, quem constabat cardinalis Sanctae Crucis secretarium esse — et illum Anglici singularibus inimicitiis insectabantur, qui ab eis Burgundorum ducem alienasset. Quae res Aeneam penitus latebant. Gravis sibi sed necessarius reditus fuit, quod frustra se maris periculo commisisset. Placuit tamen, quia populosas ditissimasque Lundonias vidit et Sancti Pauli nobile templum regumque mirificas sepulturas et Themisiam fluvium non tam velocius euntem quam redeuntem, pontemque instar urbis et villam in qua nasci caudatos homines fama praedicat, et quod omnibus nomen aufert, aureum Divi Thomae Cantuariensis mausoleum adamantibus, unionibus atque carbunculis tectum, ad quod materiam argento viliorem nefas offerre ducunt.

3 Remenso igitur mari, ad oppidum quod Bruggis vocant se contulit atque inde Clusas petiit, ubi portus est totius Occidentis frequentissimus. Ubi[16] navem ingressus dum Scotiam petit, in Norvegiam propellitur duabus maximis iactatus[17] tempestatibus, quarum altera quattuordecim horas mortis metum incussit, altera duabus noctibus et una die navim concussit atque in fundo perfregit; adeoque in[18] Oceanum et septentrionem navis excurrit ut nulla iam caeli signa nautae cognoscentes spem omnem salutis amitterent. Sed adfuit divina pietas, quae suscitatis aquilonibus navim ad continentem reppulit, ac duodecimo tandem die terram Scotiam patefecit.

4 Ubi, apprehenso portu, Aeneas ex voto decem milia passuum ad Beatam Virginem quam de Alba Ecclesia vocitant nudis pedibus profectus, cum illic horis duabus quievisset, assurgens moveri

his way back from Arras, came to his aid and ordered his release. But when Aeneas went to the king of England and asked for a safe-conduct to Scotland, he was ordered to go back again. The English feared he would plot some mischief against them with their enemy, the king of Scotland; for it was well known that he was the secretary of the cardinal of Santa Croce, who had incurred the bitter hatred of the English by alienating the duke of Burgundy from their side. Aeneas knew nothing about any of this. He was forced to return much against his will, having braved the perils of the sea to no purpose. Still he was glad to have seen the rich and populous city of London, the famous church of St. Paul, the wonderful tombs of the kings, the Thames which is swifter at the flow than at the ebb of the tide, the bridge like a city, the village where men are said to be born with tails[19] and, more famous than all the rest, the golden mausoleum of Thomas of Canterbury, which is covered with diamonds, pearls and carbuncles and where it is considered a sacrilege to offer any mineral less precious than silver.

After crossing the Channel again, he went to the town of 3
Bruges and thence to Sluys, the busiest port in the west. There he took ship for Scotland; but he was driven to Norway by two violent gales, one of which kept them in fear of their lives for fourteen hours. The other pounded the ship for two nights and a day; it sprang a leak and was carried so far north into the open sea that the sailors, who could no longer recognize the constellations, abandoned all hope. But divine mercy came to their aid, raising north winds which drove the vessel back toward land. Finally, on the twelfth day, they raised the coast of Scotland.

When they made harbor, Aeneas fulfilled a vow by walking 4
barefoot ten miles to the Blessed Virgin of Whitekirk.[20] He rested there for two hours and found, on rising, that his feet had grown so weak and numb with cold that he could not move. What saved him was the fact that there was nothing to eat there, as this forced

loco non poterat, debilitatis atque obstupefactis hiemali frigore pedibus. Saluti fuit nihil edendum illic invenisse, atque in aliud rus migrandum fuisse. Quo dum famulorum ope magis portatur quam ducitur, pedetentim terram quatiens calefactis pedibus ex insperato sanitate recepta ambulare occepit. Ad regis denique praesentiam intromissus nihil non impetravit ex his quae petitum venerat. Sumptus ei viarum restituti sunt et in reditum quinquaginta nobilia ac duo equi, quos gradarios appellant, dono dati.

: 6 :

Scotorum mores varii, et quae apud eos nascuntur, et Aeneae continentia eiusque divina ope sublatum periculum, ac per Anglia vaferrimus transitus.

1 De Scotia haec relatu digna invenit: insulam esse Angliae coniunctam, in septentrionem portentam, ducenta milia passuum longitudinis, quinquaginta latitudinis habentem; terram frigidam, paucarum frugum feracem, magna ex parte arboribus carentem; subterraneum ibi esse lapidem sulphureum, quem ignis causa defodiunt; civitates nullos habere muros, domos magna ex parte sine calce constructas, villarum tecta de caespitibus facta, ostia rusticana corio boum claudi; vulgus pauper ei incultum carnes et pisces ad saturitatem, panem pro obsonio commedere; viros statura parvos et audaces, feminas albas et venustas atque in venerem proclives; basiationes feminarum minoris illic esse, quam manus in Italia tractationes; vinum non haberi, nisi importatum; equos natura gradarios omnes parvique corporis inveniri, paucis pro semine servatis reliquos castrari solitos; neque fricari equos ferro aut ligno

him to move on to another village. While his servants were carrying, rather than leading him there, he gradually warmed his feet by kicking them against the ground until, against all hope, he recovered and began to walk. When he was at last admitted to the king's presence, he obtained all he had come to ask. He was reimbursed for his traveling expenses and given fifty nobles to accompany him on his return journey as well as two horses called trotters.

: 6 :

Various customs and products of Scotland. Aeneas's continence. Divine intervention rescues him from danger. His wanderings through England.

The following facts about Scotland seem worth recording. It is an 1
island attached to England, which extends two hundred miles to the north and is fifty miles wide. It is a cold country where few things grow and is for the most part barren of trees. Below ground there is a sulphurous rock which they dig for fuel. The cities have no walls. The houses are usually constructed without mortar, their roofs are covered with turf and in the country the doorways are closed with oxhides. The people, who are poor and rude, stuff themselves with meat and fish but eat bread as a luxury. The men are short and brave; the women fair, charming and lusty. In Scotland, a woman's kiss means less than a handshake does in Italy. They have no wine except what they import. Their horses are all small and natural trotters. They keep a few for breeding and castrate the rest. They do not curry them with iron or comb them with wooden combs or guide them with bridles. The oysters are larger than those in England and contain many pearls. Leather,

pecti,[19] neque frenis regi; ostrea illic maiora quam in Anglia reperiri, et in his plurimos uniones; ex Scotia in Flandriam corium, lanam, pisces salsos[20] margaritasque ferri; nihil Scotos audire libentius, quam vituperationes Anglorum; Scotiam duplicem dici, alteram cultam, alteram silvestrem agro carentem; silvestres Scotos lingua uti diversa, et arborum cortices nonnumquam habere pro cibo; in Scotia non inveniri lupos; cornicem novam esse, atque idcirco arborem in qua nidificaverit regio fisco cedere.

2 Dicere quoque solitus erat Aeneas, priusquam in Scotiam perrexisset, audivisse se arbores ibi esse supra ripam fluminis, quarum poma in terram cadentia marcerent, in aquam dilapsa vivificarentur atque in aves animarentur; at cum eo venisset miraculumque cupidus investigaret, comperisse id mendacii; seu verum est, ultra in Orchades insulas relegatum. Id autem verum esse asserebat: hiemali solstitio (tunc enim illic fuit) diem non ultra quattuor horas in Scotia protendi.

3 Peractis rebus cum redeundum esset, e vestigio magister navis qui eum vexerat ad[21] Aeneam accedens, locum redeunti in navi obtulit quem prius habuerat. Cui Aeneas non tam futuri praescius, quam praeteriti periculi memor 'Si frustra Neptunum,' inquit, 'accusat, qui bis periculum incidit, quid in eum dicere oportet, qui tertio naufragium patitur? Hominum ego quam maris experiri misericordiam malo.' Dimissoque nauta iter sibi per Angliam delegit. Nec mora, solvens a portu navis in conspectu omnium tempestate vexata collisa et submersa est, magistro, qui rediturus in Flandriam nuptias cum nova sponsa celebraturus erat, et omnibus aliis voragine maris absorptis praeter quattuor qui, arreptis quibusdam tabulis, nantes evasere. Tunc se divino nutu beneficioque servatum Aeneas intellegens, dissimulato habitu sub specie mercatoris per Scotiam transivit in Angliam.

wool, salt fish and pearls are exported from Scotland to Flanders. There is nothing the Scots like to hear more than abuse of the English. It is said there are two Scotlands: one cultivated, the other wooded with no open land. The Scots who live in the second part speak a different language and sometimes eat the bark of trees. There are no wolves in Scotland. Crows are rare and therefore the trees in which they nest are considered property of the king.

Aeneas also used to say that, before he went to Scotland, he 2
had heard of certain trees growing on the bank of a river there. If the fruit from these trees fell on the ground, it would rot, but if it fell into the water, it would come to life and transform into birds.[21] But when he got to Scotland and eagerly inquired after this marvel, he found that it was a lie or — if true — was now to be found in the Orkneys. This, however, he knew for a fact: at the winter solstice (for Aeneas was there then) the day in Scotland is not more than four hours long.

When he had finished his business and was ready to return, the 3
skipper who had transported him promptly came and offered him his old quarters on his ship. But Aeneas, who was not thinking so much about disasters as remembering those already past, said, "If we say a man who's been in peril twice has no credit with Neptune, what should we say about one who suffers shipwreck a third time? I'd rather trust in the mercy of men than that of the sea." So he sent the sailor away and chose to travel through England. And shortly thereafter the ship left port and in plain view ran into a storm which broke it up and sank it; and the skipper, who was going back to Flanders to marry a young bride, was drowned with everyone else on board except four men who caught hold of some planks and managed to swim to land. Then Aeneas, realizing he had been saved by a beneficent God, disguised himself as a merchant and left Scotland for England.

4 Fluvius est, qui ex alto monte diffusus utramque terram disterminat; hunc cum navigio transmeasset atque in villam magnam circa solis occasum declinasset, in domum rusticanam descendit atque ibi cenam cum sacerdote loci et hospite fecit. Multa ibi pulmentaria et gallinae et anseres afferebantur in esum, sed neque vini neque panis quicquam aderat. Et omnes tum feminae virique villae quasi ad rem novam accurrerant, atque ut nostri vel Aethiopes vel Indos mirari solent, sic Aeneam stupentes intuebantur quaerentes ex sacerdote, cuias esset, quidnam facturus venisset, Christianamne fidem saperet. Edoctus autem Aeneas itineris defectum, apud monasterium quoddam panes aliquot et vini rubei metretam receperat; quibus expositis maior admiratio barbaros tenuit, qui neque vinum prius neque panem album viderant. Appropinquabant autem mensae praegnantes feminae earumque viri, attrectantes panem et vinum odorantes portionem petebant, inter quos totum erogare necessum fuit.

5 Cumque in secundam noctis horam cena protraheretur, sacerdos et hospes cum liberis virisque omnibus, Aenea dimisso, abire festinantes dixerunt se ad turrem quandam longo spatio remotam metu Scotorum fugere, qui fluvio maris refluxu decrescente noctu transire praedarique soleant; neque secum Aeneam multis orantem precibus quoquo pacto adducere voluerunt, neque feminarum quampiam, quamvis adolescentulae et matronae formosae complures essent; nihil enim his mali facturos hostes credunt, qui stuprum inter mala non ducunt. Mansit ergo illic solus Aeneas cum duobus famulis et uno itineris duce inter centum feminas, quae corona facta medium claudentes ignem, cannabumque mundantes noctem insomnem ducebant, plurimaque cum interprete fabulabantur.

6 Postquam autem multum noctis transierat, duae adulescentulae Aeneam iam somno gravatum in cubiculum paleis stratum duxere,

There is a river,[22] rising in a high mountain, which separates the two countries. Aeneas crossed this in a small boat and around sunset reached a large settlement, where he knocked at a farmhouse and had dinner with his host and the parish priest. They served up several chickens and geese and savory dishes, but there was no bread or wine. All the men and women of the village came running as if to see a strange sight, and just as we marvel at Ethiopians or Indians, so they gazed in amazement at Aeneas, asking the priest where he came from, what his business was and whether he was a Christian. Aeneas, who had learned from experience that this route lacked certain comforts, had obtained several loaves of bread and a jug of wine from a monastery along the way. When he brought these out they excited even greater wonder among the barbarians, who had never seen wine or white bread before. Pregnant women and their husbands kept coming up to the table, touching the bread and sniffing the wine and asking for some, so that he was compelled to divide it all among them. 4

The feast continued until about two hours after sunset, when the priest and the host together with all the men and boys took leave of Aeneas and hurried away. They said they were going to withdraw to a distant tower for fear of the Scots, who often crossed the river at low tide to make raids on them in the night. Despite his urgent pleas, Aeneas could not persuade them to take him with them, nor any of the women, even though there were a number of beautiful girls and matrons. For they think the enemy can do their women no wrong, as they do not consider rape a crime. Thus Aeneas remained behind with two servants and the guide among a hundred women, who made sat up all night[23] in a circle round the fire cleaning hemp and carrying on a lively conversation with the interpreter. 5

After a good part of the night had passed and Aeneas had grown quite sleepy, two girls showed him to a chamber strewn with straw. Such being the custom of the country, they were pre- 6

dormiturae secum ex more regionis, si rogarentur. At Aeneas non tam feminas quam latrones mente volvens, quos iamiam timebat adfore, puellas a sese murmurantes reiecit veritus, ne peccatum admittens e vestigio praedonibus ingressis sceleris poenas daret. Mansit igitur solus inter vaccas et capras, quae furtim paleas ex strato suo carpentes[22] haudquaquam dormire eum sinebant.

7 Post medium autem noctis latrantibus canibus et anseribus strepentibus ingens clamor factus est; tumque omnes feminae in diversum prolapsae, dux quoque itineris diffugit, et quasi hostes adessent omnia tumultu completa.[23] At Aeneae potior sententia visa est in cubiculo (id enim[24] stabulum fuit) rei eventum expectare, ne si foras curreret ignarus itineris, cui primum obviasset, ei se praedam daret. Nec mora, reversae mulieres cum interprete nihil mali esse nuntiant, atque amicos non hostes venisse; idque tum sibi continentiae praemium Aeneas existimavit; qui ubi dies illuxit, itineri se commisit atque ad Novum Castellum pervenit, quod Caesaris opus dicunt. Ibi primum figuram orbis et habitabilem terrae faciem visus est revisere; nam terra Scotia et Angliae pars vicina Scotis nihil simile nostrae habitationis habet—horrida, inculta atque hiemali sole inaccessa.

8 Exinde Dunelmiam venit, ubi sepulchrum Venerabilis Bedae presbyteri sancti viri hodie visitur, quod accolae regionis devota religione colunt. In Eborachum quoque descendit, magnam et populosam urbem, ubi templum est et opere et magnitudine toto orbe memorandum et sacellum lucidissimum, cuius parietes vitrei inter columnas ad medium tenuissimas colligati tenentur. Inter equitandum comes ei unus ex iudicibus Angliae factus est, qui tunc Lundonias ad iudicium properebat. Hic omnia, quae apud Atrebatum gesta erant, quasi ignaro Aeneae referebat, multaque in cardinalem Sanctae Crucis maledicta iactabat, quem lupum ovina pelle vesti-

pared to sleep with him, if asked. But Aeneas was thinking less about women than about the bandits who might appear at any moment. He pushed the girls away even as they protested, for he feared that if he committed a sin, he would have to pay the penalty as soon as the bandits arrived. So he remained alone among the heifers and nanny goats, who kept him from sleeping a wink by stealthily pulling the straw from his pallet.

Some time after midnight there was a great uproar of barking 7
dogs and hissing geese. The women scattered, the guide took to his heels and the wildest confusion ensued, as if the enemy were at hand. Aeneas feared that if he rushed outside, in his ignorance of the road he would fall prey to the first person he met. So he thought it best to await events in his own room (it was the stable) and very soon the women returned with the interpreter, saying nothing was wrong and that the newcomers were friends, not enemies. Aeneas considered this a reward for his earlier continence. At daybreak he proceeded on his journey and came to Newcastle, which is said to have been built by Caesar. There for the first time he seemed to see a familiar world again and a habitable country; for Scotland and the parts of England nearest to it are utterly unlike the land we inhabit, being rude, uncultivated and untouched by the winter sun.

Next he came to Durham, where people now go to visit the 8
tomb of the holy abbot, the Venerable Bede, a shrine piously revered by the inhabitants of the region. He also went to York, a large and populous city, where there is a cathedral renowned throughout the world for its size and design and for the brilliant chapel whose glass walls are held together by the slenderest columns. As he rode along he was joined by an English judge who was hurrying up to London to court. He told Aeneas what had happened at Arras, supposing him to know nothing about it, and cursed the cardinal of Santa Croce roundly, calling him a wolf in sheep's clothing.[24] What an amazing coincidence! Aeneas was de-

tum appellabat. Quis non fortunae casus demiretur? Is Aeneam usque Lundonias securum perduxit, qui si novisset hominem, mox in carcerem coniecisset.

9 In Lundoniis autem comperit Aeneas interdictum regis esse, ne quis peregrinus absque litteris regis insula exiret, neque illas petere tutum videbatur. Corrupit igitur pecunia custodes portus, quod apud id genus hominum minime arduum est, quibus nihil est auro dulcius. Ex Dubla igitur Calesium navigavit, atque inde Basileam petiit[25] et itinere continuato Mediolanum. Ubi certior factus cardinalem Sanctae Crucis ex Florentia missum per vallem Athesis et montes quos Arelatenses appellant Basiliense concilium adire, ad eum, superatis Alpibus quas Brigae vocitant, per vallem Seduni profectus est.

: 7 :

De translatione concilii Basiliensis et Eugenii persecutione.

1 Graeci per id tempus ad Latinas terras de unione tractaturi venturos sese concilio promiserant. At gens inops et mendicandi perita in sumptum pecunias expetebat atque in eam rem auri florenorum septuaginta millia requirebat. Concilium, ut tantam summam corraderet, plenarias indulgentias remissionemque peccatorum omnium his pollicebatur qui pecuniam in hoc opus conferrent. Parum tamen valiturae indulgentiae videbantur, nisi et Romani pontificis concurreret auctoritas; neque is renuebat, sed contentio erat in conficiendis litteris. Basilienses enim sub nomine

livered safely to London by a man who, had he but known his identity, would have thrown him into prison at once.

In London, however, Aeneas found that the king had forbidden any foreigner to leave the island unless he had a royal passport, 9
and he did not think it safe to ask for one. Therefore he bribed the keepers of the port (a thing which is easy enough to do, as this class of men loves nothing more than gold) and sailed from Dover to Calais, going from there to Basel and straight on to Milan. There he learned that the cardinal of Santa Croce had been despatched from Florence and was on his way to the Council of Basel by way of the valley of the Adige and the Arlberg. Aeneas set out to join him, crossing the Alps at Brig and proceeding through the valley of Sion.

: 7 :

Transfer of the Council of Basel. Aeneas persecuted by Eugenius.

At that time the Greeks had promised the Council that they 1
would come to Latin territory to discuss the question of union. Being a poor nation, with a talent for begging, they asked to be reimbursed for their expenses. To that end they demanded some 70,000 gold florins. In order to scrape together such a sum the Council promised plenary indulgences and remission of all their sins to those who would contribute money to the cause. It appeared, however, that the indulgences would not be worth much unless backed by the pope's authority and though he did not refuse to give it, there was a dispute about the form. The delegates at Basel maintained that the indulgences should be granted in the name of the Council with the concurrence of the pope, while

concilii concurrente Romano praesule dandas indulgentias asserebant, Eugenius vero suo nomine sacro approbante concilio emittendas litteras, atque illum esse veterem et tritum usum affirmabat. Saepe et multum atque usque ad probra super ea re disputatum est. Nam et Thomas, qui postea, ut diximus,[26] Beati Petri cathedram tenuit, tunc privatus homo et cardinalis Sanctae Crucis familiaris, cum de concilii auctoritate mentio fieret, 'Quid vos,' inquit, 'concilium[27] commendatis? Non hic concilium neque Ecclesiam quisquam esse dixerit mente sanus. Synagogam sathanae, non synodum agitis, perditi homines et mancipia daemonum!' Quibus ex verbis irritati patres arripi hominem vincirique mandaverunt, sed Iuliani cardinalis Sancti Angeli prudentia[28] liberatur.

2 Cardinalis autem Sanctae Crucis ad Eugenium Bononiae manentem infectis rebus reversus, nec diu post ad Philippum Mariam ducem missus est, inter eum et Venetum populum de pace acturus. Eo usque cum eum Aeneas secutus cardinalem esset, intellexissetque Bononiae nullum Eugenio gratum esse qui rebus Basiliensibus favisset, memoriamque sibi Novariensis episcopi posse nocere, ne frustra tempus tereret in Romana Curia, permissu[29] cardinalis Basileam rediit, atque apud gravem et sanctum patrem, Iohannem Sancti Petri ad Vincula cardinalem, natione Hispanum, qui postea Ostiensis[30] creatus est, sese recepit.

: 8 :

De gestis Aeneae in concilio Basiliensi, et eius beneficiis et morbo apud Mediolanum gravissimo.

1 Referam nunc paucis quae in Basiliensi concilio Aeneae obtigerunt, et quae illic ab eo cum laude gesta sunt. Agebatur eo tem-

Eugenius insisted that the letter should be sent out in his name with the approval of the Council, this being the time-honored and usual custom. They had many long debates about this, some of them quite heated: when someone mentioned the authority of the Council, Tommaso (who later sat on the throne of Peter but was then merely a private individual in the service of the cardinal of Santa Croce) cried, "Why set so much store by the Council? No one in his right mind would say that this is a proper council or even a proper church. Sons of perdition, henchmen of demons! It's not a synod you're holding but a synagogue of Satan!"[25] The cardinals took offense at these words and gave orders to arrest and imprison him, but he was rescued by the great wisdom of Giuliano, the cardinal of Sant'Angelo.[26]

The cardinal of Santa Croce went back to Eugenius at Bologna 2
without having accomplished a thing. Soon after he was sent to Duke Filippo Maria to arrange a peace between him and the Venetians. Aeneas followed the cardinal this far; but at Bologna he learned that Eugenius could not abide anyone who had been on the side of the Council of Basel, and that any mention of the bishop of Novara might do him harm. He therefore decided not to waste his time at the Roman Curia. With the cardinal's approval he returned to Basel. There he transferred his service to Juan, the influential and holy cardinal of San Pietro in Vincoli, who was later made cardinal bishop of Ostia.[27]

: 8 :

Aeneas at the Council of Basel. The matter of his benefices. Grave illness at Milan.

I will now describe briefly what happened to Aeneas at the Coun- 1
cil of Basel and his distinguished achievements there. At the time,

pore de translatione concilii in alium locum, ad quem Graeci venturi putarentur, quattuorque in electionem loca dabantur quae pecuniam ad rem Graecorum necessariam offerebant: Florentia, Utinum, Papia et Avenio. Cumque in laudem cuiusque loci in auditorio maximo copiose peroratum fuisset, solique Papiae commendationes defuissent, quod Isidorus Rosatensis, quem Philippus Maria dux Mediolani ad eam rem miserat, inepte atque insulse verba faciens quiescere iussus erat. Motus Aeneas et urbis egregiae et principis eius contemptu, conscripta per noctem oratione sequenti die ad conventum veniens, obtenta ex auctoritate Iuliani legati copia dicendi, orationem duabus horis cum omnium singulari attentione et admiratione peroravit,[31] cuius exemplar omnes qui aderant edi postmodum sibi curaverunt.

2 Abhinc Aeneae et concilium gratius et dux Mediolanensium faventissimus fuit, namque quamvis solo psalmistatus caractere insignitus esset, tamen et scriptoris et adbreviatoris officium assecutus est; in duodecimviratu saepe fuit, quod munus quamvis trimestre tamen magni ponderis erat, nihil enim deputationes deliberare poterant nisi materiam a duodecimviris accepissent, neque ad concilium quispiam admittebatur absque horum decreto. In deputatione sua, cui 'fidei' nomen erat, saepe praesedit; claves plumbi, quo synodales litterae signabantur, frequenter in eius custodia fuerunt; inter scriptores nemo ad rescribendariatum saepius electus est; inter adbreviatores Parci Maioris locum habuit. Quotiens e nationibus aliqui ad res singulares delecti sunt, raro is unus non fuit. Legationes synodales ei ad Argentinam tres, ad Constantiam duae, ad Francfordiam una, ad Tridentum una,[32] ad Sabaudiam una demandatae sunt, atque omnes feliciter obivit.

3 Cum praepositus Sancti Laurentii Mediolanensis basilicae diem clausisset extremum, Franciscus Mediolanensium pontifex, ingenti

there was some discussion of transferring the Council to a place where the Greeks could come for a conference. The choice fell between four cities willing to pay the expenses of the Greeks: Florence, Udine, Pavia and Avignon. Eloquent speeches in praise of three of these cities resounded through the great hall; only Pavia had no one to plead its cause, because Isidoro Rosati, whom Duke Filippo Maria of Milan had sent for that purpose, had spoken so badly and stupidly that he had been told to hold his tongue. Aeneas was moved by the humiliation of this noble city and its prince, and that very night he composed a speech. Next day he went into the Council, where Giuliano, the papal legate, used his influence to get him permission to speak. For two hours he declaimed before a most attentive and admiring audience. Afterwards, everyone who heard his speech had a copy made for himself.

From that time on, Aeneas grew more popular in the Council 2
and in the favor of the duke of Milan. Although his official title was merely psalmist, he acted as secretary and abbreviator and often sat on the Committee of Twelve. This post, though it was held for only three months, was extremely influential since no deputation could engage in debate unless it had its topic approved by the Twelve, nor was anyone admitted to the Council without their permission. He often chaired his own committee, the committee on faith, and he was frequently entrusted with the keys to the lead used to seal the letters of the synod. None of the secretaries was chosen *rescribendarius* more often than he. Among the abbreviators he had the rank of the upper bar.[28] When representatives of the various nations were chosen to attend to important matters, he was almost always selected. He went on embassies for the Council three times to Strasbourg, twice to Constance, and once each to Frankfurt, Trent and Savoy; and he always met with success.

When the provost of San Lorenzo at Milan died, Francesco, 3
the bishop of Milan and a man greatly respected for his learning

et doctrina et sanctimonia commendatissimus, mox approbante concilio Aeneam illi suffecit, quamvis essent complures et doctores et magni viri natione Mediolanenses, qui se promotos optabant. At cum in contione generali res ageretur, Isidorus Rosatensis, emulus Aeneae, quo in laudanda Papia se inaudito fuisset auditus, 'Quid agitis, patres?' inquit, 'Electivam praeposituram Aeneae homini extero committitis? Ubi decretum vestrum, quod tantopere servari praecipitis? Beneficia in terra Mediolanensi absque scitu et voluntate principis de vobis optime meriti confertis? Cives et doctores spernitis, alienos eligitis? Nisi capitulum in suo iure dimittitis, ruent conatus vestri, ridebiturque provisio!'

4 Tum Aeneas 'Vehementer,' inquit, 'admiror, patres optimi, Isidorum adversum me verba iacere, qui nuper ex Mediolano reversus litteras Philippi ducis ad me detulit, quibus ille princeps gratias mihi agit, quod eius causam hoc in loco peroraverim, atque ob eam rem gratum sibi esse affirmat in eius territorio quodcunque beneficium ecclesiasticum me acceptare, cuius libenti animo possessionem sit mihi daturus. Non igitur ille me extraneum habet, neque nova res est unius regionis homines in altera dignitates habere, si modo linguam norint; nam et archiepiscopus ex Bononia Mediolanum venit. Neque movere quemquam debet, quod de decreto electionis obiicitur. Inferiores enim non concilium obligat; illis insuper capitulis electio dimittenda est quae plures graves canonicos, non quae duos tresve habent et leves et indoctos (ut in ecclesia Sancti Laurentii, de qua nunc agimus) qui tales sunt, ut habentes eligendi potestatem non eligant quidem, nisi iussi hunc aut illum eligere. Vos patres, agetis ut libebit. Nihil peto quod vestro

and piety,[29] quickly appointed Aeneas in his place. The Council approved this decision, although a number of scholars and leading citizens among the Milanese themselves had hoped for advancement. But when the matter was discussed in the general assembly, Isidoro Rosati (who was jealous of Aeneas because Aeneas had delivered a eulogy of Pavia when he himself had been refused a hearing) exclaimed, "Reverend fathers, what are you doing? Will you appoint an outsider like Aeneas to an electoral provostship? What about that decree of yours, which you bid us observe so strictly?[30] Do you mean to confer a benefice in the territory of Milan without the knowledge and consent of the prince to whom you owe so much? Do you despise his citizens and scholars? Will you chose foreigners instead? Unless you confirm the chapter in its rights, your attempt will fail and all will mock this nomination."

Then Aeneas said, "I am certainly amazed, your worships, that 4
Isidoro speaks against me, when only the other day he returned from Milan with a letter from Duke Filippo thanking me for pleading his cause here, and assuring me that he would be happy for me to accept any benefice in his domain and would be delighted to confirm my tenure. Evidently the duke does not consider me an outsider. Nor is it unheard of for a man of one state to hold positions of honor in another, provided he knows the language. Even the archbishop of Milan came from Bologna. Nor should anyone be troubled by your objection concerning the decree on elections, for that is not binding on the Council but only on those subject to its authority. Furthermore election is to be delegated only to chapters which have a number of important canons, not to such as have only two or three—and those ignorant and unimportant—as is the case with the church of San Lorenzo now under discussion. The canons there, even if they had the right of election, would not exercise it unless ordered to elect a particular candidate. Reverend fathers, you will act as you see fit. I want nothing contrary to your desires. But I should prefer to have your

honori adversum. Quod si mihi providendum duxeritis, voluntatem vestram sine possessione electioni capitulari cum possessione praetulerim.' Ad quae cum Isidorus responsurus assurgeret, universae contionis clamore correptus obticuit.

5 At Aeneas Mediolanum profectus nobilem quendam ex magna domo Landrianorum iussu ducis per capitulum ad eam praeposituram vocatum et in possessionem adductum invenit, quem sibi mox cedere compulit, tantum Aeneae et princeps et curia favit. Sed obtenta praepositura lectum aegritudinis incidit ingenti febre correptus; ad quem Philippus suum medicum, doctum et laetum virum, Philippum Bononiensem—qui postea Nicolao papae servivit—singulis diebus mittebat. In hac aegritudine cum pharmacum accepisset, neque id quicquam operatum esset, potionemque alteram sequenti nocte sumendam medicus praeparasset, ipsa hora qua ministrari secundum pharmacum debuit, moveri venter cepit atque adeo vexavit hominem ut nonaginta vicibus assurgere cogeretur. Ob quam rem mente alienatus ad portas, ut aiunt, mortis usque cucurrit. Quod si potionem alteram ebibisset, animam procul dubio extenuatus atque consumptus exalasset. Quod certissimum Dei beneficium intellegens, quamvis quinque et septuaginta dies continuo febris ardore quateretur, numquam tamen adduci potuit, ut incantatoribus auscultaret, quamvis homo ad se duceretur, quem novissime in castris Nicolai Picinini duo millia virorum ex febribus liberasse dicebant. Sed Deo fidens, cuius ope servatus in vita fuerat, adhuc febricitans iter accipiens inter equitandum liberatus Basileam reversus est.

6 Ubi cum solemnitas ageretur Divi Ambrosii, Mediolanensi invitante archiepiscopo, sermonem de laudibus sancti patris ad synodum habuit, quamvis theologi restitissent qui sibi id muneris expetebant. Sed praelatus cunctis Aeneas incredibili attentione ab omnibus auditus est.

endorsement (if you do indeed favor my nomination) and lose possession of the church, than gain it by election by the chapter." When Isidoro rose to reply to this, he was shouted down by the whole assembly and had to hold his peace.

When Aeneas arrived in Milan, however, he found that the 5
duke had ordered the chapter to appoint and install as their provost a nobleman of the great house of the Landriani. But such was the esteem Aeneas enjoyed with the prince and the court, he soon compelled his rival to surrender the post to him. After entering into it he was suddenly struck with a severe fever. The duke sent his own physician, Filippo of Bologna, to see him every day; he was a learned and delightful man, who afterward entered the service of Pope Nicholas. During this illness, after Aeneas had taken one drug with no effect, and the physician had prepared another to be taken the next night, at the very moment when the second drug was to be administered his bowels began to work. This caused him such discomfort that he was up and down some ninety times in the night, leaving him delirious and at death's door, as the saying goes. Had he drunk the second draught, he would certainly have been too weak and exhausted to survive it. Recognizing this as a clear sign of divine mercy—although the fever continued to torment him another seventy five days—he ever after refused to pay heed to miraculous healers, even when presented with a man reputed to have cured two thousand men of fever in the camp of Niccolò Piccinino. Putting his trust instead in God, by whose aid his life had been spared, Aeneas set out while still feverish and returned to Basel, recovering his health along the way.

At Basel they were celebrating the feast of St. Ambrose of Mi- 6
lan. At the archbishop's invitation,[31] Aeneas delivered the eulogy of the saint before the synod, despite the objections of the theologians who wanted to perform this function themselves. But Aeneas was preferred before them all and everyone listened to him with incredible attention.

: 9 :

De Sigismundi caesaris morte et Alberti suffectione, Aeneae pestilenti morbo et mirabili cura.

1 Interea mortuo Sigismundo caesare atque Alberto in eius locum subrogato, missus ad eum Bartholomeus Novariensis episcopus a Philippo duce Mediolani, cum Basileam venisset, Aeneas ut in Austriam sibi comes iret non parvis precibus impetravit. Nondum Albertus imperium acceptaverat adversantibus Hungaris, qui ea conditione susceptum Hungariae regnum dicebant, ne vel oblatum imperium assumeret. Incertus autem quid ageret, Albertus legatos principum qui aderant consulendos censuit, tempusque deliberantibus indulsit. Interim Bartholomeus rationes ab Aenea conscriptas accepit, quibus et imperium acceptandum et Hungari ad consentiendum induci posse videbantur; quas cum in consilio recitasset, gratiae sibi publicae actae sunt et Albertus, non consentientibus modo sed ultro suadentibus Hungaris, imperatorem se dixit.

2 At Aeneas Austriae moribus offensus, quos nondum plane norat, dimisso apud Viennam Bartholomeo cum Ludovico patriarcha Aquilegiensi, homine nobili ex ducibus Deck Basileam rediit, nescius quod magnam vitae partem in Austria postmodum esset acturus. Nulli 'Hac non ibo' dicere licet:

prudens premit deus caliginosa nocte futurum!

3 Hic annus apud Germanos neque vini neque tritici ferax fuit. In Baioaria pueri passim innuptaeque puellae ex transeuntibus pa-

: 9 :

Death of Emperor Sigismund. Succession of Albert. Aeneas miraculously cured of plague.

Meanwhile, Emperor Sigismund died. Albert was elected in his 1
place.[32] Duke Filippo of Milan despatched his legate Bartolomeo, bishop of Novara, who on arriving at Basel managed to persuade Aeneas to go with him to Austria. Albert had not yet accepted the crown on account of the opposition of the Hungarians, who claimed that he had ascended the throne of Hungary on the understanding that he would not accept the Empire even if it were offered him. Feeling unsure what to do, Albert decided to consult the envoys of the various princes who were present. During the time allowed for deliberations, Aeneas gave Bartolomeo a written statement outlining why Albert should accept the crown and suggesting how the Hungarians could be induced to consent. When Bartolomeo read it out in the council, he was publicly thanked and Albert proclaimed himself emperor, with the Hungarians not only consenting, but actually urging him to do so.

Aeneas did not care for the customs in Austria, a country 2
with which he was not yet fully acquainted, so he parted from Bartolomeo at Vienna and returned to Basel with Lodovico, the patriarch of Aquileia, a nobleman of the house of the dukes of Teck. He did not know then that a great part of his future life was to be spent in Austria. No man can say, "Here is a place I will never go," for

God in His wisdom shrouds the future in dark night.[33]

That year was not a good one in Germany for either wine or 3
wheat.[34] In Bavaria boys and girls begged bread from passersby and fought for the scraps tossed to them as dogs fight over

nem petebant, atque ut inter canes ossa proiecta, sic inter illos buccellae panis iactatae litem movebant. Nec diu post secuta est acerbissima lues, quae totam Alamaniam infecit; haec in Basilea Ludovicum patriarcham Ludovicumque protonotarium Romanum, quem dicebant iuris lumen, exstinxit, admodum multos praelatos morti dedit, infinitam plebem prostravit, tantaque rabies morbi fuit ut amplius quam trecenta cadavera una dies sepelierit. Tumque carissimos amicos Aeneas amisit: Iulianum Romanum et Arnoldum Theutonicum, quibus aegrotantibus usque ad animi transitum comes intrepidus astitit.

4 Sed neque sibi pestis ignovit; ut se tactum intellexit, vocatis comitibus ut abirent suasit, ne sibi morituro astantes inficerentur. Ex his Iacobus Cerverius territus ex Basilea recessit; Andreas Panigalius, constantioris amicitiae socius, etiamsi mori oporteret, abiturum se[33] negavit. Iohannes Steynofius Theutonicus tunc illi serviebat, ac Petrus Iuliani Romanus; cum his habito de medicis consilio cum accepisset duos esse in civitate celebres — alterum Parisiensem et doctum, sed infelicem, alterum Theutonicum indoctum et fortunatum — Aeneas fortunam scientiae praetulit, quia morbi pestiferi incertam esse curam sciebat.

5 Curatio haec fuit: quoniam sinistrum inguen laesum erat, sinistri pedis[34] aperta vena est; tum die tota et in partem noctis prohibitus somnus; exin pulvis quidam ebibitus cuius materiam revelare medicus noluit; ulceri et loco laeso nunc rafani viridis suci pleni incisae portiones, nunc madidae cretae frusta supponebantur. Inter haec aucta febris ingentem capitis dolorem ac salutis desperationem adduxit. Quibus ex rebus vocari ad se sacerdotem Aeneas iussit atque mox confessus, communicatus atque inunctus est. Nec diu post mente alienatus interrogantibus aliena respondit. Tumque fama vulgata est Aeneam mortuum esse; quae res illi Mediolanensem praeposituram abstulit, altero in possessionem re-

bones. Soon afterwards there came a terrible plague which spread through all of Germany. At Basel it took the lives of the Patriarch Lodovico and of Lodovico the Roman protonotary,[35] who was called "the light of the law"; it carried off many prelates and laid countless common people low. The sickness raged so fiercely that more than three hundred corpses were buried in a single day. At that time Aeneas lost his very close friends, Giuliano of Rome and Arnold the German, whom he courageously attended to the very end.

The plague did not spare Aeneas either. Realizing he was in- 4
fected, he called his companions and urged them to leave him on his deathbed before they fell sick themselves. Of these, Jacopo Cerveri fled in terror from Basel; but Andrea Panigali, who was a firmer friend, refused to go even if staying meant his own death. At that time Andrea had in his service a German, Johann Steinhof, and Pietro, Giuliano's son. After speaking to both about a physician, he found that there were two celebrated doctors in the city, one from Paris, who was learned but unlucky, the other a German, lucky but ignorant. Aeneas preferred luck to learning—reflecting that no one really knows how to cure the plague.

This was the treatment: since his left thigh was infected, they 5
opened a vein in his left foot. Then they kept him awake all that day and part of the night before making him drink a powder, the nature of which the physician would not reveal. Sometimes they applied chopped-up bits of green, juicy radish to the sore and infected part, and sometimes lumps of moist clay. Under this treatment the fever increased, accompanied by a violent headache, and all despaired of his life. Therefore Aeneas summoned a priest, made a quick confession and received communion and extreme unction. Soon after, his mind began to wander and he gave meaningless answers to questions. Then the rumor began to spread that he had died, a circumstance which cost him his provostship at Milan, for it was given to another man who, on account of the schism

cepto, qui propter divisionem Ecclesiae repelli non potuit. Sed miserante divina pietate post sex dies Aeneas convaluit; qui cum sex aureos medico in mercedem offerret (mira fides bonitasque viri atque in medico forsitan inaudita!) indignum se tanto praemio medicus existimans, 'Si hoc,' inquit, 'auri me vis accipere, sex pauperes sine precio aegrotos curabo' idque facturum iure iurando sese astrinxit.

6 Exin vacantibus per obitum Iohannis Andreae Poloni canonicatu et praebenda ecclesiae Tridentinae, concilium illos Aeneae summo favore contulit, quamvis competitores essent non pauci, neque contemnendi homines; ad quorum possessionem capiundam profectus Vilichinum quendam Theutonicum, litigiosum et versutum hominem qui se ex auctoritate capituli in illis intruserat, placatis canonicis et in suum favorem adductis extrusit.

: 10 :

Depositio Eugenii in concilio et Felicis creatio, eiusque secretarius Aeneas.

1 Hoc tempore Basilienses Eugenium papam suis decretis e summo pontificatu deiecerant, ac de successore solliciti ex qualibet natione octo viros assumpserant ita, ut essent duo et triginta quibus eligendi Romani pontificis potestatem concesserant. Cumque Italicos nominarent, Aeneam vocabant; et quia nondum sacris ordinibus initiatus incapax eius officii videbatur, litteras ei dedere quarum vigore una die, extra tempora a iure statuta, subdiaconatum et dia-

in the Church, could not be removed.[36] But after six days, by God's mercy, he recovered. When he offered his doctor a fee of six florins (for the man's kindness and faithfulness had been remarkable, perhaps unprecedented in a physician), the latter, thinking he was not worth so much, said, "If you really want me to have all this money, I'll attend six poor men without charge." And he swore an oath that he would do so.

At this time, with the death of the Pole, Johannes Andreas, the canonry and prebendry of the cathedral of Trent became vacant. 6
The Council conferred these benefices on Aeneas with its strongest endorsement, although there were numerous other candidates, all of them worthy.[37] When he went to take possession of his benefices, he found that a certain German named Vilichinus, a sly and quarrelsome fellow, had pushed himself into the posts with the permission of the chapter; but Aeneas won the canons over to his side and forced the man out.

: 10 :

Eugenius deposed by the Council. Felix made pope, and Aeneas his secretary.

At this time the Council of Basel issued decrees deposing Pope 1
Eugenius.[38] In order to find a successor, they chose eight men from each nation, making a total of thirty-two in whom the power of electing a pope was invested. When it came to selecting the Italians, they called on Aeneas. The fact that he was not yet in holy orders seemed to make him ineligible for this duty, so he was given a document which entitled him to disregard the fixed period required by law and so, in a single day, assume the ranks of subdeacon and deacon together with minor orders. But Aeneas did not

conatum cum minoribus ordinibus assumere posset. Sed noluit Aeneas eam ob causam sacris se imbuere, conclave tamen velut caerimoniarum clericus intravit viditque caerimonias omnes quibus usi sunt Basilienses in electione Amedei ducis Sabaudiae, quem Felicem papam Quintum appellaverunt.

2 Ad quem Aeneas adhuc heremum colentem perrexit, atque ab eo in scriniarium receptus et in Ripalia et in Thononio et in Gebennis et in Lausana et in Basilea tamdiu ei servivit, donec Fridericus Tertius Romanorum rex, qui Alberto defuncto successerat, Francfordiam et Alamaniae partes inferiores petens apud Aquas Grani regni coronam accepit; ad quem cum Felix legatos mitteret, Aeneam quoque iussit eo pergere, qui cum[35] consiliarios Federici saepius alloquitur, in amicitiam gravis et docti viri Silvestri Chiemensis episcopi recipitur.[36]

: II :

Aeneas poeta laurea donatus ab imperatore protonotarius efficitur, eiusque summa patientia et legationes variae.

1 Deinde Iacobi Treverensis archipontificis et electoris Imperii, hominis qui nobilitatem cum virtute coniunxerat, in notitiam familiaritatemque venit; atque ab his in gratiam caesaris adductus ac laurea corona poetarumque privilegiis donatus, ei ut servire suamque curiam sequi vellet rogatus est, cui Aeneas, quamvis se sub imperio natum nulli iustius quam imperatori serviturum responderet, quia tamen apud Felicem secretarii locum tenebat, indignum existimavit iniussu eius in alterius domini potestatem transire. Sed ait Basileam se reversurum Felicisque voluntatem quaesiturum, quam si assequi posset, non invitum caesaris curiam

want to enter on an ecclesiastical career for reasons such as this; he attended the conclave as clerk of ceremonies instead and witnessed all the proceedings by which the Council of Basel elected Duke Amedeo of Savoy to the Holy See as Pope Felix v.[39]

Aeneas went at once to the duke, who was still living in his her- 2
mitage. He became his secretary; and he continued in his service at Ripaille, Thonon, Geneva, Lausanne and Basel, until Frederick III, king of the Romans, who had succeeded to the imperial throne after Albert's death, was crowned at Aix on his way to Frankfurt and Lower Germany.[40] When Felix sent an embassy to Frederick, he ordered Aeneas to accompany the ambassadors; and thus Aeneas, who had frequent conversations with Frederick's counselors, became friendly with a learned and influential man, Sylvester, bishop of Chiemsee.[41]

: II :

Aeneas crowned poet laureate by the emperor and appointed protonotary. His unending patience. Various embassies.

Aeneas also met and came to know well Archbishop Jacob of 1
Trier, an imperial elector and a man as virtuous as he was noble.[42] These two introduced Aeneas to the emperor's favor: he was awarded the laurel crown and the privileges due to poets,[43] and the emperor invited him to enter his service and remain at his court. Aeneas replied that although no one had a better right to his services (since he had been born an imperial subject), nevertheless he was still Felix's secretary and it seemed improper to leave him for a new master without obtaining his permission first. He said he would go back to Basel to ask Felix for his consent, and if he could obtain it he would gladly come to the imperial court. The em-

secuturum. Caesari, qui Basilea transiturus erat, non ingratum responsum fuit.

2 At Aeneas cum ad Felicem redisset neque suopte ingenio abeundi potestatem obtinere posset, interpositis tandem amicis aegre dimissus est; qui ad Federicum transiens, cum is ex Burgundia reversus, Basileam petivisset, in secretarium admissus in Romana cancellaria protonotarii locum obtinuit. Ius iurandum apud Brixinam caesari praestitit, nam et ibi Gaspar Slichius cancellariam accepit, quam prius apud Sigismundum et Albertum caesares obtinuerat; nobilis eques ingenio prompto et facundia grata, cui vel inaudita vel rara laus obtigit, ut trium caesarum cancellarius fieret.

3 Is cum legatum caesaris apud Nurembergam ageret, regimen cancellariae Wilhelmo Taz homini Baioario et Italici nominis hosti commisit, a quo miris modis Aeneas afflictus est; qui cum statuisset malum in bono vincere, auriculas declinavit,

> ut iniquae mentis asellus
> cum gravius dorso subit onus.

Itaque, licet ultimus omnium haberetur, neque in mensa neque in cubiculo dignum se locum haberet, ac invisus ut hereticus vel Iudaeus sperneretur irridereturque, aequo animo tulit omnia.

4 Unus tamen inter consecretarios fuit, Michael Fullendorfius, qui cum mansuetiores amaret musas et studia sectaretur humanitatis, Aeneam bene sperare iubebat, quia redeunte cancellario meliorem fortunam inveniret. Neque mentitus est; nam cum redisset Gaspar atque quid Aeneas valeret nunc una nunc altera in re tentaret, cum reperiret ingeniosum, industrium et laboris patientem hominem, magni facere et praeferre eum cepit. Ad haec accessit,

peror, who was just going to Basel himself, found this answer acceptable.

When Aeneas returned to Felix, however, he was unable to obtain his release on his own. In the end, his friends intervened and Felix reluctantly set him free. Aeneas met Frederick at Basel (where the emperor had stopped on his way back from Burgundy) and was appointed his secretary and a protonotary in the imperial chancery. At Brixen he swore an oath of allegiance to the emperor.[44] There, too, Caspar Schlick was appointed chancellor, an office he had held under Sigismund and Albert. He was a noble knight, a man of ready wit and eloquent charm, who had the unprecedented or at least very rare distinction of serving three emperors as chancellor. 2

When Schlick went to Nuremberg as the emperor's legate, he delegated his authority in the chancery to Wilhelm Tacz, a Bavarian who hated all Italians. This man insulted Aeneas outrageously but Aeneas, having made up his mind to conquer evil with good,[45] laid back his ears 3

like the stubborn ass
whose burden is too heavy for his back.[46]

And so, despite the fact that he was considered last and least of all, and did not have a proper place at table or a suitable room and was hated and despised and laughed at like a heretic or a Jew, he bore everything calmly.

There was one man among his fellow secretaries, Michael Pfullendorf, who loved the gentler muses and the study of literature. He encouraged Aeneas to keep his hopes up, for when the chancellor returned he would find his fortunes improved. Nor was he mistaken, for when Caspar returned and tested Aeneas's worth in various ways, he found him talented, industrious and able to stand hard work and began to think highly of him and to show him preference. What is more, Caspar had once visited Siena: at 4

quia cum Senis ageret Gaspar eo tempore, quo Sigismundus imperator illic erat, apud Nicolaum Lollium spectatum virum eiusque coniugem, nobilem matronam Bartholomeam Ptolomeam Aeneae amitam, hospitium habuit, ac nepotem eius ex Margarita natum sacro de fonte levavit, quem suo ex nomine Gasparem vocavit.

5 Ob quas res carior Gaspari factus, cum iterum ille in legationem abiisset, gubernationi cancellariae praefectus est, eamque rexit quotiens Gaspar abfuit. At Wilhelmus, qui prius Aeneam conculcabat, vereri eum coactus est, ut intellegerent omnes humilitatem facile tolli sursum, superbiam facilius deorsum ruere. Wilhelmus tamen invidiae succumbens imperialem curiam paulo post reliquit; ceteri in gratiam cum Aenea redierunt, qui apud caesarem in dies crescens ad res magnas et arduas vocatus in consilium secretius tandem receptus est.

6 Prima ei legatio apud Tergestinos fuit, quos caesari fidelitatem iurare suasit, atque ab eis ius iurandum recepit. Exinde cum apud Nurembergam imperator et principes electores ad sublationem schismatis intenderent, quod inter Eugenium Quartum et Felicem Quintum vigebat, placuissetque ut imperator quattuor viros eligeret, elector quilibet duos et alius quivis princeps unum, qui auditis Eugenii ac Felicis oratoribus providerent ne quid res publica Christiana detrimenti pateretur, Federicus caesar hos nominavit: Silvestrum Chiemensem episcopum, Thomam Haselbachium theologum, Ulricum Sonnembergium iuris consultum et Aeneam poetam, quamvis hic adhuc rebus Basiliensibus et Felici magis quam Eugenio bene cuperet. Nondum enim ardor ille Basiliensis eum reliquerat, neque rationes tenebat quibus Eugenii causa nitebatur; qui apud unam solum partem versatus alteram contemnebat; sed pedetentim postmodum declinavit, cum Basilienses refugere iudicium animadvertit.

the time of Emperor Sigismund's visit, he had been housed in the home of the distinguished Niccolò Lolli[47] and his wife, the noble lady Bartolomea Tolomei, who was Aeneas's aunt; and he had stood godfather to their daughter Margherita's baby son, whom he named Gaspare after himself.

These things endeared Aeneas to him all the more. The next 5
time Caspar went away on an embassy, Aeneas was left in charge of the chancery. Thereafter he presided over it whenever the chancellor was away. Wilhelm, who had begun by walking all over Aeneas, was now forced to stand in awe of him, leaving all to understand that meekness is easily exalted and pride still more easily brought low. Consumed with envy, Wilhelm soon withdrew from the court. The others were reconciled with Aeneas, whose influence with the emperor increased daily. He was called on in many important and difficult matters and eventually was made a member of the privy council.

His first mission was to Trieste, where he persuaded the citi- 6
zens to swear allegiance to the emperor and administered the oath himself. Later, when the emperor and the prince electors were at Nuremberg trying to end the bitter schism between Eugenius IV and Felix V,[48] they decided to appoint a committee to hear the spokesmen of Eugenius and Felix and ensure that no harm came to Christendom. The emperor was to choose four men, each elector was to choose two, and the other princes one apiece. Frederick named the following: Sylvester, bishop of Chiemsee; the theologian Thomas Haselbach; the jurisconsult Ulrich Sonnenberg; and Aeneas the poet, even though Aeneas still favored the cause of Basel and Felix more than he did Eugenius. The enthusiasm he had felt at Basel had not yet left him, nor had he grasped the principles on which Eugenius's case rested, and associating as he did with one side only, he despised the other. (Later, however, when he realized that the representatives from Basel were trying to avoid putting their case to the test, he gradually withdrew his support.)

7 Igitur in Noremberga partes Basiliensium obnixe iuvit, atque ipsius opera conditiones pacis, quae partes oblatae sunt, non tam faciles Eugenio quam Basiliensibus dictae fuerunt. Nam cum placuisset ad reformandam Ecclesie pacem aliud concilium convocare, in quod et Eugenius et Basilienses consentirent, urbs Constantia provinciae Maguntinae pro loco concilii nominata est, quae ab Eugenio remotissima erat, Basiliensibus propinqua.

: 12 :

Sarantanae vallis descriptio et incolarum mores.

1 Interim Aeneas Sarantanae vallis parochialem ecclesiam favore caesaris assecutus est, quae aureos ei sexaginta quotannis reddidit. Sita in alpibus quae Germaniam ab Italia disterminant, ea vallis uno tantum aditu eoque altissimo et perdifficili patens, nivibus et asperrima glacie tribus anni partibus obtecta rigescit. Loci accolae totas hiemes domi se continent, cistas et quae sunt opera carpentariorum solerter agentes, quae per aestatem Bulzani Tridentique vendunt. Scaccorum ac alearum ludo temporis plurimum terunt, illumque mirum in modum callent.

2 Nullus hos belli metus occupat, neque honoris cupido cruciat, neque auri magna fames atterit. Horum opes pecora sunt, quae per hiemem faeno nutriunt, hisque vivunt; inter quos et homines invenire est, quos numquam bibisse constat, quibus pro potu est cibus lacteus. Qui procul ab ecclesia degunt, corpora hiemis tempore defuncta sub divo reponunt, atque astricta gelu in aestatem

At Nuremberg he stubbornly advanced the cause of Basel and it was owing to his efforts that the terms of peace offered to the opposing factions favored the Council rather than the pope; for when they decided to try to restore peace to the Church by calling another council to which both Eugenius and the delegates at Basel should come, the place named was the city of Constance in the province of Mainz, which was very far from Eugenius but quite near Basel. 7

: 12 :

The Sarntal and its people.

Meanwhile Aeneas received from the emperor the parish church of the Sarntal, which brought him a yearly income of sixty gold florins. This valley lies in the alps separating Germany from Italy. It has only one entrance, which is very steep and rough, and for three quarters of the year it lies buried under snow and thick ice. The inhabitants remain in their houses all winter making boxes and other pieces of carpentry, in which art they are highly skilled, and which they sell in the summer in Bolzano and Trent. They while away a good deal of time playing chess and dice, games at which they are extraordinarily clever. 1

They have no fear of war nor are they tormented by any ambition nor consumed by greed for gold. Their wealth is in their flocks, which they feed on hay in the winter and which provide them with all the means of life. There are men among them who have never tasted wine: their diet consists solely of milky porridge. In winter, those who live far from the church place the bodies of any who die out of doors and keep them frozen till summer, when the priest does the rounds of the parish at the head of a long fu- 2

servant; tum plebanus parochiam circuiens longum funens ordinem ducit, dicensque novissima verba in cimiterium plura simul cadavera recipit; illi siccis genis exequias prosequuntur. Felicissimi mortalium, sua si bona cognoscentes libidini frenum ponerent! Sed die noctuque commessati stupra et adulteria passim admittunt, neque virgo apud eos nubit.

3 Verum hanc ecclesiam Aeneas brevi dimisit, meliorem assecutus in Baioaria, Sanctae Mariae Aspacensis, non longe ab Eno flumine, quam sibi Leonardus Pataviensis episcopus, genere atque magnificentia aeque nobilis ultro contulit, litteris ei sine praedo ad Stiriam missis.

: 13 :

Aeneae legatio ad pontificem Eugenium et cum eo reconciliatio, et Thomae Sarezanei amicitia.

1 Post haec, cum iam Basilienses conditiones pacis refutassent, Aeneas ad Eugenium missus est. Qui cum Senas venisset, unanimi propinquorum voce prohibebatur Romam petere, qui Basileae infensus Eugenio fuisset. Illum enim nullius rei quam iniuriae magis memorem ac vindictae cupidum crudelemque praedicabant. Contra, Aeneas oratorem caesaris non arbitrari sese aiebat Romae non tutum, onus legationis a se receptum aut absolvendum esse aut sibi moriendum; atque parentibus invitis et flentibus Romam perrexit.

2 Gerardus Landrianus cardinalis Comanus, cum quo sibi vetus familiaritas erat, rectus pater et amicitiae tenax, ad Eugenii praesentiam ipsum introduxit. Libet hic coram summo sacerdote quibus verbis Aeneas fuerit usus referre, nam pauca sunt et memoratu

neral train. He pronounces the last words[49] and receives several bodies into the cemetery at the same time, as the people follow the procession dry-eyed. Happiest of mortals—if they would only think on their blessings and bridle their lust; but they spend day and night feasting and fornicating and no girl is ever a virgin on her wedding day.

Aeneas soon gave up this church, however, having secured a better one, that of St. Mary of Aspach in Bavaria, not far from the River Inn. Leonard, bishop of Passau, a man of noble birth and character, offered him this of his own accord and sent the presentation to him at Styria, free of all dues. 3

: 13 :

Aeneas's legation to Pope Eugenius. Their reconciliation. His friendship with Tommaso of Sarzana.

After this, the Council of Basel rejected the proposed terms of peace, and Aeneas was sent to confer with Eugenius.[50] When he reached Siena, however, his relations all tried to deter him from going to Rome because he had been opposed to Eugenius at Basel. Eugenius, they said, remembered nothing so long as an injury and was both vindictive and cruel. Aeneas replied that he could not imagine the emperor's ambassador would be in danger in Rome and that he must either perform the duty he had undertaken or die in the attempt. And so, ignoring the protests of his weeping family, he continued on his way. 1

An old intimate of his, Gerardo Landriani, cardinal of Como, an honest priest and faithful friend, introduced him to the presence of Eugenius. I should like to quote here the words Aeneas addressed to the pope, for they are brief and worth recording. Two 2

digna. Duo cardinales pontifici astabant, Comanus et Morinensis, qui prius auctoritate apostolica ab omnibus censuris Aeneam absolverant, quas favendo Basiliensibus inciderat. In conspectum ergo cum Eugenii venisset Aeneas, ad osculumque pedis, manus et oris ab eo receptus, restitutisque litteris, iussus fuisset dicere, 'Prius,' inquit, 'sanctissime praesul, quam caesaris mandata refero, de me ipso pauca dicam.

3 'Scio multa de me tuis auribus inculcata esse neque bona neque digna relatu, sed neque mentiti sunt qui me tibi detulerunt. Plurima ego dum Basileae fui adversus te dixi, scripsi et[37] feci. Nihil inficior. At non tam tibi nocere, quam Dei Ecclesiae prodesse mens mea fuit. Nam cum te persequerer, obsequium me Deo praestare putabam. Erravi (quis neget?) sed neque cum paucis neque cum parvis hominibus. Iulianum Sancti Angeli cardinalem, Nicolaum archiepiscopum Panhormitanum, Ludovicum Pontanum tuae sedis notarium sum secutus, qui iuris oculi et veritatis magistri credebantur. Quid scholam Parisiensem et alia orbis gymnasia referam, quorum pleraque adversum te sentiebant? Quis cum tantis nominibus non erraverit?

4 'Verum ego ubi errorem deprehendi Basiliensium, fateor, non statim ad te convolavi, quod plerique fecerunt; sed veritus ne ab errore in errorem prolaberer, ut saepe in Scyllam incidunt cupientes vitare Charybdim, ad eos me contuli qui neutrales habebantur, ut ab altero duorum extremorum ad alterum non sine consultatione ac mora transirem. Mansi ergo apud caesarem tribus annis; ubi dum magis ac magis contentiones audio quae inter Basilienses et tuos legatos fiunt, nihil mihi dubii relictum est, quin te penes sit veritas; atque hinc factum est, ut cupienti caesari ad tuam me clementiam viam facere non invitus paruerim, sic enim me tuam in gratiam redire posse sum ratus. Nunc apud te sum et, quia igno-

cardinals, Como and Amiens,[51] were standing by the pope. First, they invoked apostolic authority to absolve Aeneas of all the blame he had incurred by taking the side of the Council of Basel. Then Aeneas came before Eugenius. He was given permission to kiss his foot, hand and cheek; he presented his credentials and was asked to speak: "Your Holiness," he began, "before I deliver the emperor's message, I will say a few words about myself.

"I know you have heard much about me that is neither good nor fit to be repeated. Those who have told you such tales have not lied. At Basel I said, wrote and did many things against you. I deny none of them. But my intention was not so much to hurt you as to help the Church of God. For in attacking you I thought I was offering service to God.[52] I was wrong (who can deny it?) but I was not alone. I followed the lead of Giuliano, cardinal of Sant'Angelo, Niccolò, archbishop of Palermo, and Lodovico Pontano, a notary of your own see, who were considered the very eyes of the law, teachers of truth.[53] I will say nothing of the university of Paris and the other schools all over the world, so many of which opposed you. Who might not have erred in the company of such men? 3

"But I confess that when I realized the error of the Council, I did not immediately fly to your side, as many did. Instead, fearing I would slip from one error into another, as those who try to avoid Charybdis often fall into Scylla, I aligned myself with those who were considered neutral, so as not to switch from one extreme to the other without time for reflection. Therefore I stayed three years with the emperor, where I heard more and more of the dispute between the Council and your legates, till finally there remained not a shadow of doubt that the truth was on your side. Thus it happened that when the emperor desired to send me to Your Clemency, I happily obeyed, thinking I should have the chance to regain your favor. Now I stand before you and, because I 4

rans peccavi, mihi ut ignoscas oro. Deinde causam caesaris explicabo.'

5 Cui Eugenius 'Scimus te,' inquit, 'in nos graviter deliquisse, sed erratum fatenti non possumus non ignoscere. Ecclesia namque, pia mater, neganti debitum numquam remittit, fatenti numquam retinet. Tu iam veritatem tenes.[38] Cave ne relinquas eam, atque bonis operibus divinam gratiam quaerito quam malis actibus amisisti. Eo in loco iam degis ubi et veritatem tueri possis et Ecclesiae prodesse. Nos iniuriarum posthac praeteritarum obliti te bene ambulantem bene amabimus.' Atque his dictis ad res Ecclesiae ventum est; super quibus Eugenius deliberandi tempus accepit.

6 Medio tempore, dum cardinalem Aquilegiensem Aeneas peteret, Thomam Sarezaneum tunc episcopum Bononiensem forte fortuna obvium habuit; quem cum pro veteri benivolentia salutandum adiret, invitum ac sese fugientem et horrentem offendit, ut qui Aeneam Basiliensibus adhuc rebus faventem coniectabatur, quas ille singulari odio insectabatur. Quod miratus Aeneas ac paululum indignatus substitit, neque illius ultra quaesivit alloquium.

7 At cum interiectis deinde paucis diebus apud Iulianum Barattum, veterem et Basiliensem amicum, Aeneas decumberet iliorum gravi dolore oppressus, commiseratus Thomas Martinum Hispanum, fidum et probatum familiarem, ad eum misit qui consolaretur aegrotum atque in medicos offerret pecuniam. Iohannes Carvaiales, qui saepe apud imperatorem legatus fuerat ac postea cardinalatum obtinuit, nulla non die visitavit Aeneam; cardinales quoque ad eum mittebant, sed et summus pontifex Iohannem Papiensem spectatum virum misit, qui Aeneae cuncta polliceretur ad quaerendam sanitatem necessaria. Ingens illa aegritudo fuit tantaque vis doloris, ut duodecim diebus quibus Aeneas decubuit, nulla non hora mortem optaverit. Sed restitutus denique, responso

sinned in ignorance, I beg your forgiveness. After that, I shall set forth the emperor's case."

Eugenius replied, "We know that you have sinned grievously against us, but since you confess your error we must pardon you. The Church is a loving mother, who never remits the due penalty if a son denies his sin, nor insists upon it when he confesses. Now you know the truth. See that you do not let it go. Strive by good works to regain the divine grace which you lost by wicked acts. You are now in a position to defend the truth and be of service to the Church. Hereafter we shall forget past wrongs and, so long as you do well, we shall love you well." After this they proceeded to speak of ecclesiastical matters, about which Eugenius wished time to meditate. 5

Meanwhile, as Aeneas was looking for the cardinal of Aquileia,[54] he chanced to meet Tommaso of Sarzana, then bishop of Bologna. He was about to greet him as an old friend when Tommaso drew back with a shudder and tried to avoid him; for he supposed that Aeneas was still on the side of the Council of Basel, which he himself despised. Aeneas, surprised at this and somewhat indignant, stopped short and made no further effort to speak to him. 6

Some days later, however, when Aeneas lay ill with a painful attack of colic at the house of Giuliano Baratto, an old friend of his from Basel, Tommaso took pity and sent his faithful and trusted friend, the Spaniard Martino, to comfort him in his sickness and offer him money to pay his physicians. Juan de Carvajal,[55] who had often led embassies to the imperial court and was afterward made a cardinal, visited Aeneas every day; cardinals sent to inquire after him; and the pope himself sent the distinguished Giovanni of Pavia to promise him everything necessary for his recovery. His illness was very severe and the pain so intense that there was not a moment in the twelve days he lay there when he did not pray for death. Finally he recovered; and when he heard from Eugenius 7

ab Eugenio recepto (qui se missurum ad caesarem dixit) Senas repetiit et consolatus patrem, quem postea numquam vidit, salutatisque propinquis omnibus in Alamaniam rediit.

8 In via autem apud Sanctum Cassianum Thomae episcopo Bononiensi, qui Romam ibat, datus obviam gratias egit, quod sui aegrotantis memor Romae fuisset, atque ibi combibentes pristinam benivolentiam integrarunt. Non tamen adhuc vera haec reconciliatio visa est Thomae; nam cum interiecto deinde tempore legatus ad caesarem proficisceretur, Petrum Noxetanum, familiarem et propinquum suum atque Aeneae verum et antiquum amicum, interpellavit sibi ut litteras commendatitias ad eum daret. Sed minime his opus erat; Aeneas enim nullius rei suevit quam inimicitiarum facilius oblivisci. Receptis tamen Petri litteris in omne officium Thomae praestandum tanto sese magis voluntarium exhibuit, quanto duarum amicitiarum quam unius est solidior nexus. Quibus ex rebus detersa est omnis rubigo simultatis, et amicitia quae olim fuit aut eo maior innovata est.

: 14 :

Fit Aeneas Eugenii secretarius, et eius singularis cum virtute fortuna, et electorum Imperii adversus pontificem coniuratio.

1 Venit et Thomae comes qui paulo ante a caesare recesserat, Iohannes Carvaiales, atque is litteras Eugenii ad Aeneam detulit quae secretariatus apostolici sibi officium demandabant; cuius postea iuramentum Romae praebuit. Magnum, ut mihi videtur, et singulare viri praeconium! Nec scio, an alteri unquam contigerit eo fortunam unum efferre hominem, ut apud duos Romanos pontifices, unum imperatorem et unum antipapam secretariatu potiri posset! Nam Aeneas hoc muneris cum Felice primum, deinde cum Fede-

that he would send an ambassador to the emperor, he went back to Siena.[56] Then, after comforting his father, whom he never saw again, and greeting his relations, he returned to Germany.

On his way, near San Casciano, he met Bishop Tommaso of Bologna, who was on his way to Rome, and he thanked him for remembering him when he had been ill in the city. They drank together and renewed their old friendship, but even then Tommaso did not think the reconciliation was complete; for some time later, when he was travelling as ambassador to the emperor, Tommaso asked his friend and relative Piero da Noceto, who was also a loyal old friend of Aeneas, to give him a letter of recommendation to him. This was entirely unnecessary, for Aeneas forgot nothing so quickly as a grudge. Still, when he read Piero's letter, he showed himself so much the readier to do Tommaso every service as the bond of two friendships is stronger than one. Thus all the rust of dissension was scrubbed away and their friendship was renewed closer than ever. 8

: 14 :

Aeneas made secretary to Eugenius. His marvelous luck and ability. A conspiracy by the imperial electors against the pope.

Travelling with Tommaso was Juan de Carvajal, who had just returned from the emperor. He brought a letter from Eugenius appointing Aeneas apostolic secretary, a post into which he was later inducted at Rome. This seems to me an extraordinary distinction and I do not know whether anyone else has ever had the good luck to be so exalted by fortune as to serve as secretary to two popes, an emperor and an antipope. For Aeneas held this post not only 1

rico caesare, postea cum Eugenio et demum cum Nicolao non solum nomine sed re quoque obtinuit.

2 Per idem temporis electores imperii apud Francfordiam convenientes, ob depositionem Coloniensis et Iacobi Treverensis archiepiscopi ab Eugenio factam commoti, occultum inter se foedus percusserunt, nisi Eugenius irritam depositionem hanc decerneret, nationis onera tolleret et auctoritatem conciliorum (ut Constantiae declarata fuerat) profiteretur, se suam depositionem in Basilea factam amplexuros; legatosque ad caesarem miserunt, qui haec ei soli et sex iuratis consiliariis exponentes, ut foederi se adiungeret atque cum eis mitteret Romam orarent. Caesar, ut audivit electorum mentem, missurum se ad Eugenium dixit rogaturumque ut eorum petitionibus morem gereret; foedus autem sprevit, indignum atque impium dicens, nisi papa quae petuntur concesserit, ab eo descire.

3 Misit igitur Aeneam ad Eugenium, ut suaderet ei ne principes electores contemneret, maxime vero ut depositis archiepiscopis pristinam redderet dignitatem; sic enim futurum, ut Germani omnes deposita neutralitate ad eius gremium redirent; quod si durior in sententia perseveraret, timendum esse ne scandalum perpetuae divisionis oriretur. Quicquid autem electores inter se concluserant, iniuratus caesar aperuit Aeneae, atque ut papae referret imperavit. Et quia rursus in Kalendis Septembris apud Francfordiam electores habituri conventum erant, ut audito responso papae secundum foedus neutralitatem exirent, Aeneam monuit ut recta via Francfordiam peteret, ubi legatos alios conventurus, animum Eugenii eis notum efficeret.

4 Legati inter haec apostolici quid rerum principes electores in Francfordia conclusissent, quid ex caesare peterent, quid Romam

nominally but actively, first under Felix, then under Emperor Frederick, later under Eugenius and finally under Nicholas.

At this time the imperial electors met at Frankfurt.[57] Roused by 2
the news that Eugenius had dismissed the archbishop of Cologne and Jacob, archbishop of Trier,[58] they made a secret compact: unless Eugenius annulled the dismissals, relieved the nation of its burdens and recognized the authority granted to their councils at Constance, they would recognize the decrees deposing Eugenius which had been voted at Basel. They sent ambassadors to the emperor to explain these matters privately to him and to six of his sworn counselors, and to beg him to join their compact and send his representative with them to Rome. When the emperor heard of the electors' plan, he said he would send an ambassador to Eugenius and would ask him to grant their petitions; but he would have nothing to do with the compact. It would be an impious outrage, he said, to desert the pope simply because he did not grant what they asked.

Therefore he sent Aeneas to Eugenius to persuade him not to 3
defy the electors, and to beg him instead to restore the deposed archbishops to their former positions, as this would inspire the Germans to abandon their neutrality and return to his side. But if he persisted in his harsh attitude, he risked the scandal of a permanent schism. The emperor, who was not under oath, revealed all the electors' secret decisions to Aeneas and ordered him to communicate them to the pope. The electors were planning to hold another meeting at Frankfurt on the first of September, where they would hear the pope's reply and, as they had agreed, decide either for or against him. The emperor therefore told Aeneas to go straight to Frankfurt to meet the other delegates and tell them there of Eugenius's decision.

Meanwhile the apostolic legates, who had been trying for some 4
time, without success, to learn what the electors had decided at Frankfurt, what they wanted of the emperor and what message

mitterent, cum diu quaesissent nec certum aliquid excudere possent, ut alter eorum Romam pergeret decreverunt. Et quia Iohannes Carvaiales languens apud veterem hospitem suum, Iohannem Gers, mordacem et invidae mentis hominem acutis incensus febribus iacebat, Thomae Bononiensi episcopo haec provincia cessit, qui Aeneam itineris comitem accepit. Tempus tunc vernale fuit, in quo tanta celo pluvia cecidit, ut omnes in Carinthia pontes ruperit[39] et secum flumina tulerit;[40] ob quam rem per altissimos et invios montes atque abruptas et nivosas petras monstrantibus accolis triduanum iter coacti sunt pergere[41].

: 15 :

Aeneas Eugenium convenit. Aegrotatio eius, et Thomae ac Aeneae singularis prudentia in dissolvendo Francfordiensi conventu et neutralitate deponenda.

1 Cum Romam venissent, Eugenius admonente Thoma prius Aeneam quam legatos electorum audivit, facturumque se omnia promisit quae caesar suasit. Atque inde[42] Thomam ad Philippum Burgundorum ducem direxit, consensum ut archiepiscoporum restitutioni praeberet, quod nepos eius in Coloniensis et frater eius naturalis in Treverensis locum vocatus esset; itaque non videbatur illo inconsulto restitutio promittenda. Mandatum autem Thomae fuit, postquam Philippi voluntatem intellexisset, ut Francfordiam se conferret.

2 Sed cum is in expediendis litteris cunctatior[43] videretur, Aeneas, qui secum usque Parmam iturum se dixerat, praecedendum

they were sending to Rome, decided that one of them should go to Rome himself as soon as possible. Juan de Carvajal was laid up with a severe fever at the house of his old friend, Johann Gers (a very jealous and sharp-tongued person), so this duty fell to Bishop Tommaso of Bologna, who accompanied Aeneas on the journey. It was then spring, and so much rain had fallen that it destroyed all the bridges in Carinthia and swept them down the river. Therefore they were obliged to travel for three days with native guides over extremely steep and trackless mountains and precipitous, snow-covered crags.

: 15 :

Aeneas meets Eugenius. He falls ill. He and Tommaso exercise exceptional prudence in dissolving the Diet of Frankfurt and winning over the electors from their neutrality.

1 When they reached Rome, Eugenius, at Tommaso's suggestion, heard Aeneas before he heard the delegates of the electors; he promised to do everything that the emperor urged. He then ordered Tommaso to go to Duke Philip of Burgundy and obtain his consent to the reinstatement of the archbishops; for Philip's nephew had been nominated for the post at Cologne and his natural brother for that at Trier, and the pope thought he should not promise to reinstate the former bishops without consulting him. After learning Philip's wishes, Tommaso was to proceed to Frankfurt.

2 Aeneas had planned to accompany him as far as Parma, but Tommaso seemed to be dawdling, taking his time getting his documents together, so he decided to go on ahead without him. He reached Siena and was staying with his family when he suddenly

existimavit. Atque cum Senas se apud suos recepisset, e vestigio calculi aegritudinem incidit; ad quem lectulo decumbentem postridie Thomas venit, et quia festinandum erat, eo salutato recessit. Neque Aeneas vinci morbo voluit; sequenti die nondum sanus eum secutus apud Carthusiam Florentinorum apprehendit atque cum eo Pistorium Lucamque profectus est. Aeneas tamen Florentiam intravit, Thomas ingredi prohibitus qui Eugenii legatus esset, quem tum Florentini odio habebant.

3 Apud Lucam cum Petro Noxetano diem morati sunt, qui eos per vallem Carfanianae comitatus est donec ad Catherinam Thome sororem venerunt. Ea Caesaris, nobilis hominis et in valle potentis uxor erat, quae fratrem iam longo tempore non visum incredibili amore et ingenti honore suscepit.

4 Ubi relicto Petro per altos et asperrimos Sillani montes Parmam petiverunt. Illic Thomas itinere pedestri fatigatus, et quia noctes apud rusticanos hospites insomnes duxerat, acutissimas in febres cecidit; qui mox Aenea vocato flens rogavit iter suum pergeret, ne rebus agendis sua mora impedimento esset, sibique litteras apostolicas ad Iohannem Carvaialem dedit, dicens se, nisi brevi convaleret, scripturum Eugenio alium ut suo loco sufficeret.

5 Aeneas invitus aegrotum dimisit; intellegens tamen necessitatem, itineri sese dedit ac per Brixillum, traiecto Pado, Mantuam et inde Veronam venit, ac per vallem Tridentinam et montes Brixinenses Sigismundum Austriae ducem in Eni valle morantem visit; quocum venationem ingressus, id spectaculo et relatu dignum animadvertit, quod cervus mirae magnitudinis diu canibus agitatus tandem coactus est in flumen se deficere ac vivum in popinam reddere principis.

6 Illinc Aeneas discedens per Nazareth et vallem quam inferna-

fell ill of the stone. He was still in bed the following day when Tommaso arrived. The bishop stopped only to greet Aeneas and went on at once, since his business was urgent. But Aeneas would not be beaten by sickness. The next day, though he was not yet well, he followed Tommaso and caught up with him at the Certosa of Florence. They then set out together for Pistoia and Lucca. Aeneas entered Florence itself, but Tommaso was excluded because he was the legate of Eugenius whom the Florentines then despised.[59]

At Lucca they stayed a day with Piero da Noceto, who went with them through the valley of Garfagnana as far as the house of Tommaso's sister, Caterina, who had married a powerful nobleman of the valley named Cesare. She had not seen her brother for a long time and received him with extraordinary affection and great honor. 3

Leaving Piero here the others made their way to Parma over the Silanian Alps, which are extremely steep and rough. There Tommaso, who was exhausted by the long journey on foot and the sleepless nights in country inns, fell ill with a very severe fever.[60] He at once sent for Aeneas and tearfully begged him to go on without him: his delay must not interfere with their business. He gave him the apostolic letter for Juan de Carvajal and said that if he did not recover shortly, he would write Eugenius and ask him to appoint someone in his place. 4

Aeneas was reluctant to leave a man in poor health, but realizing the urgency of his mission, he carried on. He crossed the Po at Brescello and proceeded to Mantua and Verona, then up the valley of Trent and over the Alps above Brixen. He stopped to see Duke Sigismund of Austria, who was staying in the valley of the Inn. He went hunting with him and saw a sight worth telling: after a long chase the hounds drove a huge stag into the river, where he gave himself up alive to grace the prince's table. 5

From there Aeneas went by way of Nassereith and the Höllen- 6

lem vocant, superato non parvi montis dorso, ad Campidenam et Mamingam Ulmamque penetravit neque ulterius progredi poterat, latronibus omnes aditus versus Francfordiam obsidentibus. Anxius igitur ac incertus animi, dum quid agat consilium quaerit, quasi ex industria dies illic dicta ad conveniendum fuisset, mox praecursores applicant qui nocte futura Petrum Augustensem, Silvestrum Chiemensem episcopos atque Gasparem cancellarium, candidas animas, legatos caesaris adfuturos nuntiant. Nihil tum Aeneae gratius contingere potuit cum propter notitiam hominum tum propter securitatem itineris. Mox simul omnes Francfordiam petivere, ad quos intra dies paucos Iacobus Badensis et Albertus Brandeburgensis marchiones in legatione coniuncti sunt.

7 Thomas, cum decem diebus aegrotasset, tandem convalescens iter continuavit ac per Sabaudiam incognitus ad ducem Burgundorum transivit, impetratisque petitionibus circa finem conventus ad Francfordiam divertit.

8 Interea Iohannes Carvaiales et Nicolaus Cusa cum litteris quas Aeneas attulerat principibus satisfacere nitebantur. Sed frustra erant omnes conatus, cum legati principum qui Romae fuerant Eugenium asperum, superbum et nationis inimicissimum durissime sibi respondisse referrent. Itaque desperata res Eugenii videbatur, quia solus imperator adversus omnes electores declarationem facere non audebat.

9 In eo conventu egregium facinus Aeneas ausus est quod negligere nulla ratione possum. Maguntinus, qui foederi aliorum electorum et pro se et pro Federico[44] Brandeburgensi sigillum appenderat, rogantibus oratoribus caesaris ut sententiam mutaret non erat invitus, id si[45] certa posset ratione tueri, ne[46] promissi violator videretur. Tunc Aeneas bono animo collegas esse iussit, quod Ma-

thal up over a high mountain ridge to Kempten, Memmingen and Ulm; but he could get no farther because brigands were blocking all the approaches to Frankfurt. While he was anxiously debating what to do, some couriers suddenly appeared with the news that the imperial envoys would be arriving that night: Peter, bishop of Augsburg, Sylvester, bishop of Chiemsee and the chancellor, Caspar — excellent fellows, all of them.[61] It was as though they had planned in advance to meet on that day and in that spot. Nothing could have pleased Aeneas more, not only because they were his friends but also because together they could travel more safely. Very shortly, they all set out for Frankfurt; a few days later they were joined by Margrave Jacob of Baden and Margrave Albert of Brandenburg.

Tommaso had been sick for ten days when at last he began to 7
recover. He resumed his journey and passed unrecognized through Savoy to the court of the duke of Burgundy. Having obtained from him what he asked, he arrived at Frankfurt near the end of the Diet.

Meanwhile Juan de Carvajal and Nicholas of Cusa[62] were trying 8
to get the princes to accept the letter Aeneas had brought. But all their efforts were in vain, for the ambassadors of the electors who had gone to Rome reported that Eugenius had been rude, haughty and bitterly hostile to their nation and had answered them very harshly. Thus Eugenius's cause seemed desperate, for the emperor did not dare declare for him alone against all the electors.

At this diet Aeneas did a bold and remarkable thing which I 9
cannot bring myself to omit. The archbishop of Mainz[63] had affixed a seal to the concordat of the electors, both for himself and for Frederick of Brandenburg. When asked by the emperor's spokesman to change his vote, the archbishop declared he would do so if he could be assured that no one could claim he had broken his word. Then Aeneas told his companions not to fear, for he would easily satisfy the archbishop. He stayed up all night[64] and

guntino facile satisfaceret. Noctem ipse insomnem duxit, atque ex notulis principum, secundum quas Eugenium litteras dare volebant, alias notulas composuit omni expresso veneno (quod Eugenius abhorrebat) sententiasque omnes extendit, per quas et nationi provideretur, et archiepiscopi restituerentur atque auctoritas conciliorum generalium non conculcaretur.

10 Quibus peractis eas ostendi Maguntino iussit sibique dici voluntatem caesaris esse secundum eas notulas; Eugenium nationi providere; neque dubitandum esse quin illa ex eius sanctitate possent impetrari, si rursus ad eum mitterentur oratores. Visa res est Maguntino et sufficiens et iusta, moxque cum imperialibus et archiepiscoporum Magdeburgensis, Bremensis et Salzburgensis et Federici marchionis multorumque aliorum principum legatis foedus iniit, ut notulae quas Aeneas confecerat sigillis omnium munirentur mitterenturque Romam; quod sentientes electores ceterique principes animo consternati non sunt ausi contra niti, nationis enim pars maior notulas sequebatur Aeneae.

11 Ludovicus cardinalis Arelatensis ubi spe deiectum se novit; accersito Aenea, qui sibi Basileae notus, et inter familiares dilectus fuerat, mutatam eius sententiam multis verbis accusavit; cui Aeneas non se mutatum sed Basilienses non esse dicebat, qui olim fuerint; qui cum primo pacis causa transferre concilium ex Basilea in alterum locum promisissent, postea negavissent, tamquam extra Basilienses muros veritatem tueri nequirent. Iohannes quoque Lysura, vir prudens et iure pontificio consultissimus, obvius Aeneae apud Iohannem Carvaialem datus, 'Et tu,' inquit, 'ex urbe Senensi daturus legem Theutonicis advenisti? Utinam domi mansisses et nos nostram regere terram dimisisses!' Cui Aeneas transiens nihil responsi reddidit, invidiam ne sibi maiorem pararet.

from the princes' rough draft, from which they wished to compose a letter to Eugenius, he composed another, squeezing out all the venom (which would have repelled Eugenius) and amplifying all the motions concerning the provision to be made for the nation, the reinstatement of the archbishops and the respect to be shown for the authority of general Councils.

When he was finished, he gave orders that that the archbishop 10
should be shown this draft and told that it expressed the will of the emperor; that Eugenius intended to provide for the nation; and that there was no reason to doubt that they would obtain their requests from His Holiness, if they sent ambassadors to him a second time. The archbishop found this satisfactory and just, and presently he entered into an agreement with the imperial delegates and those from the archbishops of Magdeburg, Bremen and Salzburg, the Margrave Frederick and many other princes, to affix all of their seals to Aeneas's draft and send it to Rome. The electors and all the other princes were dismayed at hearing this but did not dare oppose it, for most of the nation was in favor of the draft.

When Louis, the cardinal of Arles,[65] realized that the case was 11
hopeless, he sent for Aeneas, whom he had known at Basel and counted among his intimate friends, and berated him at length for having changed his position. Aeneas replied that he had not changed; rather, the conciliar party was not what it had been. They had promised for the sake of peace to transfer the council from Basel to some other place but then had refused to do so, as though they could not defend the truth outside the walls of Basel. Likewise, when Johann of Lysura, a wise man well versed in canon law, met Aeneas at the house of Juan de Carvajal he said to him, "So you've come from Siena to dictate laws to the Germans, have you? It would have been better if you'd stayed at home and left us to govern our own country." Aeneas passed by without speaking, in order not to provoke further hostility.

: 16 :

Iohannes Carvaiales et Thomas fiunt cardinales. Aeneas Romam legatus proficiscitur; et cum omnium admiratione perorat Germanorum oboedientiam praestans.

1 Finito conventu Thomas Bononiensis antistes et Iohannes Carvaiales per Novam Civitatem Austriae transeuntes, actis caesari ingentibus gratiis qui magnos et fideles legatos ad Francfordiam miserat, dum Romam pergunt, ut qui res bene feliciterque gessissent, ad cardinalatus eminentiam provecti sunt. Caesar paucis post diebus Aeneam et nobilem equitem Procopium Rabensteynum Bohemum ad Romanam Curiam legatos instituit, hisque potestatem dedit: si Eugenius notulas in Francfordia conclusas acceptaret, concurrente praesule Maguntino et Brandeburgensi marchione, neutralitatem deponerent ac nationis nomine Sanctae Sedi Apostolicae oboedientiam restituerent.

2 Interea Iohannes Lysura, ut res suam non sequi mentem animadvertit, rebus mentem aptavit, submittensque se Maguntino archiepiscopo legationem eius ad Eugenium obtinuit; quem cum pluribus aliis oratoribus principum apud Senas legati caesaris invenerunt, atque simul Romam euntes ad primum lapidem familiam papae et cardinalium et universos Curiae praelatos obviam habuere, ac veluti duces recipi solent cum victis hostibus domum repetunt, in Urbem sunt intromissi.

3 Tertia die ad Eugenium vocati in consistorio secreto auditi sunt, quo in loco nomine omnium Aeneas oravit, quem cum papa tum cardinales mirum in modum laudaverunt. At Eugenius ea ipsa die correptus aegritudine in lectum se dedit, cardinalibusque

: 16 :

Juan de Carvajal and Tommaso made cardinals. Aeneas travels to Rome as legate and offers the obedience of the Germans in an oration admired by all.

After the Diet, Tommaso of Bologna and Juan de Carvajal returned home via Neustadt in Austria, where they stopped to thank the emperor for sending such powerful and loyal ambassadors to Frankfurt. Continuing on to Rome, they were both made cardinals in recognition of their able and successful management of affairs.[66] A few days later the emperor appointed Aeneas and the noble Bohemian knight, Procop von Rabstein, to be his ambassadors to Rome. With the consent of the archbishop of Mainz and the margrave of Brandenburg, they were instructed to abandon their neutrality and reestablish the nation's allegiance to the Holy Apostolic See, provided Eugenius accepted the proposals agreed upon at Frankfurt. 1

Meanwhile Johann of Lysura, finding that events were not going to his liking, changed his liking to suit events. He made his submission to the archbishop of Mainz, who then appointed him his ambassador to Eugenius. The emperor's envoys found him at Siena with the representatives of many other princes, and they all proceeded together to Rome. They were met at the first milestone by retainers of the pope and the cardinals and all the prelates of the Curia, who escorted them into the city like conquering heroes returning home. 2

Two days later they were summoned to a secret consistory before Eugenius where Aeneas acted as spokesman for the group; pope and cardinals alike greeted his speech with remarkable applause. But that very day Eugenius fell ill and took to his bed, leaving the matter to be handled by the cardinals. The whole affair 3

rem tractandam commisit. Cum iam res ad calcem deducta esset, plerique ex Theutonicis pedem retrahebant oboedientiamque pontifici, medicorum iudicio infra decimum diem morituro, praestandam negabant.

4 Quibus Aeneas magnis rationibus adversabatur, multumque nationi conducere affirmabat accelerari declarationem debere, cum Eugenius iam voluntati principum benivolus esset; nam quod ipse fecisset, successorem eius gratum habiturum; quod si ante moreretur Eugenius quam declaratio fieret, timendum esse ne successor nationi durus inveniretur; quamvis sive asper sive mollis successor ei daretur, nihil cum eo tractari posse quorum mandata in Eugenium sonarent. Ab Urbe vero si rebus infectis recederent, omne foedus principum solvi, nationemque nunc maiori ex parte concordem in magnas divisiones contentionesque dari; quodque gravissimum videri deberet, ad solidandum roborandumque schisma periculosissimum in Ecclesia viam, quam praecluserant, aperiri.

5 Nec Iohannes Lysura alterius sententiae fuit, qui tantopere faciendam declarationem suadebat ut, mortuis omnibus Eugenii membris, satis esse diceret si vel digitus sinistri pedis minimus viveret. Ob quam rem persuasis omnibus collegis cum iam notulas omnes Eugenius approbasset, atque litteras super his decrevisset, ad cubiculum eius omnes legati intromissi sunt, qui iacenti pontifici oboedientiam praestiterunt. Ille confestim bullas apostolicas in manus Aeneae dedit. Nec mora, rursus in consistorio publico praesidentibus cardinalibus, publicatis caesaris et aliorum principum mandatis, repetitae sunt caerimoniae.

was on the point of resolution when several of the Germans now hesitated, saying they were not sure if they should pledge obedience to a pope who, in the opinion of his doctors, would be dead in ten days' time.

Aeneas mustered powerful arguments against them, saying it would be to the nation's advantage to make the declaration now, since Eugenius was already kindly disposed to the princes; moreover, whatever he did would be approved by his successor. If, on the other hand, they made the declaration after Eugenius died, there was a risk that his successor would take a harsher line toward the German nation. And, whether the new pope proved harsh or mild, they would not be able to negotiate with him anyway, since their credentials were addressed to Eugenius. If they left Rome without settling the matter, the entire concordat of the princes would be annulled; the nation, at the moment more or less united, would be plunged into greater faction and discord; and, what should strike them as most serious of all, they would be sending the church back down the path of dangerous schism—would in fact strengthen and consolidate that schism—when they had nearly closed that path off altogether. 4

Johann of Lysura thought much the same and argued strenuously in favor of the declaration, saying that even if only the little toe of Eugenius's left foot remained alive (every other part of his body being dead!) they should still declare their allegiance to it. He thus persuaded his colleagues. Eugenius approved every one of their proposals and composed a brief in response. Next, the ambassadors were all admitted to his chamber, where they made their submission to him as he lay in bed. Eugenius at once put the apostolic bulls into Aeneas's hands.[67] Immediately the proceedings were resumed in public consistory, with the cardinals presiding, and the instructions from the emperor and the other princes were read aloud. 5

6 Inde tota Urbe ob publicam laetitiam ignes facti, et campanae tubaeque sine modo sonuerunt. Sequenti die iustitium indictum, superisque rogationes decretae; cardinales ceterique praelati cum populo in ordine procedentes Silvestri coronam, Iohannis Baptistae caput praecipuasque sanctorum reliquias ex templo Sancti Marci Lateranum[47] detulerunt, ibique sacrificatum atque de Federici Eugeniique laudibus habitus est non brevis neque inornatus sermo.

: 17 :

Aeneas ab Eugenio eligitur episcopus Tergestinus, quo non succedente fit subdiaconus. Mors Eugenii suffectioque Nicolai. Aeneas secretarius et verus Tergestinus.

1 Dum haec agerentur, rumor fuit Nicolaum episcopum Tergestinum mortem obiisse; idque primus cardinalium intellexit Thomas Bononiensis. Decanus Aquilegiensis id ei narraverat, qui ecclesiam illam ambiens cardinalis opem expetiverat. At cardinalis re cognita Iohannem Sancti Angeli eiusdem ordinis parva cedula certiorem facit, dicens iam tempus datum, quo possent Aeneam provehere. Is forte fortuna apud Iohannem cenatus diversa ex more fabulabatur; cui Iohannes, schedulam legendam porrigens, quid sibi videretur percunctatus est. Ad quem Aeneas, 'Dignitatem,' inquit, 'imparem meis meritis non petam, at ultro datam non recusabo.'

2 Sequenti die, cum Ludovicus cardinalis Aquilegiensis ecclesiam Tergestinam decano suo, alii aliis peterent, omnes ab Eugenio re-

Then the whole city erupted in celebration. In high spirits, the people lit bonfires and rang bells and sounded trumpets. The next day public business was suspended and a general thanksgiving was decreed. The cardinals and other prelates, with the people following in procession, carried the crown of Sylvester, the head of John the Baptist and the principal relics of the saints from the church of San Marco to the Lateran for mass, during which there was a long and elaborate sermon in praise of Frederick and Eugenius. 6

: 17 :

Aeneas appointed bishop of Trieste but, unable to take up the position, is made subdeacon instead. Death of Eugenius and election of Nicholas. Aeneas becomes a secretary and, at last, bishop of Trieste.

Meanwhile rumor spread that Niccolò, the bishop of Trieste, had passed away. The first cardinal to hear the story was Tommaso of Bologna, who learned of it from the deacon of Aquileia, who had asked his aid in obtaining that church for himself. But on hearing the news the cardinal sent a short note informing his colleague Juan, cardinal of Sant'Angelo, adding that here was an opportunity to advance Aeneas. Aeneas happened to be dining with Juan; they were chatting as usual on various topics when Juan handed him the note to read and asked what he thought about it. Aeneas answered, "I would not seek an office greater than I deserve, but if it is offered, I won't refuse it." 1

The next day, Lodovico, cardinal of Aquileia, asked for the church at Trieste for his deacon, and various others proposed other candidates, but Eugenius refused them all, steadily asserting 2

pulsi sunt, qui pontificatum ipsum Aeneae sese commissurum constanter affirmavit. Sed cum certitudo vacationis exquireretur, vanum fuisse rumorem constitit. Aeneas tamen ab Eugenio in subdiaconum apostolicum assumptus est.

3 Eugenius vero post oboedientiam Germanorum receptam diebus sexdecim cum morbis ac morte pugnavit, victusque tandem in festo quod Petri Cathedram vocant nature concessit anno salutis MCCCCXLVII. Exequiis per novem dies actis, cardinales ad electionem successoris ingressi Aeneam atque Procopium cum ceteris legatis regum ad custodiam conclavis delegerunt. Ubi cum duas noctes vigilassent, Thomas cardinalis Bononiensis in summum pontificem assumptus est, dictus Nicolaus Quintus ob memoriam — ut multi arbitrantur — Nicolai cardinalis Sanctae Crucis, qui magister eius fuerat papatumque perdidisse, defuncto Martino dum legatum ageret in Francia, credebatur. Is ut aedes Sancti Petri primum ascendit, Enea ad se accersito secretariatum ei subdiaconatumque confirmavit, atque in die coronationis ante se crucem deferendam commisit.

4 Ut autem Aeneas ex Urbe recessit, post dies viginti certum nuntium de morte pontificis Tergestini maximus pontifex Nicolaus accepit, qui nullum cardinalem consulens, indicto consistorio, paludatus mitratusque in Collegium venit et admirantibus primum, deinde faventibus Sacri Senatus universis patribus, Aeneam episcopum Tergestinum pronuntiavit litterasque absque pecunia expeditas ad eum misit.

5 Federicus quoque caesar, ut eius vacationem ecclesiae cognovit: 'Hanc,' inquit 'Aeneae impetrabimus, quae nostri est dominii naturalis,' litterasque pontifici in ea re iam, se ignaro, peracta conscripsit. Atque sic nescius Aeneas cum redisset ad caesarem, ad episcopatum et papae et caesaris voto sese vocatum invenit. Neque cives

he would trust the papacy itself to Aeneas. And yet, when they checked to see if the church was really vacant, the rumor turned out to be false. Eugenius nevertheless made Aeneas an apostolic subdeacon.

For sixteen days after the submission of the Germans, Eugenius battled with disease and death until, beaten at last, he yielded up his soul. The day was the feast of St. Peter's Chair in the year of our salvation 1447. His funeral rites lasted nine days, after which the cardinals went into conclave to elect his successor, appointing Aeneas and Procop and the envoys of the other princes to guard the door. After two nights of sleepless deliberations, Tommaso, cardinal of Bologna, was elected pope.[68] He took the name of Nicholas v—in memory, many think, of Niccolò, cardinal of Santa Croce, who had been his master and was thought to have lost the papacy on the death of Martin v, because he was away on a mission to France.[69] As soon as he entered the palace of St. Peter, Nicholas summoned Aeneas, confirmed him as secretary and subdeacon and charged him with carrying the cross before him at his coronation. 3

Twenty days after Aeneas left Rome, Nicholas received reliable news of the bishop of Trieste's death. Without consulting any cardinal or calling a consistory he came into the Sacred College in robe and mitre and, at first to the amazement and then with the approval of all the members of that holy assembly, he appointed Aeneas bishop of Trieste and sent him his presentation free of dues.[70] 4

Likewise Emperor Frederick, when he heard the see had become vacant, said, "That church is mine to give, and I'm going to get it for Aeneas." He wrote to the pope about the matter, not knowing that it was already settled. So when Aeneas returned to the imperial court, knowing nothing at all of what had happened, he found himself appointed bishop by both the pope and the emperor. Nor did the people of Trieste, who were famously hostile to 5

Tergestini qui omnibus exteris infesti esse consueverunt, Aeneae restiterunt,[48] sed cum primarium civem, decanum suum, canonici elegissent, silere illum iussere possessionemque vel absenti Aeneae concordibus animis tradiderunt.

: 18 :

Conventus apud Asciafburgium, et Germanorum oboedientia ad novum pontificem. Philippi Mariae ducis mors, ac Aeneae legatio ad Mediolanenses, deinde ad Histrios.

1 Inter haec imperator apud Asciafburgium, quod est oppidum Maguntinae ecclesiae supra Muganum, conventum praelatorum et principum indixerat, eoque cum Artongo iuris consulto Aeneam misit, qui Maguntinum praesulem et alios Francfordiensis participes foederis in oboedientia Nicolai papae confirmarent,[49] atque ad eam rem traherent Ludovicum comitem Palatinum Rheni et Coloniensem archiepiscopum. Neque in cassum labor cessit: in conventu decreta sunt, quae caesar optavit; interque sacrificandum Nicolaus pontifex maximus Germanorum declaratus est, Deoque pro sua salute supplicatum.

2 Palatinus, etsi Felicis filiam uxorem habebat, in reverentiam tamen devotionemque Nicolai descendit. Coloniensis archiepiscopus eo tempore adversus Susatenses, ecclesiae suae rebelles, bellum gerebat; cumque insecurum ad eum iter esset inter dissonas gentes, Aeneas Coloniae manens litteris secum egit, et is facturum se omnia spopondit, quae caesar[50] optavit, atque aurum expensarum, quas xx diebus Agrippinae Coloniae Aeneas fecerat, ultro ei ad Viennam misit.

foreigners, resist his appointment. Even though the canons had already elected their own deacon, a prominent fellow-citizen, they made him withdraw and unanimously awarded the post to Aeneas before he had even arrived.

: 18 :

Assembly at Aschaffenburg; the Germans make their submission to the new pope. Death of Duke Filippo Maria. Aeneas's legations to Milan and Istria.

Meanwhile the emperor convened an assembly of prelates and princes at Aschaffenburg, a town on the Main in the diocese of Mainz.[71] He sent Aeneas there with the lawyer, Hartung, to confirm that the bishop of Mainz and the others who had signed the concordat of Frankfurt would now make submission to Pope Nicholas, and to induce the archbishop of Cologne and Ludwig, count palatine of the Rhine, to join them. Their efforts met with success. The diet agreed to everything the emperor wanted. At a solemn ceremony Nicholas was declared Pope of the Germans and prayers were offered for his safety. 1

The count palatine, even though his wife was Felix's daughter, nevertheless made reverent submission to Nicholas. The archbishop of Cologne, however, was engaged in a dispute with the people of Soest, who had rebelled against his rule. Since Aeneas could not travel safely among these disaffected peoples, he remained at Cologne and communicated with the archbishop by letter. The prelate agreed to everything the emperor wished and, without being asked, sent money to Aeneas at Vienna for the expenses he had incurred during the twenty days he stayed at Cologne. 2

3 Dum haec aguntur, Philippus Maria dux Mediolani ventris profluvio vitam reliquit, Alfonso rege Aragonum haerede palam nuncupato, quod ei minime licuit. Ideo Federicus caesar Aeneam Mediolanum misit et cum eo Federicum episcopum Secoviensem, Gasparem Slichium cancellarium, Iohannem magistrum camerae, Iacobum Ladronium physicum et Pancratium Rinzatem, nobiles equites, ut principatum Imperio devolutum vendicarent. Uno itaque tempore dominium potentis urbis et Federicus caesar et Alfonsus rex Aragonum et Carolus dux Aurelianensis expetebant; nam et hic se ius habere dicebat ex foedere inter suos et Philippi maiores matrimonii causa percusso.

4 At Mediolanenses libertatis avidi senatum ex primoribus urbis delegerant ac magistratus assumpserant qui rem publicam administrarent; cumque regem ducemque spernerent, audito Aenea qui caesaris nomine verba fecit, imperatorem suum dominum fassi sunt, sed habere se privilegia dixerunt quibus civitatem regere possent. Tandem vero Federicum modo certo dominantem admissuri erant, quae res etsi non debito respondebat, Aeneae tamen tempus consideranti non aliena videbatur. At collegae Theutones, dum plurima volunt, omnia perdiderunt.

5 Aeneas autem Viennam reversus astante Iohanne cardinali Sancti Angeli, Apostolicae Sedis legato, consecrationis munus accepit, atque inde Tergestum profectus, a civibus cupide susceptus rem primo divinam fecit. Nec diu moratus; in Histriam iussus ire de finibus inter caesarem et Venetos litem composuit, quamvis postea rursus excitata sit. Cum redisset Tergestum, comperit Ropertum Walseum bellum adversus Tergestinos agere, in quo sua

While this was happening, Duke Filippo Maria of Milan died of dysentery.[72] He had publicly proclaimed King Alfonso of Aragon his heir, but he had no right to do so. The emperor therefore sent Aeneas to Milan together with a group of noble knights — Frederick, the bishop of Seckau; the chancellor Caspar Schlick; his chamberlain, Johann; his doctor, Jacopo Landrono; and Pancraz Riutschad — to claim the duchy for the empire. Thus the lordship of that powerful city came to be claimed at the same time by Emperor Frederick, Alfonso of Aragon and Duke Charles of Orléans; for this last lord was also asserting his right to the title on the grounds of the marriage contract made between Filippo's father and his own.[73] 3

The people of Milan, however, wished to be free. They had elected a senate of prominent citizens and appointed magistrates to carry out the business of government. They rejected the claims of the king and the duke but, after hearing Aeneas speak for the emperor, they acknowledged Frederick as their lord, though they still claimed the right to govern their own city. As the negotiations concluded, they were on the point of accepting Frederick's rule provided certain conditions were met; and this, though less than he deserved to accomplish, seemed to Aeneas reasonably satisfactory under the circumstances. But his German colleagues, by demanding too much, lost everything.[74] 4

On his return to Vienna, Aeneas was consecrated as bishop of Trieste. His sponsor was Juan,[75] cardinal of Sant'Angelo, the apostolic legate. Aeneas then went to his city, where he was warmly received by the people and celebrated his first mass. After a short stay he was ordered to go to Istria, where he settled a dispute over the boundary between the empire and Venice, though afterwards the quarrel erupted again. On his return to Trieste he learned that the citizens were being violently assailed by Rupert von Wallsee. His own church was suffering the most, for his tenants had been driven from their lands and robbed of their cattle. When Aeneas 5

potissimum ecclesia laesa est, cuius coloni ex agro pulsi et abacta pecora sunt. Ob quam rem cum caesari questum iret, Roperti, qui eum capere magnopere studebat, sola celeritate vitavit insidias.

6 Interea Gaspar Slichius apud caesarem falso delatus ecclesiam Frizingensem, quam fratri obtinuerat, dimittere compulsus est; qui cum esset in dies invisior caesari, Aeneam quoque propter amicitiam et consuetudinem paene assiduam suspectum reddebat, itaque conditio Aeneae deterior fieri videbatur. Sed usus ipse temperamento, ne vel hinc amicitiam vel inde dominum offenderet, rursus in gratiam rediit, atque parochialem ecclesiam in Castro Vindelico admodum insignem ex munere sibi caesaris commendatam accepit.

: 19 :

Aeneae altera legatio ad Mediolanenses atque opera pro imperatoria dignitate. Franciscus Sforcia post obsidionem a Mediolanensibus caeso legato Veneto civitati dux praeficitur.

1 Per idem tempus Franciscus Sforcia vicecomes Mediolanum urbem obsidebat. Cives autem exanimati caesaris opem petebant. Eo rursus Aeneas proficisci iussus est et Artongus iuris consultus, qui obsessis civibus auxilium promitterent, si se caesari subderent. In eo itinere multa his adversa fuere. Nam cum visitato Sigismundo

went to complain to the emperor, it was only by travelling with the greatest haste that he escaped an ambush by Rupert, who had determined to take him captive.

Meanwhile, Caspar Schlick had been falsely accused before the 6
emperor and was compelled to give up the church of Freising, which he had obtained for his brother. Day by day he fell into greater disfavor with the emperor,[76] and Aeneas, on account of the friendship and almost continual association he had enjoyed with the chancellor, fell under suspicion too. His position seemed precarious; but by steering a middle course, causing offense to neither his friend nor his master, he returned to favor and obtained on the emperor's recommendation the important parish church of Castro Vindelico.[77]

: 19 :

Aeneas leads another embassy to Milan, where he argues for the emperor's rights. Francesco Sforza lays siege to the city. The Milanese kill the Venetian ambassador and make Sforza their duke.

By now, Count Francesco Sforza had laid siege to Milan.[78] The 1
panic-stricken citizens begged the emperor for help and so Aeneas was sent there a second time together with the lawyer Hartung. They were to offer aid to the besieged population in return for their submission to the emperor. The journey there was a difficult one. After visiting Duke Sigismund at Innsbruck and persuading him to support them in the Milanese affair, they came down through the towering Alps above Bormio to the Valtellina, where they found the people divided, some favoring the city of Milan and others Francesco Sforza. The territory round Lake Como was

duce apud Eni Pontem et ad rem Mediolanensem persuaso per altissimas Alpes Vormii in Vallem Tellinam descendissent, divisum populum, alios civitati Mediolanensi, alios Francisco Sforciae faventes, lacum Comanum in potestate hostium magna ex parte, nihil tutum invenere; itaque modo noctu per aquam, modo die per abruptos et devios montes viam fecere. Ubi Comum venerunt, octo et decem dies moram facere oportuit, quoniam inter Mediolanum et Comum omnia hostis tenebat, qui postquam legatos caesaris advenisse didicit, aditus custodiri iussit legatosque, si comprehendi possent, ad se vinctos deduci.

2 At illi susceptis equitibus ac peditibus admodum ducentis cum viarum gnaros[51] tres, quos guidas vocant, fideles invenissent, circa solis occasum ex Como recedunt Mediolanum petentes. Sed cum horis forte duabus iter fecissent iamque nox obscurissima supervenisset, equitatus inter tenebras retrofugit. Aderant et legati ducis Sabaudiae et plures cives Mediolanenses qui negociati per Alamaniam domum redibant; hi ubi fugam equitum cognovere, insidias veriti trementesque admodum retrocedendum aiebant. Aeneas vero, vocatis peditatus[52] ducibus, ubi eos constantes invenit et alterum eorum Senensem ex loquela cognovit, versus ad negociatores:

3 'Nolite,' inquit 'timere. Angustias montium praetergressi patentes in campos venimus. Insidias iam evasimus, quas in ardis locis instruunt. Nunc mille se nobis offerunt semitae. In manus hostium solum nos infortunium ducere potest; id bonitas summi Dei auferet. Ite mecum, vos hac nocte laribus vestris salvos reddam!' Sic profecti ad horam decimam paulo post solis ortum Mediolanum ingressi magna totius populi festivitate recepti sunt.

4 Sed iam regimen civitatis ex populo Romani nominis amante (dum Comi legati manserunt) in paucorum potentiam erat deduc-

largely in the hands of the enemy and no place was safe. Therefore they had to travel in stealth, sometimes at night by water, sometimes by day over steep and pathless mountains. When they finally reached Como, they were forced to stay there eighteen days because the whole region between Como and Milan was held by the enemy. When Sforza learned that ambassadors from the emperor had arrived, he gave orders that all the approaches should be guarded and that the ambassadors, if caught, should be brought to him in chains.

Aeneas's party managed to muster some two hundred cavalry and infantry, however, and having found three trustworthy men (called "guides") who knew the roads, they set out around sunset from Como for Milan. After an hour or two on the road, however, when the blackest night had already descended upon them, the cavalry took advantage of the darkness to desert. The party had been joined by the ambassadors of the duke of Savoy and several Milanese returning home from doing business in Germany. When these men learned of the desertion, they feared an ambush and in great terror insisted on returning to Como. But Aeneas summoned the captains of the infantry and, finding them loyal, and recognizing one of them as a Sienese by his accent, he turned to the merchants and said: 2

"Do not be afraid: the mountain passes are behind us, and we're coming down now to the open plain. We're long past the point of ambush, for such snares are set on rougher ground than this. Now we have our choice of a thousand paths. Bad luck alone can lead us into the hands of the enemy now, and God's mercy will save us from that. Follow me and I'll get you safely home by the end of the night." So they continued on their way and at about the tenth hour, a little after sunrise, they entered Milan and were received by the entire populace with great rejoicing. 3

By this point, however, the constitution of the city had passed from the people, who were devoted to Rome, into the hands of an 4

tum qui Francisci Sforciae clam partes fovebant. Eam ob causam rogavit senatum Aeneas sibi ut populi copia fieret cui caesaris verba referret. Guarnerius Castilioneus iuris consultus genere ac facundia nobilis tum primum in senatu locum tenebat, Sforciae occultus amicus. Is per leges civitatis vocationem populi prohibitam dicebat, tumultum timendum in civitate obsessa, potestatem populi omnem habere senatum, huic dicenda quicunque mandaret caesar. Contra Aeneas imperatoris iussum non teneri legibus aiebat quae ab ipso robur haberent; eius mandata quietis esse, non seditionis altricia; obsessum fatigatumque longo bello populum imperatoris legatione levandum; mirum videri si domini sui vocem noluerit audire. Atque sic invito Guarnerio, senatus populi vocationem decrevit.

5 Is cum postera die in curiam frequens convenisset, oblatis lectisque publice caesaris litteris Aeneas in hanc sententiam oravit. Ait enim Philippo mortuo caesarem ad eos misisse legatos qui gubernationem civitatis exposcerent, neque auditum quamvis aequa peteret; sed Mediolanenses ipsos nova libertate gaudentes magistratus sibi constituisse qui rem publicam administrarent, idque factum esse in eam usque diem; caesare pro sua mansuetudine, quamvis indigne spreto, nihil tamen irato; venisse interim Franciscum Sforciam vicecomitem ex amico factum hostem, municipia in potestatem suam redegisse; civitatem obsessam magnas pati cala-

oligarchy who secretly favored Francesco Sforza. (This had happened when the ambassadors were still at Como.) For this reason Aeneas asked the senate for permission to address the people and give them the emperor's message.[79] At the time, the president of the senate was one Guarniero Castiglione, a lawyer distinguished both for his eloquence and his high birth, who was secretly a friend of Sforza. He declared that the city laws forbade calling an assembly of the people; in a besieged city there was a risk of riot; the senate had the full authority of the people and the emperor's message should be delivered to it. Aeneas replied that the emperor's orders could not be overridden by laws which, ultimately, derived from his own authority; his message would encourage peace and not sedition; the people, exhausted by a long war and protracted siege, would take comfort from an imperial embassy; it seemed strange they should not wish to hear the words of their lord. And so the senate overruled Guarnerio and ordered an assembly to be called.

The next day a great crowd gathered in the senate house. After 5
displaying the emperor's letter and reading it aloud, Aeneas made a speech along these lines: he said that at Filippo's death the emperor had sent ambassadors to take control of the city but, though his demands were just, he had not been heeded. Instead, the Milanese let their new liberty go to their heads; they had elected their own magistrates to run the government, an act of rebellion that persisted down to the present day. But the emperor, mild as ever, refused to be provoked despite the injustice of his rejection. In the meantime, Francesco Sforza had appeared on the scene. Once their friend, now their enemy, he had reduced the surrounding towns to his control. Milan was under siege and enduring great hardships; the troops had deserted to Francesco; food was scarce; none of the neighboring princes would bring them aid. The emperor alone, heedless of every insult, took pity on their plight. If they would now, at last, submit to the Holy Empire and acknowl-

mitates, milites ad Franciscum defecisse, inopia frumenti premi populum; ex vicinis principibus neminem ferre opem; solum autem caesarem eorum commiserari fortunam, omnis repulsae oblitum; quod si iam tandem Sacro Imperio parere velint, dominumque caesarem recognoscere, paratum eum auxilium ferre; iamque cum Sigismundo duce, patruele suo, vicino Insubribus res orditas, brevi magnam manum superatis Alpibus in eorum agrum descensuram cogitarent; ne sibi ipsis frustra confiderent neque se libertatem amissuros putarent caesaris dominatum recipientes, nam iustis et naturalibus dominis servire, eam demum veram esse libertatem; in civitatibus quae populi nomine reguntur, inveniri semper aliquos qui plebi iugum imponunt; deinde adverterent caesarem sibi an Sforciam imperare mallent; quoniam nisi caesari se sufficiant, sic res deductas esse ut dominatum Sforciae nequeant evadere; caesarem, si ab eis recipiatur, singulares gratias, magna privilegia daturum suis civibus quos in Alamania libere negotiaturos, auream civitatem facturos et Italiae caput, aiebat.

6 Post haec Guarnerius, cum multa de libertatis dulcedine disseruisset, eligendos tandem ait ex populo viros primores, qui cum legatis de mandatis caesaris agerent. At dum res penderet, post aliquot noctes tres civitatis portae (sic enim partes vocitant) sumptis armis dominum caesarem vocavere. Sex portae in urbe sunt, atque ad earum numerum distributus est populus; quod quattuor portarum plebibus placet, id ratum esse oportet. Cum ergo iam tres Vitam Imperio! peterent, senatores, audito tumultu, priusquam portae quartae multitudo assurgeret, obequitantes urbem silere plebem ac positis armis domum petere iubebant, quoniam et ipsi dominatum caesari salvo civitatis honore commissuri essent; idque cum legatis agitent[53] sedulo. Post haec viri delecti, qui cum legatis

edge the emperor as their lord, he was ready to help them. They should keep in mind that agreements had already been made with the emperor's cousin, Duke Sigismund, a neighbor of the Lombards; in a short time a large force could cross the Alps and descend into their territory. They could not rely on themselves alone, for that would be hopeless, but neither should they imagine that acknowledging the emperor as their sovereign would mean the loss of their freedom. To serve a legitimate and natural lord was the only true liberty; in cities ruled in the name of the people, some group of men always emerged to subject the people to their will. Indeed, the choice lay between imperial rule or that of Sforza, for it had got to the point where, unless they submitted to the emperor, they would never escape the tyranny of Francesco. If they would only acknowledge the emperor, he would shower his citizens with extraordinary favors and important privileges: they would trade freely throughout Germany and make Milan a magnificent city, the capital of Italy.

After this speech, Guarniero declaimed at length on the sweet- 6
ness of liberty. He concluded, nevertheless, by recommending they choose some leading citizens to meet with the ambassadors and discuss the emperor's offer. A few nights later, with the matter still unresolved, three "gates" of the city—for so they call its divisions—took up arms and hailed the emperor as their lord. (There are six "gates" in the city and the people are distributed among them. The will of any four gates is binding on all.) Cries of "Long live the empire!" were already ringing out before three of the gates. The senators grew alarmed at the uproar and, before the people could throng to the fourth gate, they rode into the city and ordered everyone to lay down his arms and go home quietly. The senators assured the crowd that they too were ready to acknowledge the emperor's sovereignty, provided the city's honor remained inviolate, and that they were discussing the matter carefully with the ambassadors. Then their representatives conferred with the

in hanc sententiam loquebantur, si caesar opem ferret adversus Sforciam, in has leges venturos sese aiebant:

7 In Mediolano qui ius diceret Theutonicum, in aliis civitatibus quem vellet, caesar gubernatorem poneret. Appellationes quae ab aliis gubernatoribus interponerentur Mediolanensis audiret; ab eo provocationi locum non esse. Vectigalia civitatum quae Mediolanensibus servirent ad caesarem et Mediolanenses aequo iure pertinere. Ex Mediolano quotannis auri quinquaginta milia caesari, feuda ecclesiarum et nobilium collationi[54] caesaris remanere. Vasallos omnes et imperatori et civitati fidem[55] iurare. Si quod amplius oppidum aut dominium Mediolanenses armis acquirerent, id a caesare sub decenti censu in feudum debere peti. Satis ea legatis placebant, sed maiora iussi petere amplecti haec non poterant.

8 Interea Carolus Gonzaga, qui tum forte unica Mediolanensium spes videbatur, magnanimus belli dux, Aeneam intempesta nocte accessit et, Artongo vocato, iterum populi vocationem ut peterent suadebat, spondens se illo venturum incitaturumque plebem, quae sibi maxime credebat, imperatorem dominum petere; nihil se dubitare, quin deiectis magistratibus mox legatis caesaris regimen civitatis committeretur, donec aut veniret caesar, aut vicarium mitteret; idque iam se providisse apud aliquos in urbe potentes aiebat.

9 Hoc quamvis erat vero simile, tamen discriminis plenum Aeneae videbatur; et licet magnum facinus et memorabile non fieri sine periculo sciret, tamen sacerdoti sibi eam rem minime ratus convenire, quod caesar imperaverat a se factum dixit; audivisse po-

ambassadors and agreed that in exchange for the emperor's help against Sforza, they would consent to the following terms:

The emperor should appoint a German to administer justice in Milan itself, and in the other towns anyone he pleased; appeals from the other governors should be heard by the one at Milan and from his decision there should be no appeal. The revenues from the cities subject to Milan would accrue in equal parts to the emperor and to the Milanese; Milan should pay 50,000 florins a year to the emperor and he should also receive the tribute paid by the churches and the nobles. All vassals should swear allegiance both to the emperor and to the city; but if Milan should capture any new towns or territory by force of arms, the emperor alone would receive its allegiance together with the payment of a fitting sum. These terms seemed satisfactory enough to the ambassadors, but since their orders were to ask for more, they could not accept them. 7

Meanwhile Carlo Gonzaga, a brave general who at the time seemed the only hope of the Milanese, came to Aeneas in the dead of night. They summoned Hartung, and then Carlo urged them to call again for a popular assembly. He promised that he would be there to incite the people, who had the greatest confidence in him, to demand the emperor as their lord. He had no doubt they would depose the magistrates and then quickly turn the government of the city over to the imperial ambassadors until the emperor either came in person or sent his representative; and he assured them that he had already begun discussions with some of the leading men of the city to prepare for such an event. 8

The plan seemed likely to succeed, but Aeneas thought it extremely hazardous. Although he knew that no great or memorable act is achieved without some risk, still he judged that such a scheme was hardly becoming to him as a priest. He explained that he had carried out the emperor's orders; the people had heard the emperor's will and could now submit to it if they chose; to employ 9

pulum caesaris voluntatem; posset iam, si vellet, parere; vim facere neque factu facile neque mandatum; Carolum amandum caesari, qui ea cogitaverit, relaturumque suam fidem. Ille tamen posthac Aeneam Sforcie faventem praedicabat, ut nihil sit quod non sinistrorsum male mentes interpretentur.

10 At Aeneas et Artongus, ubi aliud ex Mediolanensibus exculpere non potuerunt, obtentis Sforciae litteris ad eum in castra venerunt, qui se admodum mirari aiebat quo pacto Mediolanum intrassent, suas excubias evadentes. Plura igitur cum eo Venetorum et Florentinorum legatis praesentibus fabulati sunt. Deinde amotis omnibus, soli cum eo ad horam mansere, mentem sibi caesaris exponentes, atque honorati ab eo dimissi sunt.

11 Qui redeuntes in Alamaniam caesarem apud Sanctum Vitum, quod est Carentanae oppidum, invenerunt. Placebant caesari quae Mediolanenses promiserant; verum illi, dum mensibus duobus responsum expectant, veriti ne Sforciae viribus opprimerentur, occiso Galeotto Toscano pulsisque ceteris senatoribus, foedus cum Venetis percussere; atque cum ii quoque parcius subvenirent, trucidato per tumultum Leonardo Venerio, qui legatus Venetorum apud eos agebat, Francisco Sforciae portas aperuere, eique (ut est insania populi) ducatus insignia contulerunt.

force was neither easy nor within his instructions; Carlo deserved the emperor's gratitude for his proposal and he would make sure his efforts were recognized. And yet, Carlo later spread a rumor that Aeneas had favored Sforza—which goes to show that there is absolutely nothing an ill-disposed mind cannot interpret in a bad light.

Unable to elicit anything further from the Milanese, Aeneas 10
and Hartung procured a letter to Sforza and went to him in his camp—to his complete astonishment, for he said he could not understand how they had managed to get past his sentries into Milan. They spoke with him at some length in the presence of the Venetian and Florentine envoys. Then, after all the others had been dismissed, they remained alone with him for an hour explaining the emperor's position. In the end, they were sent away with every mark of respect.

On returning to Germany they found the emperor at St. Veit, a 11
town of Carinthia. He was pleased with the promises made by the Milanese; but they, after waiting two months for the emperor to reply, began to fear they would be overpowered by Sforza's army. Therefore they murdered the Tuscan Galeotto, expelled the rest of the senators and struck an alliance with Venice. When the Venetians, too, failed to provide much help, the Milanese ran riot, murdered the Venetian ambassador Leonardo Venier, opened their gates to Francesco Sforza and hailed him as their duke.[80] Such is the madness of crowds.

: 20 :

Aeneae legatio ad Alfonsum regem de matrimonio contractando cum imperatore et Leonora, et eius opera concluso. Aeneas eligitur Senensis episcopus absens.

1 Aeneas inter haec ad ecclesiam Tergestinam cum se recepisset, in anno Iubilaei revocatus ad caesarem cum Gregorio de Populosa et Michaele de Plena Villa, Alfonsum regem Aragonum et Siciliae iussus est petere, matrimonium caesaris nomine cum Leonora, regis Portugalliae sorore, ut ibi contraheret, nam legati Portugallenses eo convenerant. Quam rem diebus quadraginta tractatam cum denique conclusissent, coram rege, cardinali Morinensi apostolico legato, Clivensi, Calabriae, Suessae Sclesiaeque ducibus et magna praelatorum comitumque multitudine, in curia Novi Castri Neapolitani de nobilitate virtuteque contrahentium orationem habuit, quae postmodum a multis conscripta est.

2 Hinc ad summum pontificem reversus circa finem Iubilaei, in consistorio publico contractum coniugium manifestavit. Sequenti anno caesarem ad coronationem venturum dixit. Concilium quod Galli petebant in Francia dissuasit, praesente Alberto Austriae duce imperatoris germano, qui Nativitatis Dominicae nocte apostolico gladio donatus fuit quamvis duci Clivensi antea promisso, dicente pontifice promissionem suam, nisi dignior advenisset, intellegendam fuisse.

: 20 :

Aeneas's embassy to King Alfonso. Negotiations for the betrothal of Leonora to the emperor, successfully concluded thanks to his efforts. While there, Aeneas made bishop of Siena.

1 In the meantime Aeneas had gone to his church at Trieste, but in the jubilee year the emperor recalled him and sent him together with Gregor Volckenstorf and Michael Pfullendorf on an embassy to King Alfonso of Aragon and Sicily. Their orders were to arrange the marriage between the emperor and the king of Portugal's sister, Leonora.[81] The Portuguese ambassadors were already gathered at Naples, and after forty days of negotiation, the matter was concluded. Aeneas then delivered an oration in the hall of the Castelnuovo at Naples in the presence of the king, the cardinal of Amiens (who was the apostolic legate),[82] the dukes of Clèves, Calabria, Suessa and Silesia and a great number of prelates and noblemen. The speech treated the nobility and virtue of the contracting parties; afterwards, many had copies of it made for themselves.

2 Leaving Naples around the end of the jubilee year, he returned to the pope. At a public consistory he announced that the marriage had been arranged and that the emperor would come the next year to be crowned; he also argued against granting the request of the French for a council in France.[83] Present on this occasion was the emperor's brother, Duke Albert of Austria, who on Christmas night was presented with the apostolic sword. Earlier this had been promised to the duke of Clèves; but the pope said that his promise was to be interpreted as binding only if a worthier candidate did not appear.

3 Neque in hac via defuerunt pericula. Ligula flumen est apud Volscos, altum et undique cinctum silvis quarum arbores aquam contegunt pontesque plurimos faciunt. Naves ibi admodum parvae sunt; quas cum Aeneas sociique conscendissent, nautarum pervicacia decepti noctuque navigare compulsi, saepius in ramos arborum impegerunt, demumque ingenti haerentes trunco, cum essent tenebrae densissime, duabus horis periclitati sunt; ibique paulo post navis una submersa est et homines undecim periere. Neque procul a Cumis, cum flumen aliud prope litus maris transituri essent, navis quae famulos vehebat, cum nimium oneris accepisset, evoluta homines et equos in fundum proiecit; sed viri funem quendam manu tenentes, equi nantes evasere.

4 Verum ut adversa retulimus, sic etiam secunda referre par est. Inter eundum cum Ferrariam Aeneas appulisset, Iacobum Ptolomeum fratrem suum patruelem invenit, insignem iuris consultum et curiae Ferrariensis iudicem, quem postea caesar Sacri Palatii Lateranensis comitem creavit. Hic se litteris uxoris instructum ait Nerium episcopum Senensem naturae fecisse satis, atque Aeneam sibi suffectum dici; quod postea Bononiae verum esse ex legato didicit.

5 Ea res sic gesta est. Mortuo Nerio Senenses bonum quendam virum, nomine Comitem, abbatem monasterii Sancti Galgani, concivem suum, regentibus acceptum, summis precibus Apostolicae Sedi commendaverunt atque unum hunc esse dixerunt quem praesulem cuperent. Cardinales alii alios provehebant; at summus pontifex, solus Aeneae memor absentis, eum Sacro Collegio nomi-

This journey, too, was not without its dangers. The Ligula, a river in the territory of the Volsci, is a very deep stream, completely overgrown with vegetation. The branches of the trees on either bank spread out so far over the water that they often meet in the middle. The boats there are very small, but Aeneas and his companions embarked, for the boatmen were stubborn and played down the risk of mishap and even compelled them to sail at night. Again and again they struck against the branches until finally, at the blackest hour of the night, they stuck fast on the trunk of an enormous tree and remained there for two hours, in danger of their lives. In that same spot, not long after, another boat sank and eleven men were drowned. Later, as they were preparing to cross another river near the coast not far from Cumae, the boat carrying their servants, which was badly overloaded, capsized and men and horses alike were tipped into the deep. But the men escaped by grabbing hold of a rope and the horses swam to safety. 3

Now since we have related the mishaps, it is only fair to recount some happy times.[84] At the start of this same journey, Aeneas had passed through Ferrara, where he found his cousin, Jacopo Tolomei, a distinguished lawyer and a judge in the city's senate, whom the emperor later made a count of the Lateran. He told Aeneas he had received a letter from his wife saying that Nerio, the bishop of Siena, was dead. Rumor had it that Aeneas had been appointed to succeed him. Afterwards, this news was confirmed by the legate at Bologna. 4

The facts were these. After Nerio's death, the Sienese asked the Apostolic See to appoint a fellow-citizen of theirs, a good man by the name of Conti, abbot of the monastery of San Galgano. The city fathers approved of this candidate: they declared he was the only man they wanted for their bishop. Various cardinals urged other candidates, but the pope, who was the only one to think of Aeneas in his absence, proposed his name to the Sacred College and persuaded them to transfer him from Trieste to his native 5

navit persuasitque ab ecclesia Tergestina in patriam transferendum. Senensibus autem egregium se pontificem dedisse respondit, qui ubi nominatum Aeneam agnoverunt, ingentes apostolico culmini gratias reddidere, quia nobilem doctumque virum, concivem suum (quod minime speraverant) in patriam rediturum intellegebant. Atque cum Senis haberet Aeneas transitum, non expectatis litteris apostolicis, in episcopali eum palatio recipere festinabant rerumque omnium ei possessionem offerebant; ipse autem expectandas litteras ait.

6 Igitur cum Romam ex Neapoli redisset, relatis summo pontifici gratiis, litteris ex Apostolica Camera (quod perrarum est) sine pecunia redemptis, urbem Senam patriamque domum repetens, obviante[56] cleri et populi processione sub umbrella exceptus aurea, tanto in urbem civium plausu tantoque honore intromissus est, quantum antea nulli episcoporum delatum aiunt.

7 In hoc quoque itinere apud Nicolaum pontificem egit, ut sanctum virum, Iohannem Capistraneum, Divi Bernardini discipulum, in Germaniam mitteret exactam tota Germania Beati Francisci regulam denuo plantaturum; quem postea Viennae praedicantem audivit, gratum populis et miraculorum effectorem creditum. Verum Aeneas in Austriam reversus non solum matrimonii contractum imperatori gratum rettulit, sed Romanum praesulem, Senenses, Florentinos, Bononienses, marchionem Estensem Venetosque ad coronationem transeunti caesari tranquillum iter daturos affirmavit, quod apud eos omnes ex sententia transegerat.

city.[85] He told the Sienese that he had given them a distinguished bishop; when they heard it was Aeneas, they thanked His Holiness in the warmest possible terms. For here was something they had not dared to hope for: a noble and learned man, and a fellow-citizen, returning to his native city. When Aeneas passed through Siena, they rushed to install him in the episcopal palace without waiting for the apostolic letter of appointment, and they offered him immediate possession of all his rights and privileges. But Aeneas said they must wait for the letter.

So when Aeneas returned to Rome from Naples, he went to 6
thank the pope and received from the Apostolic Camera the very unusual honor of a letter of appointment free of all dues. And when he returned again to Siena, the home of his fathers, the clergy and the people came out in procession to meet him and he was escorted into the city under a golden canopy with greater acclamation from the citizens and greater honor, they say, than had ever been accorded to any previous bishop.

In the course of this same journey Aeneas also persuaded Pope 7
Nicholas to send that holy man, Giovanni da Capistrano,[86] a disciple of San Bernardino, to Germany to plant there again the rule of St. Francis, which had been abolished throughout the country. (Aeneas later heard him preach at Vienna, where he was very popular with the people and it was said he performed miracles.) On his return to Austria, Aeneas brought back not only a marriage contract that pleased the emperor but also the assurance that the pope, the Sienese, the Florentines, the Bolognese, the marquis of Este and the Venetians would all give safe-conduct to the emperor when he went to be crowned; for he had negotiated favorable terms from all of them.

: 21 :

Aeneas caesaris legatus ad Bohemos, eorumque reconciliatio et haeresis.

1 Interea Bohemi, cum saepe Ladislaum regem petentes non obtinuissent, conventum regni apud Pragam indixerant rebus ut suis consulerent; quod nisi Alberti filius heresque regni ad se mitteretur, alium sese regem assumpturos minabantur. Ad eos igitur Aeneas et alii plerique proceres missi sunt; verum peste apud Pragam mirum in modum grassante, conventus in villam translatus est quae Benedicti appellatur.

2 Ibi ergo cum Aeneas publice mandata caesaris exposuisset, pupillumque regem gubernationis egentem in nulla melius quam in caesaris manu esse, eosque breve post tempus voti futuros compotes affirmasset, feroces mentes lenivit nec alium se postea vocaturos regem dixere. Multa illic cum Georgio regni gubernatore de bono pacis et unionis Ecclesiae scite locutus, hominem magis dominandi cupiditate quam haeresis errore deceptum existimavit; idque plerisque Bohemis insitum est, quibus dominari hereticis quam servire fidelibus antiquius esse videtur.

3 In hac legatione bis Thaboritas adiit, hereticos qui Bohemiam incolunt omnium pessimos, cumque his acerrime de fide disseruit. Sed quoniam mores Thaboritarum, urbis situm, gentis errores et omnem suam disputationem cardinali Sancti Angeli clarissimo viro Aeneas scripsit, deque his rebus extat epistola quam nos cum aliis ingeruimus in uno volumine, his praetermissis ad alia festinabimus.

: 21 :

Aeneas appointed imperial ambassador to Bohemia; reconciliation with the Bohemians; their heresy.

Meanwhile the Bohemians, after many vain efforts to get Ladislas for their king,[87] convened a national council at Prague to discuss their affairs. They declared that unless Albert's son, the heir to the kingdom, was sent to them, they would choose another king for themselves. Aeneas was therefore despatched together with several other noblemen to meet with them. A terrible plague was then raging through Prague, so the council was transferred to the village of Beneschau. 1

There Aeneas addressed a public assembly where he delivered a message from the emperor. He explained that the boy king needed a guardian; he could be in no better hands than the emperor's; moreover, it would not be long before they saw their wishes fulfilled. This speech soothed their anger and they promised not to call anyone else to the throne. There he also had a long conversation with the regent, George,[88] in which he discoursed knowledgably on the blessings of peace and the unity of the Church. Afterwards Aeneas decided that this man had been led astray by his lust for power rather than heretical beliefs. This is a common trait among the Bohemians, who consider it more honorable to rule over heretics than be subject to the faithful. 2

In the course of this mission he made two visits to the Taborites, the worst of all heretics in Bohemia, with whom he argued bitterly over matters of religion. He sent the illustrious cardinal of Sant'Angelo an account of Taborite customs, their city and their heresy, together with the text of his disputation. Since this letter is extant and has been included in my book of collected letters, I shall pass over these topics and hasten on to others.[89] 3

: 22 :

Apparatus Leonorae, et Aeneae cura in commeatibus perquirendis, et Senarum conditio, atque Italiae metus, et imperatrix ab Aenea deducta.

1 Annus qui sequebatur is erat quo Leonora imperatrix ex Portugallia navibus ad Thalamonis portum Senensis agri ex condicto adduci, Italiamque Federicus caesar intrare atque Romae coronam Imperii suscipere debuit. Studium autem illud erat, simul ut ambo Romam petentes ex manibus summi pontificis diademata tollerent. Delectae sunt igitur matronae nobiles et innuptae puellae duodecim, quae sponsam regiam in portu reciperent illi serviturae; nominati quoque barones duo, equites duo, qui eas minarent;[57] tum Aeneas et Michael Fullendorfius secretarius additi qui legationis onera sustinerent.

2 His autem commissum est, imperatricem apud Thalamonem postquam salutassent, Senas uti deducerent ibique caesaris praestolarentur adventum. Verum Aeneae Michaelique amplius mandatum erat, Italiae communitatibus atque principibus, maxime vero summo sacerdoti, caesaris adventum (qui iam dubius videbatur) ut certum ad festum Martini renuntiarent, transitum peterent, commeatibus aequa pretia statuerent, atque ad eam rem litterae praemissae sunt.

3 Quibus cognitis Italiae potentes trepidare, sperare tenues, nutare principes, impleri omnia rumoribus, timeri motus, quos in adventu caesarum excitatos vetustas noverat. Maxime vero Senenses timor invasit, quod Aeneam ex magna et nobili familia natum,

: 22 :

Preparations for Leonora; Aeneas in charge of arrangements for the journey; the state of affairs at Siena; fear in Italy. Aeneas escorts the empress.

1 The following year, according to their agreement, Empress Leonora was supposed to sail from Portugal to the Sienese port of Talamone,[90] while Emperor Frederick was to come to Italy to receive the imperial crown at Rome. Frederick was determined that they should go to Rome together to take their crowns from the hands of the pope. He therefore appointed twelve noble matrons and twelve maiden girls to welcome the royal bride at the port and attend her, and two barons and two knights to accompany them. Aeneas and the secretary Michael Pfullendorf also joined the party, representing the emperor. After meeting the empress at Talamone the group was to escort her to Siena and there await the emperor's arrival.

2 Aeneas and Michael were further instructed to promise the communes and princes of Italy, and above all the pope, that the emperor — whom some by that point suspected of prevarication — would most certainly arrive in time for the feast of St. Martin.[91] They were also to secure safe-conducts for him and fix fair prices for the supplies he would need; letters dealing with these matters were sent ahead.

3 At this news, the princes of Italy were filled with terror and the weak with hope; great lords lost their nerve. Rumor was rife. There was a general fear of unrest, such as had broken out in the past when emperors descended into Italy. But the Sienese were more frightened than anyone else, for they suspected that Aeneas, as a member of a great and noble family, bishop of their city and a

civitatis episcopum, apud imperatorem auditum magnoque loco habitum, novarum rerum cupidum arbitrabantur.

4 Urbs autem Senarum in Etruria prima post Florentiam habetur, quae pluribus et ambitiosis oppidis dominatur, latumque agrum possidet. In ea primum nobiles rerum potiti sunt; his inter se divisis et sua sponte cedentibus regimen in populum derivatum est. In eo quoque, ut fit, excellentiores aliis alii potentiam adepti, rem publicam per vices invasere atque horum alii 'novem', alii 'duodecim' (quamvis numerosi essent) quia totidem priores inter se dominantes instituerunt, vocati sunt; aliis, cum civitatis leges in suo regimine murosque reformassent, 'reformatorum' nomen inditum est. Ex his duodecim qui vocantur (sunt autem admodum quingenti viri) quamvis negociatores opulenti, abiecti tamen habentur, atque omni imperio abdicati vitam paene servilem ducunt. Novem et reformatores munera civitatis aequo iure cum populo[58] partiti, nobilibus certam officiorum portionem precario quodammodo tribuunt.

5 Quibus ex rebus existimabant Senenses Aeneam, natu nobilem, in adventu caesaris aliquid moliturum quo suam familiam ad pristinam dignitatem potentiamque reduceret. Eum igitur, cum Venetiis, Ferrariae, Bononiae, Florentiae quae mandata caesaris explevisset, ad se venientem timere; observare quidnam ageret; prohibere vulgo ad eum irent, quosdam etiam (ut est populi mos) incessere maledictis; odiosum regentes habere. Ridendus est mundi cursus, in quo nihil stabile, nihil securum invenitur. Anno qui praecesserat, nemo satis Aeneam intueri potuit, nemo satis commendare; nunc invisus omnibus cum intraret urbem, honoris causa nullum obvium habuit, domi a paucis salutatus est, in plateis

confidant and favorite of the emperor, would try to overthrow their government.

Siena is considered the chief city in Tuscany after Florence; it 4
rules many flourishing towns and occupies extensive territory. At first it was ruled by the nobility, but they divided into factions and gave up their power voluntarily, whereupon government passed to the people. Among them too, as is natural, some men outstripped their peers. One party after another came to power and seized control of the government. One party was called the Nine, another the Twelve—not because these were their actual numbers but because they appointed that number of priors to govern together; another group, who rewrote the city's constitution and repaired the walls during their tenure, were known as the Reformers. Of these, the Twelve (who actually number nearly five hundred) are considered insignificant. Though wealthy merchants, they have renounced all political authority and are practically slaves. Thus the Nine and The Reformers distribute all public offices. They do so justly enough among the common people, but to the nobility they allow only a small number of posts—on sufferance, as it were.

For these reasons the Sienese feared that Aeneas, as a noble- 5
man, would make some attempt to restore his family to their ancestral rank and power upon the emperor's arrival. He had already done Frederick's bidding at Venice, Ferrara, Bologna and Florence, and now he was coming to them. The Sienese were terrified; they watched to see what he would do and forbade the people to go out to meet him. Some commoners even hurled abuse at him, of the sort one expects from the mob; the ruling party held him in contempt. How ridiculous are the twists and turns of fate! Nothing in the world stays the same. Only a year before, no one could regard or praise Aeneas highly enough but now, as he rode into the city, he was despised by all. Not a soul came out to meet him. At his house there were only a few to greet him; in the piazzas he

maledicere sibi plerosque animadvertit, in suam quoque necem conspirasse aliquos rumor erat. Sed tulit omnia moderate risitque secum fortunae mutationem.

6 Accedens ergo urbis senatum, postquam caesaris legationem absolvit, rogavit magistratum ne quid de se male sentiret; se pluribus beneficiis ab eorum regimine cumulatum, nullam habere causam cur ei officere vellet; se primum in urbe honoratum, qui pontifex esset, pacem cupere, motus omnes horrere; familiam Picolominaeam, de qua sibi origo esset, inter alios nobiles a regentibus semper honestius habitam; Gregorium Lollium, nobilem iuris[59] consultum inter primos gubernatores urbis, ex Bartholomea sorore patris sui natum fratrem suum esse; sorores suas in regimine nuptas, illarum liberos heredes sibi futuros; nihil demum inveniri, quod se regentibus infestum reddere posset; caesarem praeterea Italiam non regnaturum, sed coronam accepturum petere; comites habere principes nobilissimos, potentes proceres, quietis amatores; amicos omnes venire, non hostes; nihil ab his esse timendum, qui solo transitu contenti essent; caesari numquam seditiones cordi fuisse; stabilem eius fidem, inconcussum quod promitteret. Sic pacatis aliquantisper animis tutior apud eos mansit.

7 Inter haec Michael Fullendorfius, eius collega et amicus in primis carus, febre correptus magnum et illustrem spiritum exhalavit; corpus suum Aeneas in aede Beatae Virginis magnifice sepelivit. Inde, ut invidiae amplius cederet, quia non deerant Senis murmurantes, Talamonem quantotius se cum collegis contulit, ibi ut adventantem imperatricem maneret, et ne Senis inveniri posset si caesar interim proficisceretur. Romanum autem pontificem adire

heard curses muttered against him; it was even rumored there was a conspiracy against his life. But he bore everything calmly and smiled to himself at the change in his fortunes.

He appeared before the city senate and, after discharging his business for the emperor, begged the presiding magistrate not to think ill of him: the government had bestowed countless favors upon him and he had no reason to wish to oppose it; as their bishop, their most honored citizen, he desired peace and loathed every kind of agitation; the Piccolomini family to which he belonged had, like the other nobles, always been treated honorably by the party in power; Gregorio Lolli, a celebrated lawyer and one of the chief magistrates of the city, was his cousin, the son of his father's sister Bartolomea;[92] his sisters were married to members of the ruling party and their children would be his heirs; in short, there was absolutely no reason for the government to suspect his intentions. What was more, the emperor was not coming to conquer Italy but to ask for his crown; he had with him illustrious princes and powerful nobles who were lovers of peace; all were coming as friends, not foes; there was nothing to fear from them, for they wanted only permission to pass; the emperor had never favored civil strife, his honor was to be relied on, his promises would not be broken. After this, the people calmed down a little, and he was able to remain among them in safety. 6

At this time, his dear friend and colleague Michael Pfullendorf fell ill with a fever. His soul—a great and noble one—passed away; Aeneas gave his body a splendid burial in the Cathedral of the Blessed Virgin. Immediately afterwards, making a further concession to his unpopularity with the people of Siena (for some were still whispering against him), he and his colleagues departed for Talamone. There they could await the arrival of the empress; moreover, if the emperor set out for Italy in the meantime, it would not do to be found lingering at Siena. He could not go to 7

non potuit, ne dum Romae teneretur, imperatrix portum applicaret, cuius receptio sibi potissimum commissa fuerat.

8 Pontifex, cui Romanorum mores cogniti erant, quique multos novitatis avidos intellexerat, timens populi motum—nam et Florentini vaticinium esse aiebant ante diem tertium decimum Kalendarum Aprilis vel moriturum papam, vel captione mala capiendum—iam caesari nuntiaverat adventum suum in aestatem ut differret, commeatuum penuriam causatus; Aeneae vero, ut ad se quantotius iret, imperavit.

9 Ipse autem, cum se litteris excusatum fecisset (quoniam quae caesari nuntiata fuerant, non ignorabat), mirari sese ait mutationem apostolicam, neque videri honestum Romani pontificis dictum indictum fieri; memoria se tenere pontificem maximum dixisse sibi, caesari, si venire Romam vellet, hiemale tempus eligendum, quod salubrius esset; rebusque victui necessariis magis abundaret; praestoque esse ad coronationem omnia; ultro petitum adventum; nunc mandari contraria indignum esse, quando et is accinctus itineri et coniunx eius propediem litus Italicum appulsura sciretur; accepisse se maximo pontifici metum iniectum, timerique Romae caesarem; at timorem vanum: scire caesarem iustum, Nicolai amantem, nil aeque odisse quam turbas; moriturum prius quam fidem falleret;[60] comitatum habere nobilissimum, quietis cupidum, religioni et Deo faventem.

10 Quibus verbis Nicolaus motus litteras ad caesarem scripsit, suo ex arbitrio iter ut faceret, easque ad Aeneam primum direxit, ut si sibi videretur, illas ad caesarem mitteret. Placuit Aeneae scriptum apostolicum moxque tabellarium ad caesarem direxit. Verum inte-

the pope for fear that the empress, whose reception was his personal responsibility, might land while he was detained in Rome.

The pope realized that among the Romans, whose habits he knew well, many were eager for revolution. Fearing a popular disturbance (for even the Florentines were saying it had been prophesied that the pope would either die on March 20 or be taken prisoner in a sinister plot), he sent word to the emperor advising him to put off his coming till summer, giving as a further excuse the scarcity of supplies. He told Aeneas, on the other hand, to come to him as soon as possible. 8

Now Aeneas knew full well what the emperor had been told. He sent the pope his excuses in a letter, and expressed his astonishment at his change of heart. It hardly seemed right that the bishop of Rome should go back on his word; he distinctly recalled that the pope had advised him, if the emperor wished to come to Rome, to pick a date in winter because it was a healthier time of year and supplies would be more plentiful. Moreover, everything was prepared for the coronation; the pope had asked the emperor to come; it would be unseemly to retract the invitation now, when all knew the emperor was preparing to depart and his bride could land in Italy at any moment. He had heard that the pope was nervous, that Rome dreaded the arrival of the emperor, but in truth such fears were groundless. The pope must understand that the emperor was just; he held Nicholas in high regard; there was nothing he hated so much as disorder; he would sooner die than break his word; the imperial retinue was composed of great nobles who were eager for peace and devoted to the Church and to God. 9

Nicholas was impressed by these words and wrote the emperor a letter telling him to come when he saw fit. He sent the letter to Aeneas first; if it met with his approval, he was to forward it to the emperor. Aeneas approved the pope's words and at once despatched a courier to Frederick. In the meantime, however, unrest had broken out in Austria.[93] The emperor postponed his depar- 10

rea motus in Austria excitatus dies plurimos adventum caesaris retardavit, imperatricem venti contrarii et horridae tempestates diu retinuerunt; itaque LX diebus apud Talamonem Aeneas non sine magno suo et collegarum tedio demoratus est. Vidit tamen interea montem Argentarium et non obscurum Herculis Portum, neque indignam visu Lansedoniam, cuius etsi diruta sunt aedificia, moenia tamen adhuc extant ex quadratis sectisque lapidibus ingentis magnitudinis, sine caemento mirabili iunctura connexis, in colle qui mari Tusco imminens ad Carthaginem respicit.

11 Verum mirabile dictu est: cum caesar ex Alamania in Italiam descendisset iterque celeri cursu perageret, seu divino quodam flatu, seu praecipiti casu factum est, quo is die Florentiam intravit, eodem imperatrix Liburnii portum applicuit. Aeneas quoque simul die una et imperatoris et imperatricis litteras accepit, quae se suosque collegas propere Pisas iubebant petere. Parens cum collegis ac dominabus per Grossetum et Scarlinum ac per agrum Volaterranum impigre Pisas venit.

12 Iam caesar Iohannem episcopum Ratisponensem; Vanconem Sclesiae ducem, consanguineum suum; Michaelem comitem Magdeburgensem; Iohannem magistrum camere; Ulricum Sonnenbergium Austriae cancellarium; Ulricum Montis Fortis; Iacobum Lodronium physicum et nobiles equites, ad imperatricem miserat. Nihil tamen adhuc conclusum erat. Ibi ergo cum diu de consignanda mittendaque caesari sponsa tractaretur, tandem marchio Portugallensis, qui Leonoram a fratre receperat imperatori tradendam, postquam de ceteris rebus transactum est, vocatis oratoribus et qui Pisis erant viris nobilitate claris, rogatis tabellionibus, imperatricem dextera manu apprehendens ad manus Aeneae consignavit, illam ut ad caesarem transduceret. Quae res Vanconi duci admodum molesta fuit, qui sibi hoc honoris iure sanguinis quo

ture for several days, and the empress was seriously delayed by unfavorable winds and violent storms. So Aeneas spent sixty days waiting at Talamone, days which were very dull for him and his party. Still, he had time to visit Monte Argentario and the famous Port'Ercole and Ansedonia, which is worth seeing: although its buildings lie in ruins, its walls remain standing, built of huge, square-hewn stones fitted together with extraordinary precision and without mortar, and commanding a hill above the Tuscan Sea, looking south toward Carthage.

There followed a remarkable coincidence: the emperor had come down from Germany and was making quick progress through Italy. On the very day he entered Florence, the empress—sped by some breeze from heaven, or perhaps by sheer chance—landed at Livorno.[94] And on that same day Aeneas received letters from both the emperor and the empress commanding him and his party to come at once to Pisa. Accompanied by his colleagues and the ladies in waiting, he obediently hastened to Pisa, passing through Grosseto, Scarlino and the territory of Volterra. 11

The emperor had already sent a party to the empress consisting of Johann, bishop of Regensburg; his kinsman Vanco, duke of Silesia; Michael, count of Magdeburg; his chamberlain, Johann; Ulrich Sonnenburg, the chancellor of Austria; Ulrich Starnberg; Jacopo Landrono, his physician; and various other noble knights. But as no plans had yet been finalized, there was a long debate at Pisa as to how they should officially receive the bride and send her on to the emperor. At last everything was settled. The marquis of Portugal, who had formally received Leonora from her brother and was charged with bringing her to the emperor, took the lady by the hand before an assembly of ambassadors, distinguished nobles of Pisa and notaries summoned for the occasion, and delivered her to Aeneas, who was to escort her to Frederick. This was extremely vexing to Duke Vanco, who thought that the honor 12

caesari propinquabat deberi putavit. Sed Portugallensibus ceterisque legatis caesaris aliter visum fuit.

: 23 :

Florentinorum metus. Adventus caesaris et Leonorae in Italiam, primusque congressus, ac monumentum[61] Senis erectum, et caesaris de Aenea prophetia. Aeneae oratio apud pontificem, ac pontificis et caesaris somnia.

1 Dum Pisis haec agerentur, Florentini, qui civitatem duro imperio premunt, Pisanosque omnes suspectos habent, tot adventasse illuc exteros tantamque moram facere iniqua mente ferebant. Verbis tamen Aeneae, qui eis notior erat, in diesque recessum spondebat, ne quid novitatis agerent retenti sunt.

2 Imperator interea Senas venerat ibique sponsam manebat, quam postquam properare cognovit, emissis primum civibus obviam, deinde Alberto germano duce Austriae, post Ladislao patruele Hungariae ac Bohemiae rege, quarto loco cum reliquiis sanctorum clero, postremo et ipse medius inter duos legatos apostolicos—Sanctae Susannae, Nicolai pontificis germanum, et Sancti Angeli cardinales—intra secundam et tertiam urbis portam egressus coniugem expectavit, ibique ambo ex equis descendentes in spacioso et patenti loco sese mutuis amplexibus exceperunt. Verba nomine caesaris Henricus Leubin, pontificii iuris interpres fecit; imperatricis vice locutus est Aeneas. Atque ibi paulo post Senenses marmoream columnam erexerunt, memoriale diuturnum, quo posthac imperatorem ab orienti, imperatricem ab occi-

should go to him on account of his kinship with Frederick; but the Portuguese and the imperial ambassadors thought otherwise.

: 23 :

Fear among the Florentines. The emperor and Leonora arrive in Italy and meet for the first time. Monument erected at Siena. The emperor makes a prediction about Aeneas. His oration before the pope. The pope and emperor relate their dreams.

As all this was happening at Pisa, the Florentines, who rule that city like tyrants and remain wary of its citizens, grew annoyed that so many foreigners had arrived there and were staying so long. But Aeneas, who was better known to them than the rest, gave them daily assurances that they would soon depart and so kept them from taking any action. 1

In the meantime, the emperor reached Siena, where he awaited his bride. When he heard that she was approaching, he despatched welcoming parties: first the citizens, then his brother Duke Albert of Austria, then his cousin King Ladislas of Hungary and Bohemia, and fourth and last the clergy, bearing relics of the saints. Then he himself, flanked by the two apostolic legates—the cardinal of Santa Susanna (who was Pope Nicholas's brother) and the cardinal of Sant'Angelo[95]—went out to receive the bride between the second and third gates of the city. There, in a broad, open space, they dismounted and embraced one another. Heinrich Leubing, an expert in canon law, spoke for the emperor and Aeneas for the empress. Soon afterwards the Sienese erected a marble column on the spot, a lasting memorial to remind future 2

dua solis parte venientes illic sese primum vidisse posteri cognoscant.

3 Inter haec Senenses omnes, qui ferre arma poterant ex duodecim ac nobilibus, extra urbem relegavere, maxime vero cognatos Aeneae Picolominaeos. At ubi caesaris clementiam atque mansuetudinem intellexerunt, Aeneamque vera locutum, rursus in eius admirationem conversi bonum eum et patrem et civem praedicavere, revocatisque cognatis eius suspicari desiverunt, ac legatum Aeneam ad summum pontificem designarunt.

4 Cum Cimini montis iugum, qui Viturvio imminet, ascendisset imperator, accersito inter equitandum Aenea, 'Ecce,' inquit, 'Romam petimus. Videre videor te cardinalem futurum. Neque hic tua fortuna conquiescet. Altius eveheris. Beati Petri te cathedra manet. Cave ne me contempseris, ubi hoc honoris assecutus sis!' Cui Aeneas: 'Nec pontificatum maximum mihi arrogo, neque cardinalatum.'—'At ego,' subintulit caesar, 'hoc ita futurum video.' Aeneas tamquam iocantis verba suscepit, et Romam cum eo profectus primus inter praelatos eius fuit, salutantibusque cardinalibus et Urbis primoribus qui obviarunt responsa pro caesare dedit.

5 Cumque caesar nocte extra moenia civitatis remansisset, Aeneas ad pontificem lectulo cubantem vocatus; bonam fixamque caesaris mentem esse ostendit, admiratumque sese ait tanti principis fidem in dubium potuisse venire. Cui pontifex, cum verba multorum exposuisset, 'Minus,' inquit 'timentis error quam fidentis nocet.'

6 Cum vero caesar Urbem intrasset, atque ante fores basilicae Sancti Petri sacros summi pontificis pedes exoscularetur, Aeneas

generations that an emperor from the East and an empress from the West had first met in that place.

Meanwhile the Sienese had banished from the city all those among the Twelve and the Nobles who could bear arms, especially singling out Aeneas's relations among the Piccolomini. But when they saw that the emperor was mild and gentle and that Aeneas had spoken the truth, they returned to their old admiration for him. They hailed him as their benevolent father and fellow-citizen, recalled his family from exile and ceased to hold them suspect; they also appointed him their ambassador to the pope. 3

One day, Aeneas was out riding with the emperor. Climbing the ridge of Monte Cimino above Viterbo, the emperor summoned Aeneas to his side. "Now look," he said, "We are going to Rome. It looks like you are going to be a cardinal. And your luck won't stop there. You're going to the top. The throne of Peter awaits you. When you get there, make sure you don't forget me." Aeneas replied, "I'm not looking for a cardinal's hat, and I don't want a tiara." — "And yet," the emperor said, "I can see that's how it will be." Aeneas took this as a joke. He carried on with the emperor to Rome, where he acted as the senior prelate in the imperial entourage, replying on the emperor's behalf to the cardinals and leading citizens who came out to offer their greetings. 4

The emperor spent that night outside the city walls. Next day Aeneas was summoned to Nicholas's private chamber. He assured the pope that the emperor's intentions were honorable and would not change, adding that he found it astonishing that the good faith of so great a prince could have been called into doubt. The pope replied by describing the many reports he had received, adding that a cautious man makes fewer mistakes than one who trusts too much. 5

The emperor entered the city and kissed the holy feet of the pontiff before the doors of St. Peter's. At his command, Aeneas then delivered a speech. He spoke for his lord on other occasions 6

imperatoris iussu sermonem habuit. Ei quoque in petitione Mediolanensis coronae, quae Longobardorum dicitur, in benedictione sponsalium, cum sacro maximi praesulis ore Leonora Federico iungeretur, in coronatione demum caesarea apud aram Sancti Petri, imperatorio nomine quae fierent verba commissa sunt. Inter papam et imperatorem secretas res multas absolvit.

7 Neque hic unum praetereundum arbitror, quod de somniis memoratu dignum videtur. Sequenti post coronationem die caesar cum tribus consiliariis, inter quos Aeneas fuit, Nicolaum pontificem adiit; ubi sermone ad longum producto: 'Meministi, pater,' inquit, 'dicturum me tibi somnium, postquam coronam accepissem? Id huiusmodi est. Ex Vienna cum recessisti a me ultimo, vidi per quietem nocte proxima me Romam venisse, tuisque manibus meo capiti coronam imponi. Mirabar inter dormiendum, neque me legitime coronatum putabam, quem non Romanus sed Bononiensis episcopus coronasset; evigilans autem contempsi visum. At postquam te cardinalem creatum, deinde papam assumptum, Aeneae primum litteris intellexi, e vestigio ratum credidi — quod secutum est — tuis me manibus coronandum.'

8 Tum Nicolaus, 'Saepe verum somniant, qui praesunt populis. Ego quoque,' inquit, 'nocte quae mortem Eugenii praecessit, sopori deditus in hoc me cubiculum venisse[62] videbar,[63] quod tunc (ut tu nosti, Aenea) bipartitum fuit. Eugenius pallium, deinde tunicam exuens illis me induit, mitramque longam, qualem gestare nostri milites solent, suo capiti demens imposuit meo. Postremo manu me apprehendens, ostensaque hac sella, 'Sede hinc,' inquit, 'ego ad Sanctum Petrum pergam.' Sic ille in crastinum mortuus in aedem Sancti Petri delatus est; forsitan et anima gloriosi praedecessoris consortio gaudet. Mihi post duodecim dies summus apostolatus commissus est.'

as well: when Frederick made his formal petition for the crown of Milan, called the Lombard Crown; when Frederick and Leonora received the nuptial blessing, after the pope himself had performed the wedding ceremony; and, finally, when Frederick was crowned emperor at the high altar of the basilica.[96] In each case, Aeneas was charged with making the proper responses. He also handled many private matters between the emperor and the pope.

Now I must not forget to mention one thing, a matter concerning dreams, which seems worth recording. The day after the coronation the pope gave an audience to Frederick, who came with three councilors, including Aeneas. The conversation had gone on for some time when the emperor said, "Father, do you remember, after the coronation I was going to tell you my dream. It went like this. The night after you left me at Vienna for the last time, I dreamt I had come to Rome and you were placing a crown on my head. In my dream, I was amazed by this, thinking my coronation could not be valid since it wasn't the bishop of Rome but the bishop of Bologna who was performing it. When I woke up, I forgot all about this vision, but after Aeneas wrote to say that you had been made a cardinal, and then elected pope, I knew immediately that I would be crowned by your hands—and so I have." 7

Then Nicholas said, "The dreams of princes often come true. I myself, the night before Eugenius died, imagined in my sleep that I had come into this very room, which as you know, Aeneas, was then divided into two parts. Eugenius took off his robe and tunic and put them on me, and lifted a tall hat from his head, such as our soldiers wear, and put it onto mine. Then he took me by the hand and pointed to this throne, saying, 'From this seat I go to St. Peter.' He died the next day. His body was carried into St. Peter's and perhaps his soul is even now rejoicing in the company of his glorious predecessor. Twelve days later the papacy passed to me." 8

: 24 :

Pontificis promissio de cardinalatu Aeneae, qui tamen legatus de latere factus. Fuga Ladislai. Ducatus Borsii et Aeneae oratio.

1 Dum haec agerentur, frequens opinio fuit Aeneam in cardinalatus ordinem recipiendum, qui papae carus caesarique videbatur; neque ab re. Promiserat enim imperatori Nicolaus inter primos quos creaturus esset cardinales, Aeneam primo loco nominatum iri, neque mentitus est, nullo deinde ad cardinalatum assumpto mortuus. Neque dignitas huiuscemodi semper merenti patet, quam saepe rapit indignus. Quidam tamen illam merentur, post assequuntur; quidam tum dignos ea se reddunt, cum potiuntur; nonnulli usque ad sepulchrum immeriti raptam trahunt.

2 Post haec imperator Neapolim profectus; Aeneas paulisper aegrotans Romae remansit, Ladislaique regis impuberis cum aliis curam gessit. Interim relatum est papae regem fugam meditatum; nisi custodiatur, domum exiturum. Tum pontifex quinta eius noctis hora, quae ad fugam electa ferebatur, Aeneam ad se accersivit iussitque regis domum diligenter custodiri. Aeneas regis aedes ingressus custodes eius admonuit ne malis insidiis locum darent, redeuntique caesari pignus salvum restituerent. Verum eius rei nulla postmodum certa indicia sunt reperta, quamvis pedagogus regis apud Florentiam maius flagitium tentaverit.

3 Redeunte caesare conspectuique maximi praesulis ac sacri senatus se restituente, vice sua duas orationes in auditorio publico reci-

: 24 :

The pope promises to make Aeneas a cardinal, but appoints him legate instead. Ladislas attempts flight. A dukedom for Borso and a speech by Aeneas.

As all this was happening, popular opinion held that Aeneas, who seemed to enjoy the favor of pope and emperor alike, must soon be made a cardinal. This was not an idle rumor, for Nicholas had promised Frederick that the next time he appointed any cardinals, Aeneas would be the first to be named. He did not break his word: he died without appointing anyone to that office. Such distinction does not always fall to the one who deserves it; often it is snatched away by the unworthy. Some men deserve their promotions before they attain them, while others make themselves worthy once in the post. Some take their prize to the grave without ever having done anything to deserve it. 1

The emperor then left for Naples but Aeneas, who was ill, remained in Rome a few days to look after the young King Ladislas, among other business. At this time a report reached the pope that the king was planning his escape; without a guard to watch him, he would try to make for home. At the fifth hour of the night on which he was supposed to make his attempt, the pope summoned Aeneas and told him to have the king's house watched closely. Aeneas went to the palace and advised the guards they should give no quarter to treasonous schemes; they must restore their charge safely to the emperor on his return. No firm evidence of a plot was afterwards discovered, although the king's tutor would attempt an even greater crime at Florence. 2

When the emperor returned and appeared again before the pope and the college of cardinals, Aeneas delivered two speeches in his name before a public audience. In one he thanked the pope 3

tavit. In altera gratias egit summo sacerdoti atque cardinalibus pro maximis quae caesari praestiterant beneficiis; in altera, ut generale passagium adversus Christiani nominis inimicos indiceretur atque instrueretur, papam hortatus est, ne Christicolae per Graeciam et orientem amplius vexarentur. Postremo cum caesare ab Urbe recedens, orator Apostolice Sedis cum potestate legati de latere per Bohemiam, Sclesiam, Austriam, Moraviam, Stiriam, Carinthiam Carniolamque missus est; nec diu post legationem eius instante caesare Romanus praesul ad Hungariae regnum extendit.

4 Cum Senas redisset, timeretque caesar Florentia transitum facere, quia suspectam eius moram apud Neapolim Florentinis existimabat, Aeneas ad eos praemissus iter caesari tutum reddidit, innovata publica fide. Legati Hungariae et Austriae ibi caesarem expectabant, qui Gasparem pedagogum Ladislai regis ad colloquium vocantes, persuaserunt ei regem ut ex potestate caesaris raperet. Cuius rei hunc ordinem dederant: instigandum puerum aiebant ut, postquam caesarem abeuntem ad portas urbis secutus esset, velle se Florentiae dies aliquot immorari diceret, atque petita venia retroverteret equum; daturos se apud magistratus urbis operam, caesar si vim puero velit inferre, praesto viros in armis habeant qui resistant. Sed tantum flagitium senatus Florentinus exhorruit atque honesti tenacior, increpatis internuntiis, libere[64] atque magnifice honoratum caesarem a se dimisit.

5 Qui postquam Ferrariam venit, magnis precibus rogatus est Borsium marchionem ad ducatus honorem provehere, quae res menti caesaris alienior videbatur. Victus tamen cum rationibus Aeneae, tum aliorum consiliariorum suasibus ex agro Mutinae et Regii ducatum erexit, ac Borsium ducem creavit; quod bene fac-

and cardinals for the considerable favors they had granted the emperor; in the other he implored the pope to proclaim and prepare a crusade against the enemies of Christendom and thereby prevent further suffering among the Christians of Greece and the East.[97] When Aeneas finally left Rome in the emperor's train, the pope appointed him ambassador of the Apostolic See, with the powers of a legate *de latere* to Bohemia, Silesia, Austria, Moravia, Styria, Carinthia and Carniola. Not long after, at Frederick's insistence, the pope extended his mission to include the kingdom of Hungary.

When the emperor returned to Siena, he was unsure whether 4
to carry on to Florence, for he was worried that his stay at Naples had aroused the suspicions of the Florentines. Aeneas went ahead, restored public confidence and secured a safe passage for the emperor. The envoys of Hungary and Austria were waiting for the emperor there. They invited Ladislas's tutor, Caspar, to a meeting where they persuaded him to abduct the king from the emperor's custody. Their plan went something like this: as the emperor left the city, the boy was to follow him as far as the gates of the city; he would then be prompted to say he wanted to stay in Florence a few days longer. After making this request, he should wheel his horse about; they would have arranged with the city magistrates for men-at-arms to step forward to challenge the emperor if he should try to use force on the boy. The Florentine senate was aghast at the thought of such an outrage. With unshaken integrity they rebuked the intermediaries and sent the emperor away with lavish and splendid honors.

When Frederick arrived at Ferrara, great pressure was put upon 5
him to raise the marquis, Borso, to the rank of duke. It had not been the emperor's intention to do so, but he was persuaded by Aeneas's arguments and the urging of his other counselors. He carved a principality out of the territory of Modena and Reggio and made Borso its duke. All Italy said this was good move and a

tum, bene locatum omnis Italia dixit, ut quae nondum novi principis mores norat.

6 Cum novellus dux insignibus ex more publico donaretur, de caesaris beneficentia, de laudibus domus Estensis, de virtute Borsii deque dignitatis eminentia dicendi partes ad Aeneam delatae sunt. At neque Venetias postquam ventum est, de rebus magnis apud senatum ducemque gentis alius quam Aeneas ex imperio caesaris loquendi provinciam accepit.

: 25 :

Bellum Austrialium, et Aeneae legatio promotioque ad principatum Imperii, eiusque oratio et confectio pacis.

1 Postremo, cum caesar in patriam se recepisset, Austrialesque magnum exercitum adversus eum duxissent, atque ipsum diebus nonnullis apud Novam Civitatem obsedissent bombardis et aliis belli machinis quatientes muros, intrepidus caesari comes adhaesit;[65] factisque induciis, emisso rege Ladislao, conventu apud Viennam indicto in quo de pace transigeretur, cum plurimos atque praestantes oratores eo caesar misisset, Aeneas primus omnium fuit, apud quem legati totius Alamaniae, magni praelati, clari comites, insignes barones convenerunt. Bis illic apud primores Hungariae, qui ex toto regno aderant, semel apud Bohemos caesaris nomine verba fecit; Ladislaum iam regnantem bis salutatum adiit.

2 Per hoc tempus inter Albertum marchionem Brandeburgensem et civitatem Nurembergensem in curia caesaris de rebus arduis grave iudicium magnis contentionibus agebatur, quod solos diffi-

territory well chosen. They did not yet know the new prince's character.

The new duke was publicly invested with the insignia of his 6
rank, according to tradition. Afterwards, it fell to Aeneas to deliver an oration on the graciousness of the emperor, the glories of the house of Este, the ability of Borso and the exalted rank conferred upon him. And when they got to Venice, no one but Aeneas was delegated to speak for the emperor on important matters before the senate and the doge.

: 25 :

War in Austria; Aeneas sent on an embassy and promoted to the council of princes; a speech by him and a peace agreement.

At last the emperor returned to his own country. The Austrians 1
then led a great army against him and besieged him for some days at Neustadt, pounding the walls with cannon and other engines of war. Through all this Aeneas stayed undaunted at Frederick's side. Then a truce was made, King Ladislas was sent back and a congress was convened at Vienna to discuss peace.[98] The emperor sent several distinguished ambassadors there, but Aeneas had the most authority of all. The envoys of every German state, great prelates, illustrious counts and prominent barons all met at his house. While there, he spoke on behalf of the emperor, twice before the nobles of Hungary who had assembled from all parts of the kingdom, and once before the Bohemians. He went twice to pay his respects to Ladislas, who was now ruling in his own right.

At this time an important case came before the imperial court. 2
Margrave Albert of Brandenburg and the city of Nuremberg were arguing bitterly over some difficult issues which could only be set-

nire principes oportebat. Cumque Albertus unum Austriae, duos Baioariae, unum Saxoniae, duos Sclesiae duces et plerosque alios principes, ut eloquentia potens et industria solers in suam sententiam adduxisset, coactus iam caesar videbatur iniquam ferre sententiam, nisi Aeneas intervenisset, qui iam pridem post Senensis ecclesiae delatam dignitatem inter principes Imperii per caesarem assumptus fuerat.

3 Hic enim, postquam sententiam rogatus est dicere, honorem caesaris ante omnia tenendum ait, cuius nomine sententiae promulgarentur; illum vero salvari non posse, nisi iuste iudicaret; qui suspecti nominabantur, quique belli participes fuerant quod Albertus contra Norembergenses gesserat, his iudicium minime convenire; reliquos, qui caesari assiderent, iuvenes inexpertos esse paucosque, qui rem tantam dirimerent; sibi neque iustitiae, neque animae saluti detrahendum esse, utileque illud videri consilium, si res in aliud tempus protraheretur,[66] in quo caesar plures principes causae non affectos sibi assidentes habere posset.

4 Quibus dictis Iohannes Eystetensis episcopus, ubi se tangi animadvertit (nam et is bellum Nurembergensibus intulerat) ad conscientiam reversus in sententiam Aeneae concessit; idemque Ratisponensis pontifex et Carolus marchio Badensis, qui etsi Alberti sororem uxorem duxerat, affinitatem tamen iustitiae se minime praelaturum ait—dignus, cui populi pareant, et paternae virtutis sectator adolescens!

5 Ceteri Eystetensis episcopi verbis, quae haud bene intellexerunt, ducti fuere. Sic res in aliud tempus suspensa est caesarque turpi nota liberatus, quam sine culpa paene inciderat, iniquam sententiam iudicio principum qui astabant et factione laturus. Post haec cum legati Ladislai regis ad tractandam pacem, de qua Viennae desperatum erat, ad Federicum caesarem venissent, Ae-

tled properly by princes of the realm. Albert had deployed powerful rhetoric and clever diplomacy to win a duke of Austria, two of Bavaria, one of Saxony, two of Silesia and several other princes over to his side. It seemed likely that the emperor would be compelled to return an unjust decision. But at that point Aeneas, who since becoming bishop of Siena had been considered by the emperor a prince of the realm, intervened.

When asked his opinion, he said that the honor of the emperor 3
must be maintained above all else, since the decision would be handed down in his name. But this could not be done unless the decision were just. It could hardly be made by these men here, who were named in the suit and had taken part in Albert's war against Nuremberg; the rest, sitting there by the emperor, were inexperienced youths, too few in number to decide so important a question. In his opinion, in the interests of both justice and the state of their mortal souls, it would be wise to postpone the matter till a later time, when the emperor might have more princes to assist him who were not involved in the case.

At this point Johann, the bishop of Eichstadt, realized that 4
Aeneas's words implicated him, for he too had declared war on Nuremberg. Coming to his senses, he supported Aeneas's motion, as did the bishop of Regensburg and Margrave Karl of Baden. The latter, although his wife was Albert's sister, said that he would not privilege family ties over justice. Here was a young man ready to lead, a worthy successor to his excellent father.

Everyone else was persuaded by Eichstadt's speech, though they 5
had hardly understood it. So the matter was postponed and the emperor was saved from the disgrace which, through no fault of his own, he had nearly incurred; for the dissension and bad judgment of the princes advising him had put him at risk of pronouncing an unjust decision. Later, when Ladislas's ambassadors came to Frederick to negotiate peace (for at Vienna they had given up all hope of a truce), Aeneas made the public address answering them.

neas his publice respondit; deinde tractatu durante, parum tamen spei prae se ferente, hortantibus consiliariis cubiculariisque pluribus Aeneas, vocato Ulrico Sonnenbergio, caesarem adiit eamque pacem magnis rationibus et honestam et recipiendam ostendit; quae sequenti die conclusa est.

: 26 :

Constantinopolis captivitas. Conventus Ratisponensis. Burgundi adventus, et Aeneae ad pontificem legatio atque oratio.

1 Turchi, dum haec aguntur, iam pridem Minoris Asiae et maioris Graeciae partis domini, Constantinopolim orientalis imperii sedem, quae sola in terra Thracia Mahumetis iugum obtrectabat, ingentibus copiis terra marique obsident et tredecim oppugnatam diebus expugnant, capiunt, diripiunt. Imperatorem gentis Constantinum interficiunt et omnem fere nobilitatem obtruncant, plebem in servitutem redigunt, nobilissimumque Sanctae Sophiae templum cunctasque regiae urbis basilicas spurcitiis foedant Mahumetaeis. Triste id nuntium Christianis fuit—maxime vero Nicolao Quinto pontifici Romano et Federico Tertio imperatori, quorum tempora hoc tanto Christianae religionis opprobrio non modica notata sunt ignominia. Nam quae calamitas temporum non principibus imputatur? Quaecunque accidunt mala negligentiae rectorum ascribuntur. 'Poterant,' inquit vulgus, 'pereunti Graeco prius opem ferre quam caperetur. Neglexerunt. Indigni sunt qui rei publicae praesint.'

2 Imperator re cognita, dum cupit tantam infamiae notam abolere, maiorem incurrit. Incipit enim, et non perficit: convocat Christianos ut in communi consulant, et ipse non adit.

As the negotiations dragged on with little hope of success, several councilors and chamberlains urged Aeneas to speak to the emperor. With Ulrich Sonnenberg at his side, he argued powerfully that the peace was honorable and ought to be accepted; and the very next day it was.[99]

: 26 :

The fall of Constantinople. The Diet of Regensburg. Arrival of the duke of Burgundy. Aeneas's embassy to Rome and oration before the pope.

Meanwhile the Turks, who had already occupied Asia Minor and 1
the greater part of Greece for many years, laid siege to Constantinople, the capital of the eastern empire and the only city in Thrace to resist the Muslim yoke. An enormous army surrounded the city by land and sea; the siege lasted thirteen days. Then the Turks stormed, captured and sacked the place, killing Emperor Constantine, massacring nearly all the nobility, reducing the people to slavery and polluting with their Muslim filth the famous church of Holy Wisdom and all the basilicas of the city.[100] This was woeful news for Christendom, above all for Pope Nicholas and the Emperor Frederick III, for this foul insult to the Christian religion left a terrible stain on the records of their reigns. What calamity of the times is not laid at the door of princes! Every disaster is blamed on the negligence of those who rule. "They could have helped the Greeks in their hour of need," people said, "They could have sent aid before the nation was enslaved. They didn't care. They are not fit to rule."

The emperor, seeing what had happened, endeavored to erase 2
the black mark of this disgrace. But he ended up incurring a

3 Conventum[67] apud Ratisponam, Baioariae urbem quae Danubio adiacet, iubet Germanos adesse, eoque Philippum Burgundiae ducem vocat, clarum et potentem principem, qui mox relictis Flandriae motibus ad quos comprimendos ierat, receptis imperialibus litteris,[68] longissimo itinere Ratisponam se contulit. Unus enim Christianorum erat principum qui Turchorum nomini infensissimum sese ostendebat — sive patrem ulturus, quem Turchi olim captum multo auro vendiderant, sive religionis amore, quod hac potissimum via aeternam vitam quereret, sive rumores hinc populi venaretur, cui mortalium pars maxima inservit. Multum in eius adventu auctoritatis accessit Ratisponensi concilio, nam et Baioariae dux Ludovicus, et Albertus marchio Brandeburgensis et alii complures principes, audita Burgundi profectione, excitati Ratisponam[69] petiere qui alioquin domi remansissent.

4 Imperator, quamvis spem fecerat sui adventus non tenuem, mutato tamen consilio in Austria commoratus est, veritus ne vicina Hungariae flamma suam domum incenderet. Gilles et Hancrauter, latronum principes per id temporis Austriae Stiriaeque proximi Hungariam vastabant; adversus quos[70] Iohannes Huniates regni gubernator propediem conflicturus existimabatur; et victor quisquis esset, imperatori timendus erat, qui more hominum res proprias per se ipsum, communes per legatos curare statuit. Misit igitur Ratisponam egregios ex curia sua oratores barones duos, episcopos duos, quorum alter Ulricus Gurcensis, alter Aeneas Senensis fuit, et his adiunctus est Nicolaus Sancti Petri cardinalis, qui tum apud ecclesiam suam Brixinensem morabatur. Nicolaus pontifex maximus Iohannem episcopum Papiensem eo transmisit,

greater one, for he did not finish what he had started. He called for a Christian congress to address the problem, but he himself did not attend.

He ordered the Germans to assemble at Regensburg,[101] a city of Bavaria on the Danube, and there, too, he summoned Duke Philip of Burgundy. This celebrated and powerful prince had gone into Flanders to put down a revolt but, as soon as he received the emperor's letter, he abandoned his campaign and undertook the long journey to Regensburg. For he alone among the Christian princes had declared his bitter hatred for the Turks—whether from a desire to avenge his father, whom the Turks had once taken captive and held for a huge ransom; or out of devotion to his religion, thinking this the surest path to eternal life; or because he sought to win over public opinion, which holds almost all mortal men in its thrall. The authority of the Diet of Regensburg was greatly enhanced by his arrival: for when Ludwig of Bavaria, Albert of Brandenburg and several other princes heard that Burgundy was on his way, they were roused to go to Regensburg themselves; otherwise they would have stayed at home. 3

The emperor had given them good reason to count on his coming, but at the last minute he changed his mind and stayed in Austria, fearing that the flames next door in Hungary would finally set his own house alight. At the time, the bandit princes Gilles and Hanchrauter were ravaging the border regions of Hungary, very close to Austria and Styria, and it seemed likely that John Hunyadi, the governor general of the kingdom, would soon engage them in battle. The emperor had reason to fear whoever emerged the victor. Naturally he preferred to handle his private affairs by himself and the affairs of state through ambassadors, so he sent a distinguished embassy to Regensburg, including two barons from his court, two bishops (Ulrich of Gurk and Aeneas of Siena), and Nicholas, the cardinal of San Pietro in Vincoli, who was then at his church in Brixen. Pope Nicholas sent Bishop Giovanni of 4

qui tuitionem fidei catholicae concilio commendaret et opem suam offerret.

5 Conventu iam pleno cum praelati ecclesiarum et principes Christiani multi adessent, contione in praetorio civitatis, advocata Aeneas vice imperatoris verba fecit, quibus in expugnatione Constantinopolitana quantum detrimenti Christiana res publica[71] accepisset, et quantum instaret periculum nisi Turchorum conatibus occurreretur, plane dilucideque monstravit, capiendaque publice[72] arma pro communi utilitate suasit, excusato imperatore, qui domi necessario remansisset,[73] quamquam manca omnis ratio videbatur. Habuit et orationem apostolico nomine Iohannes episcopus Papiensis, et pro Burgundo locutus est Iohannes Tullensis episcopus, quem postea Pius Secundus ad Tornacensem transtulit ecclesiam. Cardinalis quoque Sancti Petri nonnihil ad persuasionem belli effatus est, et alii non pauci pro suo quisque captu perorarunt, ut assolet in multitudine congregata.

6 Philippus, cum audisset Aeneam: 'Quid opus est,' inquit, 'multis verbis? Satis Aeneas ostendit quae nobis incumbunt. Dicant de se caeteri quae volunt; ego de me ipso loquar. Novi[74] in quo discrimine Christiana res est. Si fidem nostram, si libertatem, si vitam retinere volumus, necesse est obviam Turchis ire, eorumque vires opprimere, priusquam amplius invalescant. Cui rei neque facultates neque corpus meum negabo, modo princeps alius ad eam rem idoneus sese accingat cui possim comes ire.'

7 Laudatus est a toto conventu Philippus, et unus omnium iudicatus aptus dignusque qui rem publicam administraret. Exin sententiis cunctorum dictis, in verba Aeneae decretum factum est, nec quisquam fuit qui non expeditionem in Turchos ducendam censeret. Placuit tamen auxilia Francorum exquirere qui equites expeditioni adiungerent, et Italorum qui classem validam in Graeciam Asiamque traducerent ac Turchorum praecipuas infestarent sedes; Germanorum vero alium conventum esse cogendum apud Francfordiam Mugano adiacentem, qui Rhenum e regione Maguntiae

Pavia to commend to the Diet the protection of the Catholic faith and to offer his assistance.[102]

5 The delegates, including many prelates and Christian princes, assembled in the town hall for the plenary session. Aeneas then delivered a speech on behalf of the emperor, in which he stated clearly and simply how great a blow the fall of Constantinople was for all of Christendom, and what terrible dangers would ensue if no action were taken to check the Turks; he then issued a general call to arms in defense of the common good.[103] He also presented the apologies of the emperor, who had been obliged to remain at home, though all his excuses sounded lame. The speech for the pope was delivered by Bishop Giovanni of Pavia, and that for Burgundy by Bishop Jean of Toul, whom Pius II later transferred to the church at Tournai.[104] The cardinal of San Pietro also spoke in support of a crusade, and a good many others harangued to the best of their ability, as is usually the case in a large assembly.

6 When Philip heard Aeneas, he said, "What's the use of further discussion? Aeneas has shown us clearly enough what we must do. Others may say what they like; I will speak for myself. I know that Christendom faces a great crisis. If we want to preserve our faith, our liberty and our lives, we must take the field against the Turks and crush their power before it grows any stronger. To this cause I dedicate all my resources and my very self—provided, that is, some other prince who is fit for the enterprise is prepared to undertake it with me."

7 The whole assembly cheered, hailing Philip as the only man there capable and worthy of governing a state. Then, after everyone had expressed his opinion, Aeneas's motion was put to a vote. Not one person opposed launching a crusade against the Turks. Nevertheless, they decided to ask the French for help, in the form of cavalry, and to ask the Italians to send a strong fleet to Greece and Asia to blockade the chief Turkish ports. As for the Germans, they were to convene another diet at Frankfurt on the Main (a

influit, ut ibi delectus militum fieret et altrices belli pecuniae perquirerentur. Haec et alia pleraque Germanorum propria Ratisponae acta.

: 27 :

Alius conventus Francfordiae celebratus et per Aeneam ad bellum contra infideles accensus.

1 Dissoluto concilio Aeneas, ad imperatorem reversus, Italiam revisere statuerat atque in patria, quod[75] vitae supererat, vivere. Quod cum peteret a caesare, non impetravit; retentus est ad Francfordiense concilium, vicem ibi ut imperatoris ageret, quando is unus esse videbatur in palatio de tuenda religione curiosissimus, et qui dicendo persuadere aliquid posset.

2 Adveniente concilii die, et sibi et Gurcensi antistiti, et Brandeburgensi Badensique marchionibus ea provincia demandata est; qui Francfordiam accedentes admodum paucos ibi convenerunt, et eos ipsos imperatori atque papae infensos. Post dies aliquot adfuerunt Theodericus Maguntinus et Iacobus Treverensis archiepiscopi ac legati ex tota fere Germania; ex Italia pontifex maximus et duo marchiones, Estensis et Mantuanus, oratores misere; Alfonsus rex Siciliae et Veneti tardiores fuere, quorum legati iam dimisso conventu Germaniam ingressi sunt. Hungari et Burgundi adfuere: illi petentes auxilium, hi offerentes. Aderat et Iohannes Capistranus, Ordinis Minorum professor, vitae sanctimonia et assidua verbi Dei praedicatione clarus, quem populi veluti prophe-

river which flows into the Rhine near Mainz) to levy troops and raise funds to finance the expedition. These measures and many others concerning German affairs were passed at Regensburg.

: 27 :

Aeneas exhorts the Diet of Frankfurt to war against the infidels.

After the Diet adjourned, Aeneas went back to the emperor. He had made up his mind to return to Italy and live out his life in his native city, but when he asked the emperor's permission, Frederick refused. He kept Aeneas on to serve as his spokesman at the Diet of Frankfurt, for he seemed the only man at court who cared at all about the defense of the faith, and the only one whose rhetoric was at all effective. 1

As the date of Diet approached, the emperor appointed his delegates: the bishop of Gurk, the margraves of Brandenburg and Baden, and Aeneas. On reaching Frankfurt, they found only a handful of others there, all of them hostile to both emperor and pope. Some days later Bishop Theodoric of Mainz arrived, along with Archbishop Jacob of Trier and delegates from almost everywhere in Germany. From Italy, the representatives of the pope and the marquises of Este and Mantua had arrived, but King Alfonso of Sicily and the Venetians were slower to act: by the time their ambassadors reached Germany, the Diet was over. The Hungarians and Burgundians were represented there; the former came requesting, the latter offering aid. Present, too, was Giovanni da Capistrano, the Minorite friar renowned for his pious character and tireless preaching of the word of God. The people regarded 2

tam habebant, quamvis in bello contra Turchos suadendo parum proficeret.

3 Mutati erant Theutonum animi, nec cuiquam placebat expeditionem in Turchos fieri. Infectae veluti venenis quibusdam aures neque imperatoris nomen neque Romani praesulis ferre poterant: deceptores eos esse atque avaros dicebant, corrodere aurum velle, non bellum gerere; pulchrum id esse aucupium, expeditionem in Turchos decernere ut a Germanis aurum subtili ingenio, velut a barbaris, extrahatur; eum inter se quaestum avarissima orbis capita divisisse; sed alium futurum concilii exitum quam sibi persuasissent; nec pecuniam collaturos Germaniae populos, nec in militiam daturos nomina. Atque in eam sententiam persuasi omnes imperatori et papae maledicere, legatos eorum contemnere, Burgundos irridere, qui proni ad expeditionem videbantur, Hungaris durissima verba dare, qui cum suum regnum tueri nequivissent, nunc Germaniam suis calamitatibus involvere vellent.

4 Nec ulla spes reliqua erat rei bene gerendae, cum decretum Ratisponense prorsus reiiceretur. At cum in contionem itum est, mirabile dictu, locuto Aenea, omnium repente animi in priorem belli gerendi ardorem rediere! Oravit ille duabus ferme horis, ita intentis animis auditus ut nemo unquam screaverit, nemo ab orantis vultu oculos suos averterit, nemo non brevem eius orationem existimaverit, nemo finem non invitus acceperit. (Fuerunt et alii complures auditi, verum[76] taedio et irrisione, et praesertim Papiensis episcopus, Apostolicae Sedis legatus, qui cum mulierem quandam forma pulcherrimam sub typo Ecclesiae introduxisset sua incommoda deplorantem sibi, per quietem visam, levius orare visus est quam in tanto negotio conveniret.) Orationem Aeneae ab omni-

bus laudatam multi transcripsere, et secundum eam Ratisponense decretum de bello gerendo innovatum est, et Hungaris auxilium promissum equitum decem milium, peditum XXXII,[77] statutumque ut ad caesarem electores Imperii ceterique Germaniae principes in[78] festo Penthecostes proximo sese conferrent, ut quae reliqua essent ad expeditionem maturandam ibi absolverent. Atque ita dimisso conventu legati caesaris in Austriam rediere.

: 28 :

Conventus in Nova Civitate. Aeneae oratio. Mors pontificis Nicolai. Sarezana oppidum. Nicolai gesta. Conclave. Creatio Callisti eiusque votum.

1 Nec diu post, novi concilii tempus adfuit veneruntque ad imperatorem in Novam Civitatem Iacobus archiepiscopus Treverensis, Albertus Brandeburgensis et Carolus Badensis marchiones et alii nonnulli ex Germania principes; reliqui legatos misere. Ex Hungaria episcopi et barones praecipui auxilia petitum venere, multaque de gerendo in Turchos bello et de spe victoriae disseruerunt. Ex Italia legatus apostolicus adfuit idem, qui Ratisponam et Francfordiam adierat, Iohannes episcopus Papiensis, suo iudicio valde sapiens et eloquens, aliorum neque stultus neque dicendi prorsus ignarus, quem sequebatur Michael Ritius, Alfonsi regis Siciliae et Aragonum, in vituperando quam in laudando orator vehementior; nec Iohannes Capistranus defuit assiduis praedicationibus populum contra Turchos ad arma excitans.

2 In hoc concilio Aeneas iubente imperatore legatis Hungaris publice responsum dedit, quod in scriptis redactum editum est et in-

him as a prophet, but he had little success exhorting them into battle against the Turks.

By this point, the Germans had changed their minds: none of 3
them now favored the idea of a crusade. It was as though someone had dripped poison in their ears: the slightest mention of the emperor or the pope was insufferable. Both were greedy liars, they said, more interested in profit than holy war. It was a fine trick, to swindle the Germans of their treasure by proclaiming a crusade against the Turks—as though the Germans were mere barbarians! The lords of the world were greedily scheming to divide the spoils between them. But things would turn out very differently at the Diet than they expected, for the people of Germany would contribute neither money nor men for military service. All were persuaded of this opinion; they cursed the emperor and the pope, abused their ambassadors, jeered at the Burgundians (who seemed inclined to favor the expedition) and harshly assailed the Hungarians for first failing to defend their kingdom and now trying to involve Germany in their misfortunes.

The resolutions passed at Regensburg were being rejected out 4
of hand, and it seemed impossible to imagine that matters would turn out well. But when the Diet formally convened and Aeneas made his speech—wonderful to relate—the old enthusiasm for a crusade suddenly revived in every heart. His oration lasted nearly two hours; but the audience was so utterly absorbed that no one even cleared his throat or took his eyes off the speaker's face. No one thought the speech too long, and all were sorry to hear it end.[105] They heard numerous other delegates, but they listened to them with weariness and derision, especially to the bishop of Pavia, the Apostolic Legate. In his oration, he described how he had dreamt of a beautiful woman—by which he meant the Church—bewailing her misfortunes, a figure of speech which was judged rather more frivolous than the situation required. But Aeneas's speech was praised by all and written down by many, and

because of it the declaration of war passed at Regensburg was reaffirmed; the Hungarians were promised aid (some 10,000 cavalry and 32,000 infantry) and it was agreed that the imperial electors and the other German princes should meet with the emperor at the approaching feast of Pentecost to make final arrangements for the expedition. With this, the Diet adjourned and the imperial ambassadors returned to Austria.

: 28 :

The Diet of Wiener Neustadt and Aeneas's speech. Death of Pope Nicholas. The city of Sarzana and Nicholas's career. The conclave. Election and consecration of Calixtus.

1 The time appointed for the next diet soon approached.[106] Archbishop Jacob of Trier, Margrave Albert of Brandenburg, Margrave Karl of Baden and a few of the other German princes joined the emperor at Wiener Neustadt; the remaining princes sent delegates. The bishops and chief barons of Hungary came seeking aid; they spoke at length about the crusade against the Turks and the prospects of victory. From Italy there came the Apostolic Legate—the same as at Regensburg and Frankfurt, Bishop Giovanni of Pavia, who thought himself extremely wise and eloquent, though in the opinion of others the best that could be said for him was that he was not exactly a fool nor entirely unversed in speaking. He was followed by Michele Riccio, representing King Alfonso of Sicily and Aragon, an orator with a greater passion for invective than for praise. Giovanni da Capistrano was also there, tirelessly preaching sermons to rouse the people to arms against the Turks.

2 At this diet, Aeneas gave a public address at the emperor's command, replying to the ambassadors of Hungary. This was after-

ter eius orationes habetur. Inter haec, dum omnia propemodum conclusa sunt et spes pulcherrima est aestate proxima ingentes copias in hostes eductum iri, ecce mors Nicolai Quinti renuntiatur[79] pontificis maximi, quae telam longo iam tempore ordiri coeptam uno momento interrupit, vanasque hominum cogitationes ostendit et inanes curas. Nam quae futuri cognitio,[80] quae consilii capiundi certa ratio? Decidunt omnes humani conatus, quos dextera Dei non adiuvat. Non placuit divinae pietati per id tempus excidi Turchorum imperium. Ad correctionem[81] nostrarum iniquitatum diutius conservatur.

3 Sederat Nicolaus in Beati Petri solio annos circiter octo, non tam genere clarus, quam doctrina et animi dotibus excellens. Sarezana oppidum in Tuscia non procul a Macra fluvio situm, illi patria fuit, quamvis antiquam originem ex Lucae ducenti. Celebravit annum Iubilaeum magna populorum frequentia; Bernardinum Senensem in sanctorum catalogum assumpsit; imperatorem Federicum Tertium et imperatricem Leonoram ex Portugallia natam Romae coronavit, unxitque in basilica Sancti Petri apostolorum principis; Urbis officia magnifice instauravit, etsi plura inchoavit quam perfecit; cardinales creavit septem, inter quos fratrem suum assumpsit Philippum, Bononiensem episcopum, amoeno ingenio virum et amici amicum; et facta unione Ecclesiae, ex his qui fuerant in schismate creati, recepit aliquos; Stephanum Porcarium, non ignobili apud Romanos loco natum, res novas in Urbe et ipsum christum Domini capere atque occidere parantem, intercepit necarique iussit. Multis et magnis operibus clarus felixque fuit, verum Constantinopolitana clade infelix, quae in suum incidens pontificatum nomini eius foedam inussit notham; quam dum curat abolere, arteticis doloribus universum corpus invadentibus extinguitur, et cum eo ingentia in Turchos coepta corruerunt.

wards published and is included among his *Orations*.[107] Then, just as everything seemed on the point of being settled, and there was every reason to hope that a great army would march out the following summer to meet the enemy, they received the news that Pope Nicholas v was dead.[108] In an instant, the web so long in weaving was torn to shreds, proving that the thoughts of men are but a breath,[109] and hardly worth the trouble. What knowledge can we have of the future, what certainty on which to base our plans? All human endeavors fail unless helped by the hand of God. Divine Mercy decreed this was not the time for the Turkish empire to fall. For the rebuking of our sins, it will last a little longer.

Nicholas had sat on the throne of St. Peter about eight years. 3
He was not distinguished by birth but rather by his learning and intellectual gifts. He was born in Sarzana, a town in Tuscany not far from the Magra River, though his family originally came from Lucca. He celebrated the jubilee year, which was attended by throngs of pilgrims, he canonized Bernardino of Siena, he crowned and anointed Emperor Frederick and Empress Leonora of Portugal at Rome in the church of St. Peter, the chief of the apostles. He erected magnificent buildings in his city, though he began more than he finished. He created seven cardinals, among them his own brother, Filippo, the bishop of Bologna, a man of great charm and the most loyal of friends. After the reunion of the Church, he recognized several cardinals who had been created in the schism. When Stefano Porcari, a Roman of honorable birth, plotted to raise revolution in the city and to seize and kill the Lord's own anointed, he thwarted his designs and had him put to death.[110] In several great undertakings he achieved success and fame, but the fall of Constantinople was his great misfortune. This calamity, because it occurred in his pontificate, left a black stain on his reputation which he was trying to erase when his entire body was suddenly seized with gout. With his death, all his ambitious projects against the Turks collapsed.[111]

4 Cardinales peracto funere de successore soliciti ac conclave, ut moris est, ingressi variis factionibus agitati sunt; eratque admodum difficile, cum sibi quisque pontificatum arrogarent, duas Collegii partes in unum convenire. Scrutinioque semel atque iterum in cassum peracto, collocuti sunt inter se aliqui extra locum scrutinii, Bessarionemque cardinalem Nicenum eligere decreverunt, quod is omnium aptior ad rem publicam gubernandam videretur; conveniebatque numerus in eum sufficiens, nec dubium videbatur quin sequenti scrutinio pontifex a duabus partibus eligeretur; iamque ad eum supplicationes deferebantur.

5 Quod ubi ad alios alterius factionis delatum est, Alanus cardinalis Avinionensis nunc istum nunc illum circuiens: 'Ergo,' inquit, 'Ecclesiae Latinae Graecum pontificem dabimus, et in capite libri neophitum collocabimus? Nondum barbam rasit Bessarion, et nostrum caput erit? Et quid scimus, an vera est eius conversio? Heri et nudiustertius Romanae fidem Ecclesiae impugnavit, et quoniam hodie conversus est, magister erit noster et Christiani ductor exercitus? En paupertas Ecclesiae Latinae, quae virum non repperit summo apostolatu dignum, nisi ad Graecos recurrat! Sed agite, patres, quod libet. Ego et qui mihi credent in Graecum praesulem numquam consentiemus!'

6 Moverunt ea verba nonnullos adeo, ut due partes Collegii nullo pacto ad Bessarionem accederent; qui cum una nocte pontifex constanti multorum opinione habitus esset, adveniente luce cardinalem sese repperit, aliquanto minoris famae quam antea fuerat — ut his accidere solet qui magna e spe ceciderunt.

7 Cum ventum est denuo ad scrutinium, et via quae 'per accessum' vocatur tentata, in eum duae partes consensere de quo minor

After his funeral, the cardinals turned to the question of a successor. They entered the conclave, as is the custom, and immediately split into several factions. It was exceedingly difficult to get two thirds of the Sacred College to agree on anyone, since each man wanted the papacy for himself. After they had been polled twice, without result, a group of cardinals conferred outside the place of scrutiny and decided to elect Bessarion,[112] the cardinal of Nicea, because he seemed the man best suited for political leadership. A sufficient number were ready to agree on him and there seemed no doubt that at the next scrutiny he would be chosen pope by a two-thirds vote; indeed, petitions were already being addressed to him. 4

When this became known to the opposite faction, however, Alain, the cardinal of Avignon,[113] began to go round the room, whispering first to one man and then to the next, "So we'll give the Latin Church to a Greek pope, will we? We'll put a neophyte at the head of the book?[114] Bessarion hasn't even shaved his beard, and he's going to be our head? How do we know his conversion is sincere? Only the other day he was attacking the faith of the Church of Rome but now, since he's had a change of heart, he can be our master, in command of Christian troops? Is the Latin Church so hard up that it can't find a man fit to be pope without having to turn to the Greeks? Reverend fathers, go ahead and do as you like. But I, and those who think with me, will never accept a Greek as pope." 5

His words so influenced a number of cardinals that there remained not the slightest chance that two thirds of the college would agree on Bessarion. He who that night had been generally regarded as pope, found himself the next morning still a cardinal, and with less power than before. Such is the common fate of those who fall from high hopes. 6

When they came again to the scrutiny and tried the method known as "accession,"[115] two thirds came to an agreement—on 7

erat expectatio populi. Is fuit Alfonsus cardinalis Sanctorum Quattuor Coronatorum, natione Hispanus, ex civitate Valentia nobili loco natus, scientia iuris eminentissimus et multarum rerum experientia praeditus, verum senio gravis ac propemodum decrepitus, nam LXX annum transcenderat; qui etsi ante aliquot annos et vacante tum Sede Apostolica, suam assumptionem ferme omnibus praedixisset, seque procul dubio futurum pontificem maximum affirmasset, nullius tamen opinionem ad se traxerat, et delirare potius more senum existimabatur. Sed fuit eius vaticinium verax, quod a Beato Vincentio se habuisse narrabat, suae nationis homine iam defuncto, quem postea inter sanctos Christi confessores rettulit.

8 Alfonso in Petri cathedra constituto, Callisto Tertio nomen est inditum; qui mox votum vovit adversus impios Turchos omnia sese studia conversurum. Nec moratus bellum eis indixit, in quo militantibus peccata dimisit, ac legatos in Galliam et in Hungariam ad congregandos exercitus direxit.

: 29 :

Aeneae suasio pro pontifice et ipsius ad eum legatio pro Germanorum oboedientia praestanda.

1 Haec[82] cum audita essent in Austria, fuere non pauci qui caesari suaserint nunc tempus esse coercendi Apostolicam Sedem, ne tanta in Germania posset; conventiones, quae cum Eugenio Quarto factae fuerant, diminutas esse, nec prius oboediendum novo pontifici, quam ea concederet quae natio Germanica optaret; ancillam eam videri, libertatem aliquando mereri. Atque hoc ip-

the man generally regarded the least likely candidate. This was Alfonso, cardinal of Santi Quattro Coronati.[116] He was a Spanish nobleman from Valencia, an eminent jurist with considerable experience in many fields, but he was long past his prime, practically decrepit in fact, for he was more than seventy years old. A few years earlier, when the Holy See lay vacant, he had told almost everyone that he would be chosen, insisting there was no doubt he would be pope. But no one found his words convincing; they seemed more like signs of senility than anything else. Now his prophecy turned out to be true. He said it had come to him from the Blessed Vincent, a fellow countryman of his, now dead, whom he later canonized.[117]

Seated on the throne of St. Peter, Alfonso took the name of 8
Calixtus III and swore he would direct all his energies against the impious Turks. Without delay, he declared war on them, granted all who enlisted absolution for their sins and sent ambassadors to France and Hungary to raise armies.

: 29 :

Aeneas's arguments on behalf of the pope; his embassy to Rome to offer the German submission.

When news of this was reported in Austria, there were many who 1
tried to persuade the emperor that now was the time to exert pressure on the Apostolic See and thus reduce its power in Germany. The compacts settled with Eugenius IV had been violated, they argued; therefore they should make no submission to the new pope unless he granted the petitions of the German nation. Long regarded as a servant, Germany deserved at last to be free. This was

sum Iacobus Treverensis archiepiscopus obnixe requirebat, qui ex lite lucrum aliquod expectabat.

2 Contra Aeneas non esse e re caesaris aiebat Romani pontificis auctoritatem reprimere, ut populi gratia iniretur, quae sui natura inconstantissima est, nec multitudini relinquendas habenas quam noscet[83] principantibus inimicam; inter principes aliquando amicitiam inveniri, inter plebem et regem odium immortale; papam imperatoris et imperatorem papae auxilio indigere; stultum esse illi nocere, cuius expectes opem; cum pontificatus novus initur, tunc Romani praesulis gratiam beneficiis emerendam; quod si ab iniuriis incipias, difficile in benivolentiam patere aditum; mittendam more maiorum oboedientiam, foedusque cum novo praesule honestum ineundum, eoque pacto Germanos imperatori oboedituros.

3 Vicit Aeneae sententia, atque ipse missus est qui ea perageret quae suaserat, et cum eo profectus[84] Iohannes Inderbachius iure consultus. Prius tamen quam Romam peterent, iussi sunt in Foro Iulii litem quandam de finibus intercipere, quae Venetos inter et Austriae subditos versabatur. Pro qua re cum diebus pluribus apud Naonis Portum moram fecissent, nec pervicaces Venetorum legatos evincere possent, Venetias se contulerunt et ingressi senatum, quamvis adversaretur imperatoris causae Franciscus Foscarus, civitatis princeps eloquentia et auctoritate potens, senatores tamen Aeneae verbis persuasi decretum revocarunt, quo Naonenses cum Venetorum subditis communicare prohibebantur.

4 Exin Romam ventum est; ubi collegae ambo tanto maioribus honoribus excepti sunt, quanto diutius et avidius fuerant expectati. Coactum est in eorum adventu publicum consistorium, in quo Aeneas, praestita pro vetusta consuetudine oboedientia, orationem habuit de imperatoris et Imperii laudibus, simulque de

the policy promoted tenaciously by Archbishop Jacob of Trier, who expected to profit from the dispute.

Aeneas, however, argued that the emperor would gain nothing from an assault on the pope's authority, especially if it were done for the sake of popular opinion, which is inherently fickle. The reins of government must never be handed to the people for they, as he knew, hated the rule of princes. Between princes, friendship was sometimes possible, but between the people and a king the hatred was undying. The pope and the emperor needed each other's support, and it was folly to injure the man you hoped would help you. The start of a new pontificate was a time to win the favor of the pope by showing him kindness; if one started by lashing out, it would be difficult to then find the path to his good will. Frederick must make submission, as his ancestors had done, and negotiate an honorable treaty with the new pope; once that was agreed, the Germans would follow the emperor's lead. 2

Aeneas's advice prevailed and he himself was despatched together with the lawyer, Johann Hinderbach, to see his plan through. Before going to Rome, however, they were instructed to settle a dispute at Friuli concerning the border between Austria and the territory of Venice. After spending several days at Pordenone discussing the matter, during which time the Venetian ambassadors remained stubbornly unmoved, they took themselves to Venice for an audience with the senate. There, although Doge Francesco Foscari, a most persuasive and imposing speaker, argued against the emperor's case, Aeneas nevertheless persuaded the senators to rescind their decree, which had forbidden the people of Pordenone to have any contact with Venetian subjects. 3

The two colleagues then carried on to Rome, where they were received with all the greater honor because they had been so long and so eagerly awaited. At their arrival a public consistory was convened in which Aeneas, after making his submission in the time-honored way, delivered an oration which praised the emperor 4

bello in Turchos gerendo, quae postea rescripta in multorum manus devenit.

: 30 :

Rumor vanus de cardinalatu Aeneae eiusque modestia, et Zamorensis insana laetitia, et creatio aliorum cardinalium astu Callisti.

1 Increbuerat per idem tempus fama Callistum in quattuor temporibus Adventus, qui prope aderat, novos cardinales creaturum. Inter quos assumendum Aeneam constans extabat populi rumor adeo ut quocunque iret, digitis monstraretur tamquam cardinalis propediem assumendus, et id ipsum Callistus affirmaverat.

2 Cumque dies adesset, consistoriumque eius rei causa secretum haberetur, exiit sermo ex palatio aliquos in ordinem cardinalatus esse assumptos atque inter eos Aeneam; ad quem multi congratulatum venere dolore pedum in lectulo laborantem, qui accepto nuntio, nulla in parte mutato vultu sedatoque prorsus animo: 'Si verum est,' inquit, 'quod fertur, ante horas duas innotescet; interim in utranque partem ero accinctus, neque metu frangar, neque spe ludar inani.' Iohannes autem Zamorensis episcopus pari modo salutatus: 'Iam tandem,' inquit, 'assecutus sum, quod annis uno de quadraginta expectavi anxius!' et donato nuntio, ante Beatae Virginis effigiem genua flectens ei ac Filio gratias egit, qui suo denique voto satisfecissent. Tam dispar hominum natura est: alii, quod cupiunt, facile credunt; alii, quod metuunt.

and the empire and at the same time called for a crusade against the Turks. Afterwards, copies of this speech circulated widely.[118]

: 30 :

Idle rumors of a cardinal's hat for Aeneas. His modesty, and the excessive celebration of the bishop of Zamora. Calixtus elevates other men.

Around this time, rumors spread that Calixtus would create some new cardinals during the approaching season of Advent. Popular opinion held that Aeneas would be one of them—and this belief was so widespread that, wherever he went, people pointed him out as one who would soon receive a cardinal's hat, and as if Calixtus himself had said as much. 1

When the time came and a secret consistory was held for the purpose, a report issued from the palace that several cardinals had been created and that Aeneas was one of them. He was laid up in bed, suffering an attack of gout, when a crowd of people came to congratulate him. On hearing the news he remained completely calm and allowed no emotion to show on his face. "If it's true," he said, "it will be public knowledge in an hour or two. In the meantime, I'll prepare myself for either result. I'm not going to go mad with worry, and I won't get carried away with idle hopes." On the other hand, when Juan, the bishop of Zamora,[119] was greeted with the same news, he cried "At last! After thirty-nine years! I've got what I've been waiting for!" Then he gave the messenger a tip and knelt before the image of the Blessed Virgin to gave thanks to her and her Son for answering his prayers at last. How strange is human nature! Some men find it easy to imagine what they hope for, but others what they fear. 2

3 In consistorio vero, cum diu res agitata esset, tres cardinales creati sunt, quorum duo nepotes papae fuerunt (Ludovicus Sanctorum Quatuor Coronatorum presbyter et Rodericus, Sancti Nicolai diaconus) et tertius eiusdem ordinis Iacobus Sancti Eustachii, ex regia Portugallensium domo natus; adeo iuvenes omnes, quamvis indolis optimae, ut non ab re ioco dixerint aliqui vix annos tres cardinales natos qui uni sufficerent. Palamque factum est cardinales non eos assumi, qui consulant Ecclesiae, sed quibus Ecclesia ipsa consulat — quamvis commune hoc vitium est, dignitates homini non dignitati hominem condonari.

4 Non tamen statim publicata est creatio cardinalium, sed ita dissolutum consistorium ac si nihil actum esset, cunctis patribus silere iussis, etsi nonnulli ex thalamo pontificis coniecturam rei gestae fecerunt ex eo, quod pugillare petitum est et cardinales ipsi nonnihil nutibus indicarunt — ut est inter difficilia secretum. Iccirco autem occultam esse aliquandiu creationem voluere, quoniam speraverunt cardinales papam fallere, quem prius obiturum crediderunt, quam publicatio fieret. Sed fefellit ipse cardinales, qui per aestatem, quae primum secuta est, uno tantum cardinale astante nec adversari audente, cum ceteri caumata effugissent, publicationem fecit non sine infamia Collegii, quod volenti pontifici viros aetate maturos ac de Romana Ecclesia optime meritos cum suis nepotibus assumere, in his consensit qui minus idonei videbantur, et eos reiecit quos constabat esse dignissimos. Nec Callistus infamia caruit, qui carnis affectum Ecclesiae praetulit utilitati.

And yet, after a long debate, the consistory created three cardinals, of whom two were the pope's nephews (Luis, presbyter of Santi Quattro Coronati, and Rodrigo, deacon of San Niccolò) and the third was a Portuguese prince (Jaime, deacon of Sant'Eustachio).[120] They were all so young, though of great promise, that people joked that the three cardinals together had not years enough for one. And they had a point: clearly these cardinals had not been appointed to help the Church, but rather so that the Church could help them. It is quite a common mistake—to find a job for the man, not the right man for the job. 3

News of the cardinals' creation was not immediately announced; instead, the consistory was dissolved as if no action had been taken. The cardinals were all instructed to say nothing about it. Some of the pope's household guessed what had happened, however, because the cardinals had called for writing materials and by their gestures had indicated that something was afoot. Secrets are hard to keep. The cardinals wanted to keep the election quiet for a time in order to cheat the pope of his appointments, for they hoped he would die before the announcement could be made. But it was the pope who cheated the cardinals, for the next summer, when most of the cardinals had gone away to escape the heat and only one was present (who did not dare raise any objection), Calixtus published the appointments. This episode brought discredit on the college, for when the pope had proposed to elevate together with his nephews some older, experienced men to whom the Roman Curia owed much, the cardinals had agreed to the ones who seemed less suitable and rejected those who were generally thought most worthy of the honor. Nor did Calixtus escape censure for having preferred the ties of the flesh to the interests of the Church. 4

: 31 :

Bellum Picinini contra Senenses, et eius fuga atque necessitas. Aeneae legatio ad Alfonsum efficax, et Lucretiae amores, Alfonsique prophetia.

1 Per idem tempus, cum tota Italia recenti pace respirasset — nam potentates omnes ab armis recesserant — novus turbo exortus est, qui peccatricem terram non sineret quiescere. Iacobus Picininus, Nicolai Picinini filius, qui iam pridem Venetis militarat copiarum ductor, non ferens ocium, magna equitum manu transmisso Pado in Romandiolam penetravit, ac deinde in Tusciam adversus Senenses signa convertit, omnium Italiae potentatuum minus validos, ut eorum occupata re publica nobilis urbis tyrannus fieret; et iam sese ducem Senarum appellari sinebat.

2 Erat in Senenses subirato[85] animo rex Siciliae, Alfonsus, quod hi sibi affoederati bellique socii se minime consulto duci Mediolanensi Florentinisque pacem reddiderant, atque ob eam causam Picininum fovebat Senensem agrum vastantem. Fuerat paulo ante Senensi populo bellum adversus Ildobrandinum, Pitiliani comitem, in quo duos copiarum duces perfidia notissimos mercede conduxerant: Robertum Corrigianum et Sigismundum Malatestam cognomento Pandulfum, totius nequitiae principem, qui Picinino transfugium promiserant. Robertus in palatium vocatus repente trucidatus est et per fenestram praecipitatus in forum; Sigismundus ad maiora reservatus scelera, totius Italiae virus, fuga sibi consuluit.

3 Nec vel sic Senenses Picinini tyrannidem declinassent, qui iam Citonium ac Montem Maranum cum arcibus occupaverat,

: 31 :

Piccinino makes war on Siena; his desperate flight. Aeneas's successful embassy to Alfonso. The love affairs of Lucrezia, and a prophecy by Alfonso.

At this time, when all Italy was breathing more freely because of the recent peace in which every power had laid down its arms,[121] a new whirlwind arose to torment that sinful land. Jacopo, the son of Niccolò Piccinino, after serving Venice for a long time as a condottiere, decided he could not stand retirement; he crossed the Po with a large force of cavalry, pushed through the Romagna and from there entered Tuscany, where he marched on Siena, the weakest of all Italian powers. His plan was to seize the reins of government and make himself tyrant of that famous city; already he was allowing himself to be styled duke of Siena.[122] 1

Now King Alfonso of Sicily was annoyed with the Sienese because, despite being his sworn allies, they had made peace with Milan and Florence without his permission. For this reason he supported Piccinino as he ravaged their territory. A little earlier, when the Sienese had been at war with Count Ildebrando of Pitigliano, they had hired two captains notorious for their treachery: Roberto Corrigiano and Sigismondo Pandolfo Malatesta,[123] the prince of all wickedness. Both now promised Piccinino they would desert to his side. Roberto was summoned to the palace, where he was immediately executed, his body flung through a window onto the piazza. But Sigismondo saved himself by taking flight. The poison of all Italy, he was reserved for greater crimes. 2

Piccinino had already seized the important Sienese towns of Citonio and Monte Marano, together with their fortresses. Under such circumstances, the Sienese would never have been able to turn him back had reinforcements not arrived just then, sent 3

non ignobilia oppida Senensis agri, nisi adfuissent ilico Francisci Sforciae Mediolanensium ducis ac Venetorum ei Callisti pontificis maximi auxilia et insignes copiarum duces, qui Picininum urgentes in fugam verterunt. Cessit Picininus potentioribus, adeoque territus est ut numquam se tutum putarit donec ad Castrum Leonis, quod Alfonsus Florentinis ereptum in maritima Senensium obtinebat, celeri cursu pervenit. Quo in loco clausus dies aliquot silvestribus tantum prunis vitam egit.

4 Saluti ei fuit Lucas Sclavus, qui Urbetellum pro Senensi re publica custodiens, auro corruptus, decepto captoque arcis praefecto, Picinini praesidium et ipsum mari advectum intromisit; quo in loco rursus obsessus est Picininus. Sed erat difficilis expugnatio, his praesertim qui vincere nolebant. Animadverterant bellatores Italici, expugnato captoque Picinino, sibi ad excolendos agros redeundum fore, cum pax ubique vigeret, Picininumque quasi deum colebant, qui solus belli materiam ministraret. Suggerebant igitur famae laboranti panem, consilia ducum ad eum deferebant, neque dicto maiorum parebant; Alfonsus quoque mari alimenta mittebat. Producebatur in dies obsidio, et omnes in cassum conatus ibant.

5 Nec iam Senenses exhausti auro atque frumento sumptum ferre amplius poterant, et Callistum taedebat expensarum, nec ceteri bello socii, ut ab initio, alacres ferebant suppetias; eoque deducta res erat, ut non minus obsessores, quam obsessi periclitarentur. Unicum igitur salutis iter Senensi populo visum est Alfonsum rogare ut pacem elargiretur, opemque ab eo petere cuius societatem contempserant, quando is unus erat qui Picinino posset imperare. Tam minima est in populo cura decoris, ubi adversari videtur utilitas!

by Duke Francesco Sforza of Milan, the Venetians and Pope Calixtus. These troops were commanded by distinguished generals who attacked Piccinino and put him to flight. Yielding before their superior strength, Piccinino was so terrified that he did not think himself safe until a hasty flight brought him to Castiglione, a town on the Sienese coast which Alfonso had captured from the Florentines. Here he shut himself up for several days, living only on wild plums.

He was rescued by one Luca Schiavo, whom the Sienese had put in charge of the defense of Orbetello. He was bribed to trap and imprison the commandant of the fortress and then admit Piccinino's troops and the general himself, who had arrived by sea. There Piccinino was again besieged, but the town was a difficult one to storm, especially for men who did not really wish to succeed. The Italian mercenaries had realized that if Piccinino were overpowered and captured, they would have to go back to tilling their fields, for peace would reign everywhere. Piccinino alone could provide occasion for war, and so they worshipped him almost like a god. They gave him bread when he was starving, and smuggled him their battle plans, and refused to obey their own officers. Alfonso, too, sent him supplies by sea. The siege dragged on from day to day and every attempt to take the city ended in failure. 4

By now the Sienese had run out of money and food and were unable to support the undertaking further. Calixtus, too, was growing weary of the expense involved, and their other allies were not sending aid as readily as they had at first. It had got to the point where the besiegers were in as much danger as the besieged. It seemed to the Sienese that the only safe way out of the situation was to ask Alfonso for a truce — to seek help from him whose alliance they had spurned, since he was the only one who could control Piccinino. How little people care for honor when it conflicts with their own advantage! 5

6 Redierat iam Senas in Germaniam profecturus Aeneas. Vocant eum magistratus urbis, quos priores appellant, et hi quibus balia commissa est, multisque precibus orant, ne gravetur pro patria iter ad Alfonsum facere pacemque Tusciae ab eo petere, rogato prius Callisto ut aequo animo ferat[86] legatos Senensium Alfonsum adire. Annuit Aeneas, ne patriae in tanto discrimine deesset, quae nisi pacem assequeretur quam primum, necessario libertatem erat amissura. Rediit ergo Romam, pontificemque non sine magno labore in sententiam traxit, ut pax ab Alfonso peteretur, quem singulari odio insectabatur, neque id suae existimationi conducere arbitrabatur. Sed paruit et ipse necessitati, omnium rerum dominae, Iohannemque Solerium, insignem theologum quem postea Pius Secundus Barchinonensi praefecit ecclesiae, cum Aenea misit ut suo nomine de pace ageret. Senenses duos Aeneae comites addidere: Galganum Burgensem iure consultum et Leonardum, cognomento non aequo Benevolentem.

7 Cum esset eundum, podagra Aeneam arripuit, atque octo diebus Romae retinuit. Praecesserunt collegae, et Alfonsum apud Traiectum convenere, ubi sepulchrum prioris Aphricani ostendunt non procul ab Lyri fluvio, quem nostra aetas Garilianum vocat. Auditos Galganum et Leonardum Alfonsus durissima excepit oratione. Multa de Senensibus questus est; narravit beneficia, quae eis contulerat, et contra ingratitudinem civitatis erga se rettulit, indignumque Senensem populum dixit, cuius quisquam misereri deberet nec oratores ipsos pacificis oculis intueri poterat. At cum accessisset Aeneas, hilari vultu et honesto sermone receptus, quem ut primum rex intuitus est: 'Nunc,' inquit, 'libet de pace loqui, quando mediator accessit, quem diligimus,' moxque tractatum iniit.

Aeneas had already returned to Siena and was preparing to leave for Germany when he was summoned by the magistrates of the city, called the Priors, and those who preside over the *balìa*.[124] Again and again they begged him to go on behalf of his native city to Alfonso and to ask him for peace in Tuscany. (First, however, he would have to ask Calixtus for permission for a Sienese embassy to approach the king.) Aeneas agreed. He did not want to fail his country in such a crisis, for unless it could effect a truce immediately, it would surely lose its independence. So he returned to Rome and with some difficulty persuaded the pope to intercede with Alfonso. Calixtus absolutely despised Alfonso, nor did he think such a move would do much for his own reputation. But even he had to obey Necessity, the mistress of all. He despatched Aeneas, together with Giovanni Sogliera (a distinguished theologian whom Pius afterward appointed to the church at Barcelona), to treat for peace in his name. The Sienese sent two other ambassadors, the lawyer Galgano Borghese and Leonardo Benvogliente — an inappropriate name if ever there was one. 6

When the time came for them to start, Aeneas suffered an attack of gout which kept him in Rome for eight days. His colleagues went on ahead and met Alfonso at Trajetto, where one can see the tomb of the elder Africanus lying not far from the river Liri, which we now call the Garigliano. After Alfonso had heard Galgano and Leonardo speak, he replied with a very harsh speech in which he complained at length about the Sienese. He recalled the favors he had done them and recounted the ingratitude which the state had shown him in return. He declared that the people of Siena deserved no one's pity. He could not even bring himself to give the ambassadors a civil look. But when Aeneas arrived, he was received with a smile and gracious words of welcome. As soon as the king saw him he cried, "Now here's an envoy we like! Now we can talk about peace," and negotiations began straight away.[125] 7

8 Sed cum res multos haberet nodos, et novae in dies emergerent difficultates, ad menses aliquot producta, et modo Neapoli, modo Puteolis, et aliquando apud Turrim Graecam tractata est, quibus in locis Lucretia morabatur, speciosa mulier seu virgo erat, nobilibus inter Neapolitanos nata parentibus, si qua est in paupertate nobilitas. Hanc rex perdite amavit adeo ut in conspectu eius constitutus extra se fieret, neque videret quicquam, neque audiret quemquam, nisi Lucretiam. Oculos semper in eam habebat intentos, laudabat verba eius, sapientiam admirabatur, probabat gestus, excellentiam formae divinam esse iudicabat, et cum multa ei donasset et quasi reginam honorari iussisset, ad extremum sese illi permisit; neque enim exaudiri quisquam ea nolente potuit.

9 Mira vis amoris: rex magnus, Hispaniarum nobilissimae partis dominus, cui Baleares insulae, cui Corsica Sardiniaque et ipsa Trinacria parebat, qui plurimas Italiae provincias sibi subiecerat, viceratque potentissimos in armis duces, ad extremum victus amore quasi captivus mulierculae serviebat. Nec eam cognovit—si vera est fama—solitamque eam dicere ferunt: 'Virginitatem volenti mihi numquam rex auferet. Quod si vim tentaverit inferre, non imitabor Lucretiam Collatini coniugem, quae admisso scelere mortem sibi conscivit. Ego facinus morte praevertam!' Sed non est tam facile facere magnifice quam dicere, nec vita quae secuta est verbis par fuit; quippe quae Alfonso fatis functo Iacobi Picinini venit in castra non sine infamia perditae pudicitiae, et vulgatus rumor est scribae suo eam permisceri solitam, concepisse, tandemque peperisse infantem. Verum Alfonsus nihil ea divinius inveniri posse iudicavit, in ceteris rebus sapiens, in hoc et in venando apprime demens.

10 Quem dum Aeneas obtinendae pacis gratia etiam venantem sequitur, Baias invisit et Cumas et antiquarum cadavera civitatum.

They did not progress smoothly, however, and new difficulties arose every day. So the matter dragged on for several months, discussed now at Naples, now at Pozzuoli, and sometimes at Torre del Greco—wherever Lucrezia was.[126] She was a beautiful woman or rather, a beautiful girl, the daughter of poor but noble Neapolitan parents, if there be any nobility in poverty. The king was so desperately in love with her that he was completely beside himself in her presence, unable to hear or see anything but Lucrezia. He could not take his eyes off her, praised everything she said, marveled at her wisdom, admired every gesture, thought her beauty divine, gave her countless presents and gave orders that all should treat her as a queen. He had surrendered to her so completely that no one could get a hearing without her consent. 8

The power of love is amazing: a great king, lord of the noblest part of Spain, master of the Balearic Isles, Corsica, Sardinia and Sicily itself, who had conquered several provinces of Italy and defeated the most powerful generals, was at last brought low by love. He toiled for that woman like a slave! And yet, if the story is true, he never had intercourse with her. They say she used to boast, "I'd never let the king have my virginity! And if tried to take it by force, you wouldn't see me playing Lucretia. Collatinus's wife took her life after the outrage occurred. But I would die *before* I'd suffer such a crime." Noble acts are not so easy as noble words, however, and in later life she did not live up to her promises. After Alfonso's death she went into Piccinino's camp, where she hardly enjoyed a reputation for virtue. Rumor had it that she became the mistress of his secretary and conceived and delivered his child. Alfonso, however, thought there was nothing in the world so divine as she. Though wise in everything else, in regard to this—and to hunting—he was stark mad. 9

As Aeneas followed Alfonso around trying to secure terms of peace (he even went along when the king rode out to the hounds), he visited Baiae, Cumae and some ancient cities lying in ruins. He 10

Adiit et Salernum et Amalphium atque apostolorum Andreae et Matthei venerabiles tumulos, in quis sacra corpora exudare nobile manna traduntur.[87] Vidit et fontem Sarni fluvii, cuius tanta frigiditas est, ut missa in eo vina nigriora parvo albescant spatio. Quo in loco non diu postea eius iam pontificis et Ferdinandi regis copiae ab exercitu Gallico, dum nimis audent, fusae fugataeque sunt, et Simonetus, ecclesiasticae militiae ductor ictu lapidis tormentalis confossus interfit. Oppidum hic est ex flumine Sarni nomen sortitum. Exin Nolam venit, non minus Paulini Confessoris sanctissima vita, quam Romanorum historiis et Marcelli morte nobilitatam.

11 Reversus Neapolim cum iret die quadam ad regem in arcem Novi Castri et portam triumphalem ingrederetur, deambulans cum purpuratis suis in aula, quae portae opponitur,[88] Alfonsus vidit eum et conversus ad proceres, 'Vultisne,' inquit, 'papam vobis ostendam?' Atque illis respondentibus 'Volumus,' 'Ellum,' ait, 'episcopus Senensis, qui modo portam ingreditur, summus pontifex a Deo destinatus est, et hunc ipsum mortuo Callisto cardinales ei sufficient, nec alius quispiam est quem sibi iure merito praeferre queant.' Quod cum purpurati ipsi Aeneae retulissent eique congratularentur, respondit omnibus, 'Atqui non solent cardinales non cardinalem eligere! Nolite hoc credere, nisi rubro me prius ornatum galero videritis cuius, scio, sum indignus.'

: 32 :

Profligatio Turchorum, et pax Senensis.

1 Inter haec rumor exoritur Turchorum innumerabiles copias cum ipso imperatore suo et machinarum ingenti vi terra et aqua Thau-

also went to Salerno and Amalfi and he saw the venerable tombs of the Apostles Andrew and Matthew, whose sacred relics are renowned for the manna they exude. He also saw the source of the River Sarno, a spring so cold that the darker kinds of wine, when submerged in it, quickly turn white. This was the place where, not much later, after he became pope, his troops and those of King Ferrante overextended themselves and were routed and put to flight by the French;[127] here Simonetto, general of the papal troops, was killed by a catapult stone. There is a town nearby called Sarno, after the river. He also visited Nola, which is celebrated as much for the pious life of Paulinus the Confessor as for the death of Marcellus and its place in Roman history.[128]

One day, after he had returned to Naples, he went to see the king in Castelnuovo. Just as he was coming through the triumphal gate, Alfonso, who was strolling with his courtiers in the hall across the way, caught sight of him and turned to his nobles, saying, "Shall I show you the pope?" When they agreed, he said, "Over there: the bishop of Siena, just coming through the gate, is destined by God to be pope. When Calixtus dies, the cardinals will elect him as his successor. There's no one else they could rightly prefer over him." When the courtiers reported this to Aeneas and congratulated him, he replied to them all, "But the cardinals always elect a cardinal. Don't believe a word of this unless you see me wearing a red hat — which, I well know, I hardly deserve." 11

: 32 :

Defeat of the Turks, and peace with Siena.

Meanwhile, rumor spread that a huge Turkish army, commanded by the sultan himself and equipped with an enormous array of artillery, had besieged Taurunum by land and sea. This is a town in 1

rinum obsedisse, quod est oppidum inter confluentes Savum ac Danubium in Rascia, quae olim Superior Moesia dicta est, situm; hodie Belgradum alii, alteram Albam alii vocant. Anxius eius nuntio Alfonsus percontatus est a circumstantibus, quonam pacto subveniri obsessis posset. Cui Aeneas, 'Frustra,' inquit, 'de auxilio cogitas, neque enim Hungarica atque Turchonica bella sicut Italica sunt, in quibus perraro confligitur, et quae nostri milites pulchrae negociationes appellant. Hac ipsa hora qua loquimur, aut hostes aut Hungari profligati sunt; cuius rei mox aderit nuntius.'

2 Secuti sunt octo dies, et ecce litterae adsunt ex Hungaria Christianos crucesignatos, qui Thaurini obsidebantur, erupisse in Turchos et maxima edita hostium caede, divina magis ope quam humana, victoria gloriosissima potitos; sub mammilla Turchorum imperatorem vulneratum, disperso exercitu relictisque[89] omnibus machinis, cum parvo comitatu diffugisse trepidum. Atque ita certa res allata est, ut nihil amplioris fidei desideraretur.

3 Nec diu post, tam felix nuntium Senensium pax secuta est ea lege, ut Picininus accepta pecunia Urbetellum Senensibus redderet, Tusciaque excedens in Aprutiis et Aquilanorum hiemaret agris. His rebus absolutis Aeneas Romam rediit. Et cum vellet, revisa patria, ad imperatorem in Germaniam proficisci, a Callisto pontifice retentus est, qui remanenti cardinalatum pollicebatur. Paruit Aeneas, etsi dubius erat ne Callistus cederet cardinalibus, nil aeque horrentibus quam sociorum creationem, atque eorum praesertim, quos in summo pontificatu competitores timebant.

Serbia (once called Upper Moesia), lying at the confluence of the Danube and the Sava, which is now known as Belgrade or, sometimes, the second Alba. Alfonso was disturbed by this news and asked those around him how he could send aid to the people under siege. Aeneas said, "There's no point thinking about aid. The Hungarians and Turks don't fight wars as we do. Italian 'wars' rarely come to a pitched battle—not for nothing do our soldiers call them 'negotiations'! Right now, as we speak, either the enemy or the Hungarians are in flight; we'll hear the story soon enough."

A week passed and a letter did in fact arrive from Hungary de- 2
scribing how the Christian crusaders besieged in Belgrade had sallied forth against the Turks and, helped by divine rather than human aid, won a most glorious victory.[129] The enemy had suffered great losses: the sultan was wounded in the chest; his army was scattered, all his artillery abandoned, and he himself had fled in panic with only a few followers. The information was so precise that no further evidence could be required.

Before long, this good news was followed by peace with the 3
Sienese. According to the terms, Piccinino would receive a cash payment in exchange for giving Orbetello back to Siena, withdrawing from Tuscany and spending the winter in the Abruzzi and the territory round L'Aquila.[130] Once these matters were settled, Aeneas returned to Rome. He wanted to visit his native city and then return to the emperor in Germany, but he was waylaid by Pope Calixtus, who promised to make him a cardinal if he remained in Rome. Aeneas complied, though he suspected that the cardinals would keep Calixtus from honoring his word, for they dreaded nothing so much as the creation of new colleagues, especially those they feared could be rivals for the papacy.

: 33 :

Aeneae promotio ad cardinalatum, et omnium gentium congratulatio. Varmiensis ecclesiae adeptio, Polonorumque defensio.

1 Cum adessent Adventus Christi Salvatoris tempora, quae cardinalium propemodum comitia dici possunt, summa contentione in Senatu Apostolico certatum est, cum pontifex creare cardinales vellet, Collegium resisteret; et modo numerum cardinalium esse nimium dicerent aliqui, modo in personas quae nominabantur probra maledictaque iactarent, atque in eos more suo magis ac magis inveherentur, qui meliores iudicabantur et summo pontificio digniores. Vicit tamen Callistus, tribus quos iam assumpserat cardinalibus summopere adnitentibus, seque (ut par erat) et caput et dominum ostendit, cardinalesque novos sex creavit: Raynaldum Piscicellum archiepiscopum Neapolitanum, Lucretiae patruum quem ut illi morem gereret enixissime petebat Alfonsus; Iohannem episcopum Zamorensem, natione Hispanum, scientia iuris excellenti, qui annis uno de XL in muneribus Curiae prudenter casteque fuerat obversatus; Iohannem Papiensis ecclesiae praesulem, Castilionensi nobili domo apud Mediolanenses natum; Aeneam pontificem Senensem, quem non imperator solum, sed Hungariae quoque rex Ladislaus et cuncti ferme Germaniae principes efflagitabant; Iacobum Feretranum episcopum, natione Romanum, Simonis medici fratrem et Ricchardum Constantiae Normanicae sacerdotem, quem Carolus Francorum rex expetebat. Laudata est horum creatio, Neapolitano et Feretrano exceptis, quos non suis meritis assumptos aiebant nec dignis intercessionibus, sed alterum mulierculae impudicae, alterum medico traditum asseverabant.

: 33 :

Aeneas made a cardinal. Congratulations from all corners of the world. Adoption of the church of Ermeland. The defense of Poland.

At Advent, which is practically known as election season for cardinals, a bitter dispute broke out in the apostolic senate because Calixtus wanted to create new cardinals, but the college did not. Some members protested that there were already too many cardinals; some heaped abuse and slander on the men put forward as candidates. Typically, they complained most bitterly about those who seemed likely candidates for the papacy. But with the strong support of the three cardinals he had already created, Calixtus prevailed, justly proving himself head and master of the Church. He created six new cardinals: Rainaldo de' Piscicelli, archbishop of Naples, who was Lucrezia's uncle and whose elevation Alfonso had urged as a personal favor; Juan, bishop of Zamora, a Spaniard renowned for his knowledge of the law who had served the Curia with wisdom and integrity for thirty-nine years; Giovanni, bishop of Pavia, of the noble Milanese house of Castiglione; Aeneas, bishop of Siena, whose creation was urged not only by the emperor but by King Ladislas of Hungary and almost all the German princes; Jacopo, bishop of Montefeltro, a Roman and the brother of the physician Simone; and Richard, bishop of Coutances, a Norman priest nominated by King Charles of France.[131] All these choices were generally approved with the exception of the bishops of Naples and Montefeltro. They, it was said, had not been elevated for their merits nor at the request of proper sponsors, but rather as favors done for a loose woman and a physician. 1

2 Aeneam vero ubi donatum pileo rubeo audivit populus, mox fama exorta est successorem sibi creasse Callistum, et ingens tota Urbe laetitia fuit. Sena quoque, ut accepit suo praesuli ornamenta quae accesserant, festos dies celebravit, fuitque publice gaudium, privatim apud eos, qui urbem gubernabant, ingens in mente dolor, verentes (quod secutum est) ne pontificatum adeptus Aeneas aliquando maximum nobiles eius urbis ad munia civitatis conaretur asciscere, quos illi oderant et iam pridem a regimine procul amoverant. At Federicus imperator mirum in modum exultavit, cum accepisset legatum et consiliarium suum in ordinem cardinalatus assumptum. Nec Alfonsus Aragonum et Siciliae rex mediocri gaudio affectus est, quod ad suam prophetiam iam videret aditum patefactum. Sed et Germani omnes principes Aeneae per epistolas congratulati sunt, tamquam in eo et Germania ipsa decorata fuisset. Nec decepti, nam Aeneas Germanorum semper et laudator et defensor extitit non modo in cardinalatu, verum etiam in pontificatu maximo, et Callistus eum prae ceteris cardinalibus in rebus Germanicis audivit.

3 In Pruscia, quae olim Ulmerigia dicta est et ad mare Balteum iacet, ecclesia nobilis ac praedives fuit quam Varmiensem vocant, multis arcibus et oppidis ac latissimo imperio potens. Sed orto inter religiosos Beatae Mariae Theutonicorum qui Prusciae dominabantur, et regem Poloniae ad quem Pruteni defecerant, crudeli et asperrimo bello, ecclesia ipsa admodum defecit, partem religiosis, partem Polonis ad se trahentibus, et villas atque oppida diripientibus. Obiit interea Franciscus eius ecclesiae pontifex. Canonicorum pars maior Aeneam sibi pontificem postulavit, pars altera bifariam divisa est, et quidam Luticonem, regis Poloniae consiliarium elegerunt, quidam sacerdotem alium quendam ex his, qui cum religiosis Theutonibus erant. Possessio ecclesiae a principio Luticoni data

By contrast, as soon as the people heard that Aeneas had been given a red hat, the rumor spread that Calixtus had made him his successor and there was great rejoicing throughout the city. At Siena, too, when they heard what honors had been conferred on their bishop, they declared a public holiday and decreed general celebrations. In private, however, the party in power was greatly distressed, for they feared (as actually happened) that if Aeneas someday became pope, he would try to restore to public office the nobles of the city, whom they hated and had long ago totally excluded from government. Emperor Frederick, however, was quite delighted to hear that his ambassador and counselor had been elected to the sacred college. Nor was King Alfonso of Aragon and Sicily at all displeased, for he knew this was the first step toward fulfilling his prophecy. All the princes of Germany wrote to congratulate Aeneas, as if Germany herself had been honored by his elevation. And they were not mistaken, for Aeneas was always known as the champion and defender of the Germans — not just when he was cardinal but also once he was pope — and in regard to German affairs Calixtus listened to him more than to any other cardinal. 2

In Prussia, a territory near the Baltic Sea once known as Ulmerigia, there was a famous and very rich church in a place called Ermeland. This church possessed several castles and towns and vast stretches of territory, but after a brutal and bloody war broke out between the Teutonic Knights of St. Mary, who were then occupying Prussia, and the king of Poland to whom the Prussians had transferred their allegiance, the church itself was overwhelmed. The knights and the Poles divided it between them, sacking and plundering all its towns and farms. Meanwhile the bishop, Franz, passed away. A majority of the canons wanted Aeneas to replace him, and the rest were divided, some voting for Lutkonis, the chancellor of the king of Poland, and others for one of the priests who had sided with the Teutonic Knights. At 3

est; sed cum Callistus canonicorum postulationi annuens administrationem ecclesiae Aeneae commendasset, possessio quoque ad eius procuratorem delata est eius partis, quam Lutico obtinuerat, qui minime ausus est cardinali adversari. Aeneas vero exinde pontificium maximum assecutus Paulum Leghendorfium ei[90] ecclesiae praefecit, qui absque adversario in hanc usque diem illam gubernat.

4 Eodem ferme[91] tempore et altera ecclesia vacavit in Pruscia episcopio praedita, quam vocant Culmensem; in ea Poloni unum, religiosi Theutones alterum petebant. Dominicus cardinalis Firmanus, religiosorum protector, Polonorum causam prorsus odiosam papae cardinalibusque reddiderat, Aenea excepto. Qui cum animadverteret eo sententias in Collegio tendere ut Poloni prorsus excluderentur, et is promovendus qui possessionem minime assecuturus esset, cum ad se ventum est, rem ab exordio quomodo inter religiosos Theutones et Polonos acta esset in medio exposuit, ostenditque Polonos — quamvis iniuste, more tamen hominum — in alienam terram venisse non armis, sed accersitos a subditis religiosorum, quos illi superbe immaniterque regebant; ecclesiam, de qua sermo esset, in potestate Polonorum teneri; si praeficiatur ei amicus religiosorum, neque personae provisum iri neque ecclesiae, quia non admittetur; rursusque non mereri Polonos ecclesiam pro sua voluntate impetrare, qui alienum agrum invasissent; neutri ergo auscultandum esse, sed tertium aliquem vocandum, qui tamquam iconomus ecclesiam tamdiu regeret, quoad res in meliorem fortunam conducerentur.[92]

5 Ostenditque pluribus verbis non oportere fieri, quod iam Collegii pars maior suaserat, et Callistus amplecti cupide videbatur; qui

first, possession of the church was granted to Lutkonis, but when Calixtus, responding to the demands of the canons,[132] entrusted the administration of the church to Aeneas, his deputy was also granted possession of the part which had been held by Lutkonis, who did not dare oppose a cardinal. Later, however, after Aeneas became pope, he appointed Paul Leghendorf to the church; and to this day he governs it without opposition.

Around this time another cathedral church fell vacant in Prussia, in a place called Chelmno. The Poles wanted one man for the slot, the Teutonic Knights another. Domenico, the cardinal of Fermo,[133] who championed the interests of the knights, had succeeded in turning the pope and all the cardinals except Aeneas against the Poles. Aeneas saw that opinions in the college were inclined to ignore the Poles altogether and advance a man who was by no means likely to secure possession. When it was his turn to speak, he went back to the very beginning of the quarrel between the Teutonic Knights and the Poles. He showed that the Poles had entered foreign territory unjustly, to be sure, but not inhumanely, for they came not by force of arms but rather at the invitation of the people whom the knights were governing with arrogance and cruelty. The church in question was now held by the Poles. If a friend of the knights were made bishop, neither he nor the church would be well served, for the man would not be welcome. On the other hand, the Poles had invaded foreign territory; they ought not to get the church simply because they wanted it. In fact, neither side deserved a hearing before the college; the cardinals ought rather to call in a third party as a sort of caretaker to administer the church until matters could be put on a better footing. 4

Aeneas then made a long speech proving that the plan supported by the majority of the cardinals, which Calixtus himself seemed to be embracing with enthusiasm, was not worth pursuing. After Calixtus heard this he said, "Fermo's plan sounded good 5

audito Aenea, 'Placebat,' inquit, 'nobis Firmani sententia, sed tu, Aenea, mutasti animum nostrum, decretumque pro tuo consilio facimus.' Quae res adeo Firmanum commovit, ut multis postea diebus rogatus in Senatu sententiam dicere subticuerit, Aeneaeque admodum succensuerit suo magis incommodo quam illius, qui laudatus est, ipse irrisus. Atque ita superbis evenire necesse est; plura enim de se putantes quam res exposcit, cadunt in periculo, et rodunt se ipsos, et ab aliis irridentur.

: 34 :

Aeneae auctoritas in Senatu cardinalium et contentionibus finiendis, et Lucretiae adventus ad Urbem.

1 Nec minor circa idem tempus ignominia irrogata est Iohanni cardinali Papiensi, dum Aeneam superare vult eiusque studium impugnare. Vacavit ecclesia Ratisponensis apud Danubium in Baioaria sita, cui praefuit olim Albertus, philosophus insignis, quem Germani Magnum appellant, et quem Doctor Sanctus Aquinas audisse traditur. Hanc ecclesiam petebat Ropertus Baioarius, ex imperatorum sanguine natus; canonici praepositum suum elegerant, eumque in episcopum dari sibi magnis precibus instabant. Aeneas Ropertum iuvabat, quod eius promotio et utilior et nobilior videbatur; Papiensis electum tuebatur, non tam eius causa, quam ut in rebus Germanicis Aeneam superare videretur.

2 Callistus utrique causam audiendam commisit, ut electionis decreto et utriusque competitoris[93] meritis diligenter[94] pensatis, in

to me, Aeneas, but you've changed my mind. It's decided: we'll do it your way." The cardinal of Fermo was so furious that several days later, when he was called on to speak in the assembly, he refused to say a word. He was absolutely incensed with Aeneas, though more to his own discomfiture than that of his colleague, for everyone praised Aeneas and laughed at Fermo. So matters always turn out for the proud, for those who think more of themselves than circumstances warrant will always fail in a crisis, destroy their own reputations and end up a laughing-stock.

: 34 :

Aeneas, now a prominent member of the college of cardinals, settles disputes. Lucrezia visits Rome.

Around this time Giovanni, the cardinal of Pavia, suffered a simi- 1
lar embarrassment while trying to get the better of Aeneas and cast aspersions on his loyalty. The church of Regensburg, on the Danube in Bavaria, fell vacant. This had been the church of Albert, the distinguished philosopher whom the Germans call "the Great" and who is said to have taught St. Thomas Aquinas, the Doctor of the Church. Rupert of Bavaria, a prince of the imperial house, was campaigning for this church, but the canons had chosen their own provost and were demanding to have him for their bishop. Aeneas supported Rupert, thinking him the better and more illustrious candidate, but the cardinal of Pavia defended the man chosen by the canons — not so much for that man's sake as to be seen overruling Aeneas in a matter concerning Germany.

Calixtus appointed them both to hear the case. They were to 2
consider the decree of election and the merits of the rival candidates and then report their findings to the consistory and express

consistorio ea referrent quae invenissent, et suas dicerent sententias. Dum res discutitur, Papiensis cardinales ambit atque unumquemque domi convenit. Electum laudat, merita eius longe maiora esse dicit quam Roperti; iniquum videri, nisi eligenti capitulo mos geratur. Conventa exinde nationis Germanicae in medium affert quae magnopere electionibus favent; hunc aetatem habere, Ropertum nondum annos quinque et viginti natum. Adit et papam atque eadem repetit.

3 Et iam cardinales in Papiensis sententiam pedibus ibant, Callistus dubius erat. Sed cum in[95] consistorium ventum est et Aeneas auditus, repente omnium animi commutati sunt, et Callistus omne dubium reiecit. Monstratum est enim electionem malis artibus factam, et simoniam inter venisse, et electum extra communionem fuisse, cum eligeretur, nec frugi conversationis esse, nec tanta ecclesia dignum; contra Roperti aetatis defectum et bonam indolem et mores egregios et maiorum merita abunde supplere.

4 Expectabatur consistorii exitus non minori frequentia populi quam cum de cardinalibus agitur, et Curia in duas partes divisa. Alii hunc, alii illum suis votis exposcebant, sed longe maior opinio erat ad electum. Vicit tamen Ropertus defensore Aenea, atque is, licet annis minor, Ratisponensi ecclesiae administrator est datus. Quae res nomen Aeneae inter cardinales non parum adauxit: his duabus contentionibus cum adversarios superasset et res paene desperatas restituisset.

5 Dum haec aguntur, Lucretia cuius ante meminimus, Romam venit non minori comitatu et pompa, quam si regina esset. Callistus eam in consistorio recepit assistentibus cardinalibus, multisque modis honoravit, quod neque Aeneae placuit, neque aliis complu-

their own opinions. While the matter was under discussion, the cardinal of Pavia went round to the other cardinals, meeting each in his own house. He would praise the elected candidate, remarking that his qualifications were far superior to Rupert's. Moreover, it seemed unfair to disregard the wishes of the chapter, especially as (he would note) this was a form of election strongly endorsed by the diets of the German nation. What was more, the elected candidate was of the proper age, while Rupert was not yet twenty-five. He presented these arguments to the pope, as well.

The cardinals were beginning to shift toward Pavia's position 3
and by now Calixtus himself was unsure. But once they had gathered in the consistory and heard Aeneas speak, they immediately changed their minds, and Calixtus, too, cast off his doubts. For Aeneas showed that the election had been dishonest; simony was involved; the candidate had not been within the communion of the Church at the time he was chosen; his conduct was far from reputable and he was unfit for so important a see. By contrast Rupert, with his ability, his noble character and his family's long tradition of service, could more than make up for what he lacked in years.

The consistory's decision was awaited by a crowd as large as 4
those that gather at the election of cardinals. The Curia too was divided, with some favoring one candidate and some the other, but the majority, by far, held for the elected candidate. And yet, with Aeneas as his champion, Rupert prevailed and was appointed, though still underage, to the church of Regensburg. This affair greatly enhanced Aeneas's reputation among the cardinals. In two disputes he had defeated his opponents, rescuing causes that were just about given up for lost.

At this time Lucrezia, whom I mentioned earlier, came to 5
Rome with a retinue and pomp fit for a queen. Calixtus received her at a consistory in the presence of the cardinals and honored her in many ways. Aeneas, along with many others, disapproved

ribus, indignum esse iudicantibus eam in conspectu maiestatis apostolicae magnificari, quam turpi causa rex amaret. Et quamvis esset Aeneas Alfonsi amantissimus, non tamen amicam eius Romae visitavit, sicut alii plerique cardinales, inter quos fuit Petrus Sancti Marci, non tam caerimoniarum magister quam favorum secularium sectator egregius.

: 35 :

Ingentes terraemotus in Neapolitano. Svetiae regis eiectio. Alfonsi mors Ferdinandique successio, adversante Callisto, et eius obitus Aeneaeque divinatio.

1 Per hos dies[96] terraemotus Regnum Neapolitanum multis diebus agitavere, quales patrum nostrorum memoria neque visi sunt neque auditi. Neapoli multa et praeclara aedificia corruerunt, Arrianum et alia pleraque oppida a fundamentis cecidere; fama fuit supra triginta milia corpora hominum ruinas oppressisse. Populi passim relictis urbibus in agros migravere, et facta est publica penitentia viris ac mulieribus ieiunio et verberibus sese macerantibus. Tum quoque et in Aegeo pelago insula emersit numquam antea visa, parva circuitu, verum alta super aquas quadraginta cubitis, arsitque diebus aliquot, donec flammae defuit bitumen.

2 Per hoc tempus et Carolus rex Svetiae, cum saeviret in Christi sacerdotes et avaritiae libidinique serviret, adnitente Upsalensi archiepiscopo qui duxit exercitum, regno deiectus est; et Christigernus ei suffectus, qui usque hodie regnat.

of these actions, for they thought it unseemly that the paramour of a king should be exalted in the sight of the Apostolic Majesty. Devoted as he was to Alfonso, Aeneas did not call on his mistress at Rome. Many other cardinals did, however, including Pietro of San Marco,[134] less a master of ceremonies than an expert seeker of worldly preferment.

: 35 :

A terrible earthquake in Naples. A coup in Sweden. Death of Alfonso. Against Calixtus's wishes, Ferrante succeeds him. A prophecy concerning Aeneas and the death of Calixtus.

At this time the kingdom of Naples was racked for several days by an earthquake, the likes of which had not been seen or heard for generations. In Naples itself several splendid buildings collapsed, and Ariano and many other towns were completely destroyed. It was reported that more than thirty thousand bodies had been buried beneath the ruins. Everywhere people fled their cities for the countryside. There followed a period of public penitence, during which men and women fasted and mortified themselves with scourges. At the same time, a new island appeared in the Aegean Sea. It was only a small bit of land, but it rose some forty cubits out of the water. It blazed for several days, until there was no more bitumen to feed the flames. 1

At the same time, King Charles of Sweden was dethroned, largely through the efforts of the archbishop of Uppsala, who led an army against him. Charles had treated the priests of his kingdom with great cruelty and was a slave to avarice and lust. He was succeeded by Christopher, who still reigns there.[135] 2

3 Aeneas autem cum podagrae doloribus plus solito vexaretur, indulgente Callisto ad balnea Viturviensia sese contulit, levamen aegritudini non finem sperans, quando is morbus est quem sola mors terminat, ubi confirmatus est et altas egit radices. Inter lavandum, *Historiam Bohemicam* conscripsit atque Alfonso Aragonum et Siciliae regi dedicavit—omine non bono, prius enim ille e vita excessit quam *Historia* finiretur.

4 Ceperat Alfonsus aegrotare cum esset Aeneas in balneis, et lento morbo correptus quadraginta dies inter spem vitae et mortis metum assumpsit, fecitque demum naturae satis, instituto haerede filio Ferdinando extra matrimonium nato,[97] quem Nicolaus et Eugenius Romani pontifices regni capacem reddiderant. Religiosus principis obitus fuit, nam Christiano more peccata confessus et sacramentis ecclesiasticis communitus in alteram vitam migravit, onerato filio ut auri sexaginta milia nummum in expeditionem contra Turchos Romano pontifici traderet, legavitque multa ad pias causas, et ossa sua in Aragoniam transferenda mandavit; quae omnia superveniente bello impedita sunt.

5 Etsi enim mortuo Alfonso Regni principes ac civitates omnes Ferdinandum supra se[98] regem acceperunt et in eius verba iuraverunt, Callistus tamen pontifex maximus odium, quod in Alfonsum viventem gesserat, eo extincto in filium continuavit; Regnumque Siciliae Alfonsi obitu ad Romanam Ecclesiam devolutum declaravit eo (ut vulgatior fama fuit) animo, nepotem suum Borgiam ad Regni fastigium ut extolleret. Sed quid humana cogitatione vanius? Dum Callistus inimico rege mortuo nimis alto fertur animo, et iam sibi plana omnia censet, ipse quoque intra dies quadraginta morbo captus et extremo confectus senio fatis fungitur.

6 Iohannes Caimus, Francisci Sforciae Mediolanensium ducis orator Viturvio transitum faciens Aeneam illic adiit visitationis causa, atque inter confabulandum idcirco se missum ad Callistum ait, ut ediceret ei non placere Francisco Sforciae Ferdinandum pa-

Aeneas, meanwhile, was having more trouble than usual with his gout. With Calixtus's permission, he went to the baths at Viterbo, hoping not for a cure but for simple relief; for once this disease has taken root it can end only in death. While taking the baths, he wrote his *History of Bohemia* and dedicated it to King Alfonso of Aragon and Sicily—inauspiciously, as it turned out, for the king died before Aeneas could finish the work.[136] 3

Alfonso's health had begun to fail when Aeneas was at the baths. It was a slow sickness, which kept him lingering forty days between hope of life and fear of death. At last he paid his debt to nature. He named as his heir Ferrante, his illegitimate son, whom Popes Nicholas and Eugenius had declared eligible to rule. The king died in sanctity, for like a good Christian he confessed his sins and received the sacraments before passing to the other life. He left instructions for his son to give 60,000 gold ducats to the pope for the crusade against the Turks. He bequeathed a great deal of money to pious causes, and ordered his bones taken home to Aragon. All these projects were delayed, however, by the start of war. 4

At Alfonso's death, all the princes and states of his realm had acknowledged Ferrante as their sovereign and sworn allegiance to him. But Calixtus had always hated Alfonso and now began to persecute his son. He decreed that the Kingdom of Sicily had reverted to the Church of Rome. It was common talk that he intended to put his nephew, Borgia, on the throne. How pointless are these human machinations! As Calixtus gloated over the death of his enemy the king, imagining that the way now lay open for him to realize all his plans, he himself fell sick. Weakened by extreme old age, within forty days he was dead. 5

Giovanni Caimo, the envoy of Duke Francesco Sforza of Milan, was passing through Viterbo when he paid a call on Aeneas. In the course of conversation he mentioned that he had been sent to tell Calixtus that Sforza would not be happy if Ferrante were 6

terno regno amoveri; quod si aliter pontifici sederet in[99] animo, sciret Mediolani ducem adversum se futurum. Quo audito, 'At hoc,' inquit Aeneas, 'nuntio Callisto necem affers!' Neque aliter secutum est. Namque ut accepit pontifex maximus Franciscum sibi de Regno non assentiri, mox aegritudinem incidit ex qua mortuus est; quem sui nepotes in basilica Sancti Petri sepelierunt in loco, quem vocant Beatae Mariae Febrium; olim Apollinis templum fuit. Obiit autem VIII Idus Augusti anno Salvatoris Christi quadrigentesimo quinquagesimo octavo supra millesimum. Cardinales pro more egregias ei[100] exequias fecere.

: 36 :

Conventus cardinalium in conclavi, et quid in eo factum sit, et acerrime contentiones, Aeneaeque ad pontificatum erectio ac Pii appellatio.

1 Haec cum accepisset Philippus cardinalis Bononiensis, qui apud Balneum Regium per aestatis caumata declinaverat, Viturbium venit et cum Aenea simul ad electionem futuri praesulis[101] Romam profectus est. Cumque ambo una Urbem peterent, universam Curiam et maiorem populi partem extra moenia occurrentem invenere, affirmantibus cunctis eorum alterum in pontificem maximum electum iri. Reverterunt et ceteri cardinales intra centesimum lapidem commorantes; novem et decem in Urbe adfuere. Sed dum celebrantur exequiae, cardinalis Firmanus lenta febre correptus Callistum, cui supra modum succedere aspirabat, ad sepulchrum sequitur—vir, nisi ambitioni et iracundiae succubuisset, exemplaris et optimus. Fuit enim vitae mundissimae, doctrina et rerum experientia magnus, verum plus aequo partis Gibellinae sectator.

deposed from his father's throne; if the pope had any such intention, he should know that the duke of Milan would oppose him. Hearing this, Aeneas cried, "Your message will be the death of him!" And so it was, for when Calixtus heard that Francesco opposed him in the matter of the kingdom, he soon fell ill with the disease that killed him. His nephews buried him in the basilica of St. Peter in the chapel known as St. Mary of the Fevers, which was once a temple of Apollo. He died on August 6 in the year of our Savior 1458. As is the custom, the cardinals staged a magnificent funeral.

: 36 :

The cardinals meet in conclave. Proceedings and bitter arguments. Aeneas elevated to the papacy and hailed as Pius II.

Filippo, cardinal of Bologna, was spending the hot days of sum- 1
mer at Bagnoregio when he heard the news. He went to Viterbo and from there traveled with Aeneas to Rome for the election of the next pope. As they approached the city together, they found the entire Curia and most of the populace waiting to meet them outside the walls. All agreed that one of them would be elected pope. Every other cardinal within a hundred miles of Rome also returned, making nineteen in the city. In the course of the funeral ceremonies, however, the cardinal of Fermo came down with a slow fever. He had aspired passionately, excessively even, to follow Calixtus, and so he did—to the grave.[137] This was a man who could have been a model of virtue, had he not let ambition and a violent temper master him. His life was pure, his learning and experience great, but he was too fierce a partisan of the Ghibellines.

2 Reliqui cardinales duodeviginti, decima die post Callisti obitum, conclave ingressi sunt, tota civitate suspensa in eventum rerum, quamvis sermo communis Aeneae cardinali Senensi pontificatum maximum auguraretur, nec quisquam fuit de quo maior esset opinio.

3 Conclave in apostolico palatio apud Sanctum Petrum perstructum est, in quo duae conclusae sunt aulae et sacella duo: in maiori cellulas fecere, in quis cardinales ederent dormirentque; minus, quod Sancti Nicolai appellatur, consultationi electionique pontificis asservaverunt, deambulationi omnium aulas.

4 Ipsa die ingressus nihil actum est circa electionem; sequenti capitula quaedam edita sunt, quae observari a novo praesule statuerunt; iuraruntque singuli ea se servaturos, si sors super se caderet. Tertia die, facta re divina, cum ventum esse ad scrutinium, inventum est Philippum cardinalem Bononiensem et Aeneam Senensem paribus votis ad summum pontificatum postulari, utroque vocibus quinque vocato; ex reliquis nemo tres superavit. Vilhelmum cardinalem Rhotomagensem — sive dolus fuit, sive odium — nemo ea vice elegit.

5 Consueverunt cardinales, scrutinio facto publicatoque, considere atque inter se colloqui, si quis sit qui mutare propositum velit et vocem, quam uni dederat, in alterum transferre; qui modus eligendi 'per accessum' vocatur; sic enim concordia facilius invenitur. Quae res in primo scrutinio omissa est, impedientibus illis qui a nullis electi fuerant, cum ad eos fieri non posset accessus. Itum est ad prandium, exin multae conventiculae factae sunt. Qui potentiores erant in Collegio, auctoritate atque opibus excellentes, alios ad se vocabant et aut sibi ipsis aut amicis apostolatum quaerebant; rogabant, promittebant, minas ingerebant. Nec defuerunt, qui sine rubore omni, modestia procul reiecta, pro se ipsis verba facerent summumque sibi pontificatum arrogarent, sicut Vilhelmus Rhotomagensis, Petrus Sancti Marci et Iohannes Papiensis cardinales;

Ten days after Calixtus's death the other eighteen cardinals entered the conclave. The whole city waited in suspense for the outcome; but it was common talk that Aeneas of Siena would be pope. No one was held in higher esteem. 2

On the conclave met in the apostolic palace at St. Peter's, where two halls and two chapels were cordoned off for the purpose. In the larger chapel they constructed cells where the cardinals would eat and sleep; the smaller, called the chapel of St. Nicholas, was reserved for deliberations and voting. The halls were places where all might walk about freely. 3

The day they entered, they did nothing about the election. The next day they issued certain capitulations which all agreed should be observed by the new pope. Each swore that he would abide by them should the lot fall to him. On the third day, after mass, they took a vote and found that Filippo of Bologna and Aeneas of Siena had received an equal number of votes, five apiece. No one else had more than three. On this ballot, whether from strategy or dislike, no one voted for Guillaume, the cardinal of Rouen.[138] 4

It was the custom for the cardinals to sit and talk together after the result of a scrutiny had been announced, in case anyone wished to change his mind and transfer his vote from one to another. This is the method called "by accession," for it is an easier way to reach an agreement. This procedure was not used after the first scrutiny, for those who had received no votes objected, since they could not now be candidates for accession. They adjourned for lunch, and then a great many private conferences took place. The richer and more influential members of the college summoned others to their presence. Seeking the papacy for themselves or their friends, they begged, made promises, even tried threats. Some threw all decency aside, spared no blushes and pleaded their own cases, claiming the papacy as their right. Among these were Guillaume, cardinal of Rouen; Pietro, cardinal of San Marco; and Giovanni, cardinal of Pavia; nor did the cardinal of Lerida neglect 5

nec Ilardensis sese negligebat. Multa de se quisque praedicabat. Mira erat horum contentio, summa diligentia, inquieta dies, nox insomnis.[102]

6 Rhotomagensis tamen non tam hos quam Aeneam timebat et cardinalem Bononiensem, in quos videbat vota plurium ferri. Maxime vero Aeneam formidabat, cuius taciturnitatem non dubitabat longe valentiorem esse aliorum latratibus. Vocabat igitur modo istos, modo illos, et increpans eos dicebat: 'Quid tibi est[103] Aeneae, quod eum pontificio dignum maximo censes? Pedibus laborantem et pauperem nobis pontificem dabis? Quomodo relevabit inopem Ecclesiam inops, aegrotantem aegrotus? Ex Germania recens venit, nescimus eum; forsitan et Curiam eo traducet. Quae sunt in eo litterae? Poetamne loco Petri ponemus, et gentilibus institutis regemus Ecclesiam? At Philippum Bononiensem anteponendum existimas, durae cervicis hominem, qui neque per sese gubernare calleat, neque auscultet recta monentibus? Ego in cardinalatu senior sum, nec me imprudentem nosti; et doctrina pontificali sum praeditus, et regium sanguinem prae me fero, et amicis abundo et opibus, quibus subvenire Ecclesiae pauperi possum. Sunt et mihi beneficia ecclesiastica non pauca, quae dimissurus inter te et[104] alios dispertiar.'

7 Addebat preces multas, quae si non satis valebant, minas adhibebat. Si quis simoniam eius obstare dicebat, qui papatum venalem habiturus esset, non inficiabatur praeteritam vitam simoniaca labe infectam fuisse, sed in futurum iurabat mundas se manus habiturum. Astabat ei Alanus cardinalis Avinionensis, homo audax ac venalis, eiusque causam modis omnibus adiuvabat, non tantum quia Gallicus Gallico favebat, quantum quod ex promotione Vilhelmi ecclesiam Rhotomagensem et domum eius in Urbe et Vice-

his interests.[139] Each had a great deal to say for himself. Their rivalry was extraordinary, their energy unbounded. They neither rested by day nor slept at night.

Rouen, however, feared these men less than Aeneas and the cardinal of Bologna, for he saw that the majority of the votes were tending toward them. But he was especially afraid of Aeneas, for his silence, he was sure, would prove far more effective than the snarling of the rest. And so he would summon now some, now others, and berate them: "What's Aeneas to you? What makes you think he deserves the papacy? Will you give us a pauper and a cripple for a pope? How will a destitute pope restore a destitute church, or an ailing pope a church that is sick? He's only just come from Germany—we don't know him! What if he transfers the Curia there? And look at his writing! Shall we set a poet in Peter's place, and administer the Church by pagan laws? Or perhaps you think we should choose Filippo of Bologna instead? A stiff-necked fellow,[140] without the wit to rule himself nor listen to those who counsel right? I'm the senior cardinal. You know I'm not stupid. I'm trained in pontifical law and I can boast of royal blood. I have many friends and great resources I can draw on to relieve the Church of her poverty. What's more, I have quite a few church benefices, which I'll distribute among you and the others, when I resign them." 6

Then he would pile on appeals or, if they had no effect, resort to threats. If anyone brought up his past record of simony, suggesting that in his hands, the papacy would be for sale, he would admit that his earlier career had been tainted with that stain, but would swear that in future his hands would stay clean. He was supported by Alain, cardinal of Avignon,[141] a reckless, grasping character who lent him every assistance, not so much a Frenchman aiding a Frenchman as a man who expected, at Guillaume's election, to obtain his house in Rome, the church of Rouen and the vice-chancellorship. A good number of cardinals were swayed by 7

cancellariam[105] expectabat. Vincebantur non pauci magnis pollicitationibus, et quasi muscae capiebantur abdomine, vendebaturque Christi tunica sine Christo.

8 Convenere apud latrinas plerique cardinales, eoque loco tamquam abdito et secretiori pacti inter se sunt quonam modo Vilhelmum pontificem eligerent, scriptisque et iuramentis se astrinxerunt. Quibus ille confisus mox sacerdotia, magistratus et officia promisit, ac provincias partitus est. Dignus locus, in quo talis pontifex eligeretur! Nam foedas coniurationes ubi convenientius ineas, quam in latrinis?

9 Aderant Vilhelmo certi ex cardinalibus: duo Graeci, Genuensis, Sancti Sixti, Avinionensis, Columnensis, Papiensis et[106] vicecancellarius; Bononiensis vero, Ursinus et Sanctae Anastasiae dubii erant, pauloque momento[107] accessuri videbantur, et iam propemodum spem dederant. Et cum undecim concurrere viderentur, non dubitabant quin duodecimum statim haberent. Nam cum eo ventum est, praesto adest qui ait, 'Et ego te papam facio,' ut eam ineat gratiam. Confectam igitur iam rem existimabant, nec aliud expectabant quam lucis adventum, ut ad scrutinium veniretur.

10 Iamque noctis medium effluxerat, cum ecce Bononiensis Aeneam adit, et dormientem excitans: 'Quid ais,' inquit, 'Aenea? Nescis, quia iam papam habemus? In latrinis convenere aliquot cardinales, statueruntque Vilhelmum eligere, nec aliud expectatur quam dies. Consilium meum est, ut surgens e lectulo illum adeas, vocemque tuam illi offeras priusquam eligatur, ne si te adversante pontificatum obtineat, odiosus fiat tibi! Ego mihi consulam, ne in[108] priores incidam laqueos. Novi, quid sit inimicum habere pontificem. Callistum expertus sum, qui numquam pacificis oculis me intuitus est, quoniam[109] eum non elegissem. Mihi ex usu videtur

Rouen's splendid promises; like flies, they were victims of their own appetites. And the tunic of Christ, without Christ, was being sold.

A large group of cardinals gathered in the latrines. Here, as if in 8
a secret, private meeting place, they worked out a plan to elect Guillaume pope, binding themselves with oaths and written pledges. Guillaume felt he could rely on their support and within no time was promising benefices, offices and positions of power, and dividing provinces among them. A perfect place to elect such a pope: where better to strike a filthy bargain than in the latrines!

The cardinals who had definitely decided for Guillaume in- 9
cluded the two Greeks, Genoa, San Sisto, Avignon, Colonna, Pavia and the vice-chancellor.[142] Orsini and the cardinals of Bologna and Sant'Anastasia were wavering[143] and it seemed the slightest pressure would make them accede. Already Rouen felt his hopes were practically assured of success. And now, as it seemed they had eleven men confirmed on their side, they were certain they would get a twelfth straight away. For when it gets to this point in the process, someone is always ready to jump up and say "And *I* make you pope," to win the favor those words always bring. So they thought the matter settled, and were just waiting for dawn so the vote could be taken.

It was past midnight when the cardinal of Bologna rushed into 10
Aeneas's cell and roused him, saying, "Aeneas, what do you say! Don't you know we've already got a pope? A group of cardinals met in the latrines and decided to elect Guillaume. They're only waiting for morning. I think you should get out of bed and offer him your vote *before* he's elected, for if he makes it without your support he'll never let you forget it. I'm not falling into that trap again. I know what it means to have the pope against you—I endured the reign of Calixtus, who never gave me so much as a friendly look, and all because I hadn't voted for him. It's best to

eius, qui pontifex sit futurus, ante venari gratiam. Ego, quod mihi consilium accipio, id tibi do.'

11 Cui Aeneas, 'Consilium tuum tecum,' inquit, 'Philippe, referto! Mihi nemo suaserit ut eum Beati Petri successorem eligam, quem prorsus indignum puto. Absit a me hoc peccatum! Si alii eum eligent, ipsi viderint, ego mundus ero ab eo scelere, nec me conscientia expunget mea. Dicis durum esse papam non habere benivolum. Nihil hoc ego vereor. Scio, me non interficiet, quoniam eum non elegerim. 'At non amabit, non dabit stipem, non adiuvabit, paupertate premeris!' Non est assueto dura paupertas. Inopem vitam duxi hactenus; quid, si moriar inops? Musas mihi non auferet, quae sunt in fortuna tenui suaviores.

12 Ceterum non ego is sum, qui arbitrer passurum Deum in manu Rhotomagensis Ecclesiam sponsam suam deperire. Nam quid magis alienum est a Christi professione, quam vicarium eius simoniae atque impudicitiae deservire? Non feret divina pietas hoc palatium, quod tot sancti patres habitavere, aut speluncam latronum aut lupanar meretricum fieri. A Deo datur apostolatus, non ab hominibus. Rhotomagensi qui demandare pontificatum conspiravere homines sunt, quorum cogitationes vanas esse quis nescit? Pulchre apud latrinas coniuratio facta est: in secessum conatus ibunt, et sicut Arriana perfidia, in loco foedissimo finem accipient iniquissima machinamenta. Crastina dies ostendet Romanum praesulem a Deo eligi, non ab hominibus. Tu, si Christianus es, eum in Christi vicarium non assumes, quem nosti diaboli membrum esse!' Atque his dictis, Philippum terruit ne Rhotomagensi accederet.

13 Exin summo diluculo Rodericum vicecancellarium conveniens percontatus est, an sese Rhotomagensi vendidisset. 'Et quid vis agam?' respondit ille, 'Acta res est. Convenere apud latrinas multi

curry favor with a future pope well in advance, it seems. I'm giving you the advice I'm going to take myself."

Aeneas replied, "Away with you, Filippo, and your advice! No one's going to get me to vote for a man I think totally unfit to follow Peter. Far be it from me, such a sin! If the others want to elect him, let them look to themselves. My hands will be clean of the crime, my conscience won't prick me. You say it's hard to have the pope against you. I'm not worried about that. He won't murder me because I didn't vote for him, that I know. 'But,' you say, 'he won't be kind to you, he won't give you presents, he won't show you favor. You'll feel the pinch of poverty.' Poverty isn't hard for one who's known it well. I've been poor in the past, what does it matter if I die a poor man? He won't take my muses away, and they are all the sweeter when fortunes are low. 11

"Still, I can't believe God would let the Church, his bride, perish at the hands of the cardinal of Rouen. What could be further from the preaching of Christ than a vicar enslaved to simony and lust? Divine Mercy will not turn this palace, the house of so many holy fathers, into a den of thieves[144] or a whoring brothel. The apostleship is bestowed by God, not men. They are men who conspire to commit the papacy to Rouen; and human thoughts are but a breath[145] — who doesn't know that? It was well their conspiracy was made in the latrines; their plots will go down the drain! Like the Arian heresy, these most foul machinations will have a very filthy end. Tomorrow it will be clear that the bishop of Rome is chosen by God, not men. As for you, if you are a Christian, you will not promote to be Vicar of Christ a man you know is the arm of the devil!" Hearing these words, Filippo was too frightened to accede to Rouen. 12

Then, at first light, Aeneas met the vice-chancellor, Rodrigo, and demanded to know whether he had sold himself to Rouen. "What would you have me do?" he replied, "The thing is settled. A lot of the cardinals met in the latrines and decided to elect him. 13

atque hunc statuerunt eligere. Mihi non est ex usu cum paucis extra gratiam novi praesulis remanere. Concurro cum parte quae maior est, et causae meae consului. Cancellariam non perdam; schedulam enim promissionis habeo. Si non eligo Rhotomagensem, eligent alii, et ipse privabor officio meo.'

14 Cui Aeneas, 'O stulte,' inquit, 'iuvenis! Ergo tuae nationis hostem in apostolatu collocabis? Et schedulae fidem dabis eius hominis, qui non habet fidem? Tu schedulam habebis, Avinionensis cancellariam. Nam quod tibi promissum est, illi et promissum et affirmatum est. Illine an tibi servabitur fides? Gallo an Cathelano Gallus amicior erit? Extero an civi magis consulet? Cave tibi, inexperte iuvenis, cave, stulte! Et si non est tibi Ecclesiae Romanae cura, si religionem Christianam nihili pendis et Deum contemnis, cui talem vicarium praeparas, at saltem tui ipsius curam habeto, qui Gallo papatum tenente in postremis eris!' Audivit haec patienter ab amico vicecancellarius, seque admodum cohibuit.

15 Post haec videns Aeneas cardinalem Papiensem, 'Audio,' inquit, 'et te cum hisce[110] sentire, qui Rhotomagensem eligere statuerunt. Quid ais?' Tum ille, 'Bene,' inquit, 'audivisti. Pactus sum[111] vocem illi dare, ne solus remanerem. Iam enim certa res eius est. Tot sunt qui ei promisere.'

16 Cui Aeneas, 'Alium te,' inquit, 'virum esse existimavi, quam invenio. En, quantum a tuis maioribus degeneras! Patruus tuus, sive avunculus fuit, Branda cardinalis Placentinus, cum esset pontificatus maximus ultra montes in Germania (nam Iohannes Tertius ac Vigesimus, instituto Constantiensi concilio, Romanam Curiam trans Alpes adduxerat), numquam quievit donec in Italiam Primam Sedem reduxit; cuius arte, studio atque ingenio factum est, ut abdicatis summo pontificatu qui de eo contendebant, Martinus Quintus eligeretur natione Romanus ex domo Columnensi.

There's no point remaining with the minority and out of favor with the new pope. I've considered my interests and I'm joining the rest. I won't lose the chancellorship; I have a note from Rouen promising me that. If I don't vote for him, the others will elect him anyway and I'll lose my post."

Aeneas said to him, "Young fool! You'll put an enemy of your country in the Apostle's chair? And put your faith in a note from a faithless man? You'll have the note; the chancellorship will go to Avignon. What you've been promised, he's been promised, too, and he's had confirmation. Will Rouen keep faith with him or you? Will a Frenchman be a better friend to a Frenchman or a Catalan? Will he care more about a foreigner or his fellow countryman? You inexperienced boy! You fool! Take care! Even if you think nothing of the Church of Rome, even if you have no regard for the Christian religion and despise God—whom you'd provide with such a vicar—at least take thought for yourself, for you will find yourself among the last and least, if a Frenchman becomes pope." The vice-chancellor listened patiently to the words of his friend and then reversed his decision completely. 14

After this, Aeneas saw the cardinal of Pavia and said to him, "I hear you too have fallen in with those who are going to elect Rouen. Is it true?" He replied, "You've heard correctly. I've agreed to give him my vote so as not to be left by myself. The matter's already decided, you see. So many cardinals have declared for him." 15

Aeneas replied, "You're not the man I thought you were. How far short you fall of your forebears! Think of your father's brother (or was he your mother's?), Branda, the cardinal of Piacenza.[146] When the papacy lay beyond the mountains in Germany, when John XXIII convened the Council of Constance and conveyed the entire Curia across the Alps, he never rested until he had brought the Holy See back to Italy. It was thanks to his diplomacy, devotion and skill that, when the contestants for the papacy all withdrew, Martin V was elected pope, a Roman of the house of 16

Branda Curiam Apostolicam ex Germania in Italiam reportavit: tu eius nepos ex Italia transferes in Galliam? Italus homo Galliae melius, quam Italiae consulis? At Rhotomagensis nationem suam praeferet Italicae, et Gallus in Galliam cum summa dignitate advolabit.

17 'Dices, "Iuratum est, non ibit absque Senatus consilio extra provinciam; non consentiemus ire volenti." Et quis cardinalium est, qui sedenti in apostolico throno audeat adversari? Primus tu eris qui, obtenta aliqua divite commenda, "Ito," inquies, "quo velis, pater sancte!" Et quid est nostra Italia absque Romano praesule? Retinemus apostolatum, imperio amisso, atque hoc uno lumine videmus lumen; et hoc te fautore, suasore, adiutore privabimur. Aut ibit in Galliam pontifex Gallus, et orbata est dulcis patria nostra splendore suo, aut manebit inter nos, et serviet regina gentium, Italia, extero domino erimusque mancipia Gallicae gentis. Regnum Siciliae ad Gallos perveniet; omnes urbes, omnes arces Ecclesiae possidebunt Galli. Callistus admonere te potuit, quo sedente, nihil Cathelani non occuparunt. Expertus Cathelanos experiri Gallos cupis? Cito poenitebit expertum! Videbis Collegium Gallis plenum, neque ab illis amplius eripietur papatus. Adeone rudis es, ut non intellegas hoc pacto perpetuum imponi iugum nationi tuae?

18 'Quid de vita hominis dicam? An non pudet homini lubrico, et cui anima venalis sit, Christi vices committere? En, paranymphum egregium sponsae Christi praeparas! Ovem lupo committes! Ubi conscientia? Ubi iustitiae zelus? Ubi hominis mens? Siccine a te ipso recessisti? Num te saepe dicentem audivimus perituram Ecclesiam, si in[112] manus Rhotomagensis inciderit,[113] et te mori

Colonna. Branda brought the Apostolic Curia back from Germany to Italy; will you, his nephew, take it from Italy to France? Will an Italian prefer France over Italy? Rouen will put his own nation's interests before those of Italy; this Frenchman will fly to France, the supreme office under his wing.

"You say, 'He has sworn. He will not leave the province without 17
the college's permission, and if he asks to go, we will not consent.' What cardinal will dare to oppose him once he is seated on the apostolic throne? You'll be the first, once you've secured some rich benefice, to say, 'Go where you will, Holy Father.' And what is Italy, our country, without the bishop of Rome? We have lost the empire but we still have the papacy; in this one light do we see light![147] And now we're going to lose it, with your support, your persuasion, your help. A French pope will either go to France, leaving our beloved country bereft of its splendor, or he'll stay among us, and Italy, the queen of nations, will serve a foreign master. We'll be slaves of the French. The kingdom of Sicily will fall into French hands. The French will possess all the cities and strongholds of the Church. You might have learned from Calixtus, for when he was pope, there was nothing the Catalans did not get. You tried the Catalans, and now you want to try the French? You'll be sorry if you do! You'll see the college full of Frenchmen and we'll never get the papacy back again. Are you too stupid to see that this will lay a yoke on your nation forever?

"And what can I say about the man's life? Have you no shame? 18
To entrust Christ's succession to this slippery character, a man who'd sell his own soul? A fine bridegroom you've chosen for the bride of Christ! You're trusting the lamb to the wolf! Where is your conscience, your passion for justice, your common sense? Will you completely betray yourself this way? Haven't we heard you say over and over that the Church would be ruined if it fell into Rouen's hands and that you'd rather die than vote for the man? Why have second thoughts? Has he changed overnight

malle quam ipsum eligere? Quae causa mutationis? An ex daemonio repente in angelum lucis transfiguratus est ille? An tu ex angelo in diabolum, qui libidines eius et spurcitias et avaritiam diligas? Ubi amor patriae et vox illa semper Italiam ceteris nationibus praeferens? Existimabam recedentibus caeteris ab eius caritate, te numquam recessurum. Fefellisti me, immo vero te ipsum et patriam tuam, Italiam, nisi resipis!'

19 Obstupuit his auditis Papiensis, et correptus dolore simul ac verecundia illacrimatus est, et post aliquot suspiria, 'Pudet me,' inquit, 'Aenea, sed quid agam? Promisi. Nisi Rhotomagensem eligo, proditionis arguar.' Cui Aeneas, 'Eo ventum est,' ait, 'quantum intellego, ut quocunque te vertas, proditoris nomen incurras. Nunc eligendum est: Italiam, patriam, Ecclesiam, an Rhotomagenseni malis prodere?' Victus his, Papiensis Rhotomagensi deficere minus probri existimavit.

20 Petrus autem cardinalis Sancti Marci, cum accepisset Gallorum coniurationem, et spem amisisset potiundi pontificatus, commotus amore patriae simul et odio quo Rhotomagensem prosequebatur, circuire Italos cardinales, hortari, monere, ne patriam relinquerent; nec quievit, donec apud cardinalem Genuensem excepto Columnensi cunctos Italos congregavit; exposuitque coniurationem in latrinis factam; Ecclesiamque perituram, et Italiam in perpetuum servituram, si Rhotomagensis pontificatum assequeretur, dixit; rogavitque singulos, ut sese viros ostenderent, consulerent Matri Ecclesiae atque infelici Italiae, deponerent, si qua essent inter se odia, et Italum potius quam exterum eligerent pontificem; quod si se audirent, Aeneam ceteris praeferrent. Aderant cardinales septem: Genuensis, Ursinus, Bononiensis, Sancti Marci, Papiensis, Senensis et Sanctae Anastasiae; cuncti verba Petri approbavere praeter Aeneam, qui se tanto munere indignum censebat.

from a demon to an angel of light?[148] Or have you changed (from angel into devil!) so you now adore his lust and filth and greed? Where is your love for your country, your consistent support for Italy over every other nation? I used to think that even if everyone else abandoned their devotion to her, you never would; but you've failed me. No, rather, you've failed yourself and your country—Italy!—unless you come to your senses."

Pavia was stunned by these words and burst into tears, over- 19
come by grief and shame alike. Then, stifling his sobs, he said, "I *am* ashamed, Aeneas. But what can I do? I've promised. If I don't vote for Rouen, I'll be accused of treachery." Aeneas answered, "As far as I can see, you're at the point where you'll be guilty of treachery whatever you do. The choice is this: do you want to betray Italy, your country, and the Church, or will you betray Rouen?" Pavia was convinced: there would be less shame in failing Rouen.

When Pietro, cardinal of San Marco, heard about the conspir- 20
acy of the French, he despaired of getting the papacy himself. Then, spurred equally by patriotic fervor and hatred of Rouen, he went round all the Italian cardinals, urging and cajoling them not to abandon their country. He did not rest till he had gathered all the Italians, except Colonna, in the cell of the cardinal of Genoa. There he revealed the conspiracy made in the latrines. If Rouen obtained the papacy, he said, the Church would be ruined and Italy a slave forever more. He implored each and every one of them to act like men, to protect the interests of Mother Church and miserable Italy, to put aside their rivalries and make an Italian pope, and not a foreigner. What was more, if they cared for his opinion, they should prefer Aeneas over any other. Seven cardinals were present: Genoa, Orsini, Bologna, San Marco, Pavia, Siena and Sant'Anastasia.[149] They all accepted Pavia's plan except Aeneas, who thought himself unworthy of such an honor.

21 Itum est deinde ad rem divinam, qua peracta, scrutinium incoepere. Calix aureus in ara positus est, et tres cardinales eum observavere — Rutenus episcopus, Rhotomagensis presbyter et Columnensis diaconus — inspicientes ne qua fraus intercederet. Reliqui cardinales suis in locis consederunt, et surgentes ex ordine dignitatis ac senii, accedentes altare schedulas in calicem mittebant, in quis nomina eorum inscripta erant quos ad pontificatum eligebant. Cumque iret Aeneas velletque suam papyrum in calicem mittere, expallens tremensque Rhotomagensis, 'En,' inquit, 'Aenea, habeto me commendatum!' Temeraria prorsus vox eo in loco, in quo non licebat mutare scripturam; sed vicit prudentiam ambitio. Aeneas vero, 'Mihi te,' inquit, 'vermiculo commendas?' Nec plura locutus in suum locum abiit, schedula in calicem proiecta.

22 Cumque omnes idem fecissent, mensa in medio aedis posita est, et tres cardinales memorati super ea schedularum calicem everterunt, schedulasque legentes singulas alta voce nomina eorum annotaverunt qui erant in illis conscripti; nec quisquam erat cardinalium, qui non pari modo nominatos annotaret, ne qua posset intervenire machinatio. Quae res ex usu Aeneae fuit. Namque cum fieret dinumeratio votorum, et lector Rhotomagensis Aeneam votis octo expeti pronuntiasset, et cuncti silerent in alieno damno, nequaquam passus est se fraudari, dixitque lectori: 'Inspice melius schedulas, nam votis novem flagitor!' eique omnes assensere. Rhotomagensis, quasi errasset, subticuit.

23 Modus schedularum hic erat. Scripserat quilibet manu propria: 'Ego, Petrus (sive Iohannes, sive alio nomine fuerit[114]) eligo in Romanum pontificem Aeneam cardinalem Senensem et Iacobum Ulisbonensem.' Nam et unum et duos et plures eligere permissum est, tacita conditione, ut prior nominatus praeferatur; quod si non

Then they went to mass. Once that was finished, they began the scrutiny. A golden chalice was placed on the altar and three cardinals were appointed to watch over it to prevent any fraud. These were the bishop of Kiev, the presbyter of Rouen and the deacon Colonna. The other cardinals took their seats. Then, rising in order of rank and age, each approached the altar and deposited in the chalice a ballot on which he had written the names of his choices for pope. When Aeneas came up and tried to cast his ballot, Rouen blanched and trembled and cried out, "Aeneas, look! I commend myself to you." It was a rash thing to do at this point, when no one was allowed to alter the choice he had made. But ambition overcame prudence. Aeneas replied, "You commend yourself to a worm like me?" and, without another word, dropped his ballot in the cup and went back to his seat. 21

When every vote had been cast, a table was set up in the middle of the room and the same three cardinals emptied the chalice full of ballots onto it. Then they read the ballots out, one after another, noting down the names written on them as they went. And there was not a single cardinal who did not likewise make notes of those named, so there could be no possibility of fraud. This proved to be to Aeneas's advantage; for when the votes had all been counted, Rouen, who was the teller, announced that Aeneas had eight. The rest said nothing about another man's loss, but Aeneas did not let himself be cheated. "Look more carefully at the ballots", he said to the teller, "for I have nine votes." Then the others agreed with him. Rouen said nothing, as if he had merely made a mistake. 22

The ballots looked like this: each wrote in his own hand, "I, Peter (or John or whatever his name was) elect as pope Aeneas, cardinal of Siena and Jaime, cardinal of Lisbon." It is permitted to submit one or two or even more names, on the understanding that the one first named is the one preferred, but if he should not get enough votes to be elected, the next is to be counted in his place. 23

habeat vota quae sufficiant, succedat proximus, ut eo facilius in unum conveniatur. Sed quod est utiliter inventum, nonnulli ad fraudem vertunt; quod Latinus Ursinus ea die fecit nominans septem, ut eo beneficio allecti quos nominavit, vel sibi accederent in eo scrutinio, vel in alio se eligerent, quamvis ei qui fraudulentus habetur, non multum afferunt doli.

24 Publicato scrutinio compertum est, ut ante diximus, novem cardinales Aeneam elegisse: Genuensem, Orsinum, Ilerdensem, Bononiensem, Sancti Marci, Sanctorum Quatuor Coronatorum, Zamorensem, Papiensem et Portugallensem; Rhotomagensem vero[115] tantum sex, reliquos longe inferius resedisse. Obriguit Rhotomagensis, cum se adeo superatum ab Aenea vidit. Ceteri omnes admirati,[116] neque enim memoria hominum ad novem voces per scrutinium quisquam ascenderat. Cum nemo satis votorum haberet, placuit consedere et viam, quam vocant 'per accessum,' experiri si forte ea die posset haberi pontifex; atque hic rursus, spem resumpsit Rhotomagensis inanem.

25 Sedebant omnes suis in locis taciti pallidique, et tamquam in excessu mentis essent, attoniti. Nemo aliquandiu loqui, nemo hiscere, nemo partem corporis movere praeter oculos, quos varias in partes iactabant. Mirum erat silentium, et mira hominum effigies: quasi inter statuas ageres,[117] neque vox audiebatur neque motus cernebatur ullus. Mansere in eum modum aliquantisper, expectantibus inferioribus ut superiores accessum inchoarent. Exinde[118] Rodericus vicecancellarius assurgens: 'Ad Senensem,' inquit, 'cardinalem accedo.' Quae vox gladius quidam fuit in corde Rhotomagensis, adeo exanguem reddidit[119] hominem. Subsecutum est silentium, et alter alterum intuens suos nutibus indicabat affectus. Iam prope erat, ut Aeneam pontificem videre viderentur. Quod verentes aliqui e loco abiere, ut eius diei fortunam eluderent. Hi fuere Ruthenus et Sancti Sixti cardinales, necessitates causati cor-

This way a consensus can be more easily reached. But some people will exploit a useful device for their own advantage, as Latino Orsini did that day. He wrote down seven names in the hope that those he named would be swayed by the favor, either to accede to him in that scrutiny or to vote for him in another. But cheap tricks don't do much for one who is known as a cheat.

When the results were read out it was ascertained, as we have 24 said before, that nine cardinals had voted for Aeneas: Genoa, Orsini, Lerida, Bologna, San Marco, Santi Quattro Coronati, Zamora, Pavia, and Portugal.[150] The cardinal of Rouen had only six votes, and the rest far fewer. Rouen was petrified when he saw himself so far outstripped by Aeneas. All the rest were amazed, for no one in living memory had ever polled as many as nine votes by scrutiny. Since no candidate had a clear majority, they decided to resume their seats and try the method that is called "by accession," to see if they just might elect a pope that day. And here again Rouen indulged in empty hopes.

All sat in their seats, pale and silent, thunderstruck, as if in a 25 trance.[151] For some time no one spoke, no one opened his lips, no one moved any part of his body except the eyes, which kept darting about. It was a strange silence and a strange sight, men sitting there like their own statues, no sound to be heard, no movement to be seen. They remained like this for some time, the junior members waiting for their elders to begin the accession. Then Rodrigo, the vice-chancellor, rose and said, "I accede to the cardinal of Siena," which utterance was like a dagger in Rouen's heart, so pale did he turn. Silence fell again, and each man looked at the next, indicating thoughts by subtle gestures. By now it seemed certain that Aeneas would be pope. Some who feared this result left the conclave, pretending physical needs, but really with the intent of frustrating what destiny had decreed must happen that day. Those who withdrew in this way were the cardinals of Kiev and San Sisto.[152] But no one followed them, and so they soon re-

porio, sed cum nulli eos sequerentur, mox redière. Tum Iacobus cardinalis Sanctae Anastasiae, 'Et ego,' inquit, 'Senensi accedo.'

26 Exin maior omnes stupor invasit, et tamquam in domo, quae incognitis terraemotibus agitatur, cuncti vocem amisere. Una enim Aeneae tantum vox deerat, duodecim siquidem pontificem efficiebant. Quod animadvertens, Prosper cardinalis Columnensis eam sibi gloriam acquirendam putavit ut pontificem ipse pronuntiaret, surgensque voluit pro more votum cum gravitate proferre. Sed a Niceno cardinali et Rhotomagensi medius apprehensus est atque acriter increpatus quod Aeneae vellet accedere. Perseverantem autem in proposito conati sunt viribus extra locum educere, ut vel sic Aeneae pontificatum eriperent, et unus eorum bracchium dextrum, alter sinistrum tenens, abducere tentavere. Verum Prosper calumnias et inania verba flocci faciens, quamvis in[120] voto suo Rhotomagensem elegisset, Aeneae tamen veteri benivolentia coniunctus, versus ad reliquos cardinales. 'Et ego,' inquit, 'Senensi cardinali accedo, eumque papam facio!'

27 Quo audito ceciderunt[121] adversariorum spiritus et omnis fracta est machinatio, et cardinales universi nihil morati ad pedes Aeneae sese proiecerunt eumque pontificem salutarunt; et rursus in locis suis residentes electionem factam approbaverunt nullo prorsus adversante. Ibique Bessarion cardinalis Nicenus suo et eorum nomine qui Rhotomagensi faverant:

28 'Laudamus,' inquit, 'pontifex maxime, tuam assumptionem, quam ex Deo esse non dubitamus, et sane dignum te hoc munere et censuimus antea et nunc censemus. Quod autem te non elegimus, id fecit aegritudo tua; nam cum pedibus aegrotares, hoc tantum sufficientiae tuae iudicavimus deesse. Est enim Ecclesia egens viro activo, qui possit corpus exercere itineribus, et imminentibus occurrere periculis quae a Turchis formidamus. Tu contra quietis eges: hoc nos ad Rhotomagensem traxit. Quod si fuisses corpore validus,[122] nullus erat quem tibi praeferendum existimaremus. At

turned. Then Jacopo, cardinal of Sant'Anastasia[153] said, "I, too, accede to the cardinal of Siena."

This sent an even greater shock through the assembly. All were struck dumb, as if a tremendous earthquake had shaken the hall. Aeneas now needed only a single vote, for twelve would make a pope. Seeing this, Cardinal Prospero Colonna decided to seize for himself the honor of acclaiming the next pontiff.[154] He rose and was about to pronounce his vote—solemnly, and according to procedure—when the cardinals of Nicea and Rouen suddenly laid hands on him and rebuked him sharply for wanting to accede to Aeneas. When he persisted, they tried to get him out of the room by force, one seizing his right arm and the other his left—they would even resort to means like these, so determined were they to snatch the papacy from Aeneas. And yet Prospero, though he had voted for Rouen in the scrutiny, was bound to Aeneas by ties of old friendship. Ignoring their abuse and empty threats, he turned to the other cardinals and cried, "I too accede to the cardinal of Siena, and I make him pope!" 26

When they heard this, the opposition's courage failed; all their designs were shattered. Every cardinal rushed to fall at Aeneas's feet and hail him as pope. Then, returning to their seats, they unanimously ratified the election. And then Cardinal Bessarion spoke, both for himself and on behalf of those who had favored Rouen: 27

"Your Holiness," he said, "we honor your election, and we do not doubt it is God's will. We thought before and still think now that you are worthy of the office. We only voted against you because of your infirmity. Indeed, in our view, your gout was your only defect, for the Church needs an active man with the physical strength to endure long journeys and to face the terrible trials we fear the Turks are preparing for us. You, on the contrary, need rest. It was this that led us to support Rouen. Had you been a strong man, we should have preferred no one else. But if God is 28

cum Deo placueris, et nobis placeas necesse est. Ipse qui te elegit Dominus supplebit defectum pedum tuorum, et tu nostram ignorantiam non mulctabis. Nos te pontificem veneramur et denuo, quantum in nobis est, eligimus tibique fideliter serviemus.'

29 Ad haec Aeneas, 'Existimasti, o Nicene, quantum animadvertimus, de nobis longe melius, quam nos ipsi, qui nobis pedum defectum tantummodo attribuisti. Nos imperfectum nostrum latius vagari non ignoramus, defectusque nostros paene innumerabiles esse cognoscimus, quibus iure merito potuimus a summo pontificio reiici. Merita vero, quae huc nos eveherent, nulla scimus; diceremusque nos prorsus indignos neque delatum amplecteremur honorem, nisi vocantis iudicium timeremus. Nam quod duae Sacri Collegii partes efficiunt, id profecto a Spiritu Sancto est, cui non licet adversari. Oboedimus igitur vocationi divinae; ac te, Nicene, et reliquos cum quibus sensisti laudamus, si conscientiae iudicium secuti nos tamquam insufficientes non censuistis eligendos. Eritis omnes accepti nobis, qui vocationem nostram non isti aut illi attribuemus, sed toti Collegio et ipsi Deo, a quo est "omne datum optimum et omne donum perfectum." '

30 Nec plura locutus, priora exuit indumenta et albam Christi tunicam accepit; et interrogatus quo nomine vellet vocari, 'Pio,' respondit, et mox Pius Secundus appellatus est; et iuratis quibusdam capitulis nudius tertius in Collegio editis, in altari positus rursus a cardinalibus[123] adoratus est, pedes eius et manus et ora exosculantibus; atque eo facto publicata est populo pontificis electio ex alta fenestra, acclamatumque Pium Secundum pontificem haberi, qui fuerat cardinalis Senensis.

31 Tum qui erant in conclavi ministri cardinalium cellulam eius spoliavere, atque argentum—quamvis erat modicum—et libros et

satisfied, we must be satisfied too. The Lord himself, who has chosen you, will make good the defect in your feet, nor will he punish our ignorance. We revere you as pope, we elect you again, so far as is in our power, and we will serve you faithfully."

Aeneas replied, "Your Eminence of Nicea, your opinion of us, 29
as we understand it, is far better than our own. You attribute to us no defect except that in our feet. We are not unaware that our imperfections range more widely than this. We realize we possess faults well nigh beyond measure, for which we might justly have been rejected as pope. As for virtues which make us worthy of this post, we know of none; and we should declare ourselves utterly unworthy and refuse the honor offered us, did we not fear the judgment of Him who has called us. For whatever is done by two thirds of the sacred college is surely inspired by the Holy Ghost, who may not be resisted. Therefore we submit to the divine summons and we honor you, Your Eminence of Nicea, and those who voted with you. If, following the dictates of your conscience, you thought us unworthy of election, you will still be welcome among us, who attribute our calling not to this man or that but to the whole college and to God himself, from whom comes 'every good and perfect gift.' "[155]

With these words he cast off his old garments and put on the 30
white tunic of Christ. When asked by what name he wished to be called, he answered, "Pius," and was at once addressed as Pius II. Then, having sworn to observe the capitulations issued in the college two days before, he took his place at the altar and was again reverenced by the cardinals, who kissed his feet and hands and cheek. When this was done, the result of the election was made public. From a high window it was proclaimed that he who had been cardinal of Siena was now Pope Pius II.

The attendants of the cardinals in the conclave plundered 31
Aeneas's cell, shamelessly carrying off his silver (though it was very modest), his clothes and his books. In the city, a disgraceful mob

vestes turpi more diripuere, et domum eius in Urbe vilissima plebs atque infamis non expilavit tantum, sed disrupit etiam marmoribus asportatis. Fuerunt et alii cardinales affecti damno, nam suspenso in expectatione populo cum variae voces iactarentur, et modo hic cardinalis modo ille diceretur electus, procurrere vulgus ad illorum aedes ac rapinam facere; et Genuensis pro Senensi auditus partem substantiae amisit. Cumque plures nominarentur, nullius vox cum gaudio exaudita est nisi Senensis; demisere cuncti vultus, atque in terram maesti respexere, et maledixere Collegio, cum vel Rhotomagensis vel Genuensis vel Ilardensis (nam de iis rumor fuit) pontificatum obtinuisse clamatum est. Solos eos laetitia tenuit, qui erant illis aliqua familiaritate coniuncti; reliquos omnes publicus tenebat maeror.

32 At cum certum fuit Aeneam in solio Petri constitutum esse, nemo non exultavit. Vidisses non homines tantum, sed ipsa fere animalia et Urbis aedificia gestire; ubique risus, ubique gaudium, ubique voces clamantium exaudiebantur, 'Sena, Sena! O felix Sena! Vive Sena! Gaude Sena!' Et cum esset armata civitas, nec quisquam in alio quam in ferro videretur habere fiduciam, mox ut certior factus est populus Aeneae pontificatum obvenisse, deposita sunt arma, adeoque mutata Urbis facies ut quae paulo ante Martis, e vestigio non dicam Veneris, Troiani quondam Aeneae matris, sed Pacis et Quietis civitas effecta sit, ubique laeta atque secura.

33 Interim novus praesul paululum cibo recreatus in basilicam Sancti Petri ductus est et in ara maiori collocatus, sub qua iacent beatorum apostolorum corpora, et paulo post in sublimi solio ipsaque apostolica cathedra pro consuetudine sedit; quo in loco tum cardinales et episcopi, tum multi ex populo eius pedes exosculati sunt et sedentem in throno Christi vicarium adoraverunt. Nec diu moratum, cum iam advesperasceret, in Palatium reduxere. Ad-

not only pillaged his house but actually demolished it by making off with blocks of marble. Other cardinals, too, suffered losses, for rumors had been rife as the people waited in suspense. As now this cardinal and now that one was said to have been elected, the crowd would rush to their houses and plunder them. The cardinal of Genoa, whose name was mistaken for Siena, lost part of his estate. And yet, though many names were mentioned, none was received with enthusiasm except Siena. When the cry arose that Rouen or Genoa or Lerida (for these were the ones rumor named) had been elected, every face fell. Gloomily the people cast their eyes to the ground, muttering curses against the college. The only ones to rejoice were their personal friends; all the rest fell into general lamentation.

Once they knew for certain that Aeneas sat in Peter's 32
chair, however, all joined in the celebrations. You would have thought that not only the people but even the beasts and the buildings of Rome were swooning with delight; everywhere there was laughter and joy and voices shouting, "Siena! Siena! Happy Siena! Up with Siena! Siena, rejoice!" Before, the city had been in arms; no one seemed to trust in anything but the sword. But now, with the news that the papacy had gone to Aeneas, the atmosphere was completely changed. What had been a city of Mars all at once became a city of—well, I will not say of Venus, mother of Aeneas of Troy—but a city of Peace and of Quiet. Everywhere, joy and tranquility reigned.

While this was going on, the new pope took a little refreshment 33
and then was escorted to the basilica of St. Peter. He was installed at the high altar, over the bodies of the blessed Apostles, and after a little while he sat, in accordance with tradition, in the sublime seat, the apostolic throne. There both the cardinals and bishops and many of the people kissed his feet and reverenced him on his throne as the Vicar of Christ. This did not last long, for it was already beginning to get dark, and so they escorted him back to the

ventu noctis lucere in omni trivio atque in omni turre ignes, cantus exaudiri, vicinus vicinum invitare, nulla in parte cornua tubasque non sonare, nullum in Urbe locum non publico gestire gaudio. Ferebant seniores numquam se Romae tantam populi alacritatem vidisse.

: 37 :

Laetitia Romanorum et omnium gentium ex Pii pontificatu, variaeque principum legationes ad congratulationem et oboedientiam, et famae miraculosa celeritas.

1 Sequenti nocte primarii Urbis cives, equis insedentes ardentesque cereos in manu ferentes, ad Palatium salutaturi pontificem accessere, quorum ordo ex Mole Adriani ad aedem Beati Petri protendebatur. Nec Roma tantum sed multae Italiae civitates et multi principes, audita Pii pontificis assumptione, singularem laetitiam ostenderunt. Praecipue vero Senenses exultavere, quorum civis adeo exaltatus esset ut omnium in orbe primus haberetur, quamvis plerosque nobilitatis hostes[124] tacitus occupavit maeror.

2 Corsiniani, quod oppidum octoginta passuum milibus ab Urbe distat, qua hora pontifex electus est, oppidani populariter ex agris redeuntes Laudomiam, Pii sororem salutatum iere, bonum se nuntium accepisse concordi testimonio affirmantes: Aeneam cardinalem Senensem ad summum pontificatus fastigium esse assumptum. Quod vaticinium memoratu dignum sequenti die litterae ab amicis missae confirmaverunt. Mirabilius illud fuit: Cathelanus quidam, dum essent in conclavi cardinales electiones celebrantes, accersitis ex familia cardinalis Senensis Iohanne physico et non-

palace. At dusk, fires blazed on every corner and from the top of every tower; songs were sung; neighbors called to neighbors; everywhere horns and trumpets blared; there was no spot in all the city that did not join in the public celebration. Old men said they had never seen such delight among the people of Rome.

: 37 :

Rome and the nations celebrate the election of Pius. Embassies from various princes offer congratulations and submission. The news spreads with miraculous speed.

The next night, the leading citizens of the city went to the palace to greet the pope. Riding on horseback and carrying lighted tapers, they formed a procession stretching from St. Peter's to Hadrian's mausoleum.[156] Nor did Rome alone greet the news of Pius's accession with tremendous joy: so, too, did many Italian states and princes. The Sienese were especially delighted, because one of their own had been raised so high as to be considered the first of all men on earth. (Many of those who were enemies of the nobles, however, grieved in their hearts.) 1

At Corsignano, which lies some eighty miles from Rome, at the very hour the pope was elected, the villagers returned from the fields to congratulate Pius's sister Laodamia. They all reported, in strikingly similar terms, the good news that Aeneas of Siena had been elevated to the supreme position of the papacy. This remarkable presage was confirmed the next day by letters from friends. Even more extraordinary, when the cardinals were still in the conclave celebrating the result of the election, a certain Catalan summoned some of Aeneas's servants and his doctor Giovanni to his side and said, "Your master will be chosen this very hour." When 2

nullis aliis: 'Hac,' inquit, 'hora dominus vester eligitur.' Percunctantibus, quo pacto id sciret, respondit: 'Vidi hac nocte per quietem cardinales sacellum intrantes, in quo fit electio, omnesque vestrum dominum introducere tamquam pontificem futurum; duos tantum adversari, qui eum e sacello reiicere conabantur, sed non praevaluere. Estote boni animi, mox cardinalem Senensem pronuntiari audietis!' Prophetiam paulo post secuta res est. De duobus cardinalibus, qui adversati sunt, supra retulimus.[125]

3 Ferdinando Siciliae regi felix hoc nuntium fuit, qui patris amicum in sede Petri suffectum intellexit. Franciscus Sforcia dux Mediolani, etsi alium pontificem expectabat, Aeneae tamen cognita electione gavisus est, quem olim in castris contra Mediolanum honorasset. Borsius Mutinae dux militares ludos instituit, et multa magnaque suae laetitiae signa ostendit; erat enim ei cum Aenea vetus benivolentia ab eo tempore quo ducatum a Federico imperatore accepit, cuius adipiscendi Aeneas non in ultimis auctor fuit. Speravit Borsius Aenea pontificatum tenente fortunas suas et gloriam aucturum, atque idcirco Ferrariam et omnem ditionem suam singularem ostendere voluptatem novi praesulis assumptione curavit. Ut multae patent hominibus ad faenerandum viae! Marchiones Mantuae, Montis Ferrati ac Salutiarum pariter gavisi sunt, nulli enim eorum Aeneas non notus et non amicus erat.

4 Veneti tantum et Florentini ex Italis inviti hoc nuntium audivere: Veneti, quod Aeneas imperatoris legatus saepe in eorum senatu visus fuisset asperius loqui, et ipsorum tyrannidem accusare; Florentini, quod more hominum vicinos Senenses odissent, quibus adeo molesta fuit Aeneae assumptio, ut cum iter agentes ab obviantibus salutarentur, et (ut est consuetudo) auxilium Dei super eos expeteretur, indignabundi responderent, 'Atqui circa Senenses occupatus est, quos beare conatur!' Dissimulavere tamen et Veneti et Florentini et, sicut ceteri potentatus Italiae, legatos mi-

they demanded to know how he knew this, he replied, "Last night I had a dream. I saw the cardinals entering the chapel where the votes are taken. They all led your master in, as though he would be pope, but two stood opposed. They were trying to drive him out of the chapel, but they did not succeed. So be of good cheer: soon you shall hear the name of Siena proclaimed!" And shortly thereafter, the prophecy was fulfilled. Of the two cardinals who stood opposed, we have spoken already.

King Ferrante of Sicily welcomed the news, seeing that a friend 3
of his father was now seated on Peter's throne. Francesco Sforza, though he had expected a different pope,[157] was nevertheless pleased to learn of Aeneas's election; he had once received him with honor in his camp before the walls of Milan.[158] Duke Borso of Modena, showing his pleasure in grand style, declared a military tournament. His friendship with Aeneas dated from the time he received his dukedom from Emperor Frederick, a good turn in which Aeneas had played no small part. He hoped that with Aeneas as pope, his fortunes and reputation would prosper and therefore he saw to it that Ferrara and all his dominions made an outstanding display of pleasure at the accession of the new pope. How many ways there are to get interest on one's investments! The marquises of Mantua, Monferrato and Saluzzo were equally delighted, for they all knew Aeneas and counted themselves among his friends.

Among the Italians, only the Venetians and Florentines were 4
sorry to hear the news; the Venetians because they thought that Aeneas, when representing the emperor, had spoken harshly in their senate and accused them of tyranny; the Florentines, naturally, because they hated the Sienese. They were so vexed by Aeneas's accession that when passersby hailed them with the usual "God save you!" they would answer indignantly, "He's too busy blessing Siena!" But both states concealed their true opinions and, like the other Italian powers, sent distinguished ambassadors to

sere viros honoratissimos, qui Romam petentes novo pontifici congratulati oboedientiam praestitere.

Ex ultramontanis principibus admodum laetatus est imperator Federicus, ex cuius famulatu Aeneas ad cardinalatum vocatus, tandem Beati Petri solium ascendisset. Cuncti quoque Hispaniae reges, qui Christum colunt, gaudium ostendere; at Scotus, Danus, Polonus, Francus ac Hungarus et Cyprius imperatoris amicum non libenter audivere Christi vicariatum obtinuisse; Bohemus vero apprime indoluit, ut qui nosset haereticum sese pontifici notum esse. Philippo Burgundiae et Ludovico Sabaudiae ducibus Aeneae pontificatus, amici veteris, acceptissimus fuit.

Rome to congratulate the new pope and offer him their submission.

Among the northern princes, Emperor Frederick was especially pleased, since it was from his service that Aeneas had been called to the cardinalate and then ascended the throne of Peter. All the princes of Spain (the Christian ones, that is) showed their satisfaction, but Scotland, Denmark, Poland, France, Hungary and Cyprus were not happy to hear that a friend of the emperor was now Vicar of Christ. The king of Bohemia was particularly aggrieved, for he knew the pope knew him for a heretic.[159] Both Philip of Burgundy and Lodovico of Savoy were delighted at the elevation of their old friend, Aeneas.

LIBER SECUNDUS

: I :

De Pii coronatione, et de Turchorum origine et progressu.

1 Pius Secundus pontifex maximus Romae coronatus est apud basilicam Sancti Petri tertio Nonas Septembris anno salutis quinquagesimo octavo supra mille quadringentos, petiitque ipsa die Lateranum solemni pompa. Quo in loco vix necem evasit inter eos qui propter equum, quo insederat, gladiis decertabant; servatus est divina ope. Peractisque solemnibus, regale convivium apparavit non cardinalibus tantum sed omnibus legatis principum et, qui aderant, proceribus Urbis et optimatibus; eademque nocte in suas aedes ad Vaticanum rediit.

2 Atque inter omnes curas quae animum eius invasere, nulla maior fuit quam ut in Turchos excitare Christianos posset atque illis[1] bellum inferre. Hoc genus hominum ex orientali quondam Scythia digressum Cappadociam, Pontum, Bithyniam et omnem ferme Asiam quae Minor appellatur armis subegit. Nec diu post, transmisso classibus Hellesponto, maiorem Graeciae partem occupavit et usque ad Savum et Danubium memorabiles amnes signa protulit.

3 Restabat in medio Thraciae urbs regia Byzantium, quam prior Constantinus, cognomento Magnus, cum instaurasset ac mirum in modum ampliasset, Novam Romam appellavit; sed vicit obstinatio vulgi ut ab innovatore Constantinopolis vocaretur. Hanc quoque, sedente Nicolao Quinto pontifice maximo, Mahumetes Turchorum imperator obsidione cinxit et deiecta moenium parte (ut ante relatum est) vi cepit atque diripuit, Constantino eius no-

BOOK II

: I :

Pius's coronation. The origin of the Turks and their rise to power.

1 Pope Pius II was crowned in St. Peter's basilica in Rome on the third of September in the year of our salvation 1458. The same day he went in solemn procession to the Lateran, where he narrowly escaped death in the mob who fought with swords for the horse he had ridden. He was saved by the mercy of heaven. After celebrating mass, he held a royal banquet not only for the cardinals but for all the princely ambassadors, nobles and magnates of the city who were in Rome at the time. That night he returned to the Vatican palace.

2 Among all the concerns that occupied his heart, none was greater than his desire to call the peoples of Christendom to a crusade against the Turks. This race of men had long ago emerged from eastern Scythia to attack and conquer Cappadocia, Pontus, Bithynia, and almost every other part of the land we call Asia Minor. Shortly thereafter, they crossed the Hellespont, occupied most of Greece and carried their standards as far as the celebrated waters of the Sava and the Danube.[1]

3 In the heart of Thrace there stood Byzantium, the royal city. Constantine the Great, who rebuilt and greatly enlarged the place, had given it the name New Rome, but the populace insisted it be called Constantinople after its second founder. In the pontificate of Nicholas V it was besieged by Mehmed, the emperor of the Turks, as has been previously described: he broke through the walls, took the city by storm and sacked it. Constantine, the last

minis ultimo imperatore obtruncato sive, ut fama est, inter equitum turmas oppresso.

4 Qua victoria elatus ad Europae imperium aspirare coepit, coactisque ingentibus copiis per superiorem Mysiam in Hungariam traiicere statuit. Sed remoratus apud Albam, qui locus Danubio Savoque confluentibus alluitur (Thaurinum vetustas dixit) sedente Callisto Tertio Romanae Urbis antistite a Christianis crucesignatis, quos Iohannes Capistranius Ordinis Minorum professor opinione sanctitatis insignis et Iohannes Huniates Hungarici regni gubernator duxere, magnam stragem perpessus est, et castris[2] deiectus turpem fugam arripere compulsus. Non tamen aut animum aut odium in Christianos remisit, sed novos in dies exercitus comparans nunc Albanos, nunc Rascianos, nunc alios vicinos qui Christum colerent, vexare adortus est, ut qui sanctum Evangelium ac divinam Christi legem conculcare prorsus ac delere statuisset.

5 Haec gens inimica Trinitatis Mahumetem quendam pseudoprophetam sequitur, qui fuit Arabs gentili errore et Iudaica imbutus perfidia audivitque Christianos, qui Nestoriana et Ariana labe infecti erant. Crevit potentis viduae stupro, et nobilitatus adulteriis latronum manum coegit, qua dominatum inter Arabes vendicavit, et habens Veteris Novique Testamenti notitiam utrunque corrupit, ausus que prophetam se dicere et angelorum potiri alloquio, adeo rudes illexit populos ut legem iis novam dederit, et a Christo Salvatore discedere suaserit. Utebatur enim incantationibus ac praestigiis, et usum veneris ac nefarios indulgens concubitus voluptati deditam plebem facile ad se traxit, cui subtracto vino nihil

emperor of that name, was either murdered or, as some say, trampled under the hooves of the cavalry.[2]

Inflamed by this victory, Mehmed began to aspire to rule all of 4
Europe. He assembled a huge army and planned to cross Upper Moesia and invade Hungary; but in the pontificate of Calixtus III an army of Christian crusaders stopped him at Alba (a town at the confluence of the Sava and the Danube, called Taurunum in antiquity). The Christians were by led by Giovanni da Capistrano, the Minorite friar renowned for his piety, and John Hunyadi, governor of Hungary.[3] Mehmed suffered enormous losses; he was driven from his camp and forced to a humiliating and hasty retreat. Still he did not lose heart, nor his hatred for Christians. Recruiting fresh troops, increasing the size of his armies day by day, he proceeded to harry now the Albanians, now the Serbians, now other neighboring Christian peoples. He was determined to stamp out and destroy the holy gospel and sacred law of Christ.

The Turkish nation despises the Trinity. They follow a certain 5
false prophet called Muhammad, an Arab steeped in gentile error and Jewish perfidy, who received instruction in the Nestorian and Arian heresies. He advanced his fortunes by seducing a rich widow and grew notorious for his infidelities; his reputation attracted a band of brigands to his side, and with their help he made himself lord of the Arabs. Acquainted as he was with the Old and New Testaments, he perverted them both; he had the effrontery to call himself a prophet. He claimed to speak with angels. He cast such a spell over this primitive nation that he was able to persuade them to abandon Christ the Savior and accept instead the new religion he devised for them. To this end he employed magic spells and tricks and gave his sanction to sex in all sorts of unspeakable combinations; by these means he easily seduced the common people, who are slaves to sensual pleasure. With the exception of wine, there was nothing he did not allow them in his campaign to recruit them to his cult. His doctrine, though it ad-

non concessit, ut legis suae cultum persuaderet. Quae quamvis Christum Dei flatum esse fateatur ex virgine natum, mirabilium operum effectorem, ei tamen divinitatem adimit et tormenta mortisque cruciatum pro nostra redemptione toleratum; nec prophetas recipit, nec apostolorum aut evangelistarum dictis auscultat. Adeoque portentuosae[3] legis huius auctoritas crevit, ut paene omnis Asia et Africa eius veneno infecta sit, et ducentibus Turchis in Graeciam penetraverit, et Baeticam in Hispania per Mauros occupaverit. Et quamvis Romani praesules multa adversos hanc pestem arma paraverint, ea tamen hactenus paulatim aucta est et ad interiora nostra dilapsa.

: 2 :

Pii adversus Turchos deliberatio et indictio concilii Mantuani, eiusque urbis descriptio ac prophetia.

1 Timuit Pius pontifex hoc venenum et occurrere statuit ne serperet ulterius. Non tamen in se solo (hoc est, in Apostolicae Sedis viribus) confidebat, nam vincere Turchos non huius aut illius regni opus, sed totius Christianae rei publicae videbatur. Necessaria igitur eorum consilia existimavit, quorum auxilia requireret, conciliumque principum et liberorum populorum convocare decrevit, in quo de communi salute communiter ageret. Sed ubi concilium habendum esset in consultationem venit, cardinalium alii Romae, alii trans Alpes aut in Germania aut in Gallia conventum habendum esse dicebant.

2 Pio nihil horum placuit; neque enim ex honestate arbitrabatur reges, qui trans Alpes morarentur, Romam vocari, neque in Gallia aut in Germania utile concilium futurum, ad quod propter valitu-

mits that Christ was made of God, born of a virgin and able to perform miracles, yet denies that He was divine and that He suffered the agonies of death for our redemption. It neither acknowledges the prophets nor heeds the precepts of the Apostles or Evangelists.[4] The influence of this monstrous doctrine grew so great that almost all of Asia and Africa were infected with its poison. It entered Greece along with the Turks and with the Moors seized hold of Baetica in Spain. Although the bishops of Rome mounted many campaigns against this plague, still it has continued to grow in strength and penetrate to our very vitals down to the present day.

: 2 :

Pius's concern for the Turkish problem. His summons to a congress at Mantua. Description of the city and a prophecy.

Pope Pius feared this poison and determined to take action before it wormed its way in any further. But he would not rely on himself alone (that is, on the power of the Apostolic See), for he saw that the conquest of the Turks was a task not for this or that realm but for all of Christendom. He realized he would have to ask the advice of those whose aid he would soon require, and so decided to convene a congress of princes and republics to discuss the common good. First, however, he must determine where the congress should meet. Some cardinals said it should be at Rome, but other advised a location across the Alps, in Germany or in France. 1

None of these suggestions satisfied Pius: he did not think it appropriate to summon princes from the north all the way to Rome; on the other hand, holding a council in France or Germany would be pointless, since the pope's health would prevent his attending it. 2

dinem pontifex ipse transire non posset. Antiquius[4] visum est non procul ab Alpibus[5] conventum cogere in loco, qui medius inter Romanum praesulem et transalpinos reges existimaretur. Duo nominata sunt loca: Utinum in Foro Iulii, subiectum Venetis, et Mantua in Gallia Cisalpina, ut si alter negaretur, alter praesto adesset.[6] Veritus est enim pontifex id quod postea successit, ne Veneti Turchorum arma timentes Utinum clauderent.

3 Ferunt in scriptis vatum pervetustis in quibus Romanorum praesulum tempora praedicuntur, cum Pii Secundi prophetia subnectitur, haec verba reperiri: 'Et tu, Mantua, exaltaberis. Ita Deo placitum, nec falli numina possunt. Virgilius Mantuanus Aeneam Troianum cecinit, Aeneas Senensis Virgilii patriam ditavit.' Non tamen haec consideratio praesulem traxit, sed loci commoditas. Est enim urbs amplissima in solo fertili et vicina montibus qui Gallos ac Germanos ab Italia disterminant; lacui adiacens, quem Mintius efficit amnis. Is ex Benaco in Padum decurrit idque praestat utilitatis, ut ex omni Gallia Cisalpina commeatus ad Mantuanos navigio valeant importari.

4 Diu res agitata est in consilio cum cardinalibus, quorum etsi multi adversarentur (quibus res praesentes abunde suppetebant, et placebat otium in Urbe) vicit tamen praesulis constantia, et in eius sententiam itum est. Vocati sunt in sacrario Palatii episcopi, abbates, notarii, oratores regum et omnes quis munera Curiae creduntur, ut horum quoque consilia audirentur. Ibi pontifex, quod diu tectum fuerat, propositum suum publicavit.

5 Quantas in Christianos Turchi clades intulissent, quibus modis evangelicam evertere legem molirentur, exposuit; nihil sibi acerbius esse quam intueri Christianae gentis ruinam; sacratissimae religionis se curam gerere; statuisse occurrere hostium conatibus; at cum id absque auxilio Christianorum regum perficere non posset, ha-

He thought it best to hold the congress someplace near the Alps, halfway between the pope and the northern princes. Two places were suggested: Udine, a town in Friuli subject to Venice, and Mantua in Cisalpine Gaul. If they were denied the use of one, they could turn to the other, for the pope was worried that the Venetians, who were terrified of the Turks, would keep him from coming to Udine—and later on that is exactly what they did.

It is said that in the ancient books of prophecies where the 3
reigns of the popes are foretold, the oracle on Pius II proclaims: "And thou, Mantua, shall be exalted. So it has pleased God. The spirits cannot be wrong. Vergil of Mantua sang the tale of Aeneas of Troy, and Aeneas of Siena enriched the city of Vergil." It was not this that decided the pope, however, but rather the convenience of the place. A large city, it lies in a fertile plain near the mountains separating France and Germany from Italy, on a lake formed by the river Mincio. This river flows from Lake Garda into the Po, and so goods can be shipped to Mantua from every part of Cisalpine Gaul.

For a long time, the pope and cardinals debated the question in 4
council. Many prelates opposed him, for they were happy enough with the present state of affairs and liked their easy life in the capital, but the pope persevered until his plan was adopted. He then invited various bishops, abbots, notaries, royal ambassadors and all the officials of the Curia to a meeting in the palace chapel so that their advice, too, could be heard. There he made public the project he had long held in his heart.

He described the great disasters the Turks had inflicted on 5
Christendom and explained how they were scheming to overthrow the Gospel law. The fall of a Christian nation was for him the bitterest blow imaginable; he was charged with the care of their sacred religion; he had decided to take the offensive against the Turks. Since this could not be done without help from the princes of Christendom, he was determined to hold a congress either at

bere concilium aut in Utino aut in Mantua decrevisse, ut eorum ibi sententias[7] audiret quorum opem imploraturus esset; durum sibi videri Romam relinquere, Beati apostoli Petri sedem et Christianae religionis arcem; durius se pontifice sanctum Evangelium expugnari, pro cuius conservatione non Urbem solum ac Beati Petri patrimonium, sed corpus et vitam ponere statuerit; atque idcirco, quamvis senex et aegrotus, tamen Apennini iuga et Padi fluenta transire proposuerit, ut cum potentatibus Christianis de salute Christianae religionis consulat. Et multa in hunc modum graviter peroravit.

6 Laudaverunt omnes animum ac propositum eius et in caelum extulerunt, qui unus esset omnium salvandae religionis curiosus. Exin publicum de more consistorium est habitum, et litterae apostolicae recitatae sunt in quis statuta dies conventionis est, et principes ad alterum ex duobus locis vocati. Epistola eius rei ab ipso pontifice dictata in aliarum volumine continetur.

7 Romanos cognito decreto ingens maeror affecit, qui se privatum iri emolumentis Curiae animadvertebant; pontificem morbis et aetate gravem haudquaquam reversurum aliquando sperabant. Et alii Senas peti, non Mantuam aiebant, fingique conventum Mantuanum ut in itinere Senis remoraretur et pontificis patria ditaretur; alii non solum Mantuam, sed in Alamaniam quoque profecturum praesulem affirmabant, qui nutritus inter Germanos libens ad eos rediret, neque indignum putaret Apostolicam Sedem trans Alpes habere. Desperare omnes de reditu, eiulare per Urbem feminae ac pueri, blasphemare viri, maledicere senes; qui plus sensi haberent catervatim adire pontificem, damnare recessum, rogare ut in Urbe sua maneret, polliceri multa remanenti.

Udine or at Mantua to hear the opinions of those whose aid he meant to enlist. It would be hard for him to leave Rome, the seat of St. Peter the Apostle and the ark of the Christian faith, but it would be harder still to see the holy gospel destroyed in the course of his reign. To save it, he was resolved to stake not just the city and the patrimony of Peter, but his own health, indeed his very life. And so, though he was old and infirm, he proposed to cross the Apennines and the Po and confer with Christian princes about the rescue of the Christian faith. He went on to declaim on many more such topics with great seriousness.

Everyone applauded his courage and his purpose and praised him to the skies as the only man on earth who cared for the safety of the faith. Then they convened a public consistory according to established procedure. An apostolic letter was published setting the date for the congress and summoning the princes to either of the two cities. (This letter, dictated by the pope himself, appears along with others in a separate volume.)[5] 6

The people of Rome were terribly distressed when they heard of this decision, for it meant they would lose the income they derived from the Curia. They could not imagine that the pope, afflicted as he was by illness and old age, would ever return. Some said his real objective was not Mantua but Siena: he was only pretending the congress would meet at Mantua in order to make a stop at Siena on the way and thus enrich his native city. Others said he would go not just to Mantua but to Germany, the land where he had spent his youth; he was eager to return there, nor would he think there any shame in transferring the Apostolic See across the Alps. All despaired of his return to Rome. Women and children went wailing through the streets, grown men swore and old men cursed. The more sensible among them appealed to the pope in great throngs; they condemned his departure and begged him to remain in the city, holding out many inducements if he would but stay. 7

8 Solabatur eos pontifex necessitatem profectionis ostendens et reditum celerem promittens, nec tamen ipse absque lacrimis suam plebem affari poterat. Erant omnia plena luctu, nec tanta in assumptione Pii laetitia populi fuit, quanta visa est tristitia cum profectionis decretum in plebe auditum est. Adeo nullum est gaudium cui non succedat subito maeror. Reddebant iter praesulis difficilius ac periculosius nondum compositae Regni Siciliae res.

: 3 :

De Siciliae situ, nominibus et magnitudine et Regno Neapolitano, susceptisque pro eo contentionibus et bellis, et quare Callistus adversatus Ferdinando.

1 Sicilia, etsi eadem est quam prisci Trinacriam vocavere, parvo freto ab Italia discretam qua Scyllae et Charybdis monstra feruntur, hodie tamen duo Siciliae regna vulgo appellant: alterum in insula, alterum in Italiae continenti, cuius amplius quam tres partes supero et infero mari abluuntur; quod reliquum est, montibus ac fluminibus a reliqua Italia disiungitur. Longitudo eius a finibus Reatini agri, quem umbilicum Italiae dicunt, per Aquilam Marsorum urbem usque in Brutios et Leucopetram milibus passuum circiter quadringentis protenditur.

2 Multae in eo praeclarae urbes, sed omnium metropolis est Parthenope, quam divus Augustus Neapolim appellavit. Olim Capua principatum habuit, cum altera Roma diceretur nondum Romanorum et Hannibalis armis vexata. Hoc regnum directo iure ad Ecclesiam Romanam pertinet; diu gens Gallica eius feudo potita est, censum pendens annuum Romano praesuli unciarum auri

8 The pope tried to comfort his people: he explained why he had to go and promised a speedy return, but he could not speak to them without bursting into tears. Everything was tinged with grief. The public celebrations at Pius's election had not been so intense as was the public sorrow now that his decision to depart was official. Joy never comes without grief in its trail. The pope's journey was made more difficult and dangerous by the fact that the Sicilian question remained unresolved.

: 3 :

Sicily: its location, size and the names by which it is known. The Kingdom of Naples: disputes and battles for its possession. Why Calixtus opposed Ferrante.

1 The island of Sicily was known in antiquity as Trinacria; it is separated from Italy by a narrow strait where the monsters Scylla and Charybdis are said to lurk. And yet, today, we commonly speak of two kingdoms of Sicily, one on the island, the other in Italy proper. This latter kingdom of Sicily is surrounded for more than three quarters of its perimeter by the Adriatic and Tyrrhenian Seas; the remaining part is separated from the rest of Italy by mountains and rivers. It extends from the Reatine plain, the "navel of Italy," through L'Aquila to the territory of the Bruttii and the Capo dell'Armi, a distance of about four hundred miles.[6]

2 The kingdom boasts many splendid cities, but the metropolis of them all is Parthenope, which the deified Augustus named Neapolis. In ancient times Capua was its capital; before the armies of Rome and Hannibal brought it to grief, it was known as a second Rome. Legally, the kingdom belongs to the Church of Rome, though for a long time the French held it in fief, paying the

octo milium. Sed cum regina Iohanna, quae secunda eius nominis Regnum tenuit, Ludovicum Andegavensem, quem prius in filium adoptaverat, aspernari coepisset atque Alfonsum Aragonum regem ex Hispania in Regni successione vocasset, mutata est conditio et pro Gallicis Cathelani sive Aragonenses introiere.

3 Plura inter Ludovicum et Alfonsum proelia fuerunt, fortuna (ut assuevit) nunc istum, nunc illum erigente. Ludovico febribus extincto ius eius ad Rhenatum fratrem derivatum est. Regina Alfonsum modo diligere, modo habere odio; qua vita functa Rhenatus in Regnum veniens cupide a pluribus exceptus est et tamquam rex adoratus, qui non paucis annis adversus Alfonsum de Regno dimicans victus tandem abiit. Alfonsus in Regno remansit. Non tamen ab Eugenio Quarto pontifice Romano, qui Rhenatum elegisset, obtinere feudum potuit, nisi postquam constitit Rhenatum quae promiserat neglexisse, ac ius iurandum violasse. Investitus Alfonsus ab Eugenio Regnumque consecutus fuit ingratus, sed Franciscum Sfortiam, qui Picentes ab Ecclesia deficere coegerat, armis expulit et provinciam Eugenio pacatam reddidit.

4 Erat unicus Alfonso filius, Ferdinandus nomine, ex femina nobili — verum alteri nupta — genitus; hunc Eugenius ad Regni successionem idoneum reddidit, idemque fecit Nicolaus Quintus, successor eius, qui Regnum Alfonso confirmavit. Quamdiu igitur post Eugenius et Nicolaus vixere, Alfonsus absque adversario in summa pace atque otio Regnum tenuit.[8] Mortuo autem Nicolao Callistus Tertius successit,[9] in Alfonsi aula diu versatus et illi apprime obnoxius, qui eius precibus cardinalatum obtinuisset. Quas ob causas putavit Alfonsus ab eo pontifice, qui sibi aliquando servivisset, et qui suo favore magnificatus esset, nihil se frustra petiturum, eaque fiducia ductus non solum Regni feudum, sed marchiam quoque Anconitanam et alia pleraque Ecclesiae loca tradi sibi efflagitavit.

pope an annual tribute of 8,000 ounces of gold.[7] After Queen Giovanna II fell out with Louis of Anjou, whom she had adopted as her son, however, she summoned Alfonso, king of Aragon, from Spain to be her heir. Then everything changed: instead of the French, the Catalans and Aragonese arrived on the scene.[8]

Louis and Alfonso met several times in battle. Fortune, as is 3
her habit, would raise up now one and now the other; when Louis died of a fever, his rights were transferred to his brother René. The queen sometimes favored Alfonso, but sometimes held him in contempt. When she died, René made his entrance into the kingdom, and many welcomed him with enthusiasm and hailed him as their king. He fought Alfonso for the throne for several years, but in the end he was defeated and forced to withdraw, while Alfonso remained in the kingdom. He was unable officially to obtain the fief from Eugenius IV, however, because the pope favored René—until it became clear that the latter had disregarded his promises and broken his word. Then Eugenius crowned Alfonso. Once on the throne he did not show himself ungrateful: he drove Francesco Sforza, who had forced the Picenes to revolt against Church rule, out of the province and restored it in good order to the pope.

Alfonso had one son, Ferrante, by a lady who was nobly born 4
but not his wife. Eugenius declared him eligible to succeed and so did the next pope, Nicholas V, who also confirmed Alfonso as king. Thereafter, as long as Eugenius and Nicholas lived, Alfonso reigned in peace and tranquility, without opposition. When Nicholas died, he was succeeded by Calixtus III, who had spent a long time at Alfonso's court and was under a particular obligation to him, for it was at the king's behest that he had been made a cardinal. Alfonso imagined that a pope who had once been his subject and who owed his elevation to his patronage would never refuse a request from him. His confidence led him to demand not only the fief of the kingdom, but also the marches of Ancona and several other territories belonging to the Church.

5 Pontifici longe alia sententia fuit, qui cum se iam Christi vicarium esse cerneret, nec regi cedendum, nec iura Ecclesiae alienanda censuit. Exortae sunt inter eos graves inimicitiae, quae usque ad finem vitae utriusque perdurarunt; quamquam aliqui dissimulationem putarent — ii praesertim quos Florentia mirata est, et quibus opum vis pro sapientia imputabatur. Existimabant enim duos illos senes exteros odium inter se fingere, quo facilius reliquam Italiam sibi vendicarent, qui propemodum duas eius partes obtinuissent. Sed verissimae fuerunt inimicitiae atque impacabiles, quae ad sepulchrum usque perrexerunt.

6 Obiit prior Alfonsus quadraginta diebus; quod audiens Callistus nec lacrimas nec risum continuit: illacrimatus est humanae conditionis fragilitati, risit inimico sublato, et cum propheta dixit: 'Laqueus contritus est, et nos liberati sumus.' Nec Ferdinando paternum regnum petenti aures accommodavit, sed errasse principes ac populos ait, qui eum supra se regem accepissent, accersitisque cardinalibus et, qui docti ex Romana Curia videbantur, praelatis Regnum Siciliae ad Romanam Ecclesiam devolutum esse declaravit. Eratque eius animi (quod praedictum est)[10] ut armis illud vendicaret nepotique traderet; et iam non parvam militum manum coegerat, sed morte praeventus et cogitationibus suis defuit et nepoti.

: 4 :

Picinini invasio et bellum in Ecclesiam Romanam, et arcium redemptio.

1 Dum successoris electio tractatur, Iacobus Picininus, inter duces equitum non ignobilis, qui Alfonso et deinde Ferdinando adver-

The pope saw things rather differently. Now that he was the Vicar of Christ, he saw no reason to yield to the king or to alienate the Church's rightful possessions. A bitter feud arose between the two which lasted to the end of their lives. Some — especially those leading lights of Florence whose great wealth earned them a reputation for wisdom — thought it was all for show;[9] they imagined that these two aged foreigners, already masters of nearly two thirds of Italy, only pretended to hate each other so they could conquer the rest of the country more easily. In fact, their hatred was all too genuine and implacable, and it went with them to the grave. 5

Alfonso was the first to die, by some forty days.[10] When Calixtus heard the news, he could hold back neither his tears nor his laughter. He wept at the frailty of the human condition, and laughed because his enemy was gone. Like the prophet he cried, "The snare is broken and we are escaped!"[11] He turned a deaf ear to Ferrante's claims to his father's throne, saying that those princes and peoples who had acknowledged him as their king had erred. He summoned together the cardinals and those prelates of the Roman Curia with a reputation for learning and declared that the kingdom of Sicily had reverted to the Church of Rome. He intended to take it by force (as has already been mentioned) and hand it over to his nephew. He had already collected a considerable army, but death kept him from satisfying either his schemes or the hopes of his nephew. 6

: 4 :

Piccinino attacks and invades the States of the Church. Several citadels held for ransom.

When the cardinals were still in conclave deliberating the election of the next pope, Jacopo Piccinino, the celebrated commander of 1

sum Sigismundum Malatestam militaverat, hoste dimisso Asisium occupat, munitam Umbriae civitatem; praefectus arcis, natione Cathelanus auro corruptus urbem prodidit. Gualdenses quoque et Nucerini ad Picininum defecere, nam patris eius, qui aliquando eos subegisset, memoriam colebant; arx Gualdi fide et diligentia praefecti servata est. Fulginates et Spoletani et ferme omnes Umbri vix in officio prae terrore consistere, cum vacante Sede Apostolica tantus hostis ex improviso emersisset.

2 At ubi Pius electus est, subito[11] animi hominum erecti, et spes pulcherrima oblata est Ecclesiae subditis. Arx Spoletana sexdecim milibus auri nummum redempta; Narnia quoque, Sorianum, Urbs Vetus, Viturvium, Civitas Castellana (in qua Veios olim fuisse quidam opinantur, nos nihil asserimus) et alia multa oppida non nisi placatis auro praefectis recuperari potuerunt. Molem Adriani, quae olim Castrum Crescentii, nunc Sancti Angeli nuncupatur, Collegium cardinalium viginti milibus aureis a Borgia Callisti nepote redemit. Is in Urbem Vetulam et arcem munitissimam non procul a Centumcellis se recepit, ibique brevi febre correptus interiit.

3 Pius, misso vicecancellario eius fratre et simul thesaurario, locum obtinuit nec multis post diebus universum Beati Petri patrimonium recuperavit, iis exceptis quae Picininus invaserat, mira populorum inclinatione, qui se Cathelanorum iugo liberatos ad manus redisse Italas gestiebant — adeo levius suorum civium quam exterorum imperium mortales ducunt. Picininus tantum in omni agro Ecclesiae contumaci animo Pii mandata contemnere atque in armis spem ponere, quamvis oppida quae invaserat paterni iuris fuisse diceret.

cavalry who had fought for Alfonso against Sigismondo Malatesta and later fought for Ferrante, captured and occupied Assisi, a fortified city of Umbria. The commandant of the citadel, a Catalan, was bribed to surrender the city. The citizens of Gualdo and Nocera also defected to Piccinino, for they revered the memory of his father, who had once governed them; but the citadel of Gualdo was saved by the loyalty and vigilance of its captain. The people of Foligno and Spoleto and just about every other place in Umbria remained barely loyal, so terrorized were they by the unexpected appearance of this powerful enemy at the very moment when the Apostolic See lay vacant.

Pius's election immediately raised people's spirits; hopes were 2
high indeed among the subjects of the Church. The citadel of Spoleto was ransomed for 16,000 gold ducats. Likewise Narni, Sora, Orvieto, Viterbo, Civita Castellana (built, some think, on the site of ancient Veii, though we make no claims about that) and many other towns could only be recovered by purchasing their governors' good-will. The College of Cardinals redeemed the tomb of Hadrian, once known as the Castle of Crescentius and now called Castel Sant'Angelo, from Calixtus's nephew Borgia for some 20,000 ducats. Borgia withdrew to Civitavecchia, a heavily fortified city near Centocelle, where soon after he caught a fever and died.

Pius sent his vice-chancellor[12] (who was the brother of this 3
Borgia) along with his treasurer to take possession of the place, and it was not long before he had recovered all the patrimony of St. Peter except the parts that Piccinino had invaded. The local population greeted these events with enthusiasm, for they were desperate to escape the Catalan yoke and to return to Italian rule — so much easier do men find dominion by their compatriots than by foreign men. In all the lands of the Church, only Piccinino stubbornly defied Pius's orders and decided to try his luck in battle, even as he claimed that the towns he seized had lawfully belonged to his father.

: 5 :

De coronatione regis Ferdinandi et conditionibus adiectis.

1 Inter haec legati Ferdinandi Pium adeuntes memoriam Alfonsi prae se tulerunt, qui Pium apprime dilexisset cum Senensis ecclesiae pontifex legatione apud se caesaris fungeretur; oraverunt, ne filium amici sperneret, neve paternum regnum ei negaret quem populi omnes peterent.

2 Ad quos Pius, 'Alfonsum,' inquit, 'pro sua praestanti virtute et diligimus et admirati sumus; idque Ferdinandi rebus admodum conducet, si erga Romanam Ecclesiam quod suum est fecerit.' Interrogatus quid ei faciendum esset, 'Censum,' ait, 'Apostolicae Camerae debitum quotannis exsolvet;[12] pontifici Romano, quotiens auxilium petierit, libens afferet; Ecclesiarum iura non attinget; Picininum ex agro Ecclesiae iubebit excedere; nisi paruerit, armis coget; Sigismundo Malatestae eam pacem largietur quam pontifex dixerit; Beneventum Ecclesiae restituet; Terracinam in annos decem sub censu tenebit, exin Romano praesuli tradet.'

3 Durae leges Ferdinando visae, saepeque oratores missi ac remissi sunt qui mentem pontificis ad pauciora deflecterent. Quibus responsum est Pium haudquaquam mercatorem esse, qui multa petat ut vel pauca reportet; dixisse illum in primo colloquio quod in ultimo dicendum erat, nec regi conditionem sperandam fore meliorem, quamvis pontifex Roma sit abiturus; aut his legibus Regnum obtinendum, aut eo carendum esse. Victus est tandem Fer-

: 5 :

Ferrante is crowned, subject to certain conditions.

In the meantime, Ferrante's ambassadors appeared before the pope. They dwelt on the memory of Alfonso, reminding Pius how he had been warmly received by the king when, as bishop of Siena, he had represented the emperor at Alfonso's court. They begged Pius neither to reject the son of an old friend nor deny him his father's throne, especially when he had the unanimous support of his people. 1

Pius replied, "We loved Alfonso well and we admired him for his noble character, and that will help Ferrante's case a great deal—if he will but do his duty toward the Church of Rome." When asked what Ferrante had to do, he replied that he should pay an annual tax to the Apostolic Camera; and readily supply aid whenever the pope asked for it; and respect the rights of the churches; and order Piccinino to withdraw from Church territory or—should he refuse—compel him by armed force; and grant peace to Sigismondo Malatesta on terms dictated by the pope; and restore Benevento to the Church straight away; and hand Terracina back in ten years' time, having in the meantime paid the bishop of Rome annual tribute for its possession. 2

These terms seemed harsh to Ferrante. Again and again he sent his ambassadors back to try to persuade the pope to settle for less. Pius replied that he was no market trader, who bargained for much to get at least a little. What he had said in their first interview was what he would say in their last; the king could hope for no better terms, even if the pope was about to leave Rome; he must take his kingdom on these terms or do without it. At last Ferrante was beaten, for the pope's mind had remained unchanged throughout, as had his replies. The question was put to the sacred 3

dinandus, cum una semper sententia et una vox pontificis esset. Res ad Collegium deducta est. Cardinales exceptis Gallicis, qui non tam Sedis quam regis erant, pontifici auscultabant; verum et illi rationibus tandem victi consensere, et utile consilium iudicarunt Ferdinando Regnum concedi—quamvis, ne decreto subscribere cogerentur, impetravere.

4 Erat eo tempore Romae decanus Carnotensis, regis Franciae legatus, qui ad Callistum de rebus Turchorum acturus venerat. Is suae gentis studio magnopere instabat ne Regnum Ferdinando concederetur, laturum id aegre regem suum atque in Apostolicam Sedem ulturum dictitans. Advenerat et Massiliensis episcopus, homo loquax et vanus, a rege Rhenato missus, qui Regnum domino suo asservari petens ingentibus promissis Curiam replebat, si preces audirentur suae; si minus, ruituram Curiam affirmabat. Audivit eum saepenumero Pius et multa promittentem interrogavit: possetne Rhenatus Picininum Ecclesiae cervicibus imminentem armis expellere? Quod cum negaret, 'Et quid ergo est', inquit, 'Quod expectemus ab eo, si nobis pereuntibus nullam valet opem afferre? Nobis in Regno necessarius est qui et sua possit et nostra tueri. Vos Regno iam pridem caruistis, ac tamdiu carebitis, donec vires adsint quibus hostem nobis indulgentibus possitis eicere. Interea fortiori cedite!' Atque ita verbosae legationi verbis occurrit.

5 Ferdinando Regnum concessum est ex decreto Senatus, et Latinus cardinalis Ursinus, qui regem in verba Pii ac successorum eius iurantem corona donaret, in Apuliam missus; et cum eo Nicolaus Thyanensis electus, qui postea cardinalatum consecutus est, iter fecit ut occultiora quaedam cum rege transigeret.

college. With the exception of the French, whose loyalties lay less with the See than with their king, the cardinals agreed with the pope; and in the end, reason compelled even the French to concede that the prudent thing would be to give the kingdom to Ferrante. They were excused, however, from having to sign the decree.

The dean of Chartres was in Rome at the time; he had come as the king of France's ambassador to discuss the Turkish question with Calixtus. Jealously guarding his country's interests, he insisted that Ferrante must not be granted the kingdom. Again and again he said that such a move would infuriate his king, who would take his revenge on the Apostolic See. The bishop of Marseilles was in Rome as well, a garrulous and conceited character, who had come to represent King René. Seeking to get the kingdom for his master, he heaped the assembly high with grandiose promises—if they would but answer his prayers. If they would not, he declared, it would be the ruin of the Curia. Pius received him at several audiences and heard him promise much. But when he was asked whether René could send troops to dislodge Piccinino, who threatened the very life of the Church, he answered that he could not. Pius cried, "So what *can* we expect from him, if he can't help us in our darkest hour? When it comes to the Regno, we need someone who can protect our possessions as well as his own. It's been a long time since you've had that kingdom and it will be longer still before you get it again—unless you have the power to expel the enemy. Then you'll have our favor. For now, give way to the stronger man!" To this speech the wordy ambassador could not reply. 4

By decree of the college, the kingdom was granted to Ferrante. Cardinal Latino Orsini was sent to Apulia to give the king his crown and hear him swear allegiance to Pius and his successors. With him went Niccolò, bishop-elect of Teano and afterwards a cardinal, to discuss some rather delicate matters with the king.[13] 5

: 6 :

Ordinatio rei publicae Romanae et curialium constitutio.

1 Exin, vocatis ad Urbem baronibus agri Romani, mandatum est ne quis absente pontifice res novas moliretur, pacemque inter sese ut observarent iure iurando adacti sunt; qui contra fecisset, in eum ingens poena statuta. Et quoniam Romanos magnus timor invaserat ne, abeunte pontifice, in perpetuum Romana Curia privarentur, decrevit Pius annuente Senatu ut si extra Urbem claudere se diem extremum contingeret, successoris sui electionem alibi quam Romae fieri non posse, statuto dierum termino, quo cardinales qui Romae reperirentur expectare absentes deberent; et relictis nonnullis cardinalibus et auditoribus Rotae, advocatis ac litigatoribus in Urbe, toto absentiae suae tempore Romanam Curiam apud eos non minus quam secum esse declaravit.

2 Legatis civitatum ac regulorum, qui ex universo patrimonio Ecclesiae Romam venerant, privilegia quae ab antiquis pontificibus obtinuerant (quoad sine controversia iis usi fuissent) confirmavit, et amplius haud parvam censuum partem ad tres annos remisit; quae res supra octuaginta milia auri nummum ascendit. Referendarios instituit eos qui fuerant praecessoris, et novos aliquos adiecit ex omni natione, diligenter admonitos ac iure iurando adactos, ne pecuniam neve dona sui officii causa ulla reciperent; nam simoniacam pravitatem praecipuo insectabatur odio.

3 Atque ob eam rem, cum secretarios more maiorum peracto prandio aliquot diebus ad se admisisset atque, his fidem habens, epistolas quas illi attulerant obsignasset, repperissetque postea

: 6 :

The papal state put in order; organization of the Curia.

Next, the pope summoned all the barons in Roman territory to a meeting in the city. He issued a stern warning against stirring up trouble while the pope was away. The barons swore to keep the peace; if anyone broke it, the penalty would be severe. And, because the Romans were desperately worried that the pope's departure would mean the permanent loss of the Curia, Pius announced (with the approval of the college) that if he should die away from the city, the election of his successor must take place in Rome. He also set a time limit after which those cardinals who were in Rome need not wait for those who were absent to return. And he decreed that a number of cardinals, auditors of the Rota, advocates and litigators should remain in the city throughout the period of his absence; the Roman Curia would reside with them as much as with him. 1

All the cities and principalities of the papal state had sent ambassadors to Rome. Pius confirmed them in the privileges that previous popes had granted them—provided they had enjoyed them without controversy. In addition, he remitted a substantial portion of their tribute for the next three years, a sum exceeding 80,000 gold pieces. He reappointed the *referendarii* who had served under his predecessor and appointed several new ones from every nation. Solemnly he warned them and bound them by oath not to take money or gifts for their services; for he particularly abhorred the sin of simony.[14] 2

For a short while after his election he had, in the time-honored way, admitted his secretaries to his presence each day after lunch. So completely did he trust them that he signed the letters they put before him without question. But when he discovered that they 3

infideliter secum esse actum et iniqua per pecuniam absoluta negotia, deinceps aditum ad se cunctis inhibuit exceptis duobus — Iacobo Lucensi, qui postea cardinalis effectus est, et Gregorio Lollio, fratre consobrino — quorum spectata virtus ab omni labe procul aberat.

4 E manu cardinalium supplicationes noluit accipere; si quas obtulerunt, ad referendarios remisit, ne per potentiam res iniquas extorquerent. Supplicationibus iura partium concernentibus Eberardum episcopum Spoletanum, egregium iure consultum et integritate morum ac opinione iustitiae laudatissimum praefecit, qui et ipse demum rubro pileo donatus est. Ac per hunc modum et facilis expeditio rerum erat et incorrupta et Romanam Curiam sequentibus admodum accepta, quibus non fuit necesse ad fores cardinalium dies ac noctes pro precibus impetrandis excubare.

: 7 :

Iohannes Solerius ab episcopatu priore deiectus, a Pio restituitur, et Roverius ingratus punitur, Piique integritas.

1 Per idem tempus venit Romam Iohannes Solerius, Divinarum Scripturarum sublimis interpres, de quo supra mentionem fecimus.[13] Hunc Callistus vivente Alfonso rege Aragonum Barchinonensi praefecerat ecclesiae, deinde illo mortuo invitum ad alteram transtulerat in Regno Siciliae, sibique apud Barchinonenses Bartholomeum Ragazium, thesaurarium suum nominis haudqua-

had been dealing dishonestly with him, getting improper transactions approved in return for money, he refused to see them again. He made only two exceptions: Jacopo of Lucca, who later became a cardinal, and Gregorio Lolli, his own cousin. Their integrity was spotless and above question.[15]

He refused to receive petitions from the cardinals directly, and 4
if they offered him any, he sent them straight to the *referendarii* so they would not be able to peddle their influence improperly. He put Berardo, the bishop of Spoleto, in charge of petitions concerning the rights of parties — he was a distinguished lawyer, highly esteemed for his probity and his reputation for justice, who himself later received a red hat.[16] In this way, the affairs of state were administered smoothly and with honesty. This was a welcome change for those who had business with the Roman Curia, for they no longer had to wait days and nights on the cardinals' doorsteps in order to have their petitions heard.

: 7 :

Giovanni Sogliera restored by Pius to the bishopric denied him by the previous pope. Roverio punished for his ingratitude. Pius's integrity.

Around this time, Giovanni Sogliera arrived in Rome, an inspired 1
interpreter of the scriptures, as we have mentioned before.[17] During the reign of Alfonso of Aragon, Calixtus had appointed him to the church at Barcelona, but after the king's death, he transferred him against his will to another church in the kingdom of Sicily, and appointed in his place at Barcelona his own treasurer, Bartolomeo Regas, who was hardly renowned for his probity. Giovanni complained of the injury done to him; he asked for his old church

quam probati suffecerat. Iniuria se affectum Iohannes querebatur, suamque repetebat ecclesiam, atque amicitiam prae se ferebat, qua Pio pontifici apud Neapolim iunctus fuerat nondum pontificatum adepto maximum. Exaudivit amicum praesul, et abrogato[14] Callisti decreto ad priorem ecclesiam remisit, quam ille summa cum laude gubernavit accepti beneficii et memor et gratus.

2 Dispar animus erga Callistum Tertium inventus est Bernardi Roveri. Hunc haud merentem et minus doctum Callistus ad collegium auditorum assumpserat, pluribusque beneficiis et honoribus affecerat, pro quibus vita functus insignem contumeliam rettulit. Scripsit enim Roverius ecclesiae Valentinae capitulo Callistum tandem vita excessisse, sui saeculi dedecus atque ignominiam Valentinae urbis, quae illi patria fuerat; gessisse cardinalatum turpiter, papatum foedissime, rapinis ac pessimis moribus Romanam Ecclesiam deturpasse; in ultimo vitae articulo scientem se Gehennae mancipium, esse nec confiteri voluisse, nec more Christiano ecclesiastica sacramenta suscipere; laetandum tamen, quod tam horribili monstro Ecclesia tandem liberata sit.

3 Non tulit eam ingratitudinem pacato animo Pius pontifex; sceleratumque hominem, qui tanta mentitus esset, comprehensum coniecit in vincula, ac nepoti suo in arce Sancti Angeli commendavit. Ille incautus petenti cardinali Sancti Petri hominem tradidit. Increpavit nepotem Pius durissimis verbis, neque dignum venia reputavit, quamvis diceret in Romana Curia cardinali credendum esse, qui se iussa pontificis exsequi affirmaret (quae consuetudo ad praefectos arcium nequaquam extenderetur); nec mora, Roverium rursus in carcerem arripi iussit. Quae res cardinali[15] Sancti Petri et Sancti Eustachii molestissima fuit, sed utrumque contempsit pontifex indigna petentem.

back and recalled the friendship that had bound him to Pius at Naples before he became pope. The pontiff heard his old friend, annulled the decree of Calixtus and sent him back to his former church, which he went on to administer most admirably, mindful of the kindness he had received and ready to show his gratitude for it.

Very different was the stance Bernardo Roverio adopted toward 2
Calixtus. The old pope had enrolled this man in the college of auditors, though he did not deserve it and could hardly be called a scholar; he had also granted him numerous benefices and honors. In return, at his death, Calixtus suffered the grossest kind of abuse. Roverio wrote to the chapter of the church at Valencia announcing that Calixtus had finally died and calling him the scandal of his age, a disgrace to the church of his native province; he had been a shameless cardinal and an iniquitous pope; he had befouled the Church of Rome with corruption and graft; in his last moments, knowing he was a slave of Gehenna, he had refused to make his confession or to receive the sacraments like a Christian; it was a cause for celebration that the Church was at last free from the clutches of this horrible monster.

Pope Pius would not tolerate such ingratitude. He had the ly- 3
ing scoundrel seized and taken in chains to his nephew at the Castel Sant'Angelo;[18] but the young man ill-advisedly released him to the cardinal of San Pietro in Vincoli[19] at the latter's request. Pius rebuked his nephew roundly and resolved not to forgive him, even though he insisted in the Curia that a cardinal had to be believed when he said he was carrying out the pope's orders — though this rule can hardly extend the to commandants of castles. The pope immediately ordered that Roverio be arrested and returned to prison. This bitterly offended the cardinals of Sant'Eustachio and San Pietro, but the pope dismissed their protests as beneath consideration.

4 Cardinalis Sancti Eustachii regio sanguine tumens (erat enim regis Portugalliae consobrinus frater) pontificem adiit, ac prae iracundia vix verba formare potens, 'Oro,' inquit, 'pontifex, Roverium mihi dones. Nisi dederis, non avellar a tuis pedibus.' Negavit se pontifex sontem hominem et tanti criminis reum impune dimissurum. Institit[16] iterum atque iterum cardinalis, et ampullosa verba profundens longe ab ea reverentia recessit, quam summo pontifici cardinales impendere consueverunt.

5 Tum pontifex, 'Ignoscimus,' ait, 'adolescentiae tuae.' (Erat enim cardinalis tres et viginti natus annos.) 'Nondum nosti, quibus verbis alloquenda est maiestas summi pontificis.[17] Sanguine ortus regio Christi vicarium contemnis? Longe sublimior est Christi, quam tua nobilitas. Reris abeundo — si tamen possis abire — Romanam Curiam perituram, quasi tuo splendore fulgeat? Desipis? Clarum te Sedes Apostolica facit, non tu illi decus affers, quae et si numquam natus esses, suo tamen fulgore orbem illuminaret, mater ac magistra morum, lex religionis et veritatis regula. Abi! Numquam Roverius libertatem assequetur, nisi Callisti nepotes, quibus iniuria facta est, veniam ei dederint.'

6 Atque his dictis in cubiculum se recepit. Cardinalis plenus irarum domum concessit, et paulo post repetens verba pontificis ad se reversus amare flevit; nec multos moratus dies praesulem adiens errati veniam petiit, qua facile obtenta a nepotibus Callisti impetravit, ut peccatum Roverii sibi dimitterent, eiusque libertatem secum una a summo pontifice peterent. Quo facto Roverius non absque turpi notha dimissus est; neque cardinalis absque rubore abiit, qui cum summo praesule contendere fuisset ausus.

The cardinal of Sant'Eustachio came before the pope.[20] Royal blood made him arrogant—he was a cousin of the king of Portugal—and his fury was such that he could barely spit out his words: "Pope, I demand you give me Roverio. I'll not be torn from your feet until you do." The pope replied that he would never release such a criminal before he had been punished. Again and again the cardinal pressed him, pouring out a torrent of speech, all of it rather unlike the respect cardinals usually show to the pope. 4

Then Pius replied, "We are not angry, for you are young." (The cardinal was only twenty-three.) "You do not yet know what terms should be used when the majesty of the supreme pontiff is addressed. Is it your royal blood that makes you scorn the Vicar of Christ? Christ is far more noble than you. Do you think that your departure (if indeed you will be allowed to depart!) will ruin the Roman Curia, as if your light were the only thing that makes it shine? Can you be such a fool? It is the Apostolic See that gives you glory, not you who confer honor on it. Had you never been born, the Church would still light the world with its glow. She is the mother and teacher of virtue, the law of religion, the rule of truth. Away with you! Roverio will never be free unless Calixtus's nephews, who are the injured parties here, give him pardon." 5

With these words he withdrew to his chamber. The cardinal went home filled with rage, but before long, as he reflected on the pope's words, he came to his senses and burst into bitter tears. A few days later he went to Pius and begged forgiveness for his error. This was readily granted, and he then persuaded Calixtus's nephews to pardon Roverio for his offense and join him in pleading with the pope for his liberty. As a result, Roverio was released, though not without a stain on his reputation. Nor did the cardinal emerge with his honor intact, for he had dared to challenge the pope. 6

: 8 :

Petri Sancti Marci cardinalis petulantia Piique sancta redargutio.

1 Similem contumaciam et Petrus cardinalis Sancti Marci per eosdem fere dies ostendit, similemque confusionem reportavit. Unus is fuerat ex cardinalibus, qui summo conatu Pium in adipiscendo apostolatu adiuverant, atque idcirco non aequa tantum petenti sibi, sed iniqua quoque negari nefas arbitrabatur. Pius etiam[18] amicis indigna quaerentibus durus erat. Obiisse fama fuit per eos dies apud Viturbium rectorem parrochialis ecclesiae Sanctae Mariae Prunetanae agri Florentini, in qua Virginis imago est, quam mira religione populi venerantur tamquam pluviae serenitatisque donatricem, cum necessitas ingruit. Dives illic templum est et assiduis mortalium votis insigne.

2 Accepit vacationem eius cardinalis, et adiens pontificem id commendari sibi efflagitavit, nec aliud honestatis suae petitioni adiunxit, nisi familiarem suum fuisse cuius morte sacerdotium vacaret — quamquam neque hoc ipsum erat verum, sed cardinalis omnes in familia sua ascribebat, qui se aliquando salutassent. Pio indigna petitio visa est, responditque parrochialem ecclesiam, ad quam plebes multae concurrerent, cardinali non esse commendandam, et eam praesertim quae laicos haberet patronos; monuitque cardinalem, ut maiora expectans aequo animo ferret non impetrasse minora.

3 Ille indignatus, tamquam gravi contumelia fuisset affectus, 'Si parva,' inquit, 'non impetro, qui sperem magna? Non est, ut video,

: 8 :

The anger of Pietro, cardinal of San Marco, and the holy way Pius answered him.

1 Around this time Pietro, cardinal of San Marco,[21] likewise behaved intractably and likewise was confounded. He was one of the cardinals who had tried hardest to help Pius win the papacy and therefore he imagined that Pius could not justly refuse any request of his, whether honorable or not. Now Pius dealt very severely with those who made improper requests, even if they were his friends. At just this time it was reported that the rector of the parish church of Santa Maria in Impruneta, in Florentine territory, had died at Viterbo. In this church there is a statue of the Virgin which attracts extraordinary popular devotion, for the people believe she can send either rain or clear weather as necessity requires. The church is rich and renowned for the votive offerings given it by the people.

2 The cardinal heard that this church had fallen vacant. He came before the pope and begged him to give it to him. He advanced no claims in support of his petition aside from the fact that the man who had died and left the benefice vacant had been a member of his household. But even this was hardly true, for the cardinal used to enroll in his household anyone who ever paid him a call. Pius thought the petition unseemly and replied that a parish church frequented by great numbers of common people, especially one that had lay patrons, should not be assigned to a cardinal. Furthermore, he reminded Pietro that he could expect greater favors in future and so ought not to take offense if he failed to win lesser ones now.

3 The cardinal took this badly, acting as if it were a gross insult. "If I don't get small favors," he cried, "how can I hope for great

cur amplius apud te morer. Melius in ecclesia mea Vicentina serviam Deo. Sine me domum ire, atque illic tandem post multos labores otio frui!'

4 Cui pontifex: 'Perge!' ait, 'Et sine te Romana Ecclesia suam gloriam retinebit. Nemo facultatem abeundi petat, qui nolit impetrare. Decipietur! Nulli negabitur, quando nemo est in cuius locum aeque bonus aut melior suffici nequeat.

5 Cardinalis, his auditis, tamquam in alteram diem Romanam Curiam relicturus, exosculatis pontificis pedibus in aedes suas apud Sanctum Marcum concessit, iussitque ad recessum cuncta parari. Sed nocte consilium maturante, cogitare coepit quam minima est cardinalium existimatio qui absque legatione a Curia Romana[19] procul agunt, et quam contemptui sunt[20] omnibus quos sequitur pontificis odium. Nam sicut tenebrosum est lunare corpus, cum terra interposita non illustratur a sole, ita et cardinalis extra pontificis gratiam agens luce caret, et obscurus habetur atque abiectus. Interposuit igitur Philippum cardinalem Bononiensem, qui se Pio reconciliaret, et ipse mox secutus; errorem suum professus in gratiam rediit.

6 Nec diu post in alium incidit errorem, schedulam per Thomam cubicularium pontifici mittens, in qua petebat litteras omnes arrestari, quae de rebus sub ditione Venetorum consistentibus se inconsulto decernerentur; atque hoc idem a Callisto concessum asseverabat. Schedulam cum legisset Pius, 'Ergo,' inquit, 'non me Veneti, sed cardinalem Sancti Marci summum pontificem adorabunt? Si potuit Callistus superiorem ferre, non potest Pius mortalem hominem! Deo tantum et Sacris Litteris subiecta est auctoritas nostra!' Atque his dictis supplicationis papyrum in ignem proiecit. Quod cum accepisset cardinalis, subticuit ne maioribus urgeretur stimulis.

ones? There's no reason for me to hang around here anymore. I can serve God better in my own church at Vicenza. Let me go home; after all the work I've done, let me enjoy my retirement there."

The pope replied, "Go on then! The Church of Rome won't be robbed of its glory if you take your leave. No one should one ask permission to depart unless he really wants it—otherwise, he'll be sorry! I'll not refuse anyone, for there's no one who can't be replaced by someone equally good or better." 4

When the cardinal heard this, he made as if to leave the Roman Curia the next day. He kissed the pope's feet and withdrew to his palace at San Marco, where he ordered preparations for his departure. But that night he began to think better of his plan, remembering how slight are the reputations enjoyed by cardinals who dwell away from the Roman Curia (unless they are on an embassy) and how universally unpopular are those whom the pope does not love. For as the moon falls dark when the earth blocks out the light of the sun, so a cardinal out of papal favor is deprived of light and seems an obscure and dismal figure. Therefore he sent Filippo, the cardinal of Bologna, to intercede and reconcile him to Pius. He himself followed shortly thereafter and, after confessing his guilt, was restored to the pope's good graces. 5

Not long afterward, however, he fell into error again. He sent his chamberlain Tommaso to the pope with a note demanding that resolutions regarding matters under Venetian jurisdiction should be suspended if they had been drafted without consulting him; this was a concession, he said, which Calixtus had granted him. When Pius read the note he cried, "So the Venetians should revere San Marco as their pope instead of me, should they? Calixtus may not have minded, but Pius will not tolerate any mortal man above himself! Our authority is subject only to God and holy writ." And with that, he threw the note on the fire. The cardinal, when he heard of this, held his peace for fear of yet more stinging rebukes. 6

: 9 :

Promotio Bernardi ad ecclesiam Agrigentinam, et Francisci Venerei mutata fortuna.

1 Vacavit et tunc ecclesia cathedralis in Agrigento, quae urbs in Trinacria olim celeberrima fuit, et apud veteres rerum scriptores late memoratur. Hanc Pius Bernardo Bosco, praestanti iuris interpreti et auditori Rotae, nihil petenti et prorsus ignoranti commisit, quia et boni nominis erat, et olim Basileae socius eius fuerat; atque uno hoc opere et amico satisfecit, et auditores omnes in spem erexit eadem praemia suis laboribus expectantes, quae suum collegam assecutum viderant. Nec decepti sunt, nam Pius plerosque postea excellentes viros ex eis ad pontificales assumpsit ecclesias. Verum Bernardo perniciosa[21] fuit pontificis gratia, qui dum ecclesiae suae possessionem summo studio quaerit, nec assequi potest obstante non aequo rege, labore simul et taedio confectus aegritudinem incidit, quae vitam eius breviorem reddidit atque ipsum extinxit—etsi viro bono in lucro est quantocius mori!

2 Fuerat apud Callistum potens Franciscus Venerius, natione Venetus, qui ut pecuniam pontifici permultam[22] accumularet, mensariorum libros inspicere voluit, et sumpta occasione quod res Apostolicae Camerae male tractassent, grandi eos aere mulctavit. Illi apud Pium Callisto mortuo recurrentes aes omne recuperarunt, et Cosmas quidem Medices uncias auri mille quingentas vendicavit, nec Ambrosio Spinochiae minor summa restituta est, idemque circa reliquos servatum qui se male mulctatos a Francisco ferebant. Illum Callistus in extremis suae vitae diebus vinctum in Arcem

: 9 :

Bernardo promoted to the church of Agrigento; the rise and fall of Francesco Venier.

At this time the cathedral of Agrigento in Sicily fell vacant. This 1 was once a very famous city, frequently mentioned by the ancient historians. Pius granted the church to Bernardo Bosco, an eminent jurist and auditor of the Rota, even though he had not asked for it and indeed did not know the gift was forthcoming; for he was well regarded and had been one of Pius's colleagues at Basel. With this act Pius both gratified his friend and raised the hopes of all the other auditors, who now could expect the same reward for their labors which they had seen their colleague receive. Nor were they disappointed, for Pius later named several excellent men from their ranks to pontifical churches. But the pope's favor proved ruinous to Bernardo: though he tried with all his might to gain possession of his church, he was blocked by the opposition of an unjust king. Worn out by work and worry, he contracted an illness which shortened his life and ended in his death—though, of course, a good man does well to die as soon as he can.

Francesco Venier, a Venetian, had been an influential figure at 2 Calixtus's court. In an attempt to raise as much money as possible for the pope, he had asked to inspect the books of the bankers. He then claimed that they had mismanaged the affairs of the Apostolic Camera, and took this as a pretext for demanding a heavy fine. At Calixtus's death the bankers appealed to Pius and recovered all their money. Cosimo de' Medici received 1500 ounces of gold and Ambrogio Spannocchi no less a sum, and similar restitution was made to others who claimed to have been unjustly fined by Francesco. At the end of his life, Calixtus had imprisoned the man in the Castel Sant'Angelo. Pius released him from there into

Sancti Angeli miserat; Pius inde deductum senatori tradidit ut creditoribus in Capitolio satisfaceret; sed ante mortuus est quam eius facta cognoscerentur.

: 10 :

Pii discessus et eius dissuadentibus amicis constantia.

1 Sic rebus in Urbe dispositis, ad cuius regimen Nicolaus Sancti Petri cardinalis dimissus est, pontifex maximus ad XIII Kalendas Februarias, quae dies profectionis dicta est, ex palatio apostolico quod est apud Sanctum Petrum in Vaticano intempesta nocte ad aedem Sanctae Mariae Maioris in Esquilio monte se contulit; ibique sequenti die commoratus frequenti populo ac vehementer lacrimanti lacrimans ipse benedixit, et postridie sole nondum orto per thermas Diocletiani et collem Suburae ad portam Flaminiam (nunc Populi vocant) et deinde ad pontem Milvium descendit. Cardinales eo usque secuti sunt, et optimatum[23] Urbis plebisque maxima pars.

2 Ibi equitum in armis expectabant turmae quae pontificem tutum[24] deducerent. Tum dimisso populo sex cardinales delecti sunt, qui papae servirent iter agenti: Vilhelmus Rhotomagensis, e regia stirpe natus; Alanus Avinionensis, nobilis Brito; Philippus Bononiensis, Nicolai pontificis quondam frater; Petrus Sancti Marci; Prosper Columnensis; Rhodericus vicecancellarius, qui Romanorum pontificum nepotes fuerunt: Eugenii, Martini, Callisti. Cardinales reliqui, ex quis nonnulli valitudinarii fuerunt, iussi sunt Romae[25] manere, aut mitius veris tempus expectare, ac tum pone

the custody of a Roman senator in order to get him to satisfy his creditors on the Capitol, but he died before his affairs could be investigated.

: 10 :

Pius's departure; his steadfast disregard for the protests of his friends.

The pope had thus arranged matters in the city and left Nicholas, cardinal of San Pietro, in charge. On the 20th of January, the day set for his departure, he set out in the dead of night, going from the palace of St. Peter's on the Vatican hill to Santa Maria Maggiore on the Esquiline. He stayed there the next day and tearfully blessed a throng of people who were themselves all in tears. The following day he descended past the baths of Diocletian and down the hill of the Suburra to the Flaminian Gate, now called Porta del Popolo, and went from there to the Milvian bridge. The cardinals accompanied him this far together with a great many nobles and citizens of Rome. 1

Troops of armed cavalry were waiting there to guard the pope on his journey. The people were sent back and six cardinals were chosen to attend the pope as he traveled: Guillaume of Rouen, a prince of the royal house; Alain of Avignon, a nobleman of Brittany; Filippo of Bologna, the brother of Pope Nicholas; and Pietro of San Marco, Prospero Colonna and the vice-chancellor Rodrigo — who were the nephews of Popes Eugenius, Martin and Calixtus, respectively. Pius ordered the remaining cardinals, some of whom were in poor health, to stay in Rome for the duration or at least wait for spring, when the weather would be milder, before following the pope. Though he could make allowances for the ail- 2

sequi. Et cum aliorum aegritudinibus pontifex ignosceret, suae nequaquam pepercit, qui podagrico dolore et pluribus affectus morbis subire mortis periculum maluit quam constitutam profectionis diem negligere. Obstabant amici, multisque artibus remorari praesulem adnitebantur, horridam hiemem et rigidas Apennini alpes et itineris mille pericula memorantes.

3 Quae cum frustra obiectarentur, non defuere qui dicerent, 'En, pontifex, si nulla tui corporis te retinet cura, respice saltem quae tibi commissa est, Romanam Ecclesiam, et quot ei insidiae praeparentur animadverte! Et quis Patrimonium Beati Petri te absente tuebitur? Quam primum Padum transmiseris, invadent regnum tuum lupi rapaces. Nam quae terra est tyrannis, ne dicam latronibus magis fecunda, quam tua? Picenum alii, Umbriam alii, alias alii provincias dilacerabunt, nudabuntque prorsus tuam sponsam. Cum redieris, non invenies locum ubi reclines caput, quem possis tuum dicere.'

4 Ad haec pontifex, 'Meliora,' inquit, 'praestabit Deus, cuius acturi causam peregre proficiscimur. Quod si permiserit divina miseratio id fieri quod timetis, privari his temporalibus bonis Ecclesiam quam fide malumus. Nisi servamus quod promissum est, perit fides nostra, et quis amplius credet nobis? Religio quoque in discrimine ponitur, quam Turchi oppugnant, adversus quos conventus indictus est. Sin pergimus, nutat temporale regnum Ecclesiae. At hoc saepe amissum est et saepe recuperatum. Spirituali si semel exciderimus, incertum est an vendicari aliquando poterit. Pereant haec fluxa, dum solidiora illa retineamus!' Nec plura locutus iter ingressus est.

ments of others, he still had no patience for his own. Despite his gout and various other complaints, he preferred to risk his life rather than defer the day set for his departure. His friends remonstrated with him and tried various arguments to delay him, reminding him of the terrible winter weather, the snow in the Apennines and the thousand perils he would face on the road.

When none of these objections proved effective, people yet 3
came forward to say, "Your Holiness, consider this: if concern for your own health cannot make you stay, at least have some regard for the Roman Church entrusted to your care. Look at the snares that are laid for it! Who will protect the patrimony of Peter when you are away? The minute you cross the Po, ravenous wolves[22] will fall upon your kingdom; for what land breeds more usurpers, not to say brigands, than yours? Some will wreak havoc in Piceno, others in Umbria, and others in other provinces still. They will strip your bride bare. You'll return to find no place to call your own or lay your head."[23]

The pope replied, "We go to plead God's case, and He will 4
provide better than that. But even if Divine Compassion should allow that which you fear to occur, still I would rather see the Church robbed of these temporal possessions than of her honor. For if we do not keep our promise, our honor is lost, and who will ever trust us again? The Christian faith also hangs in the balance, assailed as it is by the Turks whom this congress is called to combat. If we proceed, it is true, our temporal power may decline; but this has often been lost and often recovered. If we abandon the kingdom of the spirit, though, I am not sure we can ever win it back. These transient things may slip away, provided we keep hold of what really matters." And without further ado he set out on his way.

: II :

Pontificis profectio et Asisii restitutio, Eversique callida mandata et Pii ad Picininum responsum.

1 Prima illi pernoctatio apud Campinianum fuit, qui locus Ursinorum est, passibus ab Urbe XVI milibus distans. Hic Tranensis archiepiscopus, Latini cardinalis frater, et Pium pontificem et universam Curiam magnifico apparatu excepit.

2 Nondum Picininus Asisium restituerat, nec tamen pontifex a coepto itinere destitit, etsi per agrum quem ille occupaverat[26] transeundum esset. Ibat spe plenus, nec auxilium Dei sibi quovis pacto defuturum arbitrabatur, cuius causam ageret. Neque frustrata se[27] est pia praesulis intentio, nam die sequenti, cum inter Nepesum et Civitatem Castellanam medio ferme spatio viam faceret, litterae allatae sunt quae restitutionem Asisii Gualdique ac Nuceriae certissimam nuntiavere.

3 Vix eas legerat, cum festinanter adequitans cancellarius quidam Eversi Anguillariae comitis pontificem petit, et habere magna quae referat mandante comite dicit. Iussus fari: 'Herus,' inquit, 'meus eunti tibi longinquam viam praedicit: antequam adsint Augusti Kalendae, non parvas in regno tuo oborituras turbas; tumque cogniturum te qui fidem tibi asseveraverint.'[28] Cui pontifex, 'Redito,' ait, 'ad eum qui te misit, et[29] Asisium Ecclesiae restitutum referto!' Atque his nuntium tristem dimisit; sciebat enim id molestiae futurum Everso, qui Picininum meretriculae nomen mereri aiebat, si se aliquando Asisio et tam egregia munitione extrudi sineret.

4 Picininus autem, antequam occupatas urbes restituere statuisset, saepe per internuntios papae dixerat, 'Videto quid agas, pontifex, adversus fortunae hominem arma capiens!' Ad quae pontifex,

: II :

The pope's journey. Assisi restored. A cunning order from Everso and Pius's reply to Piccinino.

The pope spent the first night at Campagnano, a town belonging to the Orsini some sixteen miles from Rome. Here the archbishop of Trani,[24] who was Cardinal Latino's brother, received Pope Pius and all the Curia with great ceremony. 1

Piccinino had yet to surrender Assisi, but the pope would not change his route even though it lay through territory still occupied by the general. He sallied forth full of hope, never doubting even for a moment that God, whose cause he was defending, would support him. Nor was his sacred trust misplaced, for the next day, as he was about halfway down the road from Nepi to Civita Castellana, he received word that Assisi, Gualdo and Nocera had been restored to him. 2

He scarcely had a chance to read the note before the chancellor of Count Everso of Anguillara dashed up on horseback and told the pope he brought an important message from the count. Commanded to speak, he said, "My master sends you a warning as you start your long journey: before the first of August there will be a great disturbance in your kingdom, and then you will learn who is loyal to you." The pope answered, "Go and tell the man who sent you that Assisi has been restored to the Church," and with these words he sent the messenger away in distress; for he knew this news would trouble Everso, who had often said that if Piccinino ever let himself be dislodged from the great ramparts of Assisi, he would deserve to be called a little whore. 3

Piccinino, before deciding to restore the cities he had seized, sent several messengers to the pope to say, "Your Holiness, consider what you do when you take arms against Fortune's favorite!" 4

'Stulte,' inquit, 'Picininus egerit, si suam fortunam experiri cum nostra tentaverit. Nam si fortunae ascribere status hominum licet, longe maior fortuna est in solio Beati Petri sedere quam equitum aliquot alas ductare; quamquam si recte loqui velimus, Deus ipse est qui regna et status omnes distribuit. Fortunae inane nomen et vana gentilium inventio.'

: 12 :

De Eversi origine et moribus.

1 Hic, quoniam Eversi mentio incidit et saepe huius hominis faciendus est sermo, pauca de ipso dicenda sunt, ut intellegant posteri cum quibus monstris Pio pontifici concertatio fuerit.

2 Anguillaria vetus est oppidum quatuordecim milibus passuum ab Urbe distans, lacui adiacens qui propter anguillarum capturam oppido nomen dedit. Hoc sibi nobiles quidam ex Germania profecti vendicarunt,[30] qui successu temporis dominatu et opibus aucti comites tandem Anguillariae dicti sunt, Ursinorum familiae foederibus et amicitia coniuncti. Horum domus nostra aetate ad duos fratres redacta est, quorum alteri Dulcis nomen fuit, Eversus alteri. Dulcis rei bellicae apprime peritus, multis facinoribus nobilitatus, relictis duobus filiis excessit e vita. Eversus nepotum tutelam iniit, etsi praedonis magis quam tutoris personam gessit, cui nihil dulcius fuit quam rapere.

3 Assuetus in armis, non minus consanguineis et amicis quam hostibus nocuit; Romanis pontificibus, quamvis dominis suis,

To each, the pope would reply, "Piccinino is a fool if he tries to pit his fortune against ours; for if men acquire rank by their fortunes, there is far greater fortune in sitting on the throne of Peter than in commanding a few squadrons of cavalry. But to tell the truth, it is God who grants every dominion and rank. Fortune is but a meaningless name, an idle pagan invention."

: 12 :

Everso's background and character.

Here, as we have mentioned Everso and as we shall have cause to speak of him again in this work, it is necessary to say a little about him, so that later generations may understand with what monsters Pope Pius had to contend.[25] 1

Anguillara is an ancient town some fourteen miles from Rome. 2 It overlooks a lake where people fish for eels, and it is from them that the town derives its name. Long ago, it was captured by a group of high-born German invaders; over time they grew rich and powerful and eventually were styled the counts of Anguillara. Ties of friendship and formal treaties bound them closely to the Orsini. In our day, the house was reduced to two brothers named Dulcio and Everso. Dulcio was a skilled commander, renowned for his many exploits; he died leaving two sons. Everso took responsibility for his nephews' welfare, but he acted more like a bandit than a guardian, for nothing gave him greater pleasure than plunder.

A practised soldier, he made war on his kinsmen and friends as 3 often as he attacked his foes. To the popes, though they were his lords, he was always hostile. He held his own possessions tenaciously and greedily craved those of others. He cared nothing for

semper infensus; sui tenax, alieni cupidus; de religione, de Deo nihil sentiens, mundum casu regi et mortales animas dictitans hominum aeque ac iumentorum, blasphemus ac crudelis, cui tam facile hominem occidere quam pecudem fuit; ad captivorum cruciatum quos oderat, durissima et prius inaudita excogitavit tormenta.

4 Subiectos praedis ac furtis aluit, qui vellent in armis servire; reliquos durissimo attrivit imperio, quos sex dierum suorum agrorum cultura fatigatos, unde soluto censu viverent, septima quaque die ut sibi laborarent coegit, quae idcirco dominica diceretur, quia domino esset obnoxia; dominum autem se ipsum esse aiebat. Uxores eorum et filias in palatium rapiens prostituebat, stupris et adulteriis cuncta permiscens; neque incestus caruit infamia, tamquam pudicitiae filiarum illuserit. Filios saepenumero everberavit ac ferro impetiit. Ecclesiarum bona diripuit. In audaces timidus, fortis adversus ignavos. Laboris et inediae patiens, cum fuit necessum; ubi quies data est, temulentus et vorax et voluptatibus serviens. Ursinorum relicto foedere Columnensibus iunctus est, cum de successione comitis Taliacozii cum illis non conveniret, diuque bellum inter Ursinos et ipsum agitatum est eventu vario. Tandem indutiae in annos triginta factae sunt. Nepotibus Anguillariam, quae fuerat eorum haereditas, abstulit occasione recepta quod Ursinorum parti faverent.

5 Haec de Everso hoc in loco dixisse sat fuerit, cuius in sequentibus saepe fiet mentio. Nunc ad Pium revertamur, qui ubi Asisium absque armis recuperatum cognovit, longe iocundior iter suum secutus est, intellegens Deum, qui coeptis aspirasset, sibi faventissimum esse et optimis auspiciis res inchoatas. Non tamen recta via

religion or God, and often maintained that the world was ruled by chance and the souls of men and beasts alike were not immortal. He was blasphemous and cruel and could kill a man as easily as he could a sheep. In order to prolong the agonies of captives he despised, he devised excruciating and unspeakable tortures.

Those subjects of his who were willing to serve in his army he 4 supported by plunder and theft; the rest he crushed under the most oppressive tyranny. Exhausted as they were from tilling their fields six days a week in order to pay their tribute and scrape together a living for themselves, he forced them to work the seventh day for him; this was called *domenica* because it belonged to the Lord and the lord, he said, was he. He raped their wives and daughters in his palace; he constantly indulged in adultery and fornication and was even accused of incest, as if the chastity of his own daughters meant nothing. He often flogged his sons and threatened them with his sword. He plundered the goods of the churches. Against brave men he was a coward; against cowards he was brave. When necessary he could endure hunger and toil, but in times of peace he was a gluttonous drunkard, a slave to appetite. He withdrew from his alliance with the Orsini and joined the Colonna because he could not agree with the former over who should succeed the count of Tagliacozzo. His war against the Orsini raged for a long time, with varying results, until at last they made a truce for thirty years. He seized Anguillara from his nephews, although it was their rightful inheritance, on the grounds that they favored the Orsini.

That is enough, for now, about Everso; we shall mention him 5 often in the following pages. Now let us return to Pius. When the pope heard that Assisi had been recovered without recourse to arms, he carried on in a much happier frame of mind, realizing that God had furthered his undertakings and was clearly on his side. Indeed, his project had begun most auspiciously. Still he thought it best not to proceed straight through Tuscany, for he did

per Tusciam eundum censuit, ut qui Senas ingredi nolebat, priusquam suis civibus conciliaretur. Erat enim eis paulum subiratus, qui nobilitatem ad urbis regimen, quamvis rogati crebro, admittere noluissent.

: 13 :

De Senarum origine atque imperio.

1 Urbs Senarum in Etruria admodum nobilis est, et agrum late patentem possidet. De conditoribus eius multa referuntur fabulosa, verum origo gentis a Romanis est, atque ab his insigne lupae receptum et infantes gemini pendentes ab ubere.[31] Quidam et permixtum his Gallorum genus esse volunt ab eo tempore, quo Galli Senones Urbem irruperunt et a Camillo duce victi fugatique sunt. Aiunt enim utriusque reliquias exercitus, ubi nunc Senae iacent, remansisse et duo edificasse oppida, quae postmodum per tempora Magni Caroli simul iuncta urbem magnam reddiderint; signumque huiusce historiae adducunt quod usque in hanc diem pars tertia civitatis a Camillo nomen retinet (Camilliam enim vocant) et Brandum fontem paulo immutatis litteris a Brenno dictum existimant Gallorum duce.

2 Nos vetustiora haec neque asserimus, neque reiicimus. Illud affirmamus: multos in hac urbe fuisse nobiles et admodum potentes, qui palatia sublimia et altas turres templaque nobilissima extruxerunt rem publicam administrantes. Sed cum inter familias nobiliores ob gubernationem civitatis lites oborirentur[32] et armis aliquando decerneretur, placuit nobilitati regimen plebi dimittere

not wish to enter Siena until he had been reconciled with his fellow citizens. He was rather annoyed that they still refused to admit the nobles into government, despite his repeated requests that they should do so.

: 13 :

The origin of Siena and the extent of its dominions.

Siena is a celebrated city of Tuscany. Its territories are extensive. 1
There are various marvelous tales of its foundation, but the truth is that the people trace their origins back to Rome and it is from there that they took their device of a she-wolf suckling twins. Some people think the Sienese mixed with Gallic stock when the Gauls invaded Rome and Camillus routed the Senonese and put them to flight. For it is said that the remnants of both armies settled in the place where Siena now stands and built two towns; and that afterwards, in the time of Charlemagne, these joined together to form a single large city. As evidence for this story, there is the fact that to this day a third of the city is called Camillia, after Camillus; some people also believe that the spring of Fontebranda was named, with a slight change of letters, after Brennus, the chieftain of the Gauls.

We can neither confirm nor deny these ancient tales, but this 2
we know for certain: a great many powerful nobles once dwelled in the city and erected lofty palaces, high towers and splendid churches as they governed the state. But when the more prominent families among them began to quarrel over politics, sometimes even resorting to arms, the nobility as a class decided to resign the administration to the people and reserve for themselves only a handful of offices. They imagined that even though the

paucis sibi muneribus reservatis, arbitrati populares, quamvis rem publicam administrarent, nihil tamen iniussu nobilium facturos quorum potentiam formidarent; quod aliquandiu servatum est. At ubi assueta regimini plebs dulcedinem honoris et potentiae fructum gustare coepit, aucta divitiis et gloria nobilitatem dedignata est, pulsisque urbe nobilium quibusdam familiis, reliquas quasi mancipia sub iugum misit, etsi minores aliquos honores cum eis partiebatur.

3 Quinque, ut supra memoratum est,[33] in urbe hominum genera fuere: alii 'novem' appellati quia dum rem publicam soli tenerent, rectores novem constituerunt; alii eadem ratione 'duodecim' dicti; alii 'reformatores' quia reformationes civitatis aliquas fecisse sunt visi; 'nobiles' a vetustate ac potentia olim vocati nomen retinuere; aliqui 'populares' nominati.

4 Duodecim iam pridem a gubernatione deiecti nullam rei publicae partem habuere; nobilibus quorundam munerum quarta pars credita, verum neque arcibus praeesse, neque inter priores in palatio residere, nec portarum claves custodire permissi. Vis tota regiminis inter novem, reformatores et populares remansit, inter quos succedente tempore, sedente Callisto Tertio, graves inimicitiae succrevere, parsque non parva regentium falso[34] insimulata est, tamquam urbem tradere Picinino conspirasset; ob quam rem quidam securi percussi sunt, nonnulli in exilium acti, alii relegati et pecunia mulctati, adeoque urbs ipsa civili discordia vexata est, ut libertatem amissura propediem cunctorum iudicio videretur.

5 Sed respexit piis oculis magnus Deus dicatam suae matri Mariae Virgini civitatem. Assumptus enim mortuo Callisto Pius pontifex mox dulcissimae patriae curam cepit. Machinamenta,

popular party would have control of the city, they would still be intimidated by the authority of the nobles and do nothing without their permission. And so it turned out, for a while. But once the people had grown accustomed to command, once they had tasted the delights of office and the fruits of power and amassed riches and renown, they turned on the nobility. They banished certain noble families from the city and put the rest under the yoke like slaves, though they did allow them to hold a few minor offices.

There were five parties in the city (as has been explained 3
above):[26] the Nine, so named because when they had sole control of the government they appointed nine chief magistrates; the Twelve, named on the same principle; the Reformers, so called because they were said to have introduced certain reforms to the state; those who were once called Nobles because of their ancient ancestry and influence still retained at least the name; the others were called Popolari.

The Twelve had long since been deposed and no longer played 4
any part in government; the Nobles were entrusted with a quarter of certain classes of office but were barred from commanding fortresses or living as priors in the palace or keeping the keys to the city gates. All political power rested in the hands of the Nine, the Reformers and the Popolari. Over time, bitter feuds grew up among these three parties; during the reign of Calixtus III many office holders were falsely accused of conspiring to betray the city to Piccinino. On this charge some were beheaded, some were driven into exile and some were banished and fined. The whole city was so torn by civil strife that all were certain her liberty would soon be lost.

But almighty God cast his loving gaze upon the city dedicated 5
to his mother, the Virgin Mary. At the death of Calixtus, Pius succeeded to the papacy and at once took thought for his beloved country. He upset the plots contrived against her and by his authority frightened off her enemies. He decided, moreover, that it

quae in illam praeparata fuerant, disiecit et omnes eius hostes auctoritate sua deterruit. Ad salutem autem urbis pertinere magnopere existimavit ut loco civium qui e regimine cecidissent, nobilitas sufficeretur, neque suae dignitati convenire arbitrabatur nobiles, ex quibus ipse natus esset, in patria sua pro servis haberi. Quod Senenses futurum existimantes, ut viam querelae praecluderent, familiam Picolominaeam ex qua Pio esset origo ad regimen vocavere, existimantes eum nil amplius quaesiturum. Verum ipse non suae domus sed totius civitatis curam gerens, nihil actum censuit nisi nobiles universi ad rem gubernandam accersirentur, missisque legatis efflagitavit ut ceteri nobiles Picolominaeis pares fierent.

6 Tumultuare hac petitione populus,[35] dicere pontificem indigna rogare; numquam id facturam civitatem, etiamsi pati obsidionem et filios fame cogatur edere. Contra Pius instare, et nisi pareant, patriae iusta neganti benignam subtracturum se manum asserere; atque ob hanc causam iter flexit et dimissa Tuscia per Umbriam profectus est;[36] Senensibus interminatus, nisi morem gererent, se patria posthabita per[37] Perusiam, Arretium et Florentiam in Galliam profecturum.

: 14 :

De Castellana Civitate et Tiberi ponte transmisso. De Narnia, Spoleto et eius arce.

1 Petiit igitur Civitatem Castellanam, quam nonnulli (ut ante diximus) Veiorum olim fuisse patriam arbitrantur et Camillum in-

would be greatly to the city's advantage if those citizens who had been removed from government should have their places taken by nobles; it did not become his present dignity that the men of this class, to whom he himself belonged by birth, should be treated like slaves in his native city. The Sienese, concerned at the way matters were developing, tried to forestall further complaint by electing the Piccolomini, Pius's own family, to office. They imagined he would demand nothing further; but Pius's care was not for his own house but for the entire state. He declared that he would not be satisfied unless all the nobles were returned to power, and he sent ambassadors to demand that every other family in the order be made equal to the Piccolomini.

At this demand the people erupted in fury; the pope's request 6
was outrageous, they said; the city would never give in, not even if they were forced to endure a siege and starved to the point of eating their own children. But Pius stood firm. He swore that, if they did not obey, he would withdraw his favor from the city on the grounds that it had refused to comply with just demands. It was for this reason, then, that he changed his route. He left Tuscany for Umbria, warning the Sienese that if they did not do as he wished, he would ignore his native country completely and proceed to Mantua by way of Perugia, Arezzo and Florence.

: 14 :

Civita Castellana and the bridge across the Tiber; Narni; Spoleto and its citadel.

And so he went to Civita Castellana. This city, as I have said be- 1
fore, is thought by some to be the site of ancient Veii, where Camillus took refuge in his flight from the judgment of his un-

gratae patriae iudicia fugientem illic exsulasse. Locus est in plano situs, verum ita praeruptis undique rupibus, ut instar altissimi montis teneat et propemodum inexpugnabilis videatur. Episcopus eius loci, vir doctus et amoeni ingenii, Pium pontificem cuius in minoribus constituti amicissimus fuisset, singulari gaudio excepit in palatio quod Nicolaus Quintus pontifex maximus quasi refugium in persecutione, si qua emersisset, magnifice construxerat. Exin Tiberim transiit pontem ligneum recens factum, hedera et virentibus arborum ramis ornatum, non procul ab oppido Malliano quod in Sabinis Romano populo paret.

2 Quacunque iter fecit, populi obviam effusi pontificem salutare; sacerdotes sacra ferentes felicem viam eunti precari; pueri innuptaeque puellae redimiti tempora lauro et olivarum ramos manu gestantes vitam et felicitatem magno praesuli optare; qui fimbrias vestimentorum contingere possent, beatos sese arbitrari. Plena ubique populi itinera et strata virentibus herbis, oppidorum et urbium plateae preciosioribus opertae pannis, domus civium templaque magni Dei praecipuis ornata modis. Sic per Narniam et Interamnem, ubi propemodum mortis periculum adiit dum cives propter equum eius inter se gladiis decertant, Spoletum usque ventum est, neque hic minor pontifici honor exhibitus.

3 Haec urbs in monte sita,[38] in cuius cacumine arx eminet nobilissima (Egidii quondam cardinalis opus), cum natura et situ loci tum murorum altitudine et humana ope munitissima, ex qua tota vallis quae appellatur Spoletana visitur. Amoenus certe locus et saluber. E regione mons est praeruptus atque sublimis in quo, velut in eremo religioni[39] dicata, multi anachoritae famulantur Deo. Insunt et monachorum nonnulla coenobia, in quis viri sanctimonia celebres degunt. Gothis in Italia regnantibus et deinde Longobardis rerum dominis ac postea Francis imperium obtinentibus, magni momenti Spoletum fuit et Umbriae caput ducumque sedes, et usque in hanc diem Spoletani ducatus manet nomen. Hic biduo

grateful country. It lies on level ground but is surrounded on all sides by such steep cliffs that it looks like a lofty mountain and seems almost impregnable. The bishop of the place,[27] a learned and delightful man who had been a great friend of Pius when he was in minor orders, received the pope in his palace with remarkable warmth. (This was a lavish edifice built by Pope Nicholas v to be a refuge in the event of attack.) Here Pius crossed the Tiber by a wooden bridge near Magliano, a Sabine town subject to Rome. It had been built very recently, and was bedecked with ivy and leafy boughs.

All along the road, people poured out to greet the pope. Priests 2
carried holy relics and offered prayers for the success of his journey as he passed; boys and girls wearing laurel crowns[28] and holding olive branches wished the great bishop long life and felicity. Those who could touch the fringe of his garments[29] thought themselves blessed. Everywhere the ways were thronged with people and strewn with fresh straw; in the towns and cities, precious fabrics carpeted the squares; private houses and churches alike were hung with splendid decorations. In this manner he passed through Narni and Terni (where he practically risked his life as the citizens fought for his horse with swords) and on to Spoleto, where he was honored in similar style.

Spoleto is built on a mountain. The famous citadel of Cardinal 3
Egidius[30] commands the summit; it is strongly fortified both by the natural terrain and by the high walls which human effort has raised. From here one has a view of the entire valley known as the Spoletana; it is certainly a charming and healthy spot. Nearby there is a tall, sheer peak where many hermits live and serve God, as if it were a desert dedicated entirely to religion. There are also several monasteries whose monks are renowned for leading saintly lives. When the Goths, Lombards and Franks ruled Italy, Spoleto was an extremely important city, the capital of Umbria and the seat of a duke; the title "Duchy of Spoleto" survives to this day.

pontifex moratus cardinalibus, qui se comitabantur, convivium apparavit et cum eis hilare epulatus est.

: 15 :

De legatione et responso ad imperatorem pro regno Hungariae suscipiendo.

1 Miserat ipse, priusquam Roma excederet, Baptistam Brendum civem Romanum iure consultum ad imperatorem Federicum, qui eum ad conventionem invitaret aut in Utino, aut in Mantua; et cum eo ire iusserat Mattheum cognomento Fugel, unum ex aulicis suis, natione Germanum, qui mores hominum nosset et regionum itinera, ut Baptistam instrueret. Convenerat iam imperatorem ille, et habito apud Gretiam Styriae oppidum colloquio, Mattheum cum responso remiserat, qui pontifici Spoleti occurrit. Summa rerum[40] erat imperatori gravia apud Austriam incumbere negotia, quae negligere non posset, nec vocatum in unum ex duobus locis alternatim nominatis ad veniendum astringi. Cui pontifex remisso Mattheo in hanc sententiam rescripsit:

2 Quamvis in Austria multa essent quae praesentiam imperatoris exigerent, non tamen idcirco fidei orthodoxae negligenda negotia; nam et Roma pontificis praesentia egeret, reliquisse se tamen et Urbem et omne regnum Ecclesiae, ut conventum peteret pro Christiana salute indictum, nec minus a nominatis locis Romam distare quam vel Gretiam vel Civitatem Austriae Novam, imperatoris sedem; pontificem annis plenum et morbis gravem longius iter acturum; indecorum videri caesarem validum et florenti aetate recusare breviorem viam; consulat honori suo, consulat Christianae religioni, neque committat ut sua negligentia Christianam

Here the pope stayed two days. He threw a banquet for the cardinals in his entourage and merrily joined them in their feasting.

: 15 :

An embassy to the emperor; the pope's advice regarding the Hungarian succession.

Before leaving Rome, the pope had despatched the Roman jurist Battista Brendo to Emperor Frederick to invite him to a congress to be held either at Udine or Mantua. He sent one of his German courtiers with him to act as an advisor: Matthias Fugel, who knew the local roads and customs. By now Battista had met the emperor, and after a conference with him at the Styrian town of Graz, he sent Matthias back with his reply. Matthias found the pope at Spoleto. The gist of his message was that the emperor was involved in very important matters in Austria which he could not leave, nor was he bound to answer a summons to "one or the other of two places." The pope sent Matthias back with a letter of reply which made the following points: 1

Many things in Austria might require the emperor's presence; still, he must not neglect the interests of the true faith. The pope was needed in Rome, but he had left the city and the whole kingdom of the Church to attend a congress convened for the salvation of Christianity. Rome was no nearer the places mentioned than Graz or Neustadt, the imperial seat. The pope, weighed down by age and illness, was ready to make the longer journey; it seemed improper that the emperor, who was young and strong, should refuse to make a shorter one. He ought to take some thought for his reputation and for the Christian religion, and do nothing that would let future generations say that Christendom had perished 2

rem publicam perisse aliquando dici possit, neque causidicorum ineptias audiat, qui subtilitate quadam iuris negant eum oboedire oportere, qui ad loca vocetur alternatim nominata; sciat summum ius summam esse iniuriam, neque utendum cavillationibus, ubi bona fides requiritur et Christiana res in discrimine sita est; neque ad incertum locum se fuisse vocatum, qui priusquam domum relinqueret, edocendus[41] erat ex duobus locis quem deberet accedere; parceret his excusationibus, quae apud viros graves ridiculae viderentur; neque Ulricum audiret iuris interpretem magis quam suam conscientiam.

3 Exin, quia scripserat imperator manu sua secretiores litteras, in quis consilium pontificis exposcebat an regnum Hungariae acceptandum sibi esset, si (ut spes erat) regni proceres eum eligerent, in hunc modum rescripsit: 'Qui te regent Hungariae sunt electuri, si fides his habenda est et regnum[42] dare possunt, non dissuademus accipere quod offertur. Sin litem offerunt[43] et belli materiam, contra sentimus, maximeque cavendum censemus ne quid agas quod expeditioni adversus Turchos instituendae impedimento sit. Vale.'

: 16 :

Reconciliatio Senensium, et Venetorum turpe foedus cum Turchis.

1 Inter haec Senenses pontificis indignatione cognita, atque admodum veriti ne se posthabitis per Florentiam peteret Mantuam, molliores facti legatos decreverunt, qui pontificem benigne salu-

by his neglect. He should not waste his time on legal nonsense and juridical hair-splitting about whether a man need obey a summons to "one or the other" of two places. He should remember, "more law, less justice."[31] Now was not the time for sophistry, when Christendom lay in peril and what was needed was good faith. The emperor had not, in fact, been summoned to an indefinite place, since he would be informed well before his departure to which of the two places he should go. He must not proffer these excuses which all serious men found absurd, nor should he pay more heed to his lawyer, Ulrich,[32] than to his own conscience.

The emperor had also sent a more private letter, written in his 3
own hand, asking the pope's advice as to whether he should accept the throne of Hungary, for it seemed likely that the princes of the realm were going to elect him. Pius sent this reply: "If you can trust those who will elect you king of Hungary, and if they have the right to confer the throne, we do not advise against accepting the offer. But if what they are offering you is contention and a pretext for war, then we oppose the matter. Moreover, we advise you to take the utmost care to do nothing that will hinder the launch of a crusade against the Turks. Farewell."[33]

: 16 :

Reconciliation with Siena. The shameful treaty between Venice and the Turks.

In the meantime the Sienese learned that the pope was displeased 1
with them and so, fearing that he would ignore them and travel to Mantua by way of Florence, they decided to adopt a milder stance. They appointed ambassadors to greet the pope courteously and persuade him to pass through his native city. The Venetians, on

tantes iter ei per patriam suaderent. Veneti vero, qui per legatos multa Romae adversus Turchos pontifici promiserant, electionem Utini pro conventu Christianorum celebrando respuerunt, ut qui Turchorum, animos quibus foedere coniuncti[44] essent, irritare vererentur; nam cum Constantinopolim Mahumetes occupasset, diffisi suis viribus Veneti et aliorum Christianorum auxilia desperantes pacem cum Turchis his legibus fecere:

2 In Asia et omni Graecia usque ad Adriaticum sinum inter Venetos Turchosque pax esto. Venetus, qui per Propontidem navigaverit, in conspectu Byzantii vela deponito et regiam urbem honorato. Mancipia si qua vehit, quae Mahumetaeis initiari sacris velint, libera dimittito. Christiani qui Turchorum arma fugerint in munitionibus Venetorum refugium non habento. Turchi ante Christianorum faciem evadentes in agris atque oppidis Venetorum liberi tutique sunto.

3 Sic Turchis obligata civitas more plebis, quae nihil generosum cum periculo audet, pontificem maximum in suis oppidis[45] excipere recusavit, non tam Christianam amans religionem, quam Turchos timens. Quod cum Pio nuntiatum esset, quamvis dolens tantam inesse potenti populo ignaviam, plenus tamen animo et in Salvatore Christo spem habens, reiecta Utini mentione, epistolis ad reges missis per quas eos Mantuam evocavit, Fulginium adiit.

: 17 :

De Fulginio et Asisio ac Divi Francisci nobili templo.

1 Haec civitas Eugenio Quarto sedente ex manibus tyrannorum ad Romanam Ecclesiam rediit. Ferunt eius urbis regulum sanctum

the other hand, though their ambassadors at Rome had promised the pope a great deal for his campaign against the Turks, nevertheless rejected the choice of Udine as the site for a congress of Christians, because they did not dare annoy the Turks with whom they were allied. For when Mehmed captured Constantinople, the Venetians had been uncertain of their own ability to resist him and, despairing of aid from the other Christian powers, had made a compact with the Turks on the following terms.[34]

In Asia and every part of Greece as far as the Adriatic Sea there 2
would be peace between Venice and the Turks. Any Venetian who sailed through the Sea of Marmara should lower his sails in sight of Byzantium and salute the royal city. If he carried any slaves who wished to be initiated into the religion of Muhammad, he should let them go free. Christians fleeing Turkish attack should not find refuge behind Venetian fortifications. Turks retreating before Christians should be free and safe in the towns and territory of Venice.

Thus the state was bound to the Turks. Like the basest com- 3
moner who shrinks from doing a kindness if there is any risk is involved, the Venetians refused to receive the pope in their territory. Their love of Christ was nothing against their fear of the Turks. When Pius heard the news, though he was distressed to see a powerful nation reduced to such shameful conduct, nevertheless, full of courage and putting his hope in Christ the Savior, he abandoned the idea of Udine, sent letters to the princes summoning them to Mantua, and himself proceeded to Foligno.

: 17 :

Foligno, Assisi and the great basilica of St. Francis.

Foligno was delivered from its tyrants and restored to the Roman 1
Church during the pontificate of Eugenius IV. They say that long

quendam virum propheticum habentem spiritum olim consuluisse, an regno sua posteritas aliquando privanda esset, illumque respondisse privandam, cum boves circum moenia civitatis evolarent. Quod cum impossibile videretur, aeternum[46] sibi posterisque imperium[47] urbis tyrannus persuasit. Verum nepotibus regnum tenentibus, Iohannes Vitellensis Alexandrinus patriarcha eo cum copiis profectus cum obsidere urbem coepisset, explicatis vexillis in quis insigne fuit par bovum, qui flante vento et agitante vexilla volare quodammodo videbantur, magnum civitati terrorem incussit; erat enim cunctis optimatibus notum vaticinium. Nec multis post diebus civitas dedita est, quae usque in hanc diem Romanis pontificibus paret; tyranni dissipati sunt.

2 Ex hoc loco Pius Asisium petiit, fuitque illa in arce quam Picininus per proditionem emerat, miratusque vehementer est hominem (ut aiebat) fortunae et rebus novis intentum adeo munitum locum et ad pacem Italiae turbandam idoneum restituisse. Nec aliud quam divinae pietatis opus arbitratus est, quae pavorem armato immiserit ne conventus Mantuanus interrumperetur.

3 Nobilitavit hanc urbem Divus Franciscus, Ordinis Minorum inventor, cui nihil paupertate ditius fuit. Huic nobile templum erectum est, in quo sua ferunt ossa iacere; et duplex ecclesia est, altera super alteram, picturis illustrata Iotti Florentini quem constat sui temporis omnium pictorum fuisse nobilissimum. Hic et Egidius cardinalis Hispanus iacet, cuius supra fecimus mentionem, qui laceratum Ecclesiae regnum et a tyrannis ferme totum usurpatum singulari virtute recuperavit ac resarcivit; quamvis nonnulli ossa eius in ecclesia Sancti Martini supra Viturvium in monte Cimino recondita dicant. Monasterium quod ecclesiae Beati Fran-

ago a prince of the city asked a certain holy man endowed with the gift of prophecy whether his heirs would ever be driven from power. The man replied that they would lose their domain when oxen flew around the city walls. Since this seemed impossible, the tyrant was convinced that he and his descendants would maintain their hold on the city forever. When his nephews came to power, however, the patriarch of Alexandria, Giovanni Vitelleschi, came with an army to besiege the city.[35] He unfurled his standards, which bore the device of a pair of oxen, and when the wind blew and fluttered the cloth it seemed that the oxen were somehow in flight. This filled Foligno with terror, for the city fathers all knew of the prophecy. Within a few days they surrendered the city, which to this day remains subject to the popes, and the tyrants were forced to flee.

From here Pius went to Assisi. He stood in the citadel which 2
had been betrayed to Piccinino for a price and marveled that a man obsessed (as he used to say) with ideas of fate and revolution should have relinquished a place that was both so strongly fortified and so ideally suited for disturbing the peace of Italy. It must have been divine mercy, he thought, that terrified the soldier and thus safeguarded the Congress of Mantua.

Assisi was made famous by St. Francis, the founder of the 3
Minorite Order, who thought poverty the greatest treasure. Here there is a splendid church, built in his name, where his bones are said to be buried. There are in fact two churches, one built over the other and decorated with frescoes by Giotto of Florence, whom all agree was the greatest painter of his day. Here also is buried the Spanish Cardinal Egidius, whom we mentioned earlier,[36] by whose great ability the kingdom of the Church was recovered and restored after it had been torn to pieces and fallen almost entirely into the hands of usurpers — but some say his bones are buried in the church of San Martino on Monte Cimino above Viterbo. The monastery attached to the church of St. Francis is

cisci cohaeret totius ordinis caput habetur, nec structura toto orbe huiusce ordinis invenitur quae hanc superet.

4 Pius arce considerata cum animadvertisset uno tantum ex loco oppugnari posse, illic turrim erigi iussit, quae postea magnis sumptibus perfecta inexpugnabile monimentum reddidit.

: 18 :

De Perusia et eius civiumque splendore, ac Braccianorum fortuna et moribus.

1 Inde Tiberi rursum transmisso Perusiam profectus est, ubi honores hi ei sunt exhibiti, qui humano ingenio potuerunt excogitari. Nam quamvis aspera saeviret hiems, non tamen aliter adornata civitas fuit quam si vernum tempus adesset. Virere tota urbs, gestire viri ac mulieres qui Romanum pontificem intuerentur, nam ante annis octoginta nemo illic Christi vicarium viderat. Pendere per omnes urbis vias insignia pontificis et lunae aureae nondum plenae, ludi militares exhiberi, omnia profusam ostendere laetitiam, cardinales et universos curiales humane ac benigne tractari.

2 Ea urbs pervetusta est et una ex duodecim civitatibus quas Etruriae principes antiqui commemorant; et adhuc murorum pars cernitur quos Caesar Augustus instauravit. Claruit iam pridem et armis et litteris et potissimum scientia iuris, in qua Bartholus excelluit et post eum Baldus et Angelus. In armis principatum obtinuit Braccius Montonius, nobili loco natus verum hostis Ecclesiae, qui cum suae patriae tyrannidem invasisset, complures Umbriae civitates sibi subiecit. Ad ultimum, cum Aquilam Marsorum urbem quatuordecim mensibus obsedisset, ab exercitu Martini pon-

considered the headquarters of the entire order; in all the world there is no Franciscan building that can match it.

Pius surveyed the citadel and observed that there was only one place where it could be stormed. He ordered a tower to be erected there; this was later built at great expense and rendered the fortifications impregnable. 4

: 18 :

Perugia and its magnificent citizenry. The fortunes and character of Braccio.

Crossing the Tiber again, Pius proceeded to Perugia, where he was shown every honor that the mind of man could invent. Although it was the depth of winter, the city was tricked out as if spring had already arrived. The whole town was hung with greenery; the men and women rejoiced to gaze upon a pope—for it was eighty years since anyone there had seen the Vicar of Christ. The papal arms and golden crescent moons hung along every street; there were military displays; and everywhere he saw signs of profuse delight. The cardinals and all the members of the Curia were welcomed with grace and kindness. 1

Perugia is very ancient, one of the twelve cities of Etruria mentioned by historians of old. One can still see a portion of the walls which Augustus Caesar built. The city has long been renowned for its soldiers and scholars, especially in the field of law, in which subject Bartolo and his followers Baldo and Angelo excelled.[37] Its greatest soldier was Braccio da Montone, a man of noble birth but an enemy of the Church, who made himself tyrant of his own city and then subjugated many other towns of Umbria.[38] Finally, after besieging L'Aquila for fourteen months, he was defeated in battle 2

tificis praelio superatus, captus atque occisus est — non sine gloria Francisci Sforciae, qui tum primum genitore mortuo exercitum ductare coeperat. Cadaver occisi Romam delatum sepulturam cum bestiis obtinuit, quamvis postea defossum Eugenio iubente ac Perusiam translatum intra ecclesiam collocatum fuerit, non sine infamia iubentis.

3 Fuit Braccius honesto corpore, quamvis sinistri lateris impotens; alloquio blandus et dulcis, verum animo truci, ut qui vel ridens torqueri et durissimis excarnificari suppliciis iuberet homines, oblectareturque altis ex turribus miseros iactari mortales. Spoleti ex alto ponte nuntium, qui adversum se litteras attulisset, praecipitari iussit. In Asisio, e turri quae est in foro sublimis, tres viros iactavit. In domo Fratrum Minorum decem et octo monachorum, qui contra se senserant, percuti atque atteri super incude testes mandavit. In aqua Viturviensi, quod Pelacanum vocant, ferventissima immergi captivum quendam cum imperasset, illeque praeter spem omnium exisset incolumis, rogantibus universis ut divina ope salvato ignosceret, 'Age,' inquit lictori, 'iterum demergito! Si exierit, liber esto!' Ille amplius non comparuit. Plurima eius saevitiae extant exempla, quae longum fuerit recensere. De superis atque inferis nihil sensit, Ecclesiae ac religionis hostis, et prorsus indignus cui ecclesiasticae concederentur exequiae.

4 Comilito eius Nicolaus Picininus fuit, rei militaris gloria non inferior verum genere ignobili, cuius genitor infimae plebis ex macello apud Perusiam sustentavit vitam. Invasit et hic suae patriae dominatum, multisque damnis Eugenio sedente Romanam affecit Ecclesiam. Etsi enim plus religionis quam Braccius videretur habere, par tamen eius in Ecclesiam persecutio viguit. Is cum Philippo Mariae Mediolanensium duci aliquandiu militasset, multasque clades Venetis ac Florentinis intulisset, videreturque om-

by the army of Pope Martin, taken prisoner and executed—an achievement which brought great glory to Francesco Sforza, for this was his first command after his father's death. Braccio's body was taken to Rome and given a burial fit for a beast, but Eugenius later had it dug up, removed to Perugia and placed in the church there—an order that did its author no credit.

Braccio was paralyzed on his left side, but he cut a fine figure. 3
He could be pleasant and charming in conversation, but in his heart he was cruel. He would laugh as he ordered men to be tortured and racked by the most excruciating torments, and he took pleasure in hurling his wretched victims off the tops of towers. At Spoleto, when a messenger brought him a hostile letter, he had him flung headlong from a high bridge. In Assisi, he pitched three men off the high tower in the piazza. When eighteen friars in the convent of the Minorites dared to oppose him, he had their testicles beaten to a pulp on an anvil. At Viterbo, he ordered a captive to be plunged into the boiling spring called the Pelacanum. To the amazement of all, the man floated to the surface unharmed, and everyone begged Braccio to pardon a man whom God had spared. But he shouted to the executioner, "Throw him in again! If he comes out this time, he can go free." The prisoner did not reappear. It would take a long time to recount the many instances of his cruelty. He did not believe in heaven or hell. An enemy of the Church and the faith, he was utterly unworthy of Christian burial.

Braccio's comrade in arms, Niccolò Piccinino, was a man 4
equally renowned for military prowess but of much less noble birth. (His father was a man of the very lowest class, who earned his living in the meat-market at Perugia). He too seized power in his own city and inflicted great losses on the Church of Rome when Eugenius was pope. Although he seemed to have more respect for religion than Braccio, he persecuted the Church just as vigorously. After serving for some time in the army of Duke Filippo Maria of Milan and several times defeating the Venetians

nium qui arma gestarent in Italia fortunatissimus ac peritissimus imperator, ad extremum in Tuscia atque in agro Arretino apud Anglariam, cum adversus Ecclesiam et Florentinos bellum gereret, victus est.

5 Nec postea dignum laude aliquid gessit, obiitque tandem inglorius Mediolani et in ecclesia maiori sepultus est. Ferunt eum post cladem in Tuscia apud Anglariam acceptam saepe solitum dicere intulisse sibi terrorem omnemque victoriae spem ademisse vexilla Ecclesiae, in quibus Beati Petri, cuius tunc festivitas aderat, claves inspexisset; ulciscitur enim Deus suas iniurias, nec perlonga est malorum hominum felicitas. Huic duo filii successerunt paterni ductores exercitus, Franciscus et Iacobus. Ille, quamvis ferox et in armis praestans, temulentiae tamen succubuit nec diu postea vita functus est; milites sui Iacobum secuti sunt, de quo saepe nobis erit dicendum.

6 Fuit et Nicolaus Stella, Braccii cognatus, copiarum dux audacissimus, qui cum maiorum vestigia sequeretur Romanamque vexaret Ecclesiam atque in Deum contumeliosus esset, suae impietatis brevi poenas dedit equo lapsus cervice fracta procumbens.[48] Fuerunt et alii complures Perusini in armis clari, inter quos Cecholinum memorant et Ludovicum Michelotium, cui capiundi Braccii gloriam dedere; erat enim factionis illi adversae.

7 Duae sunt apud Perusinos partes quae se invicem persequuntur: nobiles ac Raspantes. Ii longo tempore urbi praefuerunt. Braccius eos expulit; ab illo tempore usque in hanc diem nobilitas imperavit. Etsi enim Picininus, ut diximus, aliquando tyrannidem ibi exercuit, cum esset plebeius, partes tamen nobilium sequebatur. (Inter Raspantes, cum civitatis regimine potirentur, quatuor fratres fuere, quorum matrem, prudentissimam feminam, saepe dixisse traditum est sibi quatuor filios esse: Biordum qui et dicendo et faciendo excelleret; Cecholinum qui facere quidem

and the Florentines, it seemed he was the luckiest and most able captain of all who bore arms in Italy; but in the end he was beaten in a battle against Florence and the Church. This happened at Anghiari near Arezzo in Tuscany.[39]

After that, Niccolò achieved nothing worthy of note and died 5
in obscurity in Milan, where he is buried in the cathedral. It is said that after his defeat at Anghiari in Tuscany he often remarked that it was the sight of the standards of the Church, emblazoned with the keys of St. Peter (for it was then the season of his feast), which had made him panic and abandon all hope of victory. God indeed avenges the injuries done against him, and the success of the wicked never lasts long. Piccinino's two sons, Francesco and Jacopo, succeeded him in command of his troops. The former, though a bold and distinguished soldier, fell victim to drunkenness and did not long survive his father. His soldiers joined the forces of Jacopo, whom we shall often have cause to mention.

Niccolò Stella, a kinsman of Braccio, was another very daring 6
captain; he followed in the family tradition of harrying the Church of Rome and blaspheming against God, but he soon paid the penalty for his sins, for he was thrown from his horse and broke his neck. There have been many other Perugians renowned in arms; among them we know of Ceccolino, and also Lodovico Michelozzo, who was granted the honor of capturing Braccio, for they belonged to opposing factions.

There are two parties in Perugia which are always at each oth- 7
ers' throats: the Nobles and the Raspanti. The latter ruled the city for a long time but were driven out by Braccio, and from that day to this the Nobles have been in power. (Piccinino, who as we have said once ruled there, was a man of the people, but he too belonged to the faction of the Nobles.) When the Raspanti were in power they included in their ranks a family of four brothers. The story is that their mother, a very wise woman, would say that of her four sons, Biordo excelled in both speech and action;

egregie nosset, eloqui nesciret; Antonium cui dicendi copia cum esset, faciendi non esset; et Eganum qui et facere et dicere ignoraret).

8 Venit in hanc urbem Pius pontifex in vigilia Purificationis Beatae Mariae Virginis, matris Domini, et in die festo candelas de more largitus est. Paucis post diebus templum Divi Dominici et amplum et nobile dedicavit. Federicus Urbinas visendi pontificis gratia eo se contulit, et perbenigne acceptus est, legatique Ludovici Sabaudie ducis hic oboedientiam Romano praesuli pro veteri consuetudine praestiterunt. Occurrerunt et Senensium oratores iter ad se petentes; vidit eos pontifex non invitus, et vocari rogarique dulcem in patriam hilari animo accepit. Voluit tamen inermem reperire urbem et liberum sibi futurum, cum Senas intraret, de forma regiminis cum senatu agere; quod illi, quamvis aegre, concesserunt.

: 19 :

De Trasimeno lacu et Clusio et Sartheano.

1 Mansit Perusiae pontifex tribus hebdomadis. Exin, non sine maerore civium qui longiorem sui domini moram optabant, Senas versus iter arripuit et ad lacum Trasimenum pervenit, Romanorum clade et Hannibalis victoria nobilitatum. Huius lacus[49] tempestate nostra nullus erat exitus, ac propterea decurrentibus in eum multis rivulis paulatim creverat, et adiacentium oppidorum magnam partem demerserat. Braccius effosso monte inundantibus aquis iter per altos cuniculos praebuit et vallem, quae alioquin arida erat,

Ceccolino was distinguished in deeds but not in speech; Antonio had a ready tongue but was slow to act; and Egano was a man of neither action nor talk.

Pope Pius arrived in the city on the eve of the Purification of the Blessed Virgin Mary, mother of our Lord,[40] and on the feast day he made the traditional offering of candles. A few days later he dedicated the great cathedral of San Domenico, a splendid building. Federico of Urbino[41] came to see the pope and received a very warm welcome. Ambassadors from Duke Lodovico of Savoy[42] also came to make their submission to the bishop of Rome, according to ancient custom. Ambassadors also arrived from Siena to beg the pope to come to their city. Pius received them gladly and was delighted to be invited back to his beloved country. But he said that he expected to find the city unarmed on his arrival, and wanted to be free to open negotiations with the senate regarding the constitution. This they conceded, though much against their will. 8

: 19 :

Lake Trasimeno, Chiusi and Sarteano.

The pope remained at Perugia for three weeks and then, to the grief of the citizens, who wanted their lord to stay longer, he set out for Siena. He went by way of Lake Trasimeno, made famous by Hannibal's victory, which was a disaster for the Romans. In recent times, the lake had no outlet, and the many little streams that ran into it had gradually raised the level of the lake until it submerged considerable parts of the surrounding towns. Braccio carved deep channels through a mountain to drain away the excess water and irrigate the valley, which would otherwise have been dry. 1

humectavit, molisque plurimis ditavit atque hoc uno opere[50] laudem meruit.

2 Exagitaverat pluribus diebus, cum eo pervenit pontifex, aquas lacus[51] valida tempestas ita ut navigandi nulla pateret facultas. Tum vero quasi divino nutu repente vis omnis ventorum conquievit, et intranti navigium praesuli velut animal domitum sese praebuit mare, et undique sedatis fluctibus mira tranquillitas oborta adeo ut ingens captura piscium facta sit, dum navigatur in insulam in qua pontifex apud religiosos Divi Francisci monachos pernoctavit. Siluerunt flatus vesperi et nocte tota et mane quod secutum est donec navigium Pii ad litus pervenit; exin iterum saevire et inter se colluctari vehementer venti coeperunt ita, ut qui pontificem sequebantur vix periculum submersionis evaserint, admirantibus accolis quod per universam hiemem procellosus et intractabilis Trasimenus pontifici navigabilem se praebuerit.

3 Ventum est deinde ad Clanium amnem, seu palus est, quae Senensem agrum a Perusino dividit; illic legati Senensium magno comitatu et ingenti laetitia praesulem excepere Clusiumque duxere, antiquam urbem et Porsenae regis patriam, opibus olim et gloria pollentem, nunc vero inops oppidulum paucis incolis habitatum. Plinius hic Labyrinthum fuisse commemorat inter miracula orbis non extremum, cuius nulla extare vestigia miraculum videri potest. Hinc Sartheanum itum est, oppidum Senensi populo socium[52] magis quam subditum, quod olim ad Urbem Veterem pertinuit. Ladislaus rex Siciliae, cum adversus Florentinos copias ingentes duceret, negarentque transitum Senenses, hoc in loco tredecim diebus commoratus[53] nulla non die oppidum oppugnavit.[54] Laboratum sed frustra[55] est: tum[56] virtute defendentium, tum proditione Pauli Ursini, qui cuncta regis consilia per internuntios ad oppidanos deferebat.

He also established several mills. For this achievement alone he deserves renown.

For several days before the pope's arrival the lake had been stirred up by a storm so severe that it made sailing impossible but now, as if in deference to divine will, the violence of the winds subsided. When the pope stepped on board his ship, the sea submitted to him like a tamed beast. As the waves died down, the lake grew so extraordinarily still that they took a huge catch of fish as they crossed over to the island where Pius spent the night with the Franciscans. The weather remained calm that evening and all through the night and next morning, until his boat reached the shore of the lake again. Then violent gusts blew up, howling and thrashing against each other, so that those who were following the pope barely escaped with their lives. The locals were amazed that Trasimeno, which is always stormy and difficult in winter, had made itself navigable for the pope. 2

Next Pius came to the river — or rather swamp — called Chiana, which separates the territory of Perugia from that of Siena. Here a party of Sienese envoys welcomed the pope with great pomp and celebration. They escorted him to the ancient city of Chiusi, the birthplace of King Porsenna, which was once rich and famous but is now a poor hamlet inhabited by only a handful of people. Pliny says there was once a labyrinth here which was justly counted among the wonders of the world.[43] That no trace of it remains may seem itself a wonder. From here Pius proceeded to Sarteano, a town allied rather than subject to Siena, which once belonged to Orvieto. When Ladislas, king of Sicily, was leading his great army against Florence and the Sienese refused to let him pass, he halted here thirteen days and every day made an attack on the city.[44] But all his attempts failed, partly because of the courage of Sarteano's defenders and partly because of the treachery of Paolo Orsini, who sent messengers to report all the king's plans to the people of the town. 3

: 20 :

De Corsiniano, nunc Pientia.

1 Pontifex e Sartheano Corsinianum petiit. Mons editus est ex valle amnis Urciae surgens, in cuius vertice planities mille passus longitudinis habet, latitudinis multo minus. In eius angulo qui solem hieme orientem respicit, situm est oppidum parvi nominis, verum aere salubri et vino ac rebus omnibus, quae ad victum pertinent, optimis. Qui Romam e Senis petunt, postquam Sancti Quiriti castellum reliquere et Radicofanum recta pergunt, Corsinianum in colle relinquunt qui ad sinistram cernitur tribus milibus passuum extra viam publicam clementer elevatus.

2 Maior oppidi pars Picolominaeorum quondam fuit, et Sylvius Pii pater avitas hic possessiones habuit, atque hic natus est Pius, et hic pueritiae rudimenta peregit. Quo tunc rediens speravit voluptatem aliquam sumere eos allocuturus, quibuscum adoleverat, et aspectum natalis soli cum gaudio revisere. Sed contra evenit, quando maior pars aequalium vita excesserat, et qui adhuc spirabant, gravati senio morbisque domi detinebantur, et si qui sese exhibebant, mutatis vultibus vix agnosci[57] poterant, exhausti viribus, deformes et quasi mortis nuntii. Offendebat pontifex ubique suae senectutis indicia, non[58] poterat se non senem et cito casurum recognoscere, cum iam aetate graves filios inveniret eorum, quos pueros reliquerat.

3 Fuit oppidum mirifice ornatum, gestiente populo et nimium festivo ob praesentiam maximi praesulis, quem apud se natum gloriabantur, nec satis aut intueri aut consalutare eum poterant. Mansit hic Pius in festo quod Beati Petri Cathedram appellant ac rem divinam peregit. Statuitque hoc in loco novam ecclesiam et palatium aedificare, conduxitque architectos et operarios non parva

: 20 :

Corsignano, now called Pienza.

From Sarteano the pope went to Corsignano. There is a great mountain in the Val d'Orcia which rises up to a narrow plateau about a mile long. At the southeast corner stands a little town, not much to speak of, but possessed of a healthful climate, excellent wine, and all the other necessities of life. Traveling from Siena to Rome, one passes Corsignano on the way to Radicofani, just after the castle of San Quirico. The town sits on a gentle rise three miles from the main road. 1

The greater part of the town once belonged to the Piccolomini. 2
Pius's father, Silvio, had his ancestral estates here, and it was here that Pius was born and passed his childhood. Returning now he hoped to take some pleasure in talking with his boyhood friends and to be cheered by old familiar sights; but he was disappointed, for most of the men of his own generation had died and those who were left kept to their houses, bowed down with old age and illness, or, if they showed themselves, were so changed that he could scarcely recognize them, for they were crippled and feeble and seemed to reek of death. At every step the pope met with proofs of his own advancing age; he could not help but admit that he was an old man whose own demise was looming. Even those whom he had left as children were now the parents of grown sons.

The town was marvelously arrayed. The people were in holiday 3
mood, delighted at the presence of the pope. They reveled in the fact that he had been born among them; they could not gaze at him enough nor stop hailing him with cheers. Pius stayed at Corsignano for the feast of St. Peter's Chair and said a mass.[45] He decided to build a new church and palace in the town as a lasting memorial of his birth, and to this end he hired architects and

mercede, ut memoriale suae originis diuturnum[59] relinqueret. Concessit et indulgentias plenarias quotannis in festo Inventionis Sanctae Crucis his, qui parrochialem ecclesiam visitarent, quae postea cathedralis effecta est. De quibus rebus suo loco dicemus.

: 21 :

De Ecclesia Patavina, de Bono Conventu, de ingressu Senarum et gravissima oratione ad populum.

1 Cum abiisset ex Corsiniano praesul, inter equitandum nuntium allatum est, ex quo didicit ecclesiam Patavinam morte sui pontificis vacuam esse; vocavitque mox cardinalem Sancti Marci aitque, 'Existimasti nos erga te ingratos esse, qui iam pridem nullo te beneficio affecimus. Noluimus minutiora tibi conferre; expectavimus aliquid magni ex quo disceres te nobis carissimum esse. Id iam occurrit: vacat ecclesia Patavina dives ac nobilis; ad eam, si libet, ex Vicentina te transferemus et Gregorium Corario, notarium nostrum, Vicentinae praeficiemus; monasterium, quod ille in Verona obtinet, nepoti nostro commendabimus.'

2 Placuit cardinali oblatio praesulis et gratias egit. Cumque Bonum Conventum introissent, ubi quondam Henricus Septimus Romanorum imperator ex hostia consecrata (ut fama est) venenum hausit, celebrato consistorio cum cardinalibus qui aderant, peracta sunt quae pontifex statuerat, et silentium eius rei donec Senas perveniretur indictum. Caeca mortalium consilia et prorsus ignara futuri! Arbitratus est praesul rem se gratissimam fecisse Venetis, ex quorum nobilitate cardinalis esset. At illis nihil molestius visum est rabida invidia, et quae praesulem latebant, civili simultate agitatis.

workmen at no small expense. He also granted a plenary indulgence yearly on the feast of the Invention of the Holy Cross to anyone who visited the parish church, which was later made a cathedral. About these matters we shall speak in their proper place.

: 21 :

The church at Padua. Buonconvento. Pius's entry into Siena and solemn address to the people.

1 After the pope left Corsignano, news reached him as he rode that the church at Padua had been vacated by the death of the bishop. He immediately summoned the cardinal of San Marco and said, "You thought we were ungrateful to you because for a long time we gave you no benefice. We were unwilling to confer on you the more insignificant favors; we were waiting for something important which would show you how very dear you are to us. This has now presented itself. The church of Padua, a rich and celebrated one, lies vacant. If you like, we will transfer you there from Vicenza and appoint our notary, Gregorio Correr, to the church of Vicenza. The monastery at Verona, which is now his, we will give to our nephew."[46]

2 The cardinal was delighted by the pope's offer and gave him his thanks. When they entered Buonconvento, where once, legend has it, Emperor Henry VII was poisoned by a sacred host,[47] the pope's orders were confirmed in a consistory of the cardinals there present, and secrecy was enjoined till they should reach Siena. How blind are mortal devices, how ignorant of the future![48] Pius thought the Venetians would take great pleasure in this decision, since the cardinal came from the ranks of their nobility, but nothing could have annoyed them more, torn as they were by fierce envy and various civic dissensions of which the pope knew nothing.[49]

3 Dormivit ea nocte Pius in hospitalis Sanctae Mariae praedio, cui Cuna est nomen, sexto a Senis miliario. Sequenti die magno civium comitatu et incredibili plebis alacritate pulcherrime adornatam et festivantem ingressus est patriam, nec usquam maior ostentatio laetitiae visa est. Inter primores tamen urbis inviti non pauci praesulem intuebantur, quem nobilitati faventem sciebant; silebant autem metu plebis et prementes altum corde dolorem vultu gaudium praetendebant, haud ignari quin populi contra se furorem excitassent, si pontificem introeuntem non benigne visi fuissent admittere.

4 Secuta est paulo post solemnitas in medio Maioris Ieiunii, dominica dies cui Rosae vocabulum imposuere. Pontifex, ut civitatem honestaret,[60] rosam auream (quae quotannis dari[61] consuevit) priori priorum urbis cuius magistratus triduanus est tradidit, adhibita oratione in qua de Senensium laudibus disseruit; iussitque cardinales deferentem rosam ad palatium usque comitari medium inter ultimos euntem, quae sors in familiam reformatoriam incidit cui ex insigni bono cognomentum dedere.

5 Post haec de restitutione nobilium coepit agere, et accersito ad se urbis senatu, in hunc modum locutus est: 'Ingentes vobis gratias habemus, viri Senenses, qui gentiles nostros Picolominaeos in partem regiminis admisistis. Nobis quoque, cum in minoribus ageremus, saepe adiumento praesidioque fuistis. Verum nec nos ingrati aut onerosi patriae fuimus, qui diu procul a domo et inter exteras nationes vitam agentes (in Mediolano apud Philippum Mariam, in Basilea apud generale concilium, in Sabaudia apud Amedeum, quem pars orbis pro Christi vicario coluit Felicem appellatum, in Austria apud Federicum imperatorem, Neapoli apud Alfonsum regem et in urbe Roma apud Callistum pontificem maximum) et

The pope slept that night in the hospice of Santa Maria which is called Cuna, six miles from Siena. The following day, he entered his city. A great crowd of citizens received him; the delight of the people was astonishing; the city was in a festive mood and beautifully decorated. Nowhere had he seen a greater display of joy. And yet, among the city fathers there were still some who could not stand the sight of the pope, for they knew he had favored the nobles. They held their peace, however, in fear of the people, and concealed their misery deep in their hearts.[50] On their faces they set expressions of joy, knowing very well they would rouse the fury of the people against them if it seemed they were not welcoming the pope with good will. 3

Soon afterwards fell the Lenten Sunday known as the Sunday of the Rose. In order to honor the city, the pope himself conferred the traditional gift of a golden rose on the Prior of Priors, an office that is held for three days. Then he delivered an oration in praise of Siena and ordered the cardinals to escort the recipient of the rose to the palace. The prior, who happened to belong to a family of the Reformers named Buoninsegni, came last in the procession, flanked by two cardinals. 4

After this, Pius raised the question of recalling the nobles. He summoned the city senate and addressed them as follows: "We are deeply grateful to you, men of Siena, for having admitted our kinsmen the Piccolomini to a share in the government. To ourselves, as well, when we were in minor orders, you often gave help and protection. We have not been ungrateful, nor have we been a burden to our country. For a long time we dwelt among foreign nations far from home (in Milan with Filippo Maria; in Basel at the general council; in Savoy with Amedeo, whom part of the world revered as Christ's vicar under the name of Felix; in Austria with the Emperor Frederick; in Naples with King Alfonso; and in Rome with Pope Calixtus). Both before and during our cardinalate we supported and defended your interests with all our 5

ante cardinalatum et in cardinalatu res vestras summo studio et audivimus et defendimus. Nunc quoque, ad summum praesulatum divino vocati consilio, libertatem vestram prorsus labantem remque simul et dignitatem conservavimus. Nihil enim tam nobis cordi est, quam patriae incolumitas atque libertas, quas res per nostram assumptionem divino munere assecuti estis.

6 'Sed non erit haec felicitas diuturna, nisi alium sumitis vivendi modum, nisi vestrum regimen in melius reformatis. Non potest veritas nostra mentiri, quae ruiturum omne regnum in se divisum in Evangelio tradit. Et quae unquam civitas tam divisa fuit quam vestra? In aliis urbibus saepe duas fuisse partes constat, quae inter se dissidentes ruinam fecere; apud vos pars populi spem omnem regiminis amisit; nobilitas etsi honorum aliquarum est particeps, ex palatio tamen reiicitur; rursus qui rem publicam tenent, alii "novem," alii "reformatores," alii "populares" appellantur, neque absque invidia et simultatibus inter se vivunt, et superare alios alii ac videri meliores volunt. Nutrit procul dubio factiones in populo, et animos in diversa trahit, ipsa nominum diversitas.

7 'Et paulo ante nostrum pontificatum, quod gravius est, novum discidium emersit: cives aliquot ex his qui vobiscum urbi praesidebant, aut securi percussistis, aut in exilium misistis, aut pecunia mulctatos relegastis. Fortasse digna expenderunt supplicia, at non sine iactura civitatis! Morte affecti e numero vestro periere; qui exsulant et qui relegati sunt, reditum in patriam meditantur, vobisque dies atque noctes insidias parant; neque desunt in civitate, qui eis student vel sanguine vel benivolentia[62] illis adiuncti. Nam quanto plures e civitate deiecistis, tanto maior est numerus eorum qui vobis infensi sunt et res novas in civitate moliuntur. Haec et alia pleraque in corpore vestro sunt[63] mala; extra vero quibus ini-

might. Lately, too, in the time since Divine Wisdom summoned us to the papacy, we have taken steps to protect your fragile independence along with the state itself and its authority; for nothing is closer to our heart than the liberty and safety of our country. These blessings you have been granted since our elevation by the grace of heaven.

"But this happy state of affairs will not last long unless you adopt a different mode of life and reform your government. The truth cannot lie—our Gospel truth that says 'every kingdom divided against itself shall fall.'[51] And what state was ever so divided as yours? In other cities, it is true, two parties have often brought on disaster by their dissension. But with you, one segment of society has abandoned all hope of governing: the nobles, though they share in some privileges, are excluded from the palace. On the other hand, those who do hold power (whether the 'Nine', or the 'Reformers', or the 'Popolari') cannot function without envy and strife. Each is always trying to outdo the next, hoping to seem the better party. No doubt the variety of names itself fosters divisions among the people and encourages unrest. 6

"Moreover, and more seriously, a new schism appeared in the days before we became pope.[52] You beheaded a number of citizens who held posts in the government alongside you; others you drove into exile or banished and punished with heavy fines. It may be that these men paid a just penalty, but it was not without cost to the state. Those who died are gone forever; but the exiles and the banished intend to return to their country. Night and day they plot against you; and they have their partisans within the city, who are bound to them by ties of blood and affection. Indeed, the more you drove out of the city then, the greater is the host of your enemies now, who are preparing revolution against the state. These and many other ills lie within your body politic. The hostilities in which you are entangled abroad, you yourselves know. Those who 7

micitiis impliciti sitis, vos ipsi nostis. Vicina in vos odia sunt, amicitiae procul absunt. Quis ei civitati bene speret, quae nec foris nec intus tuta est?

8 'At salutem aperuit vobis Deus ab externa vi, qui nos in cathedra Beati Petri collocavit, in qua dum sedemus, nemo aperto Marte invadere vos audet. Norunt inimici vestri Apostolicae Sedis vires, et scientes nos huius urbis cives esse, tam vobis quam nobis ipsis inferre bellum verentur. Sub umbra nostra ab his, qui foris sunt, satis tuti estis; ab his, qui sunt intus, non est opis nostrae vos tueri. Consulere tantum possumus et id suadere, quod unicum est civitatum omnium firmissimum[64] tutamentum: id est, ut invicem ametis et concordibus animis rem publicam gubernetis. Nam difficile monimentum et insuperabile est amor civium. Nostis illud Salustianum, "Concordia res parvas crescere, discordia magnas dilabi." Concordia est, quae servat civitates.

9 'Haec perpetuo vos coniunget et hanc civitatem tuebitur, si iustitia inter vos dominabitur, quae una est mater atque regina virtutum. Iustitia aequitatis quaedam ratio est, quae pro meritis inter homines poenas ac praemia distribuit. Beata civitas, quae iustitiae utitur moderamine; et vos, Senenses, beati eritis, si honores publicos inter merentes partiemini. Quod iam diu a vobis neglectum est, qui civibus nobilitate praestantibus, quorum maiores hanc urbem condidere, et qui non coacti sed sponte sua civitatis regimen in vos transtulere, annos supra quinquaginta tamquam mancipiis usi estis. Redeundum est iam denique ad iustitiam, et honorandi sunt nobiles et eorum loco sufficiendi, quos eiecistis necastisque! Implendus est qui vacat locus, et tot amici assumendi quot inimicos fecistis! Aut enim cavendum est, ne quis nos oderit, aut si hoc non possumus assequi, parandae sunt amicitiae quae odia superent.

10 Hoc abunde praestabunt nobiles, si damnatorum loca conscen-

hate you are close at hand; your friends are far away. What hope can there be for a state that is neither secure within nor without?

8 "But God, who set us on the throne of Peter, has provided you a safeguard against external attack. While we sit there, no one dares declare outright war against you. Your enemies understand the power of the Apostolic See; knowing we are a citizen of this state, they are as afraid to march on you as they would be to march on us. In our shadow, you are safe from foes without. From foes within, however, we have not the power to protect you. We can only advise and urge upon you that which is the one sure protection for every state, namely, that you love one another and govern your state in harmony. For civic harmony is a strong and impregnable defense. You know what Sallust says: 'By concord small things grow; by discord great things fall to pieces.'[53] Cities are preserved by concord.

9 "And this one thing shall keep you forever united and your state secure: if justice, the mother and queen of the virtues, shall prevail among you. Justice is a certain principle of equity which distributes penalties and rewards among men according to their deserts. Happy is the state guided by justice. And you too will be happy, people of Siena, if you distribute public offices to those who deserve them. It is a principle you have allowed to fall into neglect. For more than fifty years you have treated your noblest citizens like slaves—those whose ancestors founded this city, those who were not forced, but who by their own free will handed over the reins of government to you. Now you must return to the path of justice. The nobles must be respected; they must be elected to the posts held by those you cast out and killed. The empty seats must be filled. You must make as many friends as you have made foes in the past. See to it that no one hates you; or, if we cannot accomplish that much, then at least forge friendships that are stronger than your enmities.

10 This the nobles will be more than able to do, if they are raised

derint. Utilitas hoc et honestas suadet. Nam quomodo grati eritis, nisi hos honoratis quorum parentes vobis rem publicam commisere et patriam hanc fundavere, et qui — licet contumeliis a vobis affecti quam plurimis[65] fuerint — numquam tamen rebellarunt, aequo animo cuncta tulerunt, et ad omne imperium vestrum praesto fuere? Potuissent aliquando per divisiones vestras cornua erigere: maluerunt in civitate per quietem servire, quam per seditionem dominari. Et quis non eiusmodi cives dignos regimine arbitretur? Bene instituta civitas et quae radices vult altius figere, malos cives poena, bonos praemio afficit. Nemo, qui sapiat, ea in urbe manendum duxerit, in qua virtuti non adsint praemia. Vos, si sapietis, nobiles, iam enim tumore divitiarum deposito vestri similes et aliquanto humiliores effectos, in societatem gubernandae civitatis amplectemini, nec vobis ipsis minores[66] esse patiemini.

11 'Atque hoc summum est retinendae libertatis et urbis conservandae remedium; hoc est consilium nostrum quod amantissime damus patriae. Si spernitis hortamenta nostra, non possumus de hac re publica bene sperare. Imminet enim divisae civitati ruina, nec pax illic habitat unde iustitia exulat. Vos si nobilitati quod sibi debetur attribuetis, si qua ingruent adversitas, nedum auxilia nostra praesto erunt, sed ipsius Dei, qui iustis partibus semper adest, omnipotenti manu adiuti et protecti eritis.'

: 22 :

De nobilitate restituta et concesso Radicofano Senensibus.

1 Haec cum dixisset pontifex, cardinales quoque qui astabant pro suo quisque ingenio in eandem sententiam verba fecere. Respon-

to the seats of those you have condemned. This is the counsel of both honor and advantage. For how can you show yourselves grateful unless you honor those whose fathers entrusted the state to you, who founded our city, who—despite countless insults from you—never rebelled but bore all with meekness and were ready to obey your every command? There were times when you quarreled with each other, when they could have raised their horns. They preferred to serve the state in peace than to rule it by sedition. Who would not think such citizens worthy to govern? A well organized state, one that wants to put its roots down deep, will punish its bad citizens and reward the good. No sane man would want to stay in a city where virtue meets with no rewards. You, if you are of sane mind, should welcome the nobles to a share in government. Now that there is nothing to fear from their wealth, they are like yourselves or even humbler; you should not allow them to occupy a place inferior to your own.

"This is the surest protection, this will preserve your liberty II
and keep your city safe. This is the advice we give our dearly beloved country. If you reject our counsel, we will not entertain much hope for the future of this state. Disaster looms over a city divided. Peace does not dwell where justice is exiled. But if you grant the nobles their due, then should any danger arise, not only will we be ready to lend our aid, but you will be helped by the omnipotent hand of God, your defender, who is ever on the side of the righteous."

: 22 :

The Nobles restored. Radicofani granted to Siena.

When the pope had spoken, the cardinals who were present made I
speeches in the same vein, each according to his ability. The reply

sum est priores urbis senatum de more coacturos, et quod ab eo decretum fuerit pontifici relaturos. Exin abeuntes inter se cives fremere, praesulem blasphemare, verba eius (etsi nonnullis placuissent) carpere, animos in diversa iactare, quicquid unquam peccasset nobilitas in medium afferre, nihil difficilius dicere quam regni socios asciscere, armis rei publicae gubernationem acquiri, non verbis. Illi partiri honores aegre ferebant, hi lucra communicare; quidam exclusum se[67] iri existimabant, si digniores nobiles[68] includerentur. Cunctos ambitio retrahebat: nemo regni comitem facile admittit. Generosi aliquando viri honores aliis cedunt, ignobiles numquam; nec plebs est, cui honesta facile suadeas; nisi utilitati cedat, vi cogenda est.

2 Difficile senatoribus videbatur negare pontifici quod peteret, difficilius concedere. Reddebantur postulata eo impetratu magis laboriosa, quod in senatu ex tribus suffragiorum partibus duas concurrere et trecentos adesse senatores per leges oportebat; nec suum satis bonum intellegere multitudo poterat odio, avaricia et ambitione corrupta.

3 Diu frustra in senatu res agitata est, cum seniores et quibus plus pensi erat, pontifici auscultandum censerent, iuniores et imperiti, quorum turba longe maior fuit, adversarentur, et conventiculas agentes exilium patribus necemque minarentur. Dolebant tam miserum rei publicae statum quis erat sanior mens; horum nonnulli, clientelis et opibus potentes, clam pontificem adeunt et quod verbis obtineri non posset, ferro quaerendum suadent,[69] haud dubium esse dicentes quin armato populo pontificis partes

came that the Priors of the city would convene a regular meeting of the senate and report its decision to the pope. Then, as they dispersed, some of the citizens murmured among themselves and cursed the pope; they found fault with his words (though some had found them pleasing) and made various wild claims. Every mistake the nobles ever made while in office was brought up. Nothing was harder than sharing power in politics, people said, and control of a state should be determined by arms and not by words. Some resented dividing the offices, others sharing the profits. Some thought they themselves would be shut out, if the nobles, who were more deserving, were admitted. Ambition restrained everyone: no one welcomes a partner in power. Men of noble birth sometimes yield their offices to others, but commoners never. It is never easy to lead the masses down the path of justice. Unless they can see some advantage in it, the people must be compelled by force.

The senators found it hard to deny the pope what he asked, 2
harder still to grant it. His request was all the more difficult to satisfy because in order to pass a resolution, the law required at least three hundred senators to be present and a two-thirds majority to vote in its favor. Nor could the people, corrupted as they were by hatred, greed and ambition, realize what was in their best interest.

The debate in the senate was long and fruitless. The elders and 3
those with most authority voted to accede to the pope's requests; the young and inexperienced, who were far more numerous, opposed them; they held secret meetings and threatened the other senators with exile and death. Those of sounder judgment deplored the wretched condition of the state. Some of them, whose wealth and patronage gave them influence, went to the pope in secret and urged him to use the sword to take what he could not get by negotiation. There was no doubt, they said, that if the people were armed, his side would prove superior; for all who had no

superiores invenirentur; cuncti enim regiminis expertes, quorum ingens multitudo est, pontificem sequerentur. Quibus pontifex, etsi victoriam suam esse ubi proelium fieret non dubitabat: 'Patriae tamen,' inquit, 'vim non afferemus. At si spernimur a civibus nostris, beneficam subtrahemus manum, et hoc ingratae civitati satis ad supplicium, nobis satis ad vindictam fuerit.'

4 Publicata est vox haec in populo, quae multorum terruit animos. Reventum est saepe in consilium, suffragia iterum atque iterum reddita, nec tamen haberi duae partes senatorum poterant qui postulata admittenda esse censerent. Sed cum pontifex urgeret ac responsum exposceret priusquam abiret, indignabundusque videretur nisi vinceret, ad extremum censuit senatus deinceps nobiles ad honores omnes admittendos esse, et munerum aliquorum quartam, reliquorum octavam partem eis indulsit.

5 Publicatum decretum universam mox urbem implevit gaudio. Senatus frequens et cuncti magistratus urbis rem gestam expositurі pontificem convenere. Pontifex, etsi non satis suo desiderio factum animadvertit, ne tamen civitatem tristitia afficeret,[70] hilarem se ostendit egitque senatui gratias, laudans quod factum erat; sperare se tamen amplius aliquid dixit, cum ex Mantua reverteretur. Ad noctem signa laetitiae passim visa per urbem, lucere ignes, campanae ac tubae[71] concentum reddere; salutare, invitare alter alterum et in amplexus ire mutuos populares ac nobiles.

6 Pontifex maximus, ut gratitudinis vicem suis civibus redderet, Radicofanum, quod est in Amiatae monte munitum oppidum et ad Romanam Ecclesiam iure directo pertinet, de consilio fratrum Senensibus perpetuo tenendum concessit praescripto censu, quem Camerae Apostolicae quotannis dissolverent; a praedecessoribus praefinitum fuerat tempus, quod iam prope desiturum erat. Id oppidum Nannes Picolominaeus, copiarum dux non illaudatus, armis olim ex manu praedonis cuiusdam eripuerat tradideratque

share in the government (and they were legion) would back him. The pope was sure that if it came to a battle, victory would be his; nevertheless he replied, "We shall not do violence to our city. If we are rejected by our fellow-citizens, we will withdraw our favor. That will be punishment enough for an ungrateful city, and vengeance enough for ourselves."

His words were leaked to the public and struck terror in many 4
hearts. The council was repeatedly brought back into session; again and again they took the vote, but it was still impossible to get two thirds of the senators to agree to the pope's terms. Then Pius grew more insistent, demanding a reply before his departure, and when it appeared that he would be truly incensed if he did not get his way, the senate finally voted to admit the Nobles to every office and to grant them a quarter share of some privileges and an eighth of the rest.

When the decree was made public, the whole city erupted in 5
celebration. The entire senate and all the magistrates went to tell the pope what had been done. The pope realized that his demands had not been fully met; still, in order not to cast gloom on the city, he appeared pleased and thanked the senate, praising what they had done and saying he hoped for something more when he returned from Mantua. That night, the evidence of their joy was everywhere to be seen. Bonfires blazed throughout the city, bells and trumpets made a cheerful din, and nobles and commoners hailed one another, exchanging embraces and invitations.

As a mark of gratitude to his fellow-citizens, the pope gave 6
Siena the fortified town of Radicofani on Monte Amiata, which was part of the patrimony of the Church. On the advice of the friars, he granted perpetual tenure of the town in return for the annual payment of a fixed sum to the Apostolic Camera (a time limit had been set by his predecessors, which was on point of expiring). The celebrated captain Nanni Piccolomini had once wrested this town from a certain bandit and handed it over to Siena. Thus it

Senensibus; atque ita factum est ut Picolominaea domus et possessionem et titulum eius loci in civitatem suam transtulerit.

: 23 :

De ecclesia Senensi metropoli facta, et Silvii ac Victoriae parentum sepulchro nobilissimo.

1 Ecclesia quoque Senensis tum primum ad metropolitici iuris honorem erecta est, Grossetana, Massana, Suanensi et Clusina ei subiecta; tantopere suam decorare patriam pontifex adnitebatur. Primus archiepiscopus Antonius fuit ex familia Picolominaea, quem sibi Pius, ut primum Petri cathedram ascendit, successorem in eadem ecclesia designaverat.

2 Mater pontificis quatuor ante annis obierat, pater bis totidem; hic Corsiniani iacebat, mater Senis, ambo in monasteriis Minorum. Pierius quidam eques ex gente Picolominaea apud Minores, qui pro foribus urbis collocati sunt, sibi suisque posteris marmoreum sepulchrum magno sumptu iam pridem struxerat, in quo et ipse et multi suorum conditi sunt. Fratres eius ordinis matrem Pii, tunc Senensis episcopi in Germania commorantis, quae apud Creulam episcopatus munitam arcem dormivisset et in monasterio Minorum sepulturam elegisset, in hoc tumulo sepelierunt. Id aegre fuit Pierio, primi Pierii nepoti, rem prorsus indignam existimanti inter ossa maiorum suorum alieni sanguinis carnem misceri. (Nam Victoria, mater Pii, quamvis nupta in domo Picolominaea fuerit, Forteguerrarum tamen, non Picolominaeorum sanguis erat.) Iussit igitur nocte quae secuta est illinc extrahi cadaver et alio quocunque loco recondi.

3 Monachi nobilem feminam intra ecclesiam apud altare maius reposuere, humi tamen et absque marmoreo lapide, sperantes

happened that the house of Piccolomini gave their native city both possession and title to the place.

: 23 :

Siena made a metropolitan see. A magnificent tomb for the pope's parents, Silvio and Vittoria.

At this time too the church of Siena was raised to metropolitan rank, with Grosseto, Massa, Suana and Chiusi subject to it. In this way the pope strove to exalt his native city. The first archbishop was Antonio Piccolomini,[54] whom Pius had designated as his successor in the see as soon as he ascended Peter's throne. 1

The pope's mother had died four years before his return to Siena, and his father four years before that. Both were buried in Franciscan monasteries, the latter at Corsignano, the former at Siena. Long ago a certain knight of the Piccolomini family named Piero had erected a sumptuous marble tomb for himself and his descendants at the Minorite convent by the city gates. Here many of his family now lie. The friars had buried Pius's mother in this tomb (for he was then bishop of Siena and far away in Germany). She had fallen asleep at Creula, a fortified stronghold of the diocese, and desired to be buried in a Franciscan house. This angered Piero, grandson of the first Piero, who thought it outrageous that the flesh and blood of a stranger should mingle with the bones of his ancestors—for Vittoria, Pius's mother, though married into the Piccolomini family, was born a Fortiguerra. Therefore Piero had given orders that the body should be exhumed that very night and interred elsewhere. 2

The monks laid the noble lady inside the church by the high altar, but only in the earth, with no marble slab to cover her, for 3

filium aliquando genetricis corpus honoraturum. Nec frustra spes fuit. Veniens enim in patriam suam Pius, iam pridem edoctus quae circa funus matris obtigerant, Silvii patris ossa ex Corsiniano Senas deferri iussit, et utrique parenti nobile sepulchrum aedificari ex candido marmore quod ex Ligusticis montibus allatum est, epitaphiumque ipse dictavit hoc disticho:

Silvius hic iaceo, coniunx Victoria mecum est.
Filius hoc clausit marmore, papa Pius.

: 24 :

Multorum legationes, maxime regis Bohemiae, et eius haeresis.

1 Dum Senis moratur praesul, imperatoris Federici legati et Henrici Castellae et Matthiae Hungariae et Alfonsi Portugalliae et Georgii Bohemiae regis et Philippi Burgundiae et Alberti Austriae ducis et Federici atque Alberti marchionum Brandeburgensium adventarunt, Christi vicarium pro veteri more adoraturi. Inter quos magni et praestantes viri fuerunt, ex quis duo paulo post ad cardinalatus honorem assumpti sunt: Iohannes episcopus Atrebas et Brocchardus praepositus Salzburgensis, alter ab imperatore missus, alter a Burgundo.

2 Verum Brocchardus et eius collegae, Iohannes Inderbachius et Artongus cognomento Capel iure consulti, cum Florentiae applicuissent, aliquandiu illic remorati sunt indigne ferentes Matthiam Hungariae regem a Romano pontifice appellatum esse, eiusque

they hoped that her son would someday do honor to his mother's remains. Nor were these idle hopes: for when Pius returned to his city (he had heard the story of his mother's death and burial some time before), he had the bones of his father Silvio moved from Corsignano to Siena and built a noble tomb of brilliant Ligurian marble for both his parents.[55] He himself composed a couplet to serve as their epitaph:

> I, Silvio, lie here, my wife Vittoria beside me.
> Our son, Pope Pius, laid us in this marble tomb.

: 24 :

Several princes send embassies, above all the king of Bohemia. His heresy.

While the pope was in Siena, ambassadors from Emperor Frederick, Kings Henry of Castile, Matthias of Hungary, Alfonso of Portugal and George of Bohemia, Dukes Philip of Burgundy and Albert of Austria, and Frederick and Albert, the margraves of Brandenburg, arrived to do reverence to the Vicar of Christ according to ancient custom. In this company there were some great and distinguished men; two of them—Jean, the bishop of Arras, and Burchard, the provost of Salzburg, representing Burgundy and the emperor, respectively—were shortly afterwards made cardinals.[56] 1

When Burchard and his colleagues, the jurists Johann Hinderbach and Hartung Kappel, arrived at Florence, however, they remained there some time, for they were outraged that the pope had recognized Matthias as king and that the Curia had received his envoys with honors usually shown a royal embassy, even though 2

oratores eos in Curia consecutos honores, qui regum legatis exhiberi consuevere, cum barones Hungariae imperatorem supra se regem elegissent, atque ipse delatum titulum accepisset. Pontifex ea re cognita iniustam esse querelam dixit, quando mos esset Apostolicae Sedis eum regem appellare, qui regnum teneret,[72] et prior ante se Callistus Matthiam regem compellasset. Atque hoc modo imperatoris legationi satisfactum est, quae deinde in templo Divae Mariae Virginis publice praestitit oboedientiam. Legatus vero Bohemiae regis in consistorio secreto idem egit, veritus ne domino suo regni partem alienaret, si eum Apostolicae Sedi palam submitteret.

3 Regnum Bohemiae bifariam divisum est: alii Romanam Ecclesiam sequuntur, alii respuunt, qui appellantur Hussitae, multis haeresibus infames, quemadmodum in *Historia Bohemica* ab ipso Pio scriptum est. Georgius Poggebragius Hussitarum partium fuit et eorum errore respersus, quorum armis atque praesidiis regnante Ladislao, Alberti filio regni gubernationem, et illo mortuo coronam arripuit vocatis ex Hungaria duobus episcopis, Iaurinensi et Vacciensi, qui se unctum coronarent. Illi homini, qui haereticus censeretur, id honoris negare, nisi errorem prius abiuraret, et Romani praesulis oboedientiae se subiiceret.

4 Georgius seu vere seu simulate (quod vero similius est), in penitiori parte palatii vocatis nonnullis testibus atque tabellionibus, Hussitarum haeresim abiuravit et Apostolicae Sedis auctoritati iussionique sese submisit. Cuius rei publica documenta episcopi acceperunt atque deinde regem coronarunt, cui mox Bohemi omnes paruere. Moravi, cum aliquantulum restitissent, postea imperata fecerunt. Apud Sclesitas maior fuit renitentia: Vratislavienses missis ad Pium legatis nullo pacto se suscepturos regem dixere, quem de fide suspectum haberent, inventoque Senis pontifice

the barons of Hungary had chosen the emperor for their king and he had accepted the title. When the pope learned of this, he declared that their complaint was unreasonable, since it was the practice of the Apostolic See to address as king the man who actually sat on the throne and Calixtus before him had so addressed Matthias. This satisfied the emperor's legates, who then made their public profession of obedience in the cathedral of the Holy Virgin. The king of Bohemia's envoy made his profession in a secret consistory, however, fearing that if he publicly made submission to the Apostolic See he might alienate part of the kingdom from his master.

The kingdom of Bohemia is divided between two sects: one fol- 3
lows the Church of Rome, the other rejects it. The latter are known as Hussites and are notorious for their many heresies, as Pius himself records in his *History of Bohemia*.[57] George of Podêbrady was a Hussite. Defiled by their errors, and with their help and support, he seized control of the government during the reign of Albert's heir Ladislas, and on the king's death usurped the throne itself, summoning from Hungary the bishops of Vacz and Raab to crown him.[58] They refused to bestow such an honor on a reputed heretic unless he first renounced his error and professed his obedience to the bishop of Rome.

George then summoned a number of witnesses and secretaries 4
into a private part of his palace, where he either sincerely or (as is more likely) falsely abjured his Hussite beliefs and made submission to the authority and jurisdiction of the Apostolic See. The bishops accepted the published record of this act in good faith and proceeded to crown him king; before long all of Bohemia accepted his rule, while Moravia put up a feeble resistance before submitting to him as well. In Silesia there was more stubborn opposition; the people of Wrocław sent an embassy to Pius to say that they absolutely refused to accept a king whose orthodoxy they suspected. These ambassadors found Pius at Siena. They bitterly de-

multa de Georgio questi sunt, qui neque hominibus neque Deo fidem servaret, indignumque esse dixerunt quem suis litteris Apostolica Sedes regem appellasset.

5 Pontifex, cum vocari ad Mantuanum conventum principes iussisset, regemne Georgium nominaret aliquandiu haesit; erant enim in utramque partem suasiones. Callistus antea regem vocaverat et ipse abiuraverat haeresim, verum simulata eius opera putabantur. Consulentibus denique cardinalibus et scribere et regem appellare placuit, verum litteras imperatori transmittere, qui si sibi videretur eas Georgio traderet, regnum enim Bohemiae Imperii feudum est, et vacante regno ad imperatorem pertinet Bohemis regem constituere. Imperator litteras apostolicas nihil moratus Georgio restituit, quas ille ingenti gaudio accepit iussitque pro sua gloria maioribus in urbibus publicari, ut intellegerent omnes Apostolicam Sedem nomen regium sibi tamquam catholico detulisse.

6 Quae res multorum offendit animos, ac praesertim Vratislaviensium, qui ob eam rem legatos, ut diximus, ad Pium misere. A quo cum facti rationes accepissent, subveniri sibi petierunt ne vel fraudibus Georgii vel armis Christianam fidem perdere cogerentur. Pontifex consilium suum esse dixit, potentis regis uti furorem declinarent; scripturum se illi ab armis abstineat, et quas habet adversus Vratislavienses Sclesitarum principes controversias, Apostolicae Sedis arbitrio dimittat; nisi paruerit, aliis se remediis usurum. Atque hoc responso Vratislaviensium legatos dimisit.

nounced George, who they said kept faith with neither God nor man. He was not worthy of the royal title which the Apostolic See had granted him in its correspondence.

When the pope proclaimed the congress at Mantua, he had 5
been a little unsure whether to address George as king. Both sides of the question had their merits. Calixtus had recognized his title and George himself had abjured his heresy; on the other hand, this was generally thought to be no more than a sham. Finally, on the advice of the cardinals, he decided he would not only write to George but also use the title of king; but he would send the letter to the emperor, who could deliver it to George if he pleased. For the kingdom of Bohemia is an imperial fief and when the throne is vacant the emperor has the right to appoint a new king of the Bohemians. Frederick sent George the apostolic letter straight away. George received it with the greatest satisfaction and ordered it to be published in the principal cities of the kingdom, both to satisfy his pride and so that all would know that the Apostolic See had deemed him a good Catholic and thus accorded him a royal title.

Many people took offense at this, especially the people of 6
Wrocław who, as I said above, despatched ambassadors to Pius. The pope explained to them the principle behind the decision, but still they begged him to come to their assistance, lest they be compelled by George's trickery or force to abandon the Christian faith. Pius replied that in order to protect them from the great king's wrath, he intended to write to George forbidding him the use of arms and commanding him to rely on the arbitration of the Apostolic See to settle his quarrel with the people of Wrocław, the leading citizens of Silesia. If he refused to obey, the pope would take other measures. With this answer he dismissed the envoys of Wrocław.

: 25 :

Dissuasio multorum a firmo Pii proposito, et perfidia Tarentini.

1 Exin Mantuam versus iter continuare decrevit. Multi hoc dissuadebant: Senenses emolumentis carituri Curiae recessuro praesuli mille instare pericula affirmabant: iter per Florentiam discrimine plenum esse; Florentinos calliditate omnibus praestare; Senensibus quos oderint, pontificem maximum invidere; timendum esse venenum et omnis generis insidias formidandas. Alii frustra praesulem Mantuam petere, in quam paucissimi conventuri essent; provocaturum in se odia principum, quasi eorum contumaciam accusaturum; satius esse manere Senis, quam ulterius proficiscentem nil aliud quam, aere magno, regum inimicitias emere, quorum reprehensurus desidiam atque ignaviam videretur.

2 Alii magnos instare in Italia motus; pontificem, si Apenninum transierit, numquam in Tusciam rediturum perditurumque Romam et patrimonium Ecclesiae universum. Nec defuerunt qui per derisionem atque contemptum Pium papam, quasi segetibus[73] benedicentem huc atque illuc peragrantem, dicerent insulsumque praedicarent, qui non exploratis regum animis ad conventum pergeret;[74] potuisse domi quiescere donec certa principum accepisset responsa. Et hi rumores passim exaudiebantur. Cardinales, quamvis consilium pontificis quod ante probaverant publice damnare non auderent, mordere tamen clanculum aliqui non verebantur, inter quos inventi sunt qui multa contra praesulem scripsere. Unius autem cardinalis litterae ad regem Franciae in hunc modum scriptae pontificis manus inciderunt:

: 25 :

Many try to dissuade Pius from his firm resolution. The perfidy of the Tarentines.

Pius then determined to continue his journey to Mantua, though many tried to dissuade him. The Sienese, who were about to lose the emoluments of the Curia, warned the pontiff as he prepared to depart that a thousand perils lay in wait for him: the road through Florence was beset with dangers; the Florentines surpassed all men in cunning; they despised all Sienese and hated the pope for being one; he must guard himself against poison and plots of every description. Some said it would be useless for the pope to go to Mantua, since hardly anyone would attend a congress there and he would merely incur the enmity of the princes, who would suspect he meant to accuse them of disobedience; he would do better to remain at Siena than proceed further, where for a great price he would acquire nothing more than the hostility of kings whose apathy and cowardice he would seem to be rebuking. 1

Others said that great disturbances were afoot in Italy. Once the pope crossed the Apennines, he would never return to Tuscany; he would lose Rome and the entire patrimony of the Church. There were some who mocked and scorned Pope Pius: he was wandering about Italy blessing cornfields, they said; it was absurd to have set out for the congress without first sounding the attitude of the princes; he should have stayed quietly at home until he had received their definite replies. Such mutterings were heard everywhere. The cardinals did not dare condemn the pope's plan in public, since they had previously approved it, but some had no scruples about attacking him in private. A few wrote at length against him. One sent a letter to the king of France which fell into the pope's hands. It read: 2

3 'Carolo Francorum regi presbyter cardinalis salutem. Apud Mantuam Christianorum conventus indictus est. Eo sese Pius pontifex confert, cuius ingens studium est ut Federicum imperatorem conveniat; quod absque tuo dedecore damnoque fieri non potest. Tu, si sapias, hanc conventionem disturbabis. Vale.'

4 Exhorruit Pius tantam inter cardinales perfidiam invenisse, nec tamen plectendum facinus existimavit, quod sine scandalo fieri non poterat. Rumores autem omnes contempsit; de Florentinis, qui viri prudentes essent et graves, nihil mali timendum esse censuit, nec sibi recta vadenti formidandas insidias; nec tam hostem humani generis metuendum, qui bonis operibus adversatur, quam Dei sperandum auxilium cuius causam acturus iret in Galliam; quod si reges conventum negligerent, illos in culpa futuros; se qui pergeret laudem mereri, neque alienam desidiam sua negligentia excusandam fore; stultam illorum videri prudentiam, qui reges prius consulendos fuisse, quam conventus indiceretur aut eo iretur, assererent; quae res longum tempus expetivisset, neque de loco neque de die inter se reges convenissent; murmura et vulgi blasphemias ab his, qui rei publicae praesunt, contemni oportere, tantoque Romanum pontificem indulgentiorem esse detractoribus, quanto prae ceteris altius ascendisset; cui non ignota est vox Salvatoris, qui discipulos suos tum beatos dixit futuros cum eis homines maledicerent.

5 Cardinalis Sancti Petri unus ex his erat qui transeundum Apenninum prorsus negabat, scripseratque pontifici ex Urbe ne Germanos proceres ea veluti contumelia afficeret, ut illis non venientibus Mantuam peteret. Cui pontifex in hunc modum rescripsit, 'Sapis qui tuae nationi cum nostra infamia demere ignominiam

"A cardinal priest[59] to King Charles of France, greeting. A congress of Christians has been called at Mantua. Pope Pius is on his way there. He is most eager that the Emperor Frederick should attend. This must necessarily involve dishonor and injury to you. If you are wise you will put a stop to this congress. Farewell." 3

Pius was horrified to discover such treachery among the cardinals, but he did not think he could punish the crime without creating a scandal. The gossip he treated with contempt. He was convinced he had nothing to fear from the Florentines, for they were sober and sensible people; nor could treachery threaten the man who travelled on the true path; nor should he fear the enemy of mankind, who ever opposes good works: rather he should hope for the aid of God whose cause he was going north to plead. If the princes ignored the congress, the fault would be theirs; if he went on, he would earn glory for his persistence, nor could the others excuse their inaction on the grounds that the pope been indifferent. Those who had counseled prudence, saying he should have consulted the princes before calling the congress or starting on his way, seemed foolish to him—such consultation would have taken a long time and the princes would never have agreed on a place or day. Heads of state should scorn the murmurs and abuse of the crowd; the pope of Rome was exalted above all other men and ought to show clemency to his detractors. He had not forgotten the words of his Savior, who said His disciples were blessed when men reviled them.[60] 4

The cardinal of San Pietro[61] was among those who violently opposed crossing the Apennines. He had written to the pope from Rome advising him not to offer the German princes what they would construe as an affront by going to Mantua while they stayed away. The pope wrote back, "Very clever, to try to reduce your own nation's shame by urging me into disgrace!" Without further delay, and with his confidence unshaken, he took leave of his na- 5

studes!' Nec moratus amplius, fidens animi et constantia praeditus, sequente extra urbem populo atque illacrimante tamquam illum ultra non visuro e patria discessit.

6 Vixque altero peracto miliario nuntiatum est Tarenti principem, qui a rege Ferdinando defecerat, interventu Bartholomei archiepiscopi Ravennatis, quem pontifex in Regnum ad res visendas miserat, et adnitentibus Venetorum legatis domino suo reconciliatum esse. Quae res perfidia principis, ut postea dicetur, infirma fuit.

: 26 :

De oppido Bonitii et occursu Galeazii et Florentiae ingressu.

1 Ingresso praesuli Florentinorum agrum legati ad oppidum Bonitii occurrerunt, primores urbis, magnificis verbis Christi vicarium honorantes. Id oppidum tempestate nostra parvi momenti est et in plano iacet apud Elsam fluvium; olim in alto monte, qui ei supereminet, situm fuit, ambitu magnum, populo plenum neque expugnatu facile. Quod cum esset Gibellinarum partium Florentinisque saepe multa attulisset incommoda, ab eis muro primum apertum est, deinde prorsus deletum et in eum locum translatum, quem ante diximus.

2 Hic pontifex nocte peracta sequenti die apud castellum Sancti Cassiani novos legatos habuit obvios, numero plures et dignitate praestantiores, qui eum non longe ab oppido in praedium pulcherrimum privati civis deduxere, atque ibi pernoctatum est. Postera die dum Carthusiam peteret pontifex, Faventinum, Foroliviensem et Corneliensem vicarios occurrentes invenit, et paulo post Galeazium, primogenitum Francisci Sfortiae Mediolanensium principis.

tive land. The people followed him to the outskirts of the city and wept as though they would never see him again.

He had just passed the second milestone when news reached 6
him that the prince of Taranto, who had previously deserted King Ferrante, had been reconciled to his master by the intervention of Bartolomeo, archbishop of Ravenna (whom Pius had sent into the kingdom to observe conditions) and by the efforts of the Venetian ambassadors. This reconciliation, as we shall explain below, did not last long thanks to the perfidy of the prince.

: 26 :

Poggibonsi. Galeazzo provides an escort for the entry into Florence.

As Pius entered Florentine territory, he was met at Poggibonsi by 1
a delegation of the chief men of the city, who showed grandiloquent respect to the Vicar of Christ. These days, Poggibonsi is a town of little note, lying in the Val d'Elsa, but once it sat high on the mountain overlooking its present site and was large and populous and difficult to storm. Because it sided with the Ghibellines and gave the Florentines a great deal of trouble, they first destroyed its walls and later razed it to the ground and moved it to the site just mentioned.

Here the pope spent the night. Next day he was met at San 2
Casciano by a new group of ambassadors, more numerous and distinguished than the last, who escorted him to a fine estate not far from town, the property of a private citizen, where he spent the next night. The following day, on his way to the Certosa, he was met by the lords of Faenza, Forlì and Imola and soon after by Galeazzo Sforza, the eldest son of Francesco Sforza, duke of Milan.

3 Adolescentulus hic egregia specie nondum sextum decimum impleverat annum, verum his moribus, ea eloquentia, eo ingenio atque industria praeditus, ut plus quam virilem prudentiam prae se ferret. Erat in vultu gestuque gravitas digna principe; loquebatur ex tempore, quod vix alius diu cogitans effari potuisset; nihil pueriliter agebat, nihil leviter; stupor fuit audire seniles ex iuvenili ore sententias, et nondum barbatum cani hominis sensa proferre. Hunc genitor ex Mediolano cum quingentis equitibus, splendido et ornatissimo comitatu Florentiam usque misit pontifici obviam; qui ad tertium lapidem paulo citra Carthusiam ei occurrens et ab equo desiliens sacros de more pedes exosculatus est.

4 Pontifici prandium in monasterio Carthusiensi apparatum, atque eo peracto in urbem properatum. Extra portam duobus circiter stadiis, Guelfarum duces partium occurrere et praetor urbis et multi magistratus; in porta, priores quos vocant dominos, qui pontifice verbis humilibus salutato et pedibus osculatis urbem et populum ei commendarunt.[75]

5 Propter aegritudinem pedum non poterat equo pontifex vehi; sella sedens aurea humeris hominum portabatur. In ipso urbis ingressu, postquam sacerdotes sacra ferentes benedictionem pontificis acceperunt et pompam ducentes praecesserunt, Sigismundus Malatesta et alii Ecclesiae vicarii, quorum supra meminimus, sellam pontificis subiere, suumque dominum humeris aliquandiu portavere — dicente non absque indignatione Sigismundo, 'En, quo deducti sumus! Urbium domini lecticarii iam tandem evasimus!' Tulit tamen vel invitus onus. Galeazius, qui minor esset et cruribus paululum invalidis, quamvis onus ferre non posset, manum tamen apposuit quasi adiutor, cupiens unus videri portantium; priores urbis hinc atque inde pedibus incedebant. Mutabantur autem portantes per dimensa loca, et honoratiores cives id sibi muneris expetebant.

This handsome youth was not yet sixteen, but his character, eloquence, intellect and diligence were such that he seemed wiser than many a grown man. In his expression and bearing he had the dignity of a prince; he gave extemporaneous speeches which most men could scarcely have declaimed after long preparation; there was nothing frivolous or immature about him. It was astounding to hear sentiments of great age issue from the mouth of a child and to listen to a beardless boy express the ideas of a grizzled old man. His father had sent him together with a splendid and magnificently accoutred escort of five hundred horsemen from Milan to Florence to meet the pope. Encountering Pius at the third milestone, a little beyond the Certosa, Galeazzo leapt from his horse and, as was proper, kissed Pius's holy feet. 3

At the monastery, a lunch had been spread for the pope. After eating, he made haste to the city, where he was met about two stades outside the gate by the leaders of the Guelf party, the Standard-Bearer[62] and many other city officials. At the gate itself stood the Lord Priors, who greeted the pope humbly, kissed his feet, and commended the city and its people to his care. 4

The pope's gout kept him from riding on horseback, but he was carried on the shoulders of his attendants in a golden chair. Just as he entered the city, after the priests carrying the sacred relics had received his blessing and advanced to their places at the head of the procession, Sigismondo Malatesta and the other vicars of the Church whom I have mentioned above raised the pope's chair on their shoulders and carried their master some distance. Sigismondo muttered with indignation the whole time—"See how low we lords of cities have sunk!" Galeazzo was too short and a little weak in the legs and so could not help with the weight, but he laid his hand on the chair so as to appear to be one of the bearers. The Priors of the city walked on either side. The bearers were changed at fixed intervals and the most distinguished citizens claimed a part in this service. 5

6 Galeazius, cum aliquantisper pedibus ambulasset, iussu pontificis equum ascendit, et paulo post Ecclesiae vicarii. Urbs plena populo fuit, et suo et alieno; vicini ex oppidis et agris novum visuri praesulem undique concurrerant. Feminarum dives ornatus visebatur, mira vestium varietas, domesticus simul et peregrinus cultus, verum dealbatae facies lituram haud dubiam ostendere. Ingressus praesul ecclesiam Sanctae Reparatae et sacellum Beati Iohannis utrobique populo benedixit. Diversorium et apud Sanctam Mariam fuit, cui Novella cognomen[76] est, ubi et Martinus et Eugenius, sui praedecessores collocati fuerunt.

: 27 :

Florentiae origo eiusque gesta et factiones.

1 Florentia, olim Fluentia dicta[77] a fluenti Arno qui eam interlabitur, Etruriae nunc caput est; crevit ex ruinis Faesularum quas Totila diruit, Gothorum imperator. Volaterras, Pistorium, Arretium, Cortonam, Pisas sub iugum misit, Lucensibus magnam agri[78] partem ademit, Senenses magnis affecit cladibus, a quibus et aliquando detrimentum passa est; Germanis imperatoribus saepenumero adversata. Henricus septimus circa moenia castra tenuit duraque urbem cinxit obsidione, domuissetque prorsus, nisi vocatus Neapolim adversus Robertum regem, dum eo pergit cum parte copiarum apud Bonum Conventum, ut ante diximus, veneno perisset. Carolus quartus ad portas usque Florentinas cum exercitu profectus Gibellinos urbe pulsos in civitatem restituit.

2 Mediolanensium duces acerrimis odiis Florentinos insecuti sunt damnisque permultis affecerunt, neque ipsi sine detrimento fuere.

When Galeazzo had walked a short distance, he remounted at the pope's command and, soon after, the vicars of the Church did as well. The city was full of people, both citizens and outsiders. They had come from everywhere, from neighboring towns and from the countryside, to see the new pope. The women were richly dressed in a marvelous variety of costumes, both domestic and foreign in style, but their whitened faces clearly betrayed their use of cosmetics. The pope visited the church of the Reparata and the baptistery of San Giovanni and in both places gave his blessing to the people. He was lodged at Santa Maria Novella, where Martin and Eugenius had been entertained before him.[63] 6

: 27 :

Florence: its origins, history and civil wars.

Florence was once called Fluentia, after the river Arno which "flows" through it, and is now the capital of Tuscany. It was built on the ruins of Faesulae after its destruction by Totila, king of the Goths.[64] The city conquered Volterra, Pistoia, Arezzo, Cortona and Pisa, deprived Lucca of much of her territory, and inflicted great harm on the Sienese, at whose hands she herself sometimes suffered. Several times Florence took a stand against the German emperors. Henry VII pitched his tents before the walls and subjected the city to a difficult siege. He almost certainly would have taken the place had he not been called to Naples to fight King Robert and, while en route there with part of his forces, died of poison at Buonconvento, as I mentioned above.[65] Charles IV advanced with an army right up to the gates of Florence and restored the Ghibellines who had been exiled from the city.[66] 1

The dukes of Milan nurtured the bitterest hatred for the Florentines and inflicted heavy losses on them, though not without 2

Franciscus Sfortia, eorum ope Mediolani ducatum assecutus, iis amicissimus fuit. Neapolitani reges modo amici, modo hostes habiti et aliquando urbis imperio potiti sunt, in qua et dux Athenarum dominatus est. Quo tandem pulso populus in libertatem se vendicavit, quamvis tum maxime servire coepit cum se liberum existimavit, ut qui uno eiecto domino multos admisit. Exagitata saepe urbs est civilibus procellis, cum optimates inter se de primatu contenderent.

3 Praestantissimi cives visi sunt aetate nostra Pallas Strogius, Nicolaus Uzanus et Rodolphus Peruzius. Pallas opibus cunctos superavit, Nicolaus prudentia, Rodolphus armis.

: 28 :

De Cosmae divitiis et potentia.

1 Adversus hos factionem excitavit Cosmas Medices, propter quam rem urbe pulsus, Uzano iam vita functo, exilium aliquandiu tulit. Deinde sub Eugenio pontifice maximo Florentiae sedente studio partium ab exilio rediit, et tumultuante civitate, deterritis qui sibi adversabantur, suum locum recuperavit; Rodolphum et Pallantem pluresque alios cives urbe pepulit, qui postea numquam rediere, quamvis Rodolphus Nicolaum Picininum adversus patriam alliciens Mugellanum agrum ingressus vastaverit, nam postea in exilio decessit. Pallas aequo animo fortunam adversam ferens Patavi

damage to themselves. The Florentines helped Francesco Sforza gain the duchy of Milan and he has remained their loyal friend. Sometimes they regarded the kings of Naples as friends and sometimes as foes; at one point Naples ruled the city. The duke of Athens also held it for a time,[67] and when he was at last expelled, the people asserted their independence. In fact, it was only then that they began to know real slavery, at the moment they believed themselves free, for they drove out one master only to admit many. The city has often been racked by civil strife as the upper classes fought with each other for power.

It is commonly held that the most distinguished Florentines of 3
modern times were Palla Strozzi, Niccolò Uzzano and Rodolfo Peruzzi. Palla surpassed all others in wealth, Niccolò in wisdom, Rodolfo in military skill.

: 28 :

Cosimo's wealth and power.

Cosimo de' Medici stirred up a faction against these men and as a 1
result was banished from the city. Uzzano was already dead and Cosimo remained in exile for some time. Then, as Pope Eugenius was holding court in Florence and various parties were contending with one another, Cosimo returned from exile. With the city in uproar, he subdued his opponents and regained his old power, driving Rodolfo and Palla and many other citizens into exile.[68] They never returned, though Rodolfo enlisted the services of Niccolò Piccinino against his country and raided and plundered the territory of the Mugello; afterwards, however, he died in exile. Palla endured adversity cheerfully and devoted his old age to the study of philosophy at Padua, where he died at nearly ninety, a

usque ad extremam senectutem philosophiam sectatus est, ibique obiit iam ferme nonagenarius, quem sui cives eiecissent indignus.

2 Cosmas deinde sublatis emulis pro suo arbitrio rem publicam administravit, easque opes accumulavit quales vix Croesum possedisse putaverim. Aedificavit in urbe palatium rege dignum, ecclesias alias instauravit, alias a fundamentis erexit; monasterium Sancti Marci miro construxit opere, in quo bibliothecam graecis ac latinis voluminibus refersit; villas magnifice adornavit. Videbatur iam praeclaris operibus invidiam superasse, sed populi excellentem virtutem omnes oderunt: inventi sunt, qui tyrannidem Cosmae ferendam negarent, eiusque conatibus multis modis obviam irent, et quidam probra in eum iacerent.

3 Aestimatio bonorum, quae quisque possideret, per idem tempus faciunda fuit. 'Catastum' Florentini vocant, Senenses 'libram,' per quam magistratus facultates civium non ignorantes ex aequo possint inter subiectos onera partiri. Suadebat catastum innovari Cosmas, inimici adversabantur; ob quam rem parlamentum fieri placuit. Quod dum cogeretur, armati undique collecti iussu Cosmae forum circumdedere, manifestumque imminere periculum ostenderunt his qui consilium eius damnarent. Decretum est catastum armorum metu, et cives qui prius contradicebant alii relegati sunt, alii aere mulctati.

4 Post haec nihil Cosmae negatum: is belli pacisque iudex et legum moderator, non tam civis quam patriae dominus haberi; consilium de re publica domi suae agitari; magistratum hi gerere quos ipse designasset; nihil sibi ad regnum nisi nomen et pompa deesse. Ob quam rem cum rogasset aliquando Pius pontifex episcopum Ortanum, quid sibi de Florentia videretur, indignumque diceret tam pulchram feminam viro carere, respondit ille, 'Viro,

man who had not deserved the banishment imposed on him by his compatriots.

After thus disposing of his rivals, Cosimo proceeded to govern 2
the state as he saw fit, amassing a fortune such as even Croesus could scarcely have owned. The palace he built for himself in Florence was fit for a king; he restored a number of churches and erected others; he established the splendid monastery of San Marco and stocked its library with Greek and Latin manuscripts; he decorated his villas in magnificent style. By these noble works, it seemed that he had almost triumphed over envy, but the people will ever despise an outstanding character. There were some who claimed that Cosimo's tyranny was intolerable and tried various means to thwart his projects; some even hurled abuse at him.

At this point, it came time to assess the property of every citi- 3
zen. The Florentines call this process *catasto,* the Sienese *libra.* It allows the magistrates to determine the resources of the citizenry and thus apportion levies fairly among them. Cosimo was in favor of a new catasto; his opponents were against it. Therefore it was decided to call a general meeting of the city. As the people were assembling, a group of armed men gathered from all quarters at Cosimo's command; they surrounded the piazza and made it clear that anyone who objected to Cosimo's plans did so at his peril. The catasto was approved under threat of violence; some of the citizens who had opposed it were banished and others were fined.[69]

After this Cosimo was refused nothing. In matters of war and 4
peace his decisions were final and his word was regarded as law, not so much a citizen as the master of his city. Government meetings were held at his house; his candidates were elected to public office; he enjoyed every semblance of royal power except a title and a court. It was for this reason that, when Pius asked the bishop of Orte what he thought about Florence and he replied it was a pity so beautiful a woman had no husband, the pope said, "Yes, but

non moecho caret,' ac si diceret, 'Tyrannum, non regem habet,' designans Cosmam, qui tamquam urbis dominus non legitimus duro plebem servitio premeret. Aegrotabat ille, cum Pius Florentiae fuit seu, quod plerique putaverunt, ne pontificem accederet aegroti faciem induit.

5 Maiores Cosmae ex Mugello in urbem venerunt. Iohannes, qui pater eius fuit, in clientelam Medicorum receptus familiae quoque nomen assumpsit, ingentesque opes liberis suis Cosmae et Laurentio reliquit. Cosmas, supra quam credibile sit, eas ampliavit per omnem Europam negotiatus et ad Aegyptum usque mercimoniis intentus. Fuit hic egregio corpore, statura plus quam mediocri, aspectu et alloquio placidus; litterae in eo plures quam mercatores assequi soleant, graecarum non prorsus ignaro. Ingenium ei perspicax et ad omnia promptum quae ageret; animus neque ignavus neque fortis. Laborem et inediam facile pertulit et noctes crebro insomnes duxit. Nihil ignoravit eorum quae in Italia gererentur, quippe quod eius consilio magna pars urbium et regulorum duceretur. Nec eum res exterae latuerunt, cui ex orbe fere toto mercatores socii responderent, et quae apud eos fierent crebris epistolis indicarent. Ad extremum podagra laboravit, cuius antea quam vita excederet successores filios ac nepotes vidit. Annum agebat Florentiam[79] transeunte pontifice supra septuagesimum.

: 29 :

De Antonio praesule Florentino eiusque sanctimonia ac morte.

1 Per idem tempus migravit in Domino Antonius, ecclesiae Florentinae archiepiscopus, Ordinis Predicatorum professor, vir memoria

she has a lover," meaning that she had a tyrant instead of a king. Pius was referring to Cosimo who, as an illegitimate lord, kept the city and its people in cruel servitude. During Pius's stay in Florence, Cosimo was ill or rather (as many believed) he pretended to be ill, so he would not have to wait on the pope.

Cosimo's ancestors came to Florence from the Mugello. His fa- 5
ther Giovanni became a client of the Medici and took the name of the family.[70] He left an enormous fortune to his sons, Cosimo and Lorenzo, which grew incredibly in Cosimo's hands. His business interests ranged over all of Europe and he traded as far as Egypt. He was of fine physique and more than average height; his countenance and speech were mild; he was more cultured than merchants usually are and had some knowledge of Greek; his mind was keen and alert to everything going on around him; his spirit was neither cowardly nor rash; he easily endured toil and hunger and often went whole nights without sleep.[71] Nothing happened in Italy without his knowledge; indeed it was his advice that guided the policy of many cities and princes. Nor were foreign events a secret to him, for his business contacts all over the world sent him a constant stream of letters which kept him abreast of affairs in their states. Toward the end of his life he suffered from gout, a disease which he lived to see his sons and grandsons inherit. When the pope passed through Florence he was more than seventy years old.

: 29 :

The sanctity and death of Bishop Antonino of Florence.

It was at this time that Antonino, the archbishop of Florence, 1
went to meet his maker.[72] A member of the Dominican Order and a man worthy of remembrance, he conquered avarice, trampled on

dignus. Domuit avaritiam, calcavit superbiam, libidinem prorsus ignoravit, potu ciboque parcissime usus est; non irae, non invidiae, non alteri passioni succubuit; doctrina theologica emicuit, scripsit plura volumina quae docti laudant; praedicator acceptus in populo quamvis scelerum insectator vehemens; correxit cleri et populi mores, lites diligenter composuit, inimicitias (quoad potuit) ex urbe pepulit; proventus ecclesiae inter Christi pauperes distribuit; in cognatos et affines suos, nisi admodum inopes essent, nihil contulit; vitreis ac fictilibus tantum vasis est usus; familia, quae parva illi fuit, contentari modico voluit et ad philosophiae leges vivere. Mortuo nobile funus ex publico ductum. In domo nihil repertum est praeter mulum quo insedere solitus erat et vilem supellectilem; cetera manus pauperum asportavere.[80] Civitas (nec vana putanda opinio est) ad vitam illum migrasse beatam putavit.

2 Magistratus urbis, ubi se tanto privatum patre, et orphanorum tutorem[81] viduarumque iudicem defecisse animadvertit, accedens Pium pontificem non istum aut illum, sed aliquem[82] ex civibus suis in eius locum surrogari petiit, qui tanto viro dignus videri successor posset. Laudavit pontifex Florentinos, qui non ut Veneti, obstinate unum aliquem petivissent, auditurumque sese ait honestas preces.

: 30 :

De viris illustribus Florentinis.

1 Superiori aetate complures viri apud Florentinos illustres fuere, quorum hodie quoque nomen extat, verum Dantes Aringherius cunctos superasse videtur, cuius insigne poema et nobilis illa de

pride, knew absolutely nothing of lust, consumed food and drink only sparingly and never gave in to anger or envy or any other passion. He was a brilliant theologian and wrote several books which were praised by scholars; he was a popular preacher even though he was violent in his denunciation of sin; he reformed the morals of clergy and laity; he worked hard to settle quarrels; he did his best to rid the city of feuds; he distributed the revenues of his church among the poor of Christ, but to his relatives and connections, unless they were very needy, he gave nothing. He used only glass and clay dishes and he desired his household (which was very small) to be content with little and to live by the precepts of philosophy. At his death he was accorded a splendid public funeral. In his house they found nothing but the mule he used to ride and some cheap furniture; the poor had taken everything else. All of Florence was sure that he had passed to a life of bliss — nor should we imagine their belief was unfounded.

When the chief magistracy[73] of the city learned that they had 2
lost such a father, such a guardian of orphans and protector of widows, they approached Pope Pius and begged him to appoint in his place some fellow citizen (they did not specify anyone in particular) who seemed worthy to succeed so great a man. The pope praised the Florentines for not insisting, like the Venetians, on a particular candidate, and he promised to grant their honorable request.

: 30 :

Some famous Florentines.

Many illustrious Florentines of ages past remain famous even to- 1
day, but the greatest of them all is Dante Alighieri. His magnificent poem with its noble description of Heaven, Hell, and Purga-

superis, inferis ac medioximis inventio doctrinam paene divinam redolet, etsi ut homo nonnihil erravit. Proximus ei Franciscus successit cognomento Petrarcha, cui vix parem inveniremus,[83] si latina eius opera his quae tusco sermone conscripsit aequari possent. Tertio loco Iohannem Bochacium haud iniuria collocaverim, quamvis paulo lascivior fuerit neque admodum tersus.

2 Hunc sequitur Colutius, qui et prosa scripsit et versu ad suam aetatem accommodato, ad nostram rudi; is dictandis epistolis apud Florentinos praefuit, cuius calamum plus sibi obesse Iohannes Galeazius Mediolanensium dux solitus erat dicere, quam Florentinorum equitum, qui sibi hostes erant, triginta cohortes. Erat enim vir prudens, et quamvis elegantiam scribendi non teneret, locos tamen egregie callebat quibus moveri homines solent, eosque scribens cautissime attingebat. Successit pluribus post annis Leonardus, natione Arretinus, verum Florentina[84] civitate donatus, graecis ac latinis litteris apprime imbutus, cuius eloquentia prope ad Ciceronem accessit, multis operibus e graeco in latinum translatis egregiam laudem assecutus. Par prope huic oratione soluta, carmine maior inventus est Carolus, et ipse Arretinus origine, privilegio Florentinus. Fuit et Poggius in hac urbe clarus, qui cum aliquandiu apud Romanos pontifices secretariatum gessisset, et aliquot opera egregia scripsisset, postremo in patriam reversus ac cancellariae praefectus inter cognatos suos vitam finivit.

3 In armis qui ex Florentinis claruerint, magna est Pipponis gloria e familia Scolarium, qui regnum Hungariae multis annis administravit, in quo rege potentior visus est. Ex Acciarolis quoque magister militiae in Regno Siciliae Nicolaus fuit praeclari nominis, cuius filius arma in Graeciam proferens Thebas atque Athenas occupavit, et posteris possidendas reliquit, quas illi nostra demum aetate perdiderunt a Mahumete Turchorum imperatore deiecti.

tory seems to breathe a wisdom almost divine—although in his life he sometimes erred. Next to him comes Francesco Petrarca, whose equal would be hard to find were his Latin works as fine as those he wrote in Italian. The third place I would justly assign to Giovanni Boccaccio, though he was a little more frivolous and his style was not highly polished.

Next comes Coluccio, who wrote prose and verse in a style that 2
suited his age, though it seems rough to ours. He was chancellor of Florence; and as Florence was then an enemy of Milan, Duke Giangaleazzo used to say that Coluccio's pen could do him more harm than thirty troops of Florentine cavalry.[74] Coluccio was a shrewd man and, though his style lacked elegance, still he had a remarkable command of the rhetorical devices that stir the human heart, and in his writing he deployed these with great skill. After several years he was succeeded in his post by Leonardo, who was born in Arezzo but became a citizen of Florence. He was deeply versed in Greek and Latin. His eloquence approached that of Cicero and he earned a brilliant reputation for himself by translating many works from Greek into Latin. Next we find Carlo, nearly Leonardo's equal in prose and his superior in verse, and likewise an Aretine by birth but a Florentine by courtesy. Poggio too was a famous citizen of Florence. After serving for many years as a papal secretary and writing several remarkable books, he at last returned to his native city, where he was appointed chancellor and ended his days among his kinsmen.[75]

Of the Florentines who have excelled in military pursuits, one 3
of the most famous is Pippo Scolari. For many years he governed the kingdom of Hungary, where he seemed to have more power than the king himself. From the Acciaiuoli family, Niccolò earned fame as the Grand Seneschal of the kingdom of Sicily. His son led an expedition into Greece, captured Thebes and Athens and left them to his descendants, who lost them only recently when they were dislodged by Mehmed, the sultan of the Turks.[76] A great

Permulti praeterea viri commemorari possent, quorum virtute Florentia et opibus et gloria est aucta.

: 31 :

De magnificentia aedificiorum Florentinorum et ludicro apparatu.

1 Florentiam qui laudant, non solum viros illustres, qui fuerunt in ea, commemorant, verum urbis amplitudinem, qua nulla est praeter Romam in Italia maior; murorum ambitum, qui praealtus est et spissitudine praecipua; viarum et platearum munditiem, quae tum amplae sunt, tum ad longum[85] directae prospectum;[86] templorum magnificentiam ac palatiorum et publicorum et privatorum, quae et altissima et ornatissima sunt. Ceterum inter aedificia nullum memorabilius est aede Sanctae Reparatae, in qua fornix est ad amplitudinem eius proxime accedens quam Romae in Agrippae templo admiramur, quod Pantheon vocavere. Proximum ei est palatium quod priores inhabitant, et tertium a Cosma aedificatum. Laudant et Divi Baptistae sacellum et aedem quam Cosmas idem Beato Laurentio construxit.

2 Afferunt pontes qui civitatem Arno discissam coniungunt, et numerosum populum et ornamenta tum virorum tum feminarum, et omnis generis opificia, et praedia et villas egregias quae civitati adiacent plenae deliciis et non minori sumptu quam civitas ipsa exaedificatae, et ingenia hominum dexterrima, quamvis in mercatura magis excellunt, quam philosophi sordidam putant; videntur et ad rem plus aequo attenta, ac propterea cum honorandi pontificis gratia primores urbis auri quatuordecim milia nummum ex plebe corrasissent, maiorem sibi partem retinuere, partem in Ga-

many more men could be mentioned whose abilities have added to the power and fame of Florence.

: 31 :

The magnificent buildings and glorious pageantry of Florence.

Those who would praise Florence must mention not only her most famous citizens but also the size of the city, which in all of Italy is second only to Rome; the height and remarkable thickness of the walls that encircle it; the elegance of the piazzas and streets, which are not only broad but straight; and the magnificence of the churches and the lofty palaces, both public and private, which are decorated in splendid style. Among all the buildings none is more worthy of note than the church of the Reparata, whose dome is nearly as large as the remarkable one in Rome in the temple of Agrippa, which we call the Pantheon. Next comes the palace of the Priors and third the palace of Cosimo. Also worth mentioning are the baptistery of San Giovanni and the church of San Lorenzo, another of Cosimo's constructions. 1

Then there are the bridges over the Arno linking the two sides of the city, and the enormous population, the beautiful costumes worn by men and women alike, the shops of every description, the great estates and splendid and delightful villas outside the walls, which cost as much to build as the city itself, and finally the quick wits of the citizens, though their greatest talent is for trade, which philosophers find sordid. They seem excessively interested in profit: for this reason, after the leading citizens had scraped together some 14,000 ducats from the people to underwrite the pope's reception, they kept most of it for themselves and used part 2

leazium eiusque pascendos comites contulere. Impensa erga pontificem minima fuit, nec in apparandis ludis magni sumptus facti, quamvis leones in forum produxerint adversus equos et alias bestias pugnaturos, et equestria instituerint certamina, in quis multo plus vini haustum quam sanguinis effusum. Hic pontifex octo diebus commoratus est, per quod tempus a Sigismundo Malatesta multis precibus oratur,[87] sibi ut pacem daret cum Ferdinando Siciliae rege bellum gerenti.

: 32 :

De Sigismundo Malatesta eiusque flagiciosis sceleribus.

1 Sigismundus ex Malatestarum nobili familia verum extra matrimonium natus, multa vi animi et corporis fuit, eloquentia militari et arte praeditus; novit historias, philosophiae non parvam peritiam habuit; quamcunque rem sectatus est, ad eam natus videbatur. Sed mali mores plus apud eum valuere: avaritiae adeo sese dedit, ut non praedari tantum sed furari quoque non vereretur; libidinis ita impatiens fuit, ut filiabus ac generis vim intulerit; adolescens[88] nupsit in feminam, et saepe muliebria passus saepe masculos effeminavit; nulla apud eum sancta fuere matrimonia, virgines sacras incestavit, Iudeas violavit; pueros ac puellas qui ei non consensere, aut neci dedit, aut crudelibus modis everberavit; mulieres, quarum filios e sacro fonte levavit, complures adulterio polluit earumque viros necavit. Barbaros omnes crudelitate vicit; cruentae manus diris suppliciis sontes et insontes affecerunt.

2 Pauperes oppressit, divitibus bona diripuit, nec viduis aut pupillis pepercit; nemo sub eius imperio securus vixit, reos nunc opes

to support Galeazzo and his retinue. They spent very little on the pope, nor did they lay on much in the way of entertainment, though they brought lions into the piazza to fight with horses and other animals, and they held equestrian tournaments in which much more wine was drunk than blood spilled. The pope stayed for a week, in the course of which Sigismondo Malatesta requested Pius to arbitrate between himself and King Ferrante of Sicily, who had just declared war against him.

: 32 :

Sigismondo Malatesta and his unspeakable crimes.

Sigismondo, of the noble house of Malatesta, was a bastard.[77] In both mind and body he was exceedingly powerful, gifted with eloquence and great military skill, a profound knowledge of history and more than a passing understanding of philosophy. Whatever he attempted he seemed born to do, but above all else he prized sin. He was a slave to avarice, prepared not only to plunder but to steal, so unbridled in his lust that he violated both his daughters and his sons-in-law. As a boy he often played the bride; later, he who had so often taken the woman's part used other men like whores. No marriage was sacred to him. He raped Christian nuns and Jewish ladies alike; boys and girls who resisted him he would either murder or torture in terrible ways. Often, if he stood godfather to a child, he would compel the mother to commit adultery, then have her husband killed. He surpassed every barbarian in cruelty; his bloody hands wreaked dire torments on innocent and guilty alike. 1

He oppressed the poor and plundered the rich; neither widows nor orphans were spared. Under his tyranny no one was safe. A man blessed with wealth or a beautiful wife or handsome children 2

nunc uxores aut liberi forma praestantes fecere. Sacerdotes odio habuit, religionem contempsit, de venturo saeculo nihil credidit, et animas perire cum corpore existimavit. Aedificavit tamen nobile templum Arimini in honorem Divi Francisci, verum ita gentilibus operibus implevit, ut non tam Christianorum, quam infidelium daemones adorantium templum esse videretur, atque in eo concubinae suae tumulum erexit et artificio et lapide pulcherrimum, adiecto titulo gentili more in hunc modum: 'Divae Isottae sacrum.'

3 Duas uxores, quas duxerat ante Isottae contubernium, alteram post alteram seu ferro seu veneno extinxit; tertiam, quae has praecesserat, nondum cognitam accepta dote repudiavit. Feminam nobilem ex Germania Romam petentem in anno Iubilaeo non procul a Verona, cum esset forma egregia, vi rapuit, ac reluctantem vulneratam et cruore madentem reliquit.

4 Rara in ore suo veritas, simulandi ac dissimulandi egregius artifex. Perfidus atque periurus, Alfonso Siciliae regi et eius filio Ferdinando, Francisco Mediolani duci, Venetis, Florentinis, Senensibus fidem abrupit, Ecclesiae quoque Romanae saepius illusit. Postremo, cum nemo esset in Italia quem prodere posset, ad Francos abiit, qui odio Pii praesulis eius secuti fidem non meliorem quam reliqui principes successum habuere. Rogatus aliquando a subditis, ut quieti tandem se traderet parceretque patriae, quae sua causa saepe rapinis exposita fuisset, 'Ite,' inquit, 'et bono animo estote! Numquam me vivo pacem habebitis!'

5 Huiuscemodi Sigismundus fuit: quietis impatiens, voluptatum sequax, quamvis laboris patiens et belli cupidus; hominum, qui unquam fuerunt quique futuri sunt, pessimus Italiae dedecus et nostri infamia saeculi.

would find himself facing a trumped-up criminal charge. He hated priests and despised religion, thought nothing of the world to come, and believed the soul died with the body. He did build a splendid church at Rimini dedicated to St. Francis, but he filled it so full of pagan works of art that it seemed less a Christian sanctuary than a temple where heathens might worship the devil. Inside, he erected a magnificent marble tomb for his mistress. The craftsmanship was exquisite. The inscription ran, in pagan style, "Sacred to the deified Isotta."[78]

Before taking Isotta for his mistress he had two wives whom he killed in succession, using violence or poison. A third, whom he had married before the other two, he divorced before ever having intercourse with her, though he kept her dowry. Once, not far from Verona, he met a noble lady on her way from Germany to Rome for the jubilee; he raped her (for she was very beautiful) and left her there in the road, wounded from her struggles and dripping with blood. 3

Truth was seldom in his mouth. He was a past master of pretense and dissimulation, a perjuror and a cheat. He broke faith with King Alfonso of Sicily and his son Ferrante; with Francesco, duke of Milan; and with the Venetians, the Florentines and the Sienese. Repeatedly he deceived the Church of Rome. Finally, when there was no one left in Italy for him to betray, he went over to the French who, out of hatred for Pope Pius, pursued an alliance with him; but they fared no better than the other princes. Once, when asked by his subjects if he would not at last retire to a peaceful life and thereby give some relief to the country which he had so often subjected to war, he replied, "Be off, and don't lose your nerve! As long as I'm alive you'll never have peace!" 4

Such was Sigismondo, a man with no tolerance for peace, a devotee of pleasure, patient of any hardship, eager for war, the worst of all men who have ever lived or ever will live, the shame of Italy, the disgrace of our age.[79] 5

6 Hunc Alfonsus in eo bello quod cum Florentinis gessit, ut sibi militaret, magno auri pondere conduxit. Ille novo auro inauratus ad Florentinos defecit atque in Alfonsum arma convertit, perfidiae suae id causae praetendens, quod non omne sibi stipendium in tempore persolutum fuisset. Gravis haec regi iactura fuit, qui eum hostem passus est quem propugnatorem paraverat. Nec dubium quin ea Sigismundi proditio rem Florentinam salvaverit. Ob quam rem, cum pax universalis facta est et inter potentatus Italiae foedus percussum, Sigismundus et Genuenses et Aestor Faventinus exclusi sunt, rege in eos qui sibi ius iurandum fidemque abrupissent liberum sibi bellum reservante.

7 Atque idcirco valida in Genuenses ab eo classis parata est, et adversus Sigismundum ultimo Callisti pontificis et suae vitae anno Picininus, Nicolai filius, cum magna militum manu transmissus, procurante id potissimum Federico Urbinate, qui privatis inimicitiis Sigismundo erat infensus. Bellum aliquandiu tractum est vivente Alfonso et, eo fatis functo, cum filius aeque ac pater Sigismundo indignaretur. Ferebant subditi pro peccato domini supplicium, et impio superbiente pauper incendebatur. Vastabatur ager tota Italia nobilis, quamvis tyranno subiectus impiissimo, directo tamen iure ad Romanam Ecclesiam pertinens.

8 Quod miseratus Pius pontifex, ut ante retulimus, inter alias leges quas Ferdinando imposuit Regno Siciliae honestato, illam adiecit ut pacem Sigismundo his conventionibus donaret, quas pontifex ipse dictaret. At cum Asisium recuperavit, haec libertas restricta est, constitutumque ut praescripto quodam modo pax

Alfonso hired him to be his condottiere in the war he was waging against Florence. He paid him a large sum, but Sigismondo soon had yet more gold to flash about: he went over to the Florentines and turned his arms against Alfonso, alleging as a reason for his treachery the fact that the whole of his stipend had not been paid on time. This was a heavy blow to the king, who now had to face as an enemy the very man he had engaged to be his champion. There is no doubt that Sigismondo's perfidy was the salvation of the Florentine cause and this is the reason why, when a general peace was concluded and a compact struck among the princes of Italy, Sigismondo was excluded along with the Genoese and Astorre of Faenza.[80] The king reserved the right to declare war on those who had foresworn themselves and betrayed him. 6

Alfonso therefore fitted out a powerful fleet against the Genoese and in the last year of his life (which was also Pope Calixtus's last), he sent a large army against Sigismondo under the command of Piccinino, the son of Niccolò. This was a move enthusiastically supported by Federico of Urbino, who had his own reasons for hating Sigismondo.[81] The war dragged on for some time, not only during Alfonso's lifetime but even after his death, for Ferrante was as furious with Sigismondo as his father had been. The tyrant's subjects suffered for their master's misdeeds; it was the poor who burned for his arrogance and impiety. His lands, famed throughout Italy and legally the property of the Church of Rome (though subject to wicked tyranny) were being laid to waste. 7

Pope Pius deplored this situation, as we have mentioned before, and among the conditions he imposed on Ferrante when he was invested with the kingdom of Sicily, he had included the stipulation that Ferrante make peace with Sigismondo on terms which the pope himself would dictate.[82] After Pius had recovered Assisi, however, his freedom to dictate was restricted and it was decided that peace should be established according to certain specific conditions or, if Sigismondo would not consent to these, that they 8

constitueretur, aut si hoc ex Sigismundo obtineri non posset, compromissum remitteretur quod liberum in pontificem factum fuerat; cautumque[89] ne ultra mensem Februarium potestas compromissi duraret. Additus postea Martius est et Aprilis mensis.

9 Restabant ex compromissi tempore quatuor tantum dies, cum Pius Florentiae fuit, nec regis procuratores aderant qui causam agerent. Advenerant tamen Federici Urbinatis et Iacobi Picinini legati, ad quos rex id negotii remiserat. Iussit pontifex quatuor cardinales audire partes et ad concordiam reducere. Frustra id fuit. Audivit et per se ipsum pontifex disceptationes et iura partium; nec dubium erat, quin reus proditionis Sigismundus esset. Ventum est ad transactionem ut delictum pecunia redimeretur, et cum illa deesset, oppignorarentur castella. Sed cum regis nomine multa peterentur, Sigismundus pauca offerret, res propemodum desperata videbatur. Illi victoriam in manu sua esse aiebant; Sigismundus nondum se victum affirmabat, passurumque prius extrema quaeque, quam ea traderet quae petebantur.

10 Cumque ferocius loqueretur, 'Tace!' inquit pontifex, 'Generi tuo, non tibi studemus; populi tibi subiecti, non tui miseremur, qui pro tuis sceleribus non satis plecti potes. Sic vixisti hactenus ut nulla ultio tuis iniquitatibus inveniri maior queat,[90] et quamvis multis te verbis excusas, nemo tamen non proditorem Alfonsi[91] iudicat. Infamis tua vita contra te est et supplicium tibi expetit. Stant pro te tantum maiorum tuorum opera,[92] qui de Romana Ecclesia benefuerunt meriti, et quod dum poena de te nocente quaeritur, innocentes luunt. His de rebus pacare te hostibus quaerimus. At si recedis a bono et aequo, in quo te gurgite repperimus

should annul the compact made when the pope was a free agent. It was added that this compact should not continue in force beyond the end of February, though this deadline was later extended to March and then April.

When Pius was in Florence, the compact had only four days left to run, and the king's agents were not there to state his case. Envoys from Federico of Urbino and Jacopo Piccinino were present, however, and as the king had delegated the matter to them, the pope directed four cardinals to hear the two parties and bring them to an agreement. When this failed, the pope himself heard each side state its arguments and claims. There was no doubt Sigismondo was guilty of treachery. It was decided that he should offer restitution for the offense in the form of a cash payment or, if he had no money to pay, by pledging his castles. But, with the king's representatives demanding much and Sigismondo offering little, the case seemed almost impossible to resolve. The ambassadors claimed that victory was theirs; Sigismondo declared he was not yet beaten; he would sooner endure every torment known to man than surrender to these demands. 9

His speech grew even hotter until Pius cried out, "Silence! We're not talking about you, but about your domains. It's not you but your subjects we pity. Your actions give you no claim to consideration, and no punishment could ever be adequate to suit your crimes. Your life up to now has been so wicked that no penalty imaginable would be too severe. No matter what you say in your own defense, everyone believes you betrayed Alfonso. Your infamous behavior both provides the charge against you and demands the sentence. The only thing in your favor is the service your ancestors performed (for they deserved well of the Church of Rome), and the fact that while we spend time trying to punish your guilt, the innocent are paying the penalty. We want to reconcile you with your enemies in this affair, but if you refuse to do what is right and just, we will leave you in the hole in which we 10

in eodem relinquemus; nec mirabimur, si pauperes ad tempus permiserit divina pietas affligi, ut tandem scelestissimus[93] omnium puniaris, et aut in bello pereas aut perdito patrimonio miser in exilium eas.'

11 Territus his auditis Sigismundus his consensit quae proxima concordiae videbantur. Sed altera pars, victorum more superba, nihil mutare ex postulatis voluit. Pontifex, quamvis arbitrari posset de Sigismundo quae vellet, indignum tamen putavit victoriam magis quam aequitatem respicere, diuque adnixus est ex voluntate partium litem dirimere. Quod postquam non successit, et regi et Sigismundo compromissum remisit, non satis intellegens bellum huiuscemodi an pax rebus Ecclesiae magis conduceret, cum[94] constaret Picininum quiescere non posse, veroque simile esse liberatum eum Sigismundi bello, adversus Ecclesiam infestis signis iturum. Iudicavit igitur voluntatem Dei esse pacem non potuisse componi. Idemque Florentini existimarunt, quibus venisse diem placebat, in qua flagitiosus tandem homo meritas daret poenas.

: 33 :

De Austria et eius ducibus.

1 Inter haec et legati Sigismundi Austriae ducis pontificem adiere, qui Svicenses propediem in armis futuros dixerunt, Austrialemque domum bello aggressuros; id si fiat, magnam Germaniae partem vexatum iri, cunctosque praesulis cogitatus adversus Turchos eo pacto[95] perituros fore.

2 Austrialis familia apud Germanos nobilissima est, atque latissime dominatur. In ea quinque fuerunt Romanorum imperatores:

find you. It would not surprise us if divine mercy allowed the poor to suffer a little longer if it meant that you, who are accursed above all men, were punished, either by falling in battle or by losing your patrimony and fleeing into miserable exile."

11 At these words Sigismondo was struck with terror. He agreed to a set of terms that seemed likely to be acceptable. But now the other side, grown insolent in victory, objected and would consent to no compromise. The pope had the power to make any decision he liked concerning Sigismondo, but nevertheless he thought it would be disgraceful to honor victory over justice. For a long time he strove to settle the quarrel to the satisfaction of both sides. When he failed, he released both the king and Sigismondo from their agreement, uncertain whether a war of this kind or peace was more advantageous to the Church, since it was common knowledge that Piccinino could not keep quiet and if he were freed from the war with Sigismondo, he would probably turn his arms against the Church. Pius therefore came to the conclusion that it was God's will that peace could not be achieved. The Florentines agreed with him and rejoiced that the day had come when a scoundrel should at last get the punishment he deserved.

: 33 :

Austria and its dukes.

1 Meanwhile envoys of Sigismund, duke of Austria, came to warn the pope that the Swiss would soon take up arms and attack the house of Austria. If this should happen, a large part of Germany would be disturbed and all the pope's hopes and plans against the Turks would fall to pieces.

2 The house of Austria is the noblest of the German principalities and rules the largest territory. It has produced five emperors of

duo Alberti, duo Federici, quorum primus praelio victus cessit Ludovico Baioario,[96] et qui prior his suscepit imperium, Rodolphus, qui non magnus in Suevia comes imperator electus adversus Octocarum Bohemiae regem, cui et Austria et Styria parebat, bellum gessit, ac praelio, ut dictum est,[97] superatum interfecit, et Austriam suis[98] possidendam reliquit; quae circa Danubium nobilis provincia est, et aliis pluribus regionibus imperat. Olim, quod est citra Danubium, Norici et Pannonii tenuere; quod ultra,[99] barbari—partim Sarmatae, partim Germani.

3 Nostra aetate tres Austriae principes fuere: Federicus et Hernestus germani fratres et patruelis eorum, Albertus, qui eam partem sortitus est, quae proprie Austria dicitur, in qua Vienna[100] prisci Flavianum dixere, urbs nobilissima, mercatura et liberalium artium schola illustris. Federicus in montibus regnavit, ex quis Athesis et Enus, memorabiles amnes defluunt, salis et argenti mineris inexhaustis.[101] Ernestus Styriae praefuit, quae olim Valeria dicta est, ac per[102] Carinthiam et Carnos usque in Adriaticum sinum protendit imperium. Albertus Bohemis atque Hungaris et deinde Romanis imperavit, sed brevi functus vita Ladislaum, filium postumum reliquit, qui editus in lucem Romano dempto Imperio in ceteris regnis patri successit, atque apud Bohemos in adolescentia, ut fama est, veneno periit.

4 Ernesto duo filii fuere, Federicus et Albertus, qui patre defuncto saepe de successione armis contenderunt. Federicus Romanum imperium sortitus est, cui in hanc usque diem praesidet, variis fortunae casibus actus. Federicus senior Sigismundum impuberem filium reliquit, cuius tutelam gessit Federicus iunior. Attigerat hic iam duodeviginti annos, nec tamen e tutela dimissus est, nisi postquam provinciales assumptis armis magistratus, quos Federicus in vallibus Athesis Enique constituerat, eiecerunt. Tum

the Romans: two Alberts, two Fredericks (the first of whom was defeated in battle and abdicated in favor of Ludwig of Bavaria) and the first of all of them, Rudolf, a petty Swabian count. After he was elected emperor, he declared war on Ottokar, king of Bohemia, who also ruled Austria and Styria. He defeated and killed him and then left Austria to his own heirs.[83] It is a fine province, centered on the Danube and including numerous other districts. The land on this side of the Danube was once held by the Norici and the Pannonians; the land beyond was home to barbarians, some of them Sarmatians and some Germans.

In our time there have been three princes of Austria: Frederick 3
and Ernst, who were brothers, and their cousin Albert.[84] To Albert fell the part properly called Austria, including Vienna, known to the ancients as Flavianum. This is a very famous city celebrated for its trade and its school of liberal arts. Frederick ruled in the mountains where the important rivers Adige and Inn have their source and where there are rich mines of salt and silver. Ernst was lord of Styria, once known as Valeria; he extended his dominion to include Carinthia and Carniola as far as the Adriatic. Albert was emperor of the Bohemians and Hungarians and finally of the Romans, but he lived only a short time. His posthumous son Ladislas succeeded to all his father's kingdoms except the Roman Empire, which was taken from him, but he died while still a boy (of poison, it is said) among the Bohemians.

Ernst had two sons, Frederick and Albert, who after their fa- 4
ther's death repeatedly took up arms against each other to secure the succession. The empire fell to Frederick, who despite various vicissitudes[85] still retains possession.[86] The elder Frederick left a minor son, Sigismund, who was put under the guardianship of the younger Frederick. Even after he turned eighteen he was not released from tutelage, until the inhabitants of the province used force of arms to expel the magistrates appointed by Frederick in the valley of the Adige and the Inn. And even then, he was only

quoque certis conditionibus emissus est, quae sibi et suis gravissimae visae sunt; receptae tamen, cum aliter Sigismundus libertatem consequi non posset.

5 Hinc multae inter eum et Federicum subortae contentiones, quae nondum sopiri potuerunt, cum alter male administratam tutelam diceret, alter non servari conventa quereretur. Sigismundi provinciae[103] Svicenses contermini sunt, quos, ut diximus, ipse in Austriales arma moturos pontifici significaverat.

: 34 :

De Svicensibus et eorum gestis atque virtute, et dalphini bello.

1 Svicenses, quamvis in Gallia siti, Germani tamen lingua et moribus habentur. Montani et feroces populi, parvam olim villam incoluere quae lacui Lucernensi adiacet.

2 Euntibus ex Mediolano Basileam per Alpem, quae Sancto Gothardo dicata est, et hunc lacum navigantibus vallis ipsa ad dextram occurrit, quam vix homines quingenti incolunt, solis pecoribus abundantes. Inter hos et Austriae duces leves ob causas graves emerserunt inimicitiae, quae armis agitatae sunt. Cumque priores insultationes prosperae Svicensibus evenissent, qui Austrialibus acie superatis Leopoldum gentis ducem interfecerunt, et animis et amicis aucti sunt adeo, ut vicinorum montium accolae et oppida permulta in eorum clientelam transierint, quorum praecipua sunt Lucerna, Sophinga, Balneum, Solotrum, Berna et alia pleraque quae, licet populosa et potentissima essent, vocari tamen Svicenses

released on certain conditions which he and his friends found very oppressive; nevertheless he accepted them because he could not otherwise obtain his independence.[87]

This gave rise to many quarrels between him and Frederick 5
which still have not subsided, for one asserted that his guardian had administered his trust dishonorably and the other complained that his ward never respected the conditions they had agreed. Sigismund's territory borders on the Swiss, and it was they who seemed about to attack the Austrians, as Sigismund informed the pope and as I have already explained.

: 34 :

The Swiss, their history and character, and their war with the dauphin.

Although the territory of the Swiss lies in France, their language 1
and customs are German. They are descended from fierce mountain tribes who settled a little town on Lake Lucerne.

If one sails across Lake Lucerne on the way from Milan to 2
Basel (taking the route, that is, over the Gotthard Alps) one passes on the right a valley inhabited by a scant fifty men whose sole wealth is in their flocks. Between these men and the princes of Austria serious differences once arose from trivial reasons, and they resorted to arms. The Swiss had the upper hand in their first encounters: they defeated the Austrians and killed their general, Leopold,[88] thus gaining both confidence and allies. All the inhabitants of the nearby mountain and several neighboring towns placed themselves under their protection. Chief among these were Lucerne, Zofingen, Basel, Solothurn and Bern, as well as many other towns which, though populous and very powerful, were not

non recusarunt, quorum nomen a lacu prope Lemanno et Rhodano fluvio usque ad Brigantinas aquas et flumen Rhenum protenditur, et ab Alpibus Italicis Basiliensem contingit agrum, facileque bellatorum triginta milia, ubi necessitas ingruit, expeditorum in armis habet virorum, qui fugere nesciant.

3 Iustitiae his hominibus praecipua cura; fures acriter puniunt, acrius latrones. Hospitalitatem diligenter observant, sacerdotes honorant, religioni parent, pace gaudent et suo contentantur. Bella non movent nisi irritati; ex praelio fugisse capitale est; eorum qui cadunt in pugna liberos atque uxores publice alunt. Robusta his pectora et insuperabiles animi. Adversus Philippum Mariam Mediolani ducem transgressi Alpes non procul a Belinzona infelici pugna decertarunt; quamvis cruentam victoriam hosti reliquere, Angelus Pergula eos delevit. Occisus est in praelio magnae staturae vir cuius cadaver Mediolanum delatum gigantis propemodum staturam prae se ferebat. Cum Thuricensibus dispari eventu bellum gessere, cum illi societate eorum dimissa ad Federicum caesarem defecissent; nam circiter octingentos viros unica pugna obtruncaverunt.

4 Austriales pluribus cladibus affecere, et partem agri illis ademerunt; postremo in quinquaginta annos pax statuta, quae tunc rupta est, cum dalphinus Viennensis, regis Franciae primogenitus, magnis equitum copiis circumdatus Basiliensibus bellum intulit; tunc enim Austriales subditi in spem erecti dalphini partes secuti foedus rupere. Miserant Svicenses quatuor milia militum auxilio Basiliensibus bello sociis, quae manus, priusquam urbem ingrederetur, non tam virtute hostium quam sua temeritate caesa est; quae cum esset pedestris, adversus ingentes equitum copias, ut postea dicetur,[104] congredi non dubitavit. Nec tamen inulta cecidit magna strage Gallorum edita.

ashamed to be called Swiss. Thus their name now extends from near Lake Geneva and the Rhone to Lake Constance and the Rhine and from the Italian Alps to Basel. When necessary they can easily put 30,000 light infantry into the field who do not know the meaning of flight.

Justice is these men's chief concern; they punish thieves with great severity and brigands with yet greater; they strictly observe the laws of hospitality, honor priests, are obedient to their religion, love peace, are contented with what they have and do not make war unless provoked. To flee the battlefield is a capital offense. The orphans and widows of those who fall in battle are supported by public funds. Their hearts are stout and their spirits unconquerable. When they crossed the Alps to oppose Filippo Maria, duke of Milan, they were defeated near Bellinzona.[89] It was a bloody victory for Milan, but Angelo Pergola still annihilated them. In this battle an enormous man was killed; his body seemed like that of a giant, and it was taken back to Milan. Against the people of Zurich, who had deserted the confederation and gone over to Emperor Frederick, the Swiss waged war with very different results, for they slew eight hundred men in a single encounter. 3

They inflicted many signal defeats on Austria and annexed part of its territory. At last they concluded a fifty-year truce,[90] but this was broken when the dauphin of Vienne, the eldest son of the king of France, attacked Basel with a large force of cavalry.[91] At that moment their Austrian subjects, elated with hope, tore up the compact and joined the dauphin. The Swiss had sent 4,000 men to aid their allies in Basel, but this force was cut to pieces before it could reach the city, thanks not so much to the courage of the enemy as to its own rashness, for they did not hesitate (as shall be explained later) to sally forth on foot against a huge force of cavalry. But they did not die unavenged, for they killed great numbers of French. 4

5 Abeunte dalphino Svicenses Albertum Austriae ducem bello persecuti sunt, et varia cum eo fortuna aliquandiu certaverunt; postremo fessis partibus et multo sanguine fuso rursus pax in quinquaginta annos redintegrata est, non ut tanto tempore quies esset, sed quod supererat priorum annorum, paci tranquillitatique cederet. Neque hoc stare posse videbatur novis litium subortis causis, et iam Svicenses veluti ferociores, et qui se laesos crederent, bellum minabantur. Quod intellegens Sigismundus Austriae dux, nec suis fidens viribus, ad pontificem qui bellum interciperet, ut ante diximus, oratum misit. Pius id minime negligendum ratus notarium suum, Stephanum Nardinum, egregia virtute virum, quem postea Mediolanensi praefecit ecclesiae, ut tantum incendium restingueret in Germaniam misit.

: 35 :

Apenninus mons quantus sit et unde dicatur.

1 Ipse pontifex Florentia discedens prima nocte in villa Cosmae, quae est in Mugello pulcherrima, quievit. Sequenti die summum Apennini iugum transmisit, et in oppido cui Florentiola est nomen pernoctavit.

2 Apenninus mons est altissimus, qui ab Alpibus descendens universam Italiam percurrit, a dextris Liguriam, Tusciam, Umbriam, Campaniam et alias complures provincias dimittens, a sinistris Galliam Cisalpinam, Flamineum, Picenum, Aprutium,

5 After the departure of the dauphin, the Swiss declared war on Duke Albert of Austria, and fought against him with varying fortunes. Finally, when both sides were exhausted and much blood had been shed, the fifty-year truce was renewed—not that there was to be peace for fifty years from that moment, but that the remaining years of the original fifty should be allowed to pass in peace and tranquility. It appeared, however, that not even this compact would hold, for new grounds for quarrels soon presented themselves. The Swiss grew more confident and, convinced that they were the injured party, threatened war. When Duke Sigismund of Austria learned of their intentions, he was uncertain of his own strength and so, as we have said before, sent to the pope to intervene against a possible war. Pius, who considered this a matter that could not be neglected, sent his notary, Stefano Nardini, a very distinguished man whom he afterward made bishop of Milan, to Germany to put out the flames of this dangerous fire.

: 35 :

The Appenines: their extent and the origin of the name.

1 After leaving Florence, the pope spent the first night in a very beautiful villa in the Mugello belonging to Cosimo.[92] The next day he crossed the ridge of the Apennines and spent the night in the town of Firenzuola.

2 The Apennines are a high mountain chain which run from the Alps down the entire length of Italy, passing on the right Liguria, Tuscany, Umbria, Campania and various other provinces, and on the left Cisalpine Gaul, Flaminia, Piceno, the Abruzzi, Apulia and other districts of Italy. From the tops of these ridges rushing streams tumble down into both the Adriatic and Tyrrhenian Seas.

Apuliam et alias Italiae partes respicit; ex cuius dorso fluentes amnes alii in superum, in inferum mare alii devolvuntur. Quidam Apenninum a Poeno dictum putant eo, quod Poenus Hannibal in eius transitu alterum oculum amisit; Illyri summa montium iuga 'planina' vocant, hinc alii vocabulum paucis mutatis litteris receptum existimant. Nobis neutrum placet, nominum interpretationem atque originem difficillimam iudicantibus; si quid tamen coniectari licet, non ab re fuerit Apenninum quasi Alpinum per diminutionem appellatum arbitrari, ut est Italiae linguae modus.

3 Florentiola dimissa alterum Apennini iugum non sine labore atque incommodo pontifex superavit, ac Planorium venit, Bononiensium legatis paulo ultra Caprennum inventis, ubi Florentinorum ac Bononiensium terminantur agri.

: 36 :

De Bononia et Baioariis et Xantho tyranno et factionibus urbis.

1 Bononiam, prius Boioniam dictam, Galli quondam Boi, eiectis Etruscis, occupavere, qui a Romanis pulsi trans Alpes migraverunt Danubioque adiacentem agrum atque omnem Eni fluminis vallem possederunt, inde Noricorum gente deiecta. Retinuerunt non parvo tempore Boiorum nomen, deinde Boioarii et postea Baioarii appellati sunt; nostra aetas corrupto vocabulo Bavaros vocat. Quibus ab orienti Austriales occurrunt, ab occidenti Suevorum gens, qua in parte fuit ager Rheticus, a meridie Italici montes, ab aquiline Francones et Bohemi, quos Boiorum reliquias nonnulli arbitrantur, quamvis eorum historia genus esse Sclavorum dicat.

2 Bononiensis ager[105] inter Apenninum et Padum iacet; regionem hanc Emiliam dixere Romani, nunc Romandiolam vocant, sic

Some say the name "Apennines" comes from Poenus (meaning Punic) because Hannibal lost an eye when he crossed them. Others think the name derives from the Illyrian word for mountaintop, *pianina*, with a few letters changed. We do not favor either view, for in our opinion the question of the origin and meaning of names is a most difficult one. But if we may hazard a guess, it does not seem unreasonable to suppose that *Apennine* is an Italian diminutive for *Alpine*.

On leaving Firenzuola the pope crossed another ridge of the Apennines, involving considerable exertion and discomfort, and arrived at Pianoro. He had been met by the Bolognese envoys a little way past Caprenno, which is on the boundary between the territories of Florence and Bologna. 3

: 36 :

Bologna and the Bavarians. Sante's tyranny and the factions in the city.

Bologna, formerly Boionia, was once occupied by the Boii, a Gaulish tribe who had driven out the Etruscans. The Boii were in turn repulsed by the Romans and moved across the Alps, where they seized land along the Danube and all of the valley of the Inn, dislodging the Norici. For a long time they kept the name Boii, but later were called Boioarii and then Baioarii. In our day the name has been corrupted to Bavari. They are bordered on the east by Austria, on the west by Swabia (which encompasses ancient Rhaetia), on the south by the Italian Alps and on the north by Franconia and Bohemia. Some think the Franconians are the remnants of the Boii, but their history indicates that they are Slavs. 1

The territory of Bologna lies between the Apennines and the Po, a region the Romans called Emilia but which is now known as 2

enim intrantibus Italiam Longobardis eam Cisalpinae Galliae partem vocare placuit, quae in officio cum Romanis mansit. Civitas ad radicem Apennini sita est, in quam parvi Rheni fluvii pars derivatur. Abundat urbs tritico vinoque, sericum plurimum colligit; aer hic saluber et laetus; schola insignis legum ac philosophiae, verum mores bonos non tam cives quam exteros docet.

3 Civitas Ecclesiae Romanae iure subiecta est, verum[106] male parens populus factionibus studet, nec regere novit, nec regentem ferre; rapinae avidus atque in caedes pronus. Saepe nostra aetate tumultuavit; nunc Bentivolii, nunc Cannetuli seu Iambeccharii excusso Ecclesiae iugo illic tyrannidem exercuere. Martinus Quintus urbem amisit, Eugenius Quartus recuperavit; sed cum Antonium Bentivolium, nobilem equitem aut imperasset aut permisisset gladio percuti, rursus Ecclesiae perdidit. Hannibal, Antonii filius, et Baptista Cannetolus Nicolaum deinde[107] Picininum, pulso praesidio Ecclesiae, cum equitatu intromisere. Nec Picininus longo tempore placuit: Franciscus eius filius hic captus malo modo mulctatus est. Baptista insidiatus Hannibali hominem obtruncavit; nec mora, oborto tumultu fugatis Cannetoli partibus, Baptista e latebris eductus in quas effugerat, multis vulneribus confossus scelerum poenas dedit; cadaver lacerandum canibus et suibus traditum; nec defuerunt qui more ferarum rabidi cruorem eius ebiberint corque commanducarint.

4 Tum Bentivolii et Malvetii et Maliscotti urbis principes facti; at cum Bentivolii capite carerent (nemo enim erat in ea familia ad regimen urbis aptus) et filius Hannibalis Iohannes impuber egeret

Romagnola, because when the Lombards invaded Italy they gave that name to the part of Cisalpine Gaul that remained loyal to Rome. The city lies at the foot of the Apennines and part of the little river Reno has been diverted through it. The area abounds in wheat and wine and harvests a great deal of silk, and the climate is pleasant and healthy. Bologna has a famous school of law and philosophy but in matters of moral behavior it instructs foreigners rather better than its own citizens.

Legally, the city is subject to the Church of Rome, but the peo- 3
ple are rebellious and given to factions. They know neither how to rule nor how to obey a ruler; they are greedy for plunder and ever ready to shed blood. In modern times there have been several revolutions, with now the Bentivogli, now the Canetoli, now the Zambeccari throwing off the Church's yoke and seizing power. Martin v lost the city; Eugenius iv regained it, but because he ordered the murder of the noble knight Antonio Bentivoglio (or at least allowed the crime to happen), the city again slipped from the Church's possession. Antonio's son Annibale and Battista Canetoli drove out the papal garrison and admitted Niccolò Piccinino and his cavalry. But Piccinino did not remain in favor long, either, and his son Francesco was arrested and terribly maltreated. Battista then lay in wait for Annibale and murdered him, and soon afterwards there was another revolution. The party of the Canetoli was banished and Battista was dragged from the hiding-place where he had taken refuge and stabbed repeatedly, thus paying the penalty for his crimes. His body was thrown to the dogs and swine to be torn to pieces, and there were actually men who drank his blood and gnawed his heart like raging beasts.[93]

Then the Bentivogli, the Malvezzi and the Marescotti became 4
lords of the city. But because the Bentivogli were without a chief (for there was no one in that family fit to rule) and Annibale's son Giovanni needed a guardian, they called in a certain weaver named Sante from Florence, whom they believed to be a bastard of

tutore, Xanthum quendam nomine lanificem ex Florentia vocaverunt, quem Bentivoliorum sanguine natum, quamvis ex adulterio, putabant. Memorabile[108] dictu: ignotus homo, lanificio et quidem vilissimo vitam ducens et nihil prorsus tale expectans, ad tutelam nobilis pupilli et ad gubernationem potentis atque indomiti populi favore incredibili est assumptus. In quibus rebus ita se gessit, ut non tam sordidam qua vixerat artem, quam sanguinem ex quo natus dicebatur, prae se ferre et inter urbis principes primum tenere locum haud iniuria videretur, ac si cum vestibus et ingenium mutasset et animum. Interea, cum obiisset Eugenius Nicolausque illi suffectus esset, qui adolescens olim in ea urbe nutritus ac episcopatum postea sortitus fuisset, civitas cum eo in gratiam rediit, praescriptisque nonnullis legibus legatum admisit, qui verius 'ligatus' appellari potuit, cum omne urbis imperium penes sexdecim viros esset, quorum princeps Xanthus habebatur, qui miserabili servitute civitatem oppressit, quando aliter rapax et inquietus populus in officio retineri non poterat.

5 Is cum accepisset Pium pontificem statuisse Mantuam petere, accersitis factionis suae ducibus, 'Quid agimus?' inquit, 'Si nobis praetermissis Mantuanum concilium adierit pontifex, amaro in nos esse animo iudicabitur. Exulibus nostris cum spe crescet animus, et auxilia praestabunt amici quibus nos urbe pellant. Si hac iter habuerit, populus, qui nos odit, omne ad eum imperium deferet et nostra peribit auctoritas.'

6 Diu res agitata est in consilio, cum anceps periculosaque videretur. Tandem suadente Francisco Sfortia Mediolanensium duce, quem ea de re consultum habuere, Iacobum cognomento Ingratum Romam misere, qui pontifici Mantuam ituro, suam Bononiam ut inter eundum viseret, quam efficacissimis precibus supplicaret, idque magistratibus et universae civitati gratissimum futurum diceret; verum cum exularent in agro Ferrariensi complures Bononienses, qui res novas per omnes dies molirentur, et urbis

Bentivoglio blood. It was a remarkable thing: this unknown character, earning his living by weaving—and very cheap weaving at that—became by an incredible twist of fate, and to his great surprise, guardian of a noble youth and governor of a fierce and powerful people. His performance in these duties testified not so much to the mean trade by which he had previously lived as to the blood from which he was said to have sprung, and it seemed perfectly just that he should take precedence over the leaders of the state, as if along with his clothes he had changed both his character and his spirit. Later, when Pope Eugenius died and was succeeded by Nicholas (who had spent his youth in Bologna and was later made its bishop), the state was reconciled to the pope. After imposing several conditions, the city admitted the papal legate, who ought more truly to have been called a 'ligate;' for all power in the city was vested in sixteen men with Sante at their head.[94] He had reduced the state to miserable slavery, as there was no other way to keep the ruthless and restless population in check.

When Sante learned that Pope Pius had decided to go to Mantua, he summoned the chiefs of his party and said, "What are we to do? If the pope passes us by on his way to the congress at Mantua, people will think he hates us; this will give our exiles hope and courage and their friends will help them to drive us out of the city. But if he comes here the people, who hate us, will deliver the government into his hands and our regime will be destroyed." 5

The question was debated for a long time in the council, for it was a delicate and dangerous matter. They called on Francesco Sforza, duke of Milan, for advice, and on his suggestion they sent Jacopo Ingrato to Rome. His orders were to use every means possible to beg the pope to make a stop at his city of Bologna on his way to Mantua; he was also to say that both the magistrates and the state as a whole would warmly welcome such a visit, but since a great many Bolognese exiles had taken shelter in the territory of Ferrara and were every day hatching new plots, and since malcon- 6

non satis pacata plebs illis aliquando aures accommodaret, opus esse non parva militum custodia, qui providerent ne res Bononiensis per ingressum pontificis aliquid detrimenti pateretur; ad quam rem Mediolanense praesidium quaerere statuissent.

7 Intellexit pontifex quorsum ea tenderent verba, remque in utramque partem pensitans, neque armatam intrare Bononiam neque civitatem Ecclesiae praeterire honestum censuit; responditque demum[109] ituro sibi ad conventum animum esse Bononia transitum habere, nec causam sibi occurrere cur Bononienses metuant; consulerent tamen suo timori, et armarent si possent formidinem, urbemque pro suo arbitrio custodirent, dum milites ad custodiam accersiti in verba Pii iurarent.

8 Placuit ea conditio Bononiensibus, qui accersita ex Mediolano magna equitum manu, in adventu pontificis urbem armis complevere. Cohortes decem affuere, quarum duces ad Planorium pontifici occurrentes iuramento se illi astrinxere. Galeazius, cui parere omnes iussi erant, in manu Pii Florentiae iuraverat et praecedens eum Bononiam venerat, ubi equitatu patris accepto, iterum pontifici obviam factus est cohortibus non aliter instructis quam si praelium essent inituræ, catafractis equis et fulgentibus armis insignes.

: 37 :

Ingressus pontificis in Bononia, et Bornii oratio, Bononiensiumque licentia.

1 Intravit Pius Bononiam ingenti plebis alacritate, primoribus urbis sellam eius portantibus. Sequentique die, apud Sanctum Petro-

tents among the lower classes in the city sometimes paid them heed, a strong guard would be needed to ensure that the arrival of the pope brought no harm to Bologna; and to this end, they had determined to ask for a garrison from Milan.

The pope understood the import of this message and, on thinking over both sides of the question, decided it would not be right for him to enter Bologna if the city was under armed guard, but neither should he pass by a state belonging to the Church. In the end, he replied that he intended to pass through Bologna on his way to the congress and could think of no reason why the Bolognese should be apprehensive; nevertheless, they should do what was necessary to calm their fears, strengthening their resolve by arms, if possible, and guarding the city as they saw fit—provided the soldiers they called in swore allegiance to Pius. 7

The Bolognese agreed to this condition. They sent to Milan for a large body of cavalry and filled the city with ten companies of armed men in advance of the pope's arrival. Their captains met the pope at Pianoro and took the oath of allegiance. Galeazzo, who was their commander-in-chief, had already sworn allegiance to Pius at Florence. He went ahead to Bologna, where he took over his father's cavalry, and then returned to meet the pope with his troops equipped as if for battle. With their mail-clad horses and flashing swords, they were a striking sight. 8

: 37 :

The pope's entry into Bologna. An oration by Bornio; the lawlessness of the citizens.

Pius entered Bologna to a rapturous public reception,[95] seated on a chair carried by the leading citizens of the state. The next day, 1

nium peracta re divina, populo publice benedixit, et reversus in palatium dicendi quae vellent civibus qui frequentes aderant copiam fecit; venerant enim pontifici gratias acturi qui suam visere urbem haud aspernatus fuisset.

2 Orandi partes Bornio iure consulto demandatae sunt, viro qui multa legisset et cuius os dulce sonaret. Is non quod iussus erat, sed quod sibi placuit, longo sermone disseruit; laudato enim pontifice quantum sufficere arbitratus est, de Bononiensis agri fertilitate, de caeli clementia, de litterarum studiis, de templis, de moenibus, de privatis et publicis aedificiis multa pulchre locutus est. Invectus autem in cives miro modo: hos legum hostes, boni et aequi inimicos, nullis teneri frenis ait, alieni avidos, sui prodigos; neque matrimonii iura neque hospitii foedera custodire; nihil sanctum apud eos inveniri, qui neque fidem neque iuris iurandi religionem colerent; alios tyrannos esse, alios servos; et illos rapere, hos furari; illos gladio inimicos occidere, hos veneno; illos adulteros esse, hos lenones; scelera et turpitudines omnes hic sibi proprium domicilium elegisse, nec ullius esse tam foedam urbis faciem quam Bononiae; orare igitur, ut urbis suae curam gereret, daretque operam ut eliminatis vitiis civitas tandem reformaretur, quando superum ope eo sospes adventasset.

3 Quae cum audacter atque intrepide et in modum torrentis fluenti oratione depromeret, cives qui aderant contra se magnopere excitavit, exteros in admirationem adduxit. Quis enim de sua patria quemquam talia dicturum expectasset? Patriae omnes ignoscunt, cuius dedecus suum ducunt. Caeterum oratio Bornii vera est habita, et ipse non tam orator existimatus quam philosophus. Pontifex facundiam eius doctrinamque laudavit, et ad reformandos

after mass at San Petronio, he gave his blessing to the people and then, retiring to his palace, he gave the citizens who thronged inside an opportunity to say whatever they desired; for they had come to thank the pope for condescending to visit his city.

The task of making a speech had been assigned to the jurist Bornio,[96] a man of wide reading and an elegant speaker. He delivered a long oration in which he said what it pleased him to say—and not what he had been told to recite. First, he gave a eulogy of the pope, no longer than he thought sufficient. He followed this with a long and elegant speech in praise of the fertility of Bolognese soil, the mildness of the climate, the city's universities, churches and walls and its buildings both public and private. After this he launched into an extraordinary attack on the people, calling them enemies of the law and of all that was good and just. They were ungovernable scoundrels, greedy for the goods of others and wasteful of their own, observing neither the laws of marriage nor the bonds of hospitality, holding nothing sacred, contemptuous of religion and disrespectful of oaths. Some were tyrants, others slaves; some plundered, others robbed; some killed their enemies by violence, others with poison; some were adulterers, others panders. Every sort of crime and disgrace had chosen Bologna for its home; no city had so foul a countenance. And so he begged the pope, who by the grace of God had somehow reached the city in safety, to show some concern for his property and take steps to root out vice and reform the state. 2

It was a bold and courageous speech. The torrents of his oratory offended the citizens who were present but deeply impressed the foreigners, for who would have thought that anyone could say such things about his own country? All men make excuses for their state, for they think any shame that befalls it befalls themselves. But Bornio's speech seemed to ring true, and he himself appeared not so much an orator as a prophet. The pope praised his eloquence and learning and promised to take steps to reform the 3

civitatis mores suam operam[110] est pollicitus, si tamen eum populum inveniret qui coerceri legibus posset.

4 Schola Bononiensis non apud Italos tantum, sed apud exteros quoque clarissima est, multosque viros erudivit, qui postea sapientiae civilis arcem tenuere, cum suorum civium tum aliorum quorum commentaria vigorem quodammodo legis habent. Nec philosophia hic sterilis fuit, cuius auditores adeo profecerunt, ut multis postea in locis cathedras rexerint. In armis non extat ingens Bononiensium laus, quos domi crudeles magis quam fortes, foris esse ignavos constat. Opinione sanctitatis duos aetate nostra memoria dignos novimus: Nicolaum cardinalem Sanctae Crucis, ordinis Carthusiensium professorem, et Franciscum Parvipassus, qui Mediolanensi praefuit ecclesiae; ille Francis Burgundos conciliavit, iste in bello quo Braccius hostis Ecclesiae Romanae cecidit, Martini papae vices gessit.

: 38 :

De Orlando praesule Florentino et eius stulta morte.

1 Mansit Bononiae Pius sex diebus, et in primo consistorio quod illic habuit, Orlandum Florentinum causarum Sacri Palatii auditorem patriae suae praesulem designavit, qui eius rei accepto nuntio prae gaudio illacrimatus est. Fuerat enim in omni vita pauper, verum doctus et iustitiae tenax, et quamvis bene de Pio speraret, numquam tamen episcopatum urbis alicuius ambivit; satis se felicem arbitrabatur, si aureos quotannis trecentos ex minoribus dignitatibus consequi posset. At cum certior factus est Florentinam sibi ecclesiam esse creditam, more hominum insanire coepit, qui

city if he could—that is, if the people could in fact be restrained by law.

The University of Bologna is famed not only throughout Italy 4
but also abroad. Many of the scholars trained there, citizens of other states as well as Bolognese, have risen to the top of the legal profession and their opinions in some respects have the force of law. The study of philosophy has flourished here as well, for Bologna graduates have been named to professorial chairs in many places. The Bolognese have won no great glory in war; it is generally agreed that they are cruel rather than brave at home, and cowardly abroad. We know of two men in our generation whose reputations for piety make them worthy of mention: Niccolò, cardinal of Santa Croce, a member of the Carthusian Order, and Francesco Pizzolpasso, bishop of Milan.[97] The former made peace between France and Burgundy; the latter represented Pope Martin in the war in which Braccio, the enemy of the Church, was killed.[98]

: 38 :

Orlando made bishop of Florence but dies a pointless death.

Pius stayed in Bologna for six days. In the first consistory he held 1
there, he appointed a new bishop of Florence: Orlando, a native of that city and an auditor of cases in the Vatican.[99] When Orlando heard the news he burst into tears, for though he was a fiercely just and learned man, all his life he had been poor. He had hoped for advancement from Pius but had never asked for a bishopric, thinking he would be lucky to get three hundred florins a year from minor posts. But when he was told that the cathedral of Florence had been committed to his care, he began to take leave of his senses, like a man who can never ascend to any height without

numquam adeo sublimem gradum ascenderunt, quin altiora quaerant, et tum miserrimi sunt cum felices esse videntur.

2 Existimavit Orlandus, cum tam facile atque insperato[111] pontificatus sibi obvenisset, cardinalatum longe[112] facilius obventurum — tantum sibi[113] de pontificis benivolentia blandiebatur. Ad quam rem si non satis sua sponte insaniebat, necessariorum et amicorum verbis instigabatur, nihil de Pio desperandum esse dicentium, qui sibi absenti et prorsus ignoranti archiepiscopalem mandasset honorem. Ille infelix adeo spem hanc arripuit, ut numquam ad se nuntium ex Curia venientem viderit, quin sibi allatum pileum existimaret; atque idcirco creatis postea cardinalibus cum sui nullam mentionem factam intellexisset, maerore confectus morbum incidit ex quo mortuus est. Pius amicum occidit, dum honestare contendit: adeo parum est quod mortalibus ex sententia cadit.

: 39 :

De Ferraria eiusque origine, et Estensium spurcitia.

1 Ipse deinde relicta Bononia per flumen Rhenum et deinde per Padum Ferrariam petiit. Borsius eius loci pro Romana Ecclesia vicarius ad agri[114] fines obviam factus est magno nobilium comitatu stipatus.[115]

2 Ferraria in una ex insulis Padi fluminis sita est. Priusquam civitatis nomen sortiretur, ecclesiae Ravennati paruit. Ferunt Ravennatem praesulem tribus oppidis suis ex tribus metallis indidisse nomen: Aureolum ex auro, Argentam ex argento, ex ferro Ferrariam appellasse, quae vilior ceteris videretur. Smaragdus patricius et exarchus Italiae primus hanc urbem muro cinxit, quae vastanti-

wanting to rise higher, and who is most miserable at just the moment when he seems to have been blessed.

Orlando imagined that the bishop's miter would not have come to him so easily and unexpectedly unless a cardinal's hat were soon to follow — so much did he pride himself on the pope's good will. And as if his own madness in this matter were not enough, he was egged on by his friends and family, who kept telling him there was nothing he might not hope for from Pius, who had made him an archbishop when he was far away from the Curia and expecting nothing of the sort. The wretched fellow was obsessed by this hope; he never saw a messenger arrive from the Curia without thinking he had come to make him cardinal; and it was for this reason that, when he found his name did not appear in the next list of appointments, he died of a broken heart. Pius, by promoting his friend, had killed him. Rarely do things turn out as mortal men expect. 2

: 39 :

The origins of Ferrara and the sordid family of Este.

The pope then left Bologna and proceeded along the Reno and the Po to Ferrara.[100] Borso, who was the Roman Church's vicar there, met him at the border of the territory with a large company of nobles. 1

Ferrara is built on one of the islands in the Po. Before it became an independent state it was subject to the church of Ravenna. They say the bishop of Ravenna named three of his towns after metals: Oriolo for gold, Argenta for silver, and Ferrara, because it seemed to be worth less than the rest, for iron. The patrician Smaragdus, exarch of Italy, first walled the city, and it staunchly 2

bus Italiam Longobardis, in Ravennatium Romanorumque partibus constantissime perseveravit; victor Carolus Magnus inter alias Ravennatis exarchatus urbes Ferrariam quoque Romanae Ecclesiae et Beato Petro dono dedit. Persequentibus Ecclesiam nonnullis Germanorum imperatoribus haec urbs ad eos defecit, sed comitissa Mathildis, fama excellens femina, Henrico Tertio armis eam eripuit Ecclesiaeque restituit.

3 Salinguerra deinde, privatus civis suasu marchionum Estensium et auxiliante Federico Primo, perfidia usus tyrannidem arripuit; hunc Innocentius Quartus pontifex maximus expulit. Paulo post marchiones Estenses Ecclesiae deiecto praesidio introiere; qui cum annos octo et sexaginta regnassent, a Venetis sunt repulsi. Hos pontifex maximus Clemens Quintus extra communionem Ecclesiae fecit, et bona eorum per Gallias diripi iussit; cum neque hoc modo parerent, misso legato armis aggressus est victorque civitatem recuperavit, ac marchiones Estenses, qui auxilio fuissent et egregiam operam in bello navassent, vicarios in ea constituit; qui postea in hoc usque tempus Ecclesiae censum praebuere. Eugenius Quartus decem mille aureos, quos illi singulis annis Apostolicae Camerae dissolvebant, ad quattuor milia reduxit, et concilium Latinorum ac Graecorum in ea urbe celebravit, quod eius opes mirum in modum auxit.

4 Ii marchiones Francorum sese genus esse dicunt, neque Franciae reges id negant, a quibus insigne liliorum acceperunt. Nonnulli ex Maguntia profectos asserunt, et sanguinem esse Gayni, quem prodidisse Francos in bello adversus Saracenos infeliciter gesto fama est. Veri periculum in medio relinquimus, quamvis et Gaynum Francum fuisse tradunt. Illud in hac familia singulare, quod patrum nostrorum memoria, nemo legitime natus ad princi-

supported Ravenna and the empire when the Lombards invaded Italy. A triumphant Charlemagne included Ferrara among the cities of the exarchate of Ravenna which he presented to St. Peter and the Church of Rome. When some of the German emperors made war on the Church, Ferrara went over to their side, but the celebrated Countess Matilda wrested the city from Henry III by force of arms and restored it to the Church.[101]

Later, a private citizen by the name of Salimguerra used treachery to seize control of the state; he was encouraged by the marquises of Este and backed by Frederick I, but Pope Innocent IV expelled him. Soon afterwards, the marquises of Este entered the city, dislodged the papal garrison and ruled there for sixty-eight years, before they in turn were driven out by Venice.[102] Clement V, who was an over-zealous champion of the Este princes, excommunicated the Venetians and allowed their possessions to be plundered and dispersed throughout France. When even this did not reduce them to obedience, he sent his legate to attack Ferrara and triumphantly recovered it.[103] He appointed the marquises of Este as his vicars there, to reward them for their valuable support and the service they had shown him in battle. Ever since, they have been tributaries of the Church. Eugenius IV reduced the annual payment they owed the Apostolic Camera from 10,000 florins to 4,000; he also held a congress of Latins and Greeks at Ferrara which increased the city's wealth to an extraordinary degree.[104] 3

The marquises of Este say they are of Frankish origin, and the kings of France, who granted the family their emblem of lilies, do not deny the claim. Some say they came from Mainz and are descended from that Ganelon who, as the story goes, betrayed the Franks in their disastrous war against the Saracens. The truth of the matter we leave to braver souls—but Ganelon too is said to have been French. Here is an extraordinary fact about the family: within recent memory no legitimate son has ever inherited the title; fortune has smiled so much more on the children of the mis- 4

patum pervenit, adeo concubinarum quam uxorum filii fortunatiores fuere, res non Christianis modo sed omnium fere gentium legibus adversa.

5 Nicolaus nostro tempore extra matrimonium genitus eius gentis princeps fuit, magno vir ingenio, verum sequax voluptatis; felicem putasset vulgus, nisi comperto uxoris ac filii adulterio utrumque gladio percussisset. Digna Dei ultio, qui alienas nuptias percrebro foedavit, thalami sui corruptorem perpessus est filium! Huic plures fuerunt nati cum ex matrimonio tum ex adulterio. Legitimos iudicium patris exclusit, Leonellum ex concubina Senensi genitum successorem constituit, qui regis Alfonsi filiam (et ipsam spuriam) duxit uxorem, cum prius ex domo Gonzagae duxisset alteram. Leonello frater successit Borsius eadem matre natus. Filius praeteritus est, sive quod legitimus esset, sive quod aetate minor.

: 40 :

De Borsio et dubiis eius moribus, et ingressu Ferrariae.

1 Borsius egregio corpore fuit, statura plus quam mediocri, crine pulchro et aspectu grato; multiloquus auscultavit se ipsum dicentem, ut qui sibi magis quam auditoribus placeret. Multa in eius ore blandimenta commixta mendaciis. Magnificus ac liberalis videri magis quam esse cupiebat, quamvis Federicum caesarem Romam euntem atque inde redeuntem magnis honoribus ac donis prosecutus fuerit, a quo Mutinae comitatum in ducatum erigi et se

tresses than on those of the wives. It is a circumstance contrary not only to Christian teaching but to the law of almost every nation.

In our time, the bastard in charge was Niccolò, a man of great 5
ability but a devotee of pleasure. The common crowd would have thought him happy had he not discovered his wife in bed with his son and killed them both with his sword. Here was just vengeance from the Lord: he who repeatedly violated the marriages of others found his son polluting his own marriage bed. Niccolò had several children, some legitimate and some not. He barred the former from succession and named instead Lionello, his son by a Sienese concubine. Lionello first married a daughter of the house of Gonzaga and then wed the daughter of King Alfonso, who was herself illegitimate. He was succeeded by Borso, his brother by the same mother, and not by his son; the boy's claims were ignored either because he was legitimately born or because he was a minor.[105]

: 40 :

Borso and his dubious morals; the pope's entry into Ferrara.

Borso was a handsome man, taller than most, with beautiful hair 1
and an attractive face. A garrulous talker, he liked the sound of his own voice and he spoke to please himself not those who heard him. In his mouth, blandishments mingled with lies. He wanted to appear magnificent and generous — rather than genuinely to be so. Still, when Emperor Frederick passed through Ferrara, first on his way to Rome and then again on his return, Borso lavished him with honors and gifts and thereby persuaded him to raise Modena from a county to a duchy and make him the duke, as we mentioned earlier.[106] He never married; most of his energy went into

ducem creari, ut ante diximus, obtinuit. Uxorem numquam duxit, venationi magnam operam dedit. Statuam sibi viventi[116] in foro erexit, quae sedens ius dicere videretur; adiecti sunt et tituli, quos palpans adulatio excogitavit; nihil enim Borsio laude fuit dulcius. Coemit lapillos preciosos quam plurimos, et numquam non gemmis ornatus in publicum prodiit. Supellectilem domus ditissimam cumulavit, argenteis et aureis vasis etiam ruri usus.

2 Is, cum Pius electus est, multa ostendit laetitiae signa: ludos militares instituit, victoribus praemia posuit, donavit nuntios, ignes tota in ditione sua incendi iussit, epulumque amicis fecit, inter quos Pium sibi affinem esse gloriabatur, quoniam mater eius Senensis fuisset ex domo Ptolomaea, quae Picolominaeae sanguine iungitur. Agebat quoque Deo gratias, qui eum sibi pontificem dedisset, a quo nihil impetrare non posset; neque id falso fuisset opinatus, si concessu digna petivisset. At cum indigna quaereret, repperit apud Pium praesulem non tanti benivolentiam esse quam honestatem.

3 Petiit enim Ferrariae se ducem creari, censum sibi remitti, et Franciscum Ferrariensem episcopum non damnatum a sua ecclesia removeri. Non est exauditus; noluit enim pontifex aut Romanam Ecclesiam suo censu privare, aut pontificatum incognita causa laudato viro auferre; ducatum concessisset tributo retento, quem ille contempsit. Obtinuit tamen concessiones alias magni ponderis, speravitque maiores in dies accipere; atque ob eam rem et quod aliorum exemplis admonebatur, summis honoribus Pium excepit, adnixusque eos superare per quos iter fuerat habitum, in porta claves urbis pontifici obtulit, pedesque ad sellam eius inter portantes tamdiu profectus est, quoad equum ascendere iuberetur.

hunting. In his lifetime the citizens erected a statue in the piazza representing him seated and administering justice; the inscription dripped with flattery, for Borso loved nothing so much as praise. He bought as many precious stones as he could and never appeared in public without jewels. He furnished his household extravagantly, and even in the countryside he ate off gold and silver plates.

When Pius was elected pope, Borso made a great display of his delight; he arranged military tournaments and offered prizes for the victors; he gave presents to the couriers who brought the news; he ordered bonfires to be lit throughout his domains, gave a banquet to his friends and boasted to them that Pius was a connection of his, for his mother had been a Sienese of the Tolomei family which is kin to the Piccolomini. He thanked God for sending him a pope who would deny him nothing. He would not have been mistaken in this view, had he asked for proper favors; but when he made improper requests, he found that in Pius honor prevailed over benevolence. 2

He petitioned the pope to make him duke of Ferrara, to remit his tribute and to have Francesco, bishop of Ferrara, removed from his church even though he had not been convicted of any misdeed. His request was not granted, for the pope did not want to deprive the Church of Rome of its revenue nor to remove a man of such distinction from his bishopric without a hearing. He did grant him the dukedom, but he continued to require the tribute, an offer which Borso spurned. Still, he obtained some other valuable concessions and he hoped every day for more. Because of this, and also because he was mindful of the example others had set, he received the pope with the highest honors and tried to outdo those whose lands he had already traversed. At the city gates he presented Pius with the keys to the city and walked beside his chair between the bearers till he was bidden to mount his horse. 3

4 Tecta pannis omnis via fuit et strata floribus per quam itum est ad maiorem ecclesiam, adornatae domus, et omnia plena cantibus ac personatibus erant, acclamante populo, 'Pio pontifici vita!' Cardinalibus et universae Curiae ministrata ex palatio cibaria, ludi multiplices exhibiti, orationes complures ab oratoribus disertissimis habitae. Celebritas hic Sacratissimi Corporis Domini acta est, solemnis pompa per forum ducta pontifice populo benedicente et Hostiam Immaculatam portante.

5 Mansum est hic octo diebus. Multa in secreto colloquio pro negatis sibi petitionibus questus est Borsius, quem pontifex facile confutavit. Rettulit et ad consistorium litem quam contra episcopum suum haberet et in arbitrio pontificis posuit; qui cognito negotio pollicitus duci est, quamprimum facultas adesset, episcopum ad aliam ecclesiam se translaturum, idque Senis postea factum est, spoponditque dux in conventu Mantuano sese minime defuturum, ut qui rem Christianam inter omnes qui viverent conservari maxime cuperet.

: 41 :

De Guarrino, Aurispa, Poggio et Iannotio oratoribus et eorum morte.

1 Guarrinus Veronensis, grandaevus et venerabilis senex, magister fere omnium qui nostra aetate in humanitatis studio floruerunt, pontificem adiit dignamque suo nomine suisque moribus orationem habuit. Adiit et Iohannes Aurispa Siculus, graecae atque la-

The street to the cathedral was covered with carpets and strewn with flowers along its entire length; the houses were festooned with decorations; and everywhere there was singing and cheering as the people kept up a continuous cry of "Long live Pope Pius!" The cardinals and the entire Curia were served refreshments from the palace, various pageants were performed and there were a number of speeches by very eloquent orators. That day was the feast of Corpus Domini; a solemn procession made its way through the piazza, in which the pope blessed the people and carried the host aloft. 4

Pius remained in Ferrara for a week. In private conversations Borso continued to complain bitterly that his petitions had been refused, but the pope easily refuted his arguments. He also brought before the consistory a dispute he had had with his bishop; he left the decision to the pope, who after investigating the matter promised the duke that as soon as an opportunity presented itself, he would transfer the bishop to another church. This was done later at Siena. The duke promised he would not fail to appear at Mantua for the congress, maintaining it was his dearest wish to see the Christian religion secure among all peoples. 5

: 41 :

Deaths of the orators Guarino, Aurispa, Poggio and Giannozzo.

Guarino of Verona, an aged and venerable man, whose school was attended by almost every scholar who has attained distinction in the liberal arts in our day, then appeared before the pope and delivered an oration worthy of his reputation and character. The Sicilian Giovanni Aurispa also addressed the pope, a distinguished 1

tinae linguae peritissimus, annum prope nonagesimum agens, qui paulo post mortem obiit. Fuit hic annus trium eloquentissimorum virorum dormitionibus insignis; nam et Poggius, cuius ante meminimus, Florentiae et Iannottius Manettus Neapoli ex hac luce migravit. Iannottius et ipse Florentinus fuit, vir admodum doctus, qui cum latinis graecisque litteris coniunxit hebraeas. Horum nemo de naturae legibus conqueri potuit; septuagesimum cuncti annum excessere, et sortem vicere communem. Iniurius est qui plus sibi deberi censet.

: 42 :

Padi fluminis origo et magnitudo.

1 Relicta Ferraria pontifex[117] adverso Pado Rovarium navigio petiit, marchionis Mantuani oppidum. Padus in Alpibus Cocciis ortum habet, omnemque Galliam Cisalpinam percurrens multis amnibus, quorum plerique navigantur, in se receptis quinque[118] ostiis in Adriaticum mare defertur. Graeci Eridanum vocavere, Heliadum fabulis et Phaetontis incendio, cui restitisse creditur, memorabilem; eorum qui sunt in Europa fluminum nulli cedentem, quamvis Rhenus et Ister longiora dimensi spatia pluribus fluviis augeantur.

2 Navigante Pio duae inter se classes concurrere, altera ducis, marchionis altera; illa Pium ferebat, ista ferre optabat. Tubicines hinc atque inde omnes circum valles mirabili clangore replebant; vexilla ventis agitata instar silvae prae se ferebant. Accolae in utraque ripa consedentes pontificis benedictionem exposcebant, ac benedicenti Vitam! acclamabant. Postquam marchionis in fines[119] navigatum est et pontifex novi hospitis navigium intravit, Borsius

scholar of Greek and Latin who was almost ninety at the time; he died soon afterwards. This year was marked by the death of three great orators, for Poggio, whom we have mentioned above, departed this world at Florence, as did Giannozzo Manetti at Naples. Giannozzo was also a Florentine, a most learned man who added knowledge of Hebrew to his mastery of Greek and Latin. Not one of them could accuse nature of injustice, for all were over seventy and had lived beyond the common span. No man has the right to expect more.[107]

: 42 :

The source and length of the Po.

1 After leaving Ferrara, Pius sailed up the Po to Revere, a town subject to the marquis of Mantua. The Po rises in the Cottian Alps and flows through Cisalpine Gaul; it has many tributaries, most of them navigable, and it empties into the Adriatic through three different mouths. The Greeks called this river the Eridanus and it is by this name that it is celebrated in the myth of the daughters of the Sun and the immolation of Phaethon, whose flames it is said to have doused. No river in Europe is greater, though the Rhine and the Danube are longer and have more tributaries.

2 As the pope sailed along, the duke's flotilla met that of the marquis;[108] the former was carrying Pius, the latter was hoping to take him. Buglers from both sides made the surrounding valleys resound with an extraordinary din; they lifted aloft a forest of banners, all tossing in the wind. The locals thronged the banks of the river and implored the pope's benediction; when he gave it, they roared back with cries of "Viva!" After they had sailed into the marquis's territory and the pope had boarded the ship of his new

salutato marchione et impetrata a Pio potestate discedendi[120] retro abiit. Secuta nox Rovarii peracta est, quo in loco regium palatium semiaedificatum structura et artificio singulare architecti ostendit ingenium.

: 43 :

De Mintio flumine et Virgilii villa. De Mantuae origine et Mathildis dominatione, et Gonzagae strumositate, et Ludovici praestantia.

1 Postera die ad ostium Mintii fluminis perventum[121] et in stagnum usque navigatum, in cuius sinistro litore tumulus ostenditur sacer habitus, in quo divini Maronis fuisse lares affirmant; villa circum parva iacet, quae tantum peperit vatem. Ab eo loco secundo[122] ferme miliario, in praedio principis pontifex pernoctavit, ut sequenti die urbem ingrederetur.

2 Mintius amnis ex lacu Benaco defluit, stagnumque efficit quod Mantuam magna ex parte ambit. Ipsa urbs in paludibus iacet, neque adiri potest nisi pontibus aut navibus. Ampla est et ingentis populi capax; multae in ea splendidae domus et palatia regibus apta, verum aestate pulvis, hieme lutum incolas molestat; populus perhumanus et amans hospitum. Monasteria multa insunt virorum et feminarum, in quis sanctae degunt animae.

3 Etrusci trans Apenninum in Gallia et ultra et citra Padum duodecim colonias condidere, quarum unam fuisse Mantuam tradunt, opus nobile Bianoris, Tyberini regis et Mantonis filii. Multas haec

host, Borso greeted the marquis and, with the pope's permission, took his leave. The next night they spent at Revere, where there is a princely palace which, though only half completed, displays in its layout and construction the consummate genius of the architect.[109]

: 43 :

The River Mincio and Vergil's hometown. The origins of Mantua and its conquest by Matilda. Skin problems among the Gonzaga. The accomplishments of Lodovico.

The following day the pope arrived at the mouth of the Mincio and sailed upriver as far as the lake. On the left-hand shore there is a hill which the Mantuans hold sacred, for they say that this was where the divine Vergil made his home. At the base of the hill lies the little village where the great poet was born. The pope spent the night on an estate belonging to the duke about two miles from here, so that he could make his entrance into the city the following morning. 1

The Mincio runs down from Lake Garda and spreads into a marsh which surrounds most of Mantua. The city itself stands in a swamp and can be reached only by bridge or boat. It is an expansive place and can support a large population and there are many splendid houses and palaces fit for kings, but the inhabitants are plagued by dust in summer and mud in winter. The people are very kind and hospitable. There are many convents, for both men and women, where pious souls dwell. 2

The Etruscans founded twelve colonies beyond the Apennines in Gaul, on either side of the Po, and Mantua was one of them. Its foundation was the noble work of Bianor, son of King Tiberinus 3

urbs perpessa est calamitates. Nam praeter illud quod ait Virgilius,

Mantua, vae, miserae nimium vicina Cremonae!

et Hunnorum et Gothorum et Longobardorum et Baioariorum armis invasa nunc direpta, nunc deiectis moenibus immunita prorsus relicta. Memoriae proditum est per tempora Caroli Magni sanguinem hic Domini nostri Salvatoris Christi miraculosum apparuisse, atque ad eum visendum Leonem Secundum pontificem maximum accessisse, qui rem cognoverit atque probaverit. Hic Carolus Calvus, Magni filius, veneno interfit, quod Hebraeus medicus propinavit. Hic Nicolaus Secundus urbis Romae praesul concilium celebravit, in quo statutum est Romani pontificis electionem per cardinales faciendam esse.[123] Mathildis, gloriosa mulier, cuius supra meminimus, huius olim[124] urbis dominatum habuit; qua defuncta multae regiminis mutationes factae sunt, et modo imperatores Germani, modo Romani pontifices imperium[125] tenuere. Postremo nobiles, quis Gonzaga cognomen dedit, favore populi ad principatum pervenere, eoque longo tempore potiti sunt.

4 Primus eius familiae dominatum arripuit Aloysius Gonzaga, cuius posteri adeo clementes habiti sunt, ut tyrannidem in iustum imperium commutaverint, vicariatumque urbis a Romanis imperatoribus obtinuerint. Demum vero Iohannes Franciscus, magno vir ingenio et armorum gloria illustris, aetate nostra a Sigismundo caesare, cum Roma rediret in Germaniam, marchionatus honorem adeptus est; cui coniunx clarissima fuit Paula, moribus et litteris excellens, cuius sollertia monachi omnes qui Mantuam incolunt instituta patrum ad unguem, ut aiunt, usque in hanc diem custodiunt.

5 Ex his ortus est Ludovicus, qui per tempora Pii papae huic urbi praefuit, armorum et litterarum peritia clarus, nam et parentis gloriam militans adaequavit et Victorinum oratorem audiens praecep-

and Manto. The city has suffered many disasters. Aside from Vergil's

> Alas for Mantua, too close a neighbor to wretched
> Cremona![110]

it has been invaded by armies of Huns, Goths, Lombards and Bavarians. It was sometimes sacked, sometimes left utterly defenseless, with its walls in ruins. It is recorded that during the reign of Charlemagne the blood of our Lord and Savior Jesus Christ miraculously appeared, and that Pope Leo, who came to inspect it, acknowledged and gave his sanction to the marvel. Here Charlemagne's son, Charles the Bald, was poisoned by a Jewish physician. Here Pope Nicholas II held the council in which it was determined that popes should be elected by cardinals.[111] At that time, the illustrious Matilda, whom we have mentioned above, ruled the city. After her death there were many political upheavals, with now the German emperors, now the popes of Rome ruling over it as lords. Finally, with the support of the people, the Gonzaga obtained sovereign authority; they have held it for a long time.

The first member of the family to seize power was Lodovico 4
Gonzaga.[112] His descendants had such a reputation for clemency that they transformed tyranny into just rule and were appointed imperial vicars of the city. In our day, Gianfrancesco, a man famed for his great abilities and military exploits, was made a marquis by the Emperor Sigismund on his return to Germany from Rome.[113] His wife Paola was a lady of great character and learning, and it is thanks to her efforts that to this day the monks of Mantua all observe the precepts of their fathers "down to the fingertips,"[114] as the saying goes.

Their son, Lodovico, ruled the city during the reign of Pope 5
Pius. Lodovico was famous for his prowess in both arms and letters, for he matched his father in military glory and nearly

toris propemodum doctrinam assecutus est; mitis ingenii et iustitiae observantissimus. Uxorem duxit ex familia Brandeburgensi Barbaram nomine, praestanti animo atque ingenio feminam, et quae dominandi artem calleret, quaeque viro prolem pulcherrimam peperit, quamvis gibbus et struma in nonnullis apparuit postquam pueritiam exivere. (Quod in ea puella accidit, quae prior Galeazio Mediolanensi desponsata est; propter quod repudiata in monasterio se clausit, sorori cedens quae in locum eius surrogata est.) Divina haec ultio creditur in ea familia propter aliqua parentum delicta; frequenter enim pulcherrimi pueri, postquam adoleverunt, deformes facti sunt. Felix alioquin domus, subditorum et vicinorum benivolentia gaudens.

: 44 :

De Blanca ducissa Mediolani et Ippolita filia ac dignissima prole, et de ingressu Mantuae in pompa triumphali, et Ippolitae puellae oratione pereleganti.

1 Ingressus est Mantuam Pius sexto Kalendas Iunii, quinque diebus ante praestitutum terminum. Civitas plena hospitum fuit, vicinarum urbium populi frequentes aderant. Et Blanca Mediolanensium princeps affuit, Philippi Mariae quondam ducis filia, tunc Francisci Sfortiae coniunx, magni animi et singularis prudentiae mulier; et cum ea nobilissima proles utriusque sexus, mares quatuor non alio aspectu quam missi e caelo angeli, et desponsata filio Siciliae regis puella, Ippolita nomine, vultu moribusque praestans; multae insuper virgines ac matronae nobiles et illustrium virorum comitatus.

equalled his teacher, the rhetorician Vittorino, in erudition.[115] He was a mild character, but very strict in the observance of justice. He married Barbara of Brandenburg, a lady of high spirit and intellegence who was well acquainted with the arts of government. She bore her husband beautiful children, though after they grew up, some of them developed humps and goiters. This happened to the daughter who was first betrothed to Galeazzo of Milan, and it was for this reason that he repudiated her. She became a nun, thus making way for the sister who was chosen to take her place. This affliction is thought to be God's vengeance on the family for certain ancestral sins: the fairest children often grow deformed on reaching adolescence. In other respects fortune has smiled on the house, which rejoices in the goodwill of its subjects and neighbors.

: 44 :

Bianca, duchess of Milan, her daughter Ippolita and her remarkable sons. The pope's triumphant entry into Mantua. Ippolita delivers an accomplished speech.

Pius entered Mantua on May 27, five days before the appointed 1
date. The city was filled with foreigners and crowds of people had come in from the neighboring towns. Among them was Bianca, duchess of Milan, the daughter of the late Duke Filippo Maria and the wife of Francesco Sforza, a woman of high spirit and extraordinary wisdom. She had with her a noble brood of sons and daughters, four boys as beautiful as angels from heaven and a girl, called Ippolita, lovely of face and character, who was betrothed to the son of the king of Sicily.[116] Her retinue also included many girls and noble matrons and important gentlemen.

2 Blanca in suggestu apud ecclesiam maiorem apparato et Barbara simul pontificis adventum expectavere, qui pompam huiuscemodi ducens intravit urbem: praecesserunt servitia Curiae et cardinalium ministri, tum minoris ordinis curiales, exin equi candidi absque sessoribus duodecim, frenis sellisque aureis ornati; tum vexilla tria, in primo signum Crucis resplenduit, in altero clavium Ecclesiae, in tertio quinque lunarum, quod est Picolominaeorum insigne, et ea viri nobiles armis tecti et phaleratis insedentes equis portavere. Mox umbella secuta est rubro et croceo colore distincta; proximi sacerdotes urbis diviti apparatu sacra ferebant; post hos regum et principum legati, tum crucem auream comitantes subdiaconi apostolici, auditores palatii, scriniarii et advocati. His arcula iungebatur aurea equo albo vecta et multis luminaribus circundata, in qua condita fuit Eucharistia, id est Hostia Salvatoris sacrata, et sericaeum desuper umbraculum. Huic proximi Galeazius Mediolanensis et Ludovicus marchio, et post eos cardinalium venerabilis ordo. Tum pontifex ipse sella sublimi sedens, sacerdotali paludamento et onusta divitibus gemmis mitra fulgens, nobilium procerum portatus humeris, benedicens populo incedebat, et iuxta eum cubicularii et corporis custodes. Episcopi et notarii et abbates et ingens praelatorum turba pontificem sequebantur.

3 In porta urbis Ludovicus equo desiliens claves civitatis pontifici obtulit. (Idem fecere omnes ad quos Pius in itinere declinavit, praeter Senenses et Florentinos, qui populari oppressi tyrannide retentis clavibus videri liberi voluerunt.) A porta urbis usque ad ecclesiam Sancti Petri, quae cathedralis est, nihil non tectum pannis fuit, et parietes undique et floribus et aulaeis ornati. Mulieres, pueri ae puellae fenestras ac tecta compleverant, nec tamen pres-

Bianca and Barbara awaited the pope on a platform erected before the cathedral. Pius entered the city in a procession arranged as follows: first came the servants of the Curia and the cardinals' attendants, followed by minor officials of the Curia; then twelve white horses, riderless and bedecked with saddles and bridles of gold; then three banners, the first gleaming with the sign of the Cross, the second with the keys of the Church and the third with five crescent moons, the emblem of the Piccolomini. These were carried by noblemen clad in armor and mounted on richly caparisoned horses. Next came a red and yellow canopy and after that the priests of the city, dressed in splendid robes and carrying sacred relics. They were followed by the ambassadors of various kings and princes and, crowding around a golden cross, the apostolic subdeacons, auditors of the palace, scribes and advocates. Then a white horse carried a golden tabernacle under a silk canopy, surrounded by several torches; this held the eucharist, that is, the sacred host of our Savior. Galeazzo of Milan and the Marquis Lodovico rode next, followed by the venerable college of cardinals and, finally, the pope himself, raised high on his throne in his papal robes, his miter blazing with precious gems. He was carried on the shoulders of noblemen, and he blessed the people as he went. Behind him came the gentlemen of his bedchamber and his personal attendants, followed by bishops, notaries and abbots and a great throng of priests. 2

At the city gates Lodovico dismounted and presented the pope with the keys to the city. Every city the pope visited on his journey had done the same except Siena and Florence, for they both—though under the heel of popular tyranny—wanted to make a show of independence by keeping their keys. From the gate all the way to the cathedral of San Pietro, every foot of ground was covered with carpets and the facades on either side were draped with flowers. Women, boys and girls crowded the windows and roofs, but still there were great crowds in the streets, and all the ap- 3

sura defuit cunctis aditibus populo occupatis. Altaria multis in locis incenso thure fumabant, nec alia vox exaudiebatur quam populi clamantis, 'Vita Pio pontifici maximo!'[126]

4 Ubi ad ecclesiam ventum est, supplicationibus Deo factis et hymno decantato et annuntiata cunctis qui aderant plenaria peccatorum remissione, pontifex in amplissimo palatio exceptus est, et mansiones suas quisque petiere. Postridie Blanca et Barbara pontificem visitarunt, exobsculatisque sacris pedibus spirituales, quas optaverunt, gratias impetravere. Ippolita, Blancae filia, latine coram pontifice oravit adeo eleganter ut omnes qui aderant in admirationem adduxerit.

proaches were thronged with people. Incense smoked at several altars along the way, and no voice was heard except the shouts of the people crying, "Long live Pope Pius!"

When the procession reached the church, prayers were said and a hymn sung and a plenary remission of sins was proclaimed for all who were present. Afterwards, a reception was held for the pope in a splendid palace, and then everyone went home to his own quarters. The next day, the pope gave an audience to Bianca and Barbara, who kissed his holy feet and obtained the sacred blessings they had come to seek. Bianca's daughter Ippolita delivered a Latin oration[117] before the pope; her style was so elegant that all who heard her were lost in wonder and admiration. 4

Note on the Text and Translation

The Latin text in these volumes is based on the two most important manuscript witnesses. The older is *A*, a manuscript written partly in Pius's own hand and partly in that of his secretary, Agostino Patrizi. The later witness is *B*, a fair copy, dated 1464 (the year of Pius's death), written by the professional scribe Joannes Gobellinus of Linz. It contains the text as revised by Giannantonio Campano on the explicit command of Pius himself.[1] In general we have preferred the readings of *B*, as they represent what Pius intended to be the final version of the *Commentarii*. Occasionally, however, we have resorted to *A* when grammar or semantics or scribal error seemed to require it.[2] We have silently corrected obvious errors of spelling or syntax, and have omitted from the apparatus any notice of orthographical variants, minor word-inversions, erasures, *notabilia*, or marginal and interlinear corrections. Nor have we attempted to identify individually all the autograph parts of *A*. Readers interested in such questions are advised to consult the editions of van Heck and of Bellus and Boronkai, where they are treated more fully.

Both *A* and *B* contain a list of rubrics for individual chapters of the *Commentaries*, copied out separately from the text itself. In *B* the rubrics also appear within the text; hence, we have reproduced them in both the text and translation.

In accordance with the preference of this series, spelling, punctuation and capitalization have been modernized throughout. An exception to this rule has been made in the case of certain proper names, where the imposition of standardized forms was impractical and might cause confusion to readers.

The text of the *Commentarii* first appeared in print at Rome in 1584, in an edition based on *B* but heavily edited by Cardinal Francesco Bandini Piccolomini, a distant relative of Pius. The cardinal silently excised numerous words, phrases and, occasionally, whole passages deemed impious or otherwise unflattering to the majesty of the Holy See. He also contrived to have the work published under the name of the scribe Gobel-

linus; Pius's stylistic decision to report the story of his life in the third person naturally facilitated the misattribution of his work. The expurgated text was reprinted at Frankfurt in 1614.[3] In 1883 Giuseppe Cugnoni printed a list of the omitted words and passages, derived from a manuscript in the Chigi library of which he was the keeper.[4] Within a decade, the papal historian Ludwig Pastor had announced the discovery of *A* in the Vatican library;[5] the importance of *B* was recognized soon afterwards. It was not until 1984, however, that two complete, critical editions of the full text appeared. The translation by Florence Alden Gragg, produced directly from *A*, thus provided the most complete account of the text for several decades.[6]

Gragg's translation has provided the foundation for the English text presented here. Her text has been thoroughly revised in order to bring it into line with the present edition (which is based on *B* rather than *A*). Some minor errors of translation, prosopography and geography have also been corrected. Although an attempt has been made to preserve the flavor of Gragg's text, and in many places her wording is followed quite closely, the text as a whole has been completely overhauled and in many places largely retranslated.

In compiling the notes to the translation, reference was made in the first instance to the extensive commentary by Leona Gabel that accompanied the original publication of Gragg's translation. The substance and, in a few cases, the wording of slightly less than half of Gabel's notes has been retained, most of them in greatly abbreviated form. Where a substantial amount of her work has been retained (either *verbatim* or in paraphrased form), the cipher (*LG*) appears at the end of the passage in question.

To this apparatus we have added occasional notes on the sources of biblical and classical quotations and basic information on the historical and political context of the events described, above all those taking place in Italy. Occasional reference is made to Aeneas's collected letters, his other historical works, and to the monumental researches of his modern biographers—especially those of Voigt, Pastor, Paparelli and Mitchell. These primary and secondary works could easily have provided the material for a full, line-by-line commentary on the contents of the *Commen-*

taries; readers interested in the historical background to the events described, or in testing the overall veracity of the work, will find a great deal more information in these works than we have been able to supply.

SIGLA

A Vatican City, Biblioteca Apostolica Vaticana, MS Regin. lat. 1995
B Rome, Biblioteca Corsiniana, MS Corsini 147

NOTES

1. See the important letter of Campano to Cardinal Iacopo Ammannati, in Pius II, *Commentarii rerum memorabilium quae temporibus suis contigerunt* (Frankfurt, 1614), 472; also printed in the edition of Bellus and Boronkai, text volume, 619–624.

2. See Concetta Bianca, "La terza edizione moderna dei *Commentarii* di Pio II," *Roma nel Rinascimento*, 12 (1995): 5–16.

3. We concur with van Heck in finding no trace of a Roman edition of 1589, mentioned by Pastor.

4. *Aeneae Silvii Piccolomini Senensis qui postea fuit Pius II pontificis maximi opera inedita*, ed. G. Cugnoni (Rome, 1883), 495–549.

5. Pastor, II, 323, n. 2, and III, 42–4 and 415–18.

6. For a more detailed treatment of the textual history of the work see the accounts of Pastor, mentioned above; Leona Gabel, in her introductions to Gragg's translation (*Smith College Studies in History* 22 (1936), 3–5 and 43 (1957), vii–xii); and van Heck, in his edition of the *Commentarii*, 5–13.

Notes to the Text

PREFACE

1. quod Christiani simul et philosophi nobilissimi tradunt *after* dimissa *A*
2. quem mortales *A*

BOOK I

1. rexerant *A*
2. possedit *A*
3. Picolomina *AB*
4. sectatus est *A*
5. intermittere *omitted in A*
6. aeditum *A*
7. paene *A*
8. verum *A*
9. concessurus] ut sese conferret *A*
10. de *A*
11. delatum *A*
12. recepit *A*
13. suum *A*
14. a iuramento *A*
15. securus *A*
16. Ibi *A*
17. iactus *A*
18. intra *A*
19. pectinari *A*
20. salsos *omitted in A*
21. ad *omitted in A*
22. rapentes *A*
23. impleta *A*
24. enim *omitted in A*
25. repetiit *A*
26. ut diximus *omitted in A*
27. tantopere *after* concilium *A*
28. summa prudentia *A*
29. ex placitu *A*
30. episcopus Ostiensis *A*
31. recitavit *A*
32. ad Tridentum una *omitted in B*
33. sese *A*
34. sinistri pedis] ex pede sinistro ei *A*
35. dum *A*
36. receptus est *A*
37. et *omitted in A*
38. nosti *A*
39. ruperint *A*
40. tulerint *A*
41. agere *A*
42. exinde *A*
43. morosior cunctatiorque *A*
44. marchione *A*
45. se *A*

46. nec *A*
47. ad Lateranum *A*
48. repraestiterunt *A*
49. confirmaret *A*
50. caesar *omitted in B*
51. ignaros *A*
52. peditibus *A*
53. agerent *A*
54. collocationi *A*
55. fidelitatem *A*
56. obvia *A*
57. comitarentur *A*
58. plebe *A*
59. iure *A*
60. fallere *A*
61. matrimonium *B*
62. vidisse *B*
63. videbatur *A*
64. liberum *A*
65. haesit *A*
66. proveheretur *A*
67. re cognita . . . Conventum *omitted in B*
68. apicibus *A*
69. audita . . . Ratisponam] audito Burgundi motu commoti sunt et Ratisponam *A*
70. quos profectus *A*
71. publica *omitted in A*
72. publicitus *A*
73. mansisset *A*
74. Nosco *A*
75. quod demum *A*
76. verum cum *A*
77. XXXII milium *A*
78. in *omitted in B*
79. nuntiatur *A*
80. cognitio est *A*
81. correptionem *A*
82. Quae *A*
83. nosset *A*
84. profectus est *A*
85. amarulento *A*
86. ferret *A*
87. tradunt *A*
88. apponitur *B*
89. -que *omitted in B*
90. eidem *A*
91. fere *A*
92. fortunam conducerentur] formam reducerentur *A*
93. competitionis *B*
94. abunde *A*
95. ad *A*
96. Per hos dies] Dum haec aguntur *A*
97. genito *A*
98. sese *A*
99. in *omitted in B*
100. ei *omitted in B*
101. pontificis *A*
102. nox insomnis] nox his insomnis fuit *A*
103. et *B*
104. atque *A*
105. cancellariam *B*
106. et *omitted in A*
107. memento *B*
108. *omitted in A*

109. cum *A*
110. his *A*
111. Promisi *inserted in B*
112. in *omitted in A*
113. incideret *A*
114. fuit *A*
115. vero *omitted in A*
116. admirati sunt *A*
117. ageres] sors ageretur *A*
118. Exin *A*
119. reddit *A*
120. in *omitted in A*
121. cecidit *A*
122. valido *A*
123. singulis *after* a cardinalibus *A*
124. infensos *before correction in B*
125. Corsiniani . . . retulimus (= §1.37.2) *omitted in A*

BOOK II

1. his *A*
2. campo *A*
3. potentuose *B*
4. illud *A*
5. non . . . Alpibus] apud Alpes *A*
6. esset *A*
7. consilia *A*
8. possedit *A*
9. natione valentinus *after* successit *A*
10. (quod . . . est) *omitted in A*
11. mox *A*
12. dissolvet *A*
13. de quo . . . fecimus *omitted in A*
14. cassato *A*
15. cardinalibus *A*
16. instetit *A*
17. praesulis *A*
18. et *B*
19. Romana *omitted in A*
20. sint *B*
21. noxia *A*
22. quam multam *A*
23. magnatum *A*
24. securum *A*
25. aut Romae *A*
26. possidebat *A*
27. se *omitted in A*
28. asservaverint *A*
29. et *omitted in A*
30. vendicaverunt *A*
31. ab ubere] ad ubera *A*
32. exorirentur *A*
33. ut . . . est *omitted in A*
34. falso *omitted in A*
35. populares *A*
36. profectus est] iter habuit *A*
37. per *omitted in B*
38. sita est *A*
39. religione *B*
40. responsionis *A*
41. certiorandus *A*
42. regni possessionem *A*
43. afferunt *A*

44. foedere coniuncti] affoederati *A*
45. suis oppidis] suo territorio *A*
46. aeternam *A*
47. possessionem *A*
48. equo . . . procumbens] occisus in proelio *A*
49. laci *A*
50. uno opere] unum eius opus fuit, in quo *A*
51. laci *A*
52. affoederatum *A*
53. remoratus est *A*
54. oppugnans *A*
55. frustratus *A*
56. cum *A*
57. cognosci *A*
58. nec *A*
59. quam diuturnum *A*
60. ut . . . honestaret] ut civitati blandiretur *A*
61. dono dari *A*
62. caritate *A*
63. insunt *A*
64. firmissimum *omitted in A*
65. pluribus *A*
66. minoris *B*
67. se *omitted in A*
68. nobiles] se nobiles *A*
69. suadent *omitted in A*
70. contristaret *A*
71. campanas ac tubas *A*
72. possideret *A*
73. segetes *A*
74. pergere *B*
75. commendaverunt *A*
76. Mariam . . . cognomen] Mariam, cui Novella est nomen, consignatum *A*
77. dicta est *A*
78. territorii *A*
79. Florentia *B*
80. asportaverunt *A*
81. tutore *B*
82. unum *A*
83. invenerimus *B*
84. Florentia *B*
85. ad longum *omitted in A*
86. prospectum *omitted in A*
87. oratus est *A*
88. saepe *after* adolescens *A*
89. cautumque est *A*
90. possit *A*
91. te *A*
92. merita *A*
93. sceleratissimus *A*
94. cum satis *A*
95. facto *A*
96. quorum . . . Baioario *omitted in A*
97. ut dictum est *omitted in A*
98. posteris *A*
99. ultra est *A*
100. Vienna est *A*
101. mineris inexhaustis] minerae dives *A*
102. per *omitted in B*

103. territorio *A*
104. ingentes . . . dicetur] decem millia equitum *A*
105. Bononiense territorium *A*
106. verum *omitted in B*
107. deinde *omitted in A*
108. mirabile *A*
109. demum *omitted in A*
110. suam operam] suas operas *A*
111. ex insperato *A*
112. sibi *after* longe *A*
113. sibi *omitted in A*
114. territorii *A*
115. circumdatus *A*
116. populus *after* viventi *A*
117. pontifex *omitted in B*
118. tribus *A*
119. regnum *A*
120. potestate discedendi] licentia *A*
121. perventum est *A*
122. secundo *omitted in B*
123. Hic Nicolaus . . . esse *omitted in B*
124. eo tempore *A*
125. dominium *A*
126. maximo *omitted in A*

Notes to the Translation

ABBREVIATIONS

CMH	*The New Cambridge Medieval History,* VII: *c. 1415–c. 1500,* ed. C. Allmand. Cambridge, England, 1998.
DBF	*Dictionnaire de biographie française.* Paris, 1933–.
DBI	*Dizionario biografico degli Italiani.* Rome, 1960–.
ER	*Encyclopedia of the Renaissance,* ed. P. Grendler. 6 vols. New York, 1999.
Hay and Law	D. Hay and J. Law, *Italy in the Age of the Renaissance, 1380–1530.* London and New York, 1989.
Mansi	*Pii II Pontificis Maximi olim Aeneae Sylvii Piccolominei Senensis Orationes politicae et ecclesiasticae,* ed. J. D. Mansi. 3 vols. Lucca, 1755–1759.
Mitchell	R. J. Mitchell, *The Laurels and the Tiara: Pope Pius II, 1458–1464.* London, 1962.
NCE	*The New Catholic Encyclopedia,* 2nd ed. 15 vols. New York, 2003.
ODP	J. N. D. Kelly, *The Oxford Dictionary of Popes.* Oxford and New York, 1986.
Opera	Pius II, *Opera omnia,* Basel, 1551.
Paparelli	G. Paparelli, *Enea Silvio Piccolomini: L'umanesimo sul soglio di Pietro.* 2nd ed., Ravenna, 1978.
Pastor	L. Pastor, *The History of the Popes from the Close of the Middle Ages,* trans. F. I. Antrobus. London, 1891–.
Voigt	G. Voigt, *Enea Silvio de' Piccolomini als Papst Pius der Zweite, und sein Zeitalter.* 3 vols. Berlin, 1856–1863.
Wolkan	*Der Briefwechsel des Eneas Sylvius Piccolomini,* ed. R. Wolkan. 3 vols. Vienna, 1912–1918.

PREFACE

1. John 8:48.

2. John 13:16, 15:20.

BOOK I

1. The nobility of Siena were barred from high office in 1277.

2. Vergil, *Aen.* 1.240.

3. During his time at the university, Aeneas lived in the house of his aunt, Bartolomea Tolemei (his father's half-sister), and uncle, Niccolò Lolli. He developed a close friendship with his cousin, Gregorio (or Goro) Lolli, also a university student at the time, whom he later appointed to be his private secretary. Lolli's letter to Jacopo Ammanati, written after the pope's death in 1464, gives a detailed description of this phase of Aeneas's life, published in Pius II, *Commentarii* (Frankfurt, 1614), 493–5.

4. The War of Lucca (1429–33), in which Siena allied with Milan, Genoa and others to oppose Florentine attempts to seize Lucca. The chronology of activities is not quite accurate: Aeneas spent 1429–31 travelling around various Italian universities and schools, and studying for a time with Francesco Filelfo at Florence. On his return to Siena in 1431, it seems the prospect of unemployment, rather than war, led him to seek employment with Capranica: see Mitchell, *Laurels and Tiara,* 56–9.

5. Bishop of Fermo, made cardinal by Martin V in 1430 but deposed by Eugenius IV in 1431. He arrived in Siena in the autumn of that year and took Aeneas into his service. They reached Basel in the spring of 1432.

6. The Council of Basel, 1431–1449, convened to explore issues of church reform, union with the Greek Orthodox Church and the limits of papal power. See the Introduction to this volume.

7. One of Aeneas's closest friends, he likewise served Cardinals Capranica and Albergati in turn.

8. Filippo Maria Visconti (1392–1447), duke of Milan.

9. Sigismund received the Iron Crown of the Lombards in Milan on November 25, 1431. Early in 1432 he departed for Siena, where he stayed for nine months before proceeding to Rome for his coronation by Eugenius IV on May 31, 1433.

10. Eugenius IV, born Gabriele Condulmer, reigned 1431–1447. Eugenius had fled Rome on June 4, 1434, after a Roman mob revolted against his

policy of heavy taxation; he very rarely returned to the city until 1443: see *ODP*, 241–3.

11. Aeneas seems to have been unaware of the nature of the letter he carried from the bishop of Novara to Piccinino. Both were in the service of the duke of Milan and were plotting to seize the pope as he left Florence. The details and motives of the plot remain obscure. (*LG*) For Piccinino see the sketch at 2.18.4; for the history of the plot from the Florentine point of view, see J. Hankins, "Unknown and Little-known Texts of Leonardo Bruni," *Rinascimento* n.s. 38 (1998): 125–161, reprinted in his *Humanism and Platonism in the Italian Renaissance*, vol. I (Rome, 2003), 19–62, esp. 33–40.

12. Niccolò Albergati.

13. Tommaso Parentucelli da Sarzana, reigned as Nicholas V, 1447–1455: see *ODP*, 244–5; for a fuller account of his career see 1.28.3.

14. He was elected Felix V on November 5, 1439: see *ODP*, 243–4 and 1.10.1.

15. The Congress of Arras (summer of 1435), where representatives of Charles VII of France and Henry VI of England attempted to bring the Hundred Years' War to a close.

16. According to Campano, Pius's biographer, the real object of the mission was to stir up hostilities against England (after the English withdrawal from the peace congress at Arras), with a view to preventing Henry VI from interfering in the reconciliation of France and Burgundy. In this, Aeneas was not successful, though James I did agree to put diplomatic pressure on Henry to keep the peace. See Campano's *Vita Pii II*, in L. Muratori, *Rerum Italicarum Scriptores*, III.2 (Milan, 1734), 967 and 969–70; Mitchell, *Laurels and Tiara*, 65.

17. The Battle of Ponza, August 5, 1435, a serious setback in the campaign by King Alfonso V of Aragon (1396–1458) to seize the kingdom of Naples after the death of the Angevin Queen Giovanna II (on which see 2.3.2–3). The Genoese, traditional opponents of Aragonese expansion in the Mediterranean, delivered Alfonso to their overlord Filippo Maria Visconti of Milan. The two men promptly struck a deal to recognize and support one another in their respective "spheres of influence" in Italy, and

Alfonso was set free. Milanese support enormously strengthened his position in the south. See J. H. Bentley, *Politics and Culture in Renaissance Naples* (Princeton, 1987), 11–13.

18. Henry Beaufort, second son of John of Gaunt.

19. Strood in Kent. The inhabitants of this district were said to have cut off the tail of St. Thomas à Becket's horse, for which crime they received this congenital retribution. (*LG*)

20. A renowned place of pilgrimage near Dunbar.

21. I.e., the legendary barnacle geese, whose spontaneous generation was a commonplace of medieval natural history.

22. The Tweed.

23. *Noctem insomnem:* Vergil, *Aen.* 9.166–7, one of the author's favorite figures of speech (see 1.15.4, 1.15.9, 2.28.5).

24. Matthew 7:15.

25. Revelation 2:9.

26. Giuliano Cesarini (1398–1444), cardinal of Sant'Angelo in Pescaria, whom Martin V appointed to preside in his name at the Council of Basel and who continued to perform this office under Eugenius IV: see *DBI*, XXIV, 188–95.

27. Juan Cervantes (d. 1453).

28. The psalmists were clerks appointed to lead the antiphonal singing in liturgical services. The College of Abbreviators consisted of chancery officials responsible for drafting papal briefs and other documents. There were three ranks, of which the highest was *de parco maiori,* or 'of the upper bar.' The College of Scriptures consisted of the copyists, or 'secretaries,' and was headed by the *rescribendarius.* Appointed for a six-month term, his duties included distributing work equally among the copyists and computing their fees. (*LG*)

29. Francesco Pizzolpasso (d. 1443), archbishop of Milan, one of Aeneas's closest friends and early protectors.

30. The decree passed in the twelfth session of the Council (on July 13, 1433) restricted the pope's ability to provide benefices. Cathedral chapters

and monastic establishments were to regain their right of free election, and papal reservations were to be abolished unless guaranteed by canon law or imposed in territories subject to Rome. (*LG*) See also Black, *Council and Comune*, 40–1.

31. Pizzolpasso, again.

32. Sigismund of Hungary died on December 9, 1437 and was succeeded by his son-in-law, Duke Albert V of Austria, who became king of Hungary and Bohemia and on March 18, 1437 was elected king of the Romans with the title Albert II: *CMH*, 355–6. (From the 11th to the 16th century the elected candidate took the title "King of the Romans" until his coronation at Rome by the pope; only after this was he officially styled "Emperor." (*LG*)

33. Horace, Carm. 3.29.29.

34. 1439.

35. Lodovico Pontano, a celebrated canon lawyer.

36. On the provostship see 1.8.3. The post went to a certain Leonardo of Vercelli, the candidate previously appointed to the vacancy, who along with the duke's nominee had been set aside in favor of Aeneas. (*LG*) See his letter on the subject in Wolkan, I.1, 117–118.

37. The narrative momentarily skips forward a few years: the plague struck Basel in 1439, but Aeneas was not awarded the offices in Trent until three years later, after a bull of Felix V dated October 26, 1442 assured him of appointment to the next benefice to fall vacant in the diocese there. (*LG*)

38. The decree of suspension against Eugenius was passed on January 24, 1438; the Council officially deposed him on June 25, 1439: *ODP*, 243.

39. Felix was elected on November 5, 1439. He continued to claim the allegiance of the Council of Basel until its final dissolution in 1449, whereupon he resigned. He died in 1451: *ODP*, 243–4.

40. Albert II died October 27, 1439. Frederick III was elected his successor on February 2, 1440, but his coronation at Aix did not take place till June 17, 1442: Voigt, I, 247, 256, 267.

41. Sylvester Pflieger, bishop of Chiemsee from 1438 to 1454.

42. Jacob von Sirk, archbishop of Trier from 1439 to 1456.

43. Diploma dated at Frankfurt, July 27, 1442, printed in J. Chmel, *Regesta chronologico-diplomatica Friderici III Romanorum Imperatoris*, 2 vols (Vienna, 1859), I, Appendix 29.17.

44. January 1443.

45. Romans 12:21.

46. Horace, *Serm.* 1.9.20–1.

47. Aeneas too had stayed in the Lolli household, during his time at the University of Siena: see 1.2.3.

48. August 1444.

49. Vergil, *Aen.* 6.231.

50. Spring 1445.

51. Jean de Centay.

52. John 16:2.

53. All of them leading conciliarists: Giuliano Cesarini, the president of the Council; Niccolò Tudeschi, called Panormitanus, the celebrated canon lawyer; and Lodovico Pontano, also an eminent canonist (mentioned at 1.9.3).

54. Lodovico Scarampo, patriarch of Aquileia (he succeeded Lodovico von Teck, see 1.9.2, in 1439) and cardinal of S. Lorenzo in Damaso.

55. Juan de Carvajal (c. 1400–1469), auditor of the Rota and throughout the 1440s a frequent papal emissary to Germany. His efforts were crucial in persuading Frederick and the German princes to abandon their neutrality and support Eugenius IV against the Council: see *NCE*, III, 197; *ER*, IV, 316–17.

56. Aeneas left Rome on April 1, 1445.

57. March 1446.

58. I.e., Dietrich von Mörs, a powerful German prince, and Jacob von Sirk: see 1.11.1. A papal bull of February 9, 1446 gave their sees to Adolph, duke of Clèves, a nephew of Philip of Burgundy, and John, bishop of Cambrai, Philip's natural brother: see Voigt, I, 357, and 1.15.1.

59. Eugenius had come to terms with Alfonso of Aragon in June 1443 (by the Treaty of Terracina) and shortly afterwards recognized his bastard son Ferrante as the legitimate heir to the throne of Naples. The rapprochement brought Naples, Rome and Milan together to the discomfiture of Florence: Bentley, *Renaissance Naples*, 16–17.

60. *Noctes insomnes:* Vergil, *Aen.* 9.166–7.

61. *Candidas animas:* Horace, *Serm.* 1.5.1.

62. Nicholas of Cusa (1401–1464), the celebrated scholar and reformer, made cardinal of S. Pietro in Vincoli in 1448; like Carvajal he was dedicated to re-establishing papal authority in Germany: see *ER*, IV, 317–20.

63. Dietrich von Erbach, who controlled the vote of the elector of Brandenburg in addition to his own.

64. Vergil, *Aen.* 9.166–7.

65. Louis Alleman (1385–1450), cardinal of S. Cecilia and Cesarini's successor as president of the Council of Basel. (In 1438 Cesarini had obeyed Eugenius's order to transfer his office to the Council of Ferrara. Alleman took charge of the disaffected remnant in Basel; he personified the extreme anti-papal stance of the Council in its final phase.) See *DBF*, II, 168–71.

66. In December 1446.

67. The documents, known as the Concordat of the Princes, were dated February 5 and 7, 1447: see Voigt, I, 387ff.

68. Eugenius died on February 23, 1447. On March 6, Tommaso Parentucelli of Sarzana was elected as Nicholas V: see *ODP*, 244–5, *ER*, IV, 316–17.

69. Niccolò Albergati, who had also employed Aeneas (see 1.4.1).

70. April 19, 1447.

71. July 1447.

72. August 13, 1447.

73. Charles of Orléans's father, Louis, had married Valentina Visconti, Filippo Maria's sister, in 1387. As Filippo Maria died without legitimate issue, Charles claimed the succession as his nephew. Other claimants in-

cluded Francesco Sforza, who had married the duke's illegitimate daughter, Bianca, and Lodovico of Savoy, whose sister, Bona, was the duke's widow.

74. Aeneas's report to Frederick shows that he himself determined it would be impossible to accept the first proposals put forward by Milan: see Wolkan, II, 263ff. The Milanese had offered a vague recognition of imperial overlordship which left them virtually free, in return for defense against their enemies. The terms offered to the imperial ambassadors on their second mission (see 1.19.7) were quite different in character. (*LG*)

75. Carvajal (see 1.15.8).

76. The reasons for his fall are obscure. He died soon afterwards, on July 16, 1449. (*LG*)

77. A parish in Augsburg (Augusta Vindelicorum)?

78. 1449. The mercenary captain (*condottiere*) Francesco Sforza (1401–1466) became duke of Milan in 1450.

79. The pope's narrative agrees with other contemporary accounts of the political turbulence in Milan in 1449–50, but it is difficult to appraise his account of his own activities in the city. In most contemporary accounts, Aeneas's presence in Milan is not even mentioned. (*LG*)

80. February 26, 1450.

81. Leonora was the niece of Alfonso of Aragon. The negotiations were concluded on December 10, 1450. Volckenstorf's first name was actually Georg: see Voigt, II, 107.

82. Jean de Centay.

83. Nicholas V had promised to hold a council in a French town, presumably Toulouse, after the close of the jubilee year. This promise was virtually the price of French mediation to secure the resignation of Felix V and the dissolution of the Council of Basel. (*LG*)

84. Pius here describes earlier events, occurring on his journey south from Germany and during his stay in Naples.

85. The letter of appointment is dated September 23, 1450.

86. The Franciscan preacher and future saint (1386–1456), a tireless advocate for a new crusade against the Turks. See D. H. Farmer, *Oxford Dictionary of Saints* (Oxford, 1978), 217.

87. Ladislas (1440–1457), the posthumous son of Emperor Albert II (see 1.10.2) and heir to the kingdoms of Bohemia and Hungary. He was then eleven years old. Frederick III had appointed himself Ladislas's guardian at his birth and kept him a virtual prisoner throughout his childhood. Aeneas dedicated his treatise *De educatione puerorum (On the Education of Boys)* to the boy king; see *Humanist Educational Treatises*, ed. Craig Kallendorf, ITRL 5 (Cambridge, Mass., 2002) for the Latin text and an English translation.

88. George of Podêbrady (d. 1471), Czech baron and Hussite, *de facto* ruler of Bohemia during the minority of Ladislas Postumus. See D. Hay, *Europe in the Fourteenth and Fifteenth Centuries*, 2nd ed. (London and New York, 1989), 251–3.

89. The Taborites were extreme, iconoclastic Hussites. Aeneas's letter on the Taborites, addressed to Juan de Carvajal, cardinal of Sant' Angelo, is in Wolkan, III.1, 22ff. See also chapter 25 of Aeneas's *Historia Bohemica*, in *Opera*, 81–143.

90. Leonora was to land on November 1, 1451.

91. November 11.

92. Gregorio Lolli later became Pius II's confidential secretary: see 2.6.3. For Aeneas's relations with the Lolli family see 1.2.3 and 1.11.4.

93. Frederick's decision to take Ladislas with him to Italy prompted a number of Austrian nobles, prelates and towns to band together to ask for the return of the young king. Frederick's failure to comply with the league's demands led to open rebellion under the leadership of the powerful Ulrich Eizinger. (*LG*) See 1.25.1, also Voigt, II, 30ff.

94. February 2, 1452. She was received by Frederick at Siena on February 24: see Voigt, II, 39, Pastor, II, 147.

95. Filippo Calandrini, Nicholas's step-brother (see Pastor, II, 146) and Juan de Carvajal.

96. Frederick and Leonora entered the city on March 9, the wedding took place on the 16th, and the imperial coronation on the 19th. The party departed for Naples on March 24: see Pastor, II, 154–8.

97. Frederick arrived back in Rome on April 22, and left four days later with Aeneas: see Pastor, II, 159. Aeneas's oration is printed in his *Opera*, 928–32.

98. November to December 1452. The author gives little indication here of the precariousness of the emperor's position. The leader of the Austrian opposition, Eizinger, had joined forces with Hunyadi, the governor of Hungary, and George of Podebrady in Bohemia. Their display of force at the walls of Neustadt speedily led Frederick to propose a truce and turn Ladislas over to the rebels. (*LG*) See also Voigt, II, ii.

99. Aeneas sent Carvajal an account of these proceedings, including the text of his speech to the emperor, on April 10, 1453: see Wolkan, III.1, 126ff.

100. Constantinople fell to the Ottoman Sultan Mehmed II on May 29, 1453. The loss of the city profoundly disturbed Aeneas. From this moment until his death at Ancona, Aeneas's desire to rouse the princes of Europe to a new crusade against the Turks would dominate his oratory, political philosophy and policy. For his initial reaction to the news, see his letters to Nicholas V (July 12, 1453), Nicholas of Cusa (July 21) and Leonardo Bentivoglio (September 25) in Wolkan, III.1, 189–215, 279.

101. On April 23, 1454: see Voigt, II, 101.

102. The imperial embassy included the "barons" Johann Ungnad and Georg Volkenstorf, Ulrich Sonnenberg, Aeneas and Cardinal Nicholas of Cusa. The pope's representative was Giovanni Castiglione, bishop of Pavia.

103. The text of the oration is in Wolkan, III.1, 538–47.

104. Apparently *Guillaume* Fillastre, bishop of Toul from 1449 to 1460, and translated from there to Tournai. (*LG*)

105. The speech circulated widely in manuscript and was printed three times in the fifteenth century. It appears under the title *De Constantinopolitana clade* in *Opera*, 678–89.

106. February 26, 1455.

107. I.e., it was copied in manuscript collections of his speeches; it is printed in Mansi, I, 288–333.

108. March 25, 1455.

109. Psalm 93:11.

110. The conspiracy occurred in 1453: see Pastor, II, ii.

111. See *ODP*, 244–5.

112. The celebrated Greek scholar and theologian (1403–1472), archbishop of Nicea (1437) and one of the architects of the act of union between the Greek Orthodox and Roman Catholic Churches agreed at the Council of Ferrara/Florence (1438–1439). In recognition of his services to Rome, he was made a cardinal by Eugenius IV in Dec. 1439. From 1440 until his death he remained in the West, an ardent campaigner for the crusade against the Turks, and a friend and patron of numerous Byzantine émigré scholars. In 1463 he became titular patriarch of Constantinople: see *DBI*, IX, 686–96.

113. Alain de Coëtivy, (1407–1474), one of the leaders of the French party in the Curia: see *DBF*, IX, 104–5.

114. I.e., at the head of the Church. See Psalm 39:8–10 and Hebrews 10:7.

115. See 1.36.5.

116. Alfonso Borgia, elected Calixtus III on April 8, 1455.

117. St. Vincent Ferrer.

118. It is printed in *Opera*, 923–8.

119. Juan de Mella, made a cardinal along with Aeneas in 1456: see 1.33.1.

120. Juan Luis de Mila and Rodrigo Borgia (the future Alexander VI); and Jaime, son of the Infante Pedro of Portugal: see Pastor, II, 450, 451, 459.

121. The Peace of Lodi, signed on April 9, 1454 in response to the Turkish capture of Constantinople, bound the papacy, Venice, Milan, Florence and Naples in a truce united against external aggression: see Pastor, II, 287–97.

122. The Peace of Lodi left mercenary captains like Piccinino dangerously unemployed: see Hay and Law, 160; J. Burckhardt, *The Civilization of the Renaissance in Italy,* transl. S.G.C. Middlemore, (London and New York, 1990), 33–4.

123. Lord of Rimini, another powerful *condottiere,* notorious for his cruelty, lawlessness and disregard for the Church. He was, nevertheless, a generous patron of arts and letters and a formidable mercenary captain, whom most of the Italian powers, Eugenius IV included, employed at one point or another. (*LG*) There is a vivid sketch of his character at 2.32.1–5, one which has perhaps excessively influenced his later biographers. For a balanced account see P. J. Jones, *The Malatesta of Rimini and the Papal State* (Cambridge, Eng., 1974); Hay and Law, 161.

124. A temporary civic commission in charge of conducting wars.

125. In early March 1456.

126. Lucrezia di Alagno.

127. July 7, 1460, in the war between Anjou and Aragon over the throne of Naples: see Pastor, III, 103–4.

128. Paulinus Confessor, bishop of Nola, d. 431. The Roman commander Marcus Claudius Marcellus famously saved Nola from Hannibal in the Second Punic War; but his death, in 208 B.C., occurred at Venusia in Apulia.

129. July 21, 1456.

130. The peace with Alfonso was actually concluded on May 31, 1456, before the final battle at Belgrade.

131. More fully: Rainaldo de' Piscicelli (Naples), Juan de Mella (Zamora); Giovanni da Castiglione (Pavia); Aeneas Silvius Piccolomini (Siena); Jacopo Tebaldo (Montefeltro); Richard Ollivier de Longueil (Coutances). The appointments were announced on December 17, 1456: see Pastor, II, 458–9.

132. Voigt, II, 231, n. 3., calls this assertion a presumptuous falsehood. The canons at this time had been scattered in three groups, six at Gross-Glogau, who voted for Aeneas, seven at Königsberg who elected their

own candidate, and three at Danzig who chose a third. The account here is thus quite misleading. See also Voigt, II, 225. (*LG*)

133. Domenico Capranica, Aeneas's first employer (see 1.3.1).

134. Pietro Barbo, nephew of Eugenius IV and later Pope Paul II (1464–1471).

135. The text reads Christopher, but this is incorrect. In 1458, the year of Alfonso's death, Charles VIII (Karl Knutsson) of Sweden was deposed and succeeded by Christian I, formerly Count of Oldenburg, d. 1481. From 1440 to 1448, however, the same monarch ceded the throne to Christopher of Bavaria—presumably the Christopher mentioned here. (*LG*)

136. The *Historia Bohemica* was Aeneas's last work before his elevation to the pontificate. It was first printed in 1475; it also appears in his *Opera*, 81–143. The later chapters on Ladislas are largely identical with the account given in his *Historia Friderici III*: see Voigt, II, 331ff. Alfonso died on June 27, 1458: Pastor, II, 467.

137. August 14, 1458: see Pastor, II, 494.

138. Guillaume d'Estouteville (c. 1412–1483), created cardinal by Eugenius IV in 1439, a powerful and wealthy prelate with a distinguished record of service to the Church. Eugenius and Nicholas V both entrusted him with important missions to France, in the course of which he often championed the interests of the papacy against those of the Valois kings. In the following chapters he is portrayed as entirely the tool of French policy—not an entirely fair assessment. See *NCE*, V, 379.

139. I.e., Guillaume d'Estouteville (Rouen); Pietro Barbo (San Marco); Giovanni da Castiglione (Pavia) and Antonio de la Cerda (Lerida) .

140. Exodus 32:9, 33:3, 34:9

141. Alain de Coëtivy.

142. Respectively, Cardinals Bessarion, Isidore of Kiev, Fieschi, Juan de Torquemada, Alain de Coëtivy, Prospero Colonna, Giovanni da Castiglione and Rodrigo Borgia (the vice-chancellor). Borgia had been appointed to this post by his uncle Calixtus III in 1457; he held it through four pontificates until his own election as Alexander VI in 1492.

143. Latino Orsini, Filippo Calandrini and Jacopo Tebaldo.

144. Jeremiah 7:11, Matthew 21:13; Mark 11:17, Luke 19:46.

145. Psalm 93:11.

146. Branda da Castiglione, 1350–1443, a key figure at the Council of Constance.

147. Psalm 35:10.

148. 2 Corinthians 11:14.

149. I.e., the Italians Fieschi, Orsini, Calandrini, Barbo, Castiglione, Piccolomini and Tebaldo. Tebaldo, however, did not vote for Aeneas in the first scrutiny, but acceded to him afterwards.

150. All of them Italian or Iberian prelates: Fieschi, Orsini, de la Cerda, Calandrini, Barbo, de Mila, de Mella, Castiglione, and Jaime, the Portuguese prince. Pastor, III, 14–15, stresses that interventions by Milan and Naples were crucial in Aeneas's election: Ottone del Carretto, the Milanese envoy, secured for Aeneas the votes of Cardinals de la Cerda, de Mila and Borgia (though Borgia did not vote for Aeneas in the first scrutiny, but was the first to accede to him afterwards).

151. Acts 10:10.

152. Isidore of Kiev and Juan de Torquemada.

153. Jacopo Tebaldo.

154. Ottone del Carretto's report to Francesco Sforza of August 20, 1458, one of the chief sources of information on the conclave, suggests that Colonna's support had already been secured by previous agreement: see Pastor, III, 14ff.

155. James 1:17.

156. The Castel Sant'Angelo, on the bank of the Tiber.

157. Sforza had hoped for Capranica. Carretto, in his report of August 14, 1458 (Pastor, III, Appendix I), refers to the death of Capranica as having spoiled the hopes of Milan.

158. See 1.19.10.

159. George of Podêbrady (see 1.22.2) was elected king of Bohemia on March 2, 1458, a few months after the death of Ladislas Postumus: see Pastor, II, 441.

BOOK II

1. The Seljuk Turks emerged from of Central Asia ("eastern Scythia") in the eleventh century and conquered much of Byzantine Anatolia. A successor state ruled by the Ottoman dynasty emerged in northwest Anatolia about 1300; in 1352, the Byzantine pretender John Cantacuzenus summoned a group of Ottoman mercenaries into Thrace, where they soon turned on their master, capturing several important fortresses. In 1361 they took Adrianople (Edirne), which remained the Ottoman capital until Mehmed II captured Constantinople in 1453. See H. Inalcik, *The Ottoman Empire: The Classical Age* (London, 1973), 5–10.

2. Constantine XI Palaeologus, whose body was never recovered. See the account of the city's fall at 1.26.1.

3. The Battle of Belgrade, 1456. See 1.32.2.

4. The author here draws on most of the standard topics of medieval Christian polemic against Islam. See B. Z. Kedar, *Crusade and Mission: European Approaches to the Muslims* (Princeton, 1984), 85–93; J. V. Tolan, *Saracens: Islam in the Medieval European Imagination* (New York, 2002). For the recycling of these commonplaces in Renaissance crusade rhetoric see R. Schwoebel, *The Shadow of the Crescent: The Renaissance Image of the Turk*, Nieuwkoop, 1967; J. Hankins, "Renaissance Crusaders: Humanist Crusade Literature in the Age of Mehmed II," *Dumbarton Oaks Papers*, 49, 1995, 111–207.

5. The *Bull Vocavit nos Pius*, issued October 13, 1458, designated June 1, 1459 for the opening of the congress: see Pastor, III, 24, with a note discussing its date.

6. The Bruttii were an ancient Italic people of Calabria, where the Capo dell'Armi forms the toe of the "boot" of Italy.

7. The eleventh-century Norman conquerors of Naples had sworn an oath of fealty to the pope, but in 1265 Urban IV proclaimed Charles of

Anjou king as part of his campaign to remove Manfred and Conradin, the heirs of Frederick II and his Norman forebears, from the kingdom. Later French claims on Naples ultimately derived from Urban's grant to Charles of Anjou.

8. In 1420, Giovanna II, a direct descendant of Charles of Anjou, rejected her distant cousin Louis in favor of Alfonso of Aragon (his family had occupied parts of Sicily since the late thirteenth century). Less than three years later, however, she reconciled with Louis, who died in 1434, leaving his brother René to challenge Alfonso for the kingdom after Giovanna's death in 1435. Eugenius IV recognized Alfonso as king in 1443, in which year he made a triumphant entry into Naples: see J. H. Bentley, *Politics and Culture in Renaissance Naples* (Princeton, 1987), 7–12.

9. I.e., means the Medici, especially Cosimo, whose name appears in a marginal note opposite this passage on f. 72ᵛ of MS BAV Reg. 1995. (*LG*)

10. Alfonso died on June 27, 1458, Calixtus on August 6. See 1.35.4–5.

11. Psalm 123:7.

12. Rodrigo Borgia.

13. Niccolò Forteguerri, a relative of Pius's mother Vittoria, was made cardinal of S. Cecilia in March, 1460: see Pastor, III, 297. His secret mission was to negotiate the betrothal of the pope's nephew, Antonio Piccolomini, to the natural daughter of Ferrante. (*LG*)

14. The *referendarius* received petitions and reported them to the pope, an office which lent itself to bribery. (*LG*)

15. Jacopo Ammanati (1422–1479), humanist scholar and protégé of Pius, who appointed him bishop and then cardinal of Pavia (in 1460 and 1461, respectively) and adopted him into the Piccolomini family: see *DBI*, II, 802–3. Ammanati wrote his own *Commentaries* as a continuation of Pius's work, in close imitation of the pope's style. The texts are printed together in the Frankfurt edition of 1614. Gregorio (or Goro) Lolli, a close friend from Pius's student days in Siena, was the son of his aunt Bartolomea Tolomei (see 1.2.3).

16. Berardo Eroli, made cardinal of S. Sabina in 1460: see Pastor, III, 297.

17. 1.31.6.

18. Niccolò d'Andrea Piccolomini, whom Pius had appointed commandant of the fortress: see Voigt, III, 554.

19. Nicholas of Cusa.

20. Jaime, son of the Infante Pedro of Portugal: see 1.30.3.

21. Pietro Barbo, the future Paul II.

22. Matthew 7:15.

23. Matthew 8:20, Luke 9:58.

24. Giovanni Orsini.

25. Everso, count of Anguillara, d. 1464: see *DBI*, III, 302–3.

26. 1.22.4.

27. Niccolò Palmieri.

28. Vergil, *Georg.*, 1.349, *Aen.* 3.81.

29. Matthew 9:20, 14:36.

30. The papal legate Egidio Albornoz (1295–1367): see *DBI*, II, 45–53.

31. Cicero, *Off.* 1.33.

32. Ulrich Riederer.

33. This ambiguous reply reflects the dilemma in which Pius found himself. Matthias Corvinus, who was actually in possession of royal power in Hungary and thus a usurper in the eyes of Frederick III, was already engaged in war against the Turks. Pius had no desire to antagonize this active ally in the cause of Christendom while trying to enlist the aid of the reluctant Frederick. A good account of these relations is given by Voigt, III, 660ff. (*LG*)

34. The treaty was agreed on April 18, 1454: see F. Babinger, *Mehmed the Conquerer and his Time,* transl. R. Manheim (Princeton, 1978), 110–111, who characterizes the terms as fairly advantageous to Venice.

35. In 1439.

36. 2.14.13.

37. Bartolo of Sassoferrato (1314–1357), the most famous jurist of the late Middle Ages. Baldo degli Ubaldi (1327–1400) and his brother Angelo (d. 1423) were famous pupils of his.

38. Andrea d'Oddo Fortebraccio, Count of Montone, captured Perugia in 1416 and carved a state for himself from its territory; he died shortly after a failed attempt on L'Aquila in 1424: see M. Mallett, *Mercenaries and their Masters* (London, 1974), 69–75.

39. In 1440.

40. February 1.

41. Federico da Montefeltro (1422–1482), count of Urbino, the celebrated *condottiere* and patron of arts and letters.

42. The son of Duke Amedeus VIII, who had died in 1451.

43. Pliny the Elder, *Hist. nat.* 36.91.

44. In 1414: see P. Partner, *The Papal State under Martin V* (London, 1958), 19–29.

45. February 22.

46. Francesco de' Todeschini Piccolomini, later Pope Pius III (1503).

47. He died at Buonconvento in 1313.

48. Vergil, *Aen.* 4.508.

49. The Venetian Senate had designated its own candidate and resented Pius's infringement of its traditional control over ecclesiastical appointments. (*LG*)

50. Vergil, *Aen.* 1.209.

51. Luke 11:17.

52. A conspiracy discovered early in 1457 revealed that the nobles had been plotting with Piccinino to seize control of the government. Among those punished by heavy fines and exile were friends and relatives of Pius, including Goro Lolli: see Voigt, III, 32. (*LG*) See also 2.13.4.

53. Sallust, *Jug.* 10.6.

54. Antonio d'Andrea da Modanella-Piccolomini, yet another relation of Pius's, not the Antonio betrothed to Ferrante's daughter (see note to 2.5.5).

55. The tomb, in the church of S. Francesco, was destroyed by fire in the seventeenth century but portrait busts of the couple survive and are still displayed in the choir of the church.

56. Jean Jouffroy, bishop of Arras, made cardinal December 18, 1461, and Burchard of Weissbriach, appointed in March, 1460; his elevation was not published till May 31, 1462.

57. See 1.21.2–3 and 1.35.3.

58. See 1.37.5.

59. Although Pius does not reveal the author's name, the title "Cardinal-Presbyter" seems to point to Alain de Coëtivy, bishop of Avignon, a leader of the French party in the Curia. (*LG*)

60. Matthew 5:11.

61. Nicholas of Cusa.

62. The *gonfaloniere della giustizia*, the ceremonial head of the Florentine government.

63. Pius stayed in Florence from April 25 to May 5.

64. Pius's account is based on Leonardo Bruni's *History of the Florentine People*, as the reference to Totila shows. Bruni's history argued that it had been Totila, not Attila the Hun, who had destroyed Florence in late antiquity. See Leonardo Bruni, *History of the Florentine People*, ed. J. Hankins, ITRL 3 (Cambridge, Mass., 2001), 1.76.

65. 2.21.2.

66. Emperor Charles IV (r. 1346–1378), who travelled through Tuscany twice, in 1355 and 1368, never actually approached the city. Both journeys were invoked in later political rhetoric to encourage patriotic resistance to outside aggression: see G. Brucker, *The Civic World of Early Renaissance Florence* (Princeton, 1977), 291, 343, 382.

67. Walter of Brienne ruled Florence 1342–1343.

68. Cosimo de' Medici (1389–1464). He was exiled in 1433 but returned in triumph the next year. For a brief account of his career see J. R. Hale, *Florence and the Medici: The Pattern of Control* (London, 1977), 20–42; *ER*, IV, 90–93.

69. The political and fiscal issues leading up to the *parlemento* of August 1458 were rather more complicated than Pius suggests: see Hale, *Florence and the Medici*, 37–38.

70. Cosimo's grandfather Averardo was nicknamed Bicci, and his son Giovanni was known as Giovanni di Bicci; they were a minor branch of the Medici family, but there is no truth to the claim they were adopted. (*LG*)

71. Vergil, *Aen.* 9.166–7.

72. Antonio Pierozzi (called Antonino), d. May 2, 1459, canonized in 1523.

73. I.e., the Priors, known collectively as the Signoria or town council.

74. Giangaleazzo Visconti (1351–1402), duke of Milan

75. Coluccio Salutati (1331–1406), Leonardo Bruni (1370–1444), Carlo Marsuppini, (1398–1453), Poggio Bracciolini (1380–1459).

76. Filippo Scolari (1369–1426) who served Sigismund of Hungary for many years; Niccolò Acciaiuoli (1310–1365) whose adopted son, Neri (c. 1394), seized the duchy of Athens from the Catalans in 1388: *DBI*, I, 85–86, 87–90. Athens fell to Mehmed II in 1460.

77. See note to 1.31.2.

78. Isotta degli Atti, buried in the famous *Tempio Malatestiano* (the church of S. Francesco a Rimini, rebuilt to designs by Leon Battista Alberti).

79. Ovid, *Met.* 8.97.

80. Astorre Manfredi.

81. See M. G. Pernis and L. Schneider Adams, *Federico da Montefeltro and Sigismondo Malatesta: The Eagle and the Elephant* (New York, 1996).

82. See 2.4.1–3.

83. Rudolf of Habsburg, elected in 1273, defeated Ottokar in the battle of Marchfeld in 1278.

84. All were grandsons of the Duke Rudolf IV of Austria, who divided the Habsburg possessions in Austria among his offspring. Ernst (d. 1424) was lord of Styria, and Frederick IV (d. 1439) regent of the Tyrol; their

cousin was Albert IV, duke of Austria (d. 1404). Pius most likely refers here, however, to his son, Albert V (d. 1439), who in 1438 was elected Emperor Albert II and was the father of Ladislas.

85. Vergil, *Aen.* 1.240.

86. I.e., Frederick V of Austria (1415–93) and his brother Albert VI (1418–1463). 1439 saw the death of this Frederick's uncle, Frederick IV of the Tyrol, and of his father's cousin, Emperor Albert II. Frederick immediately assumed guardianship of his young cousins: Frederick IV's son Sigismund of the Tyrol and Albert's posthumously born son Ladislas (1440–1457), thus making himself the leader of the crowded House of Habsburg. It was from this position of strength that he was elected king of the Romans, with the title Frederick III, in 1440. See V. Press, 'The Habsburg Lands: The Holy Roman Empire, 1400–1555," in *Handbook of European History 1400–1600,* eds. T. A. Brady, H. A. Oberman and J. D. Tracy, 2 vols (Leiden, 1994), I, 441–4.

87. In 1446.

88. In the battle of Sempach, 1386.

89. In 1422.

90. In 1412.

91. Summer 1444.

92. Cafaggiolo.

93. *Baldassare* Canetoli murdered Annibale Bentivoglio in 1445; he was executed three years later. For these events and the rule of Sante see C. Ady, *The Bentivoglio of Bologna: A Study in Despotism* (London, 1937), 15–59.

94. Pius's joke: a "legate" is one who is sent (in this case one sent by the pope to rule the city); a "ligate", from *ligatus,* is one who is bound or tied up.

95. Pius stayed in Bologna May 9–16.

96. Bornio di Beltrame da Sala: *DBI,* XII, 801–3.

97. Both Niccolò Albergati and Francesco Pizzolpasso were early patrons of Aeneas: see 1.4.1 and 1.8.3. Albergati's negotiations with France and Burgundy occasioned Aeneas's mission to Scotland.

98. See 2.18.2.

99. Orlando Bonarli, appointed in a brief dated May 11, 1459.

100. Pius stayed in Ferrara from May 17 to 25.

101. In 1101, when Henry IV (1056–1106), not III, was emperor. Countess Matilda of Tuscany (1046–1115), allied with the papacy against the empire in the conflict over investitures.

102. In 1240.

103. In 1309.

104. The Council of Ferrara-Florence, which began in Ferrara in 1438 before moving to Florence in 1439; its primary task was to bring about a union between the Greek Orthodox and Roman Catholic Churches. See 1.7.1.

105. Niccolò d'Este died in 1441, Lionello in 1450. Borso ruled 1450–1471: see *ER*, II, 293–5.

106. See 1.24.5.

107. Guarino da Verona (1370–1460), distinguished humanist educator and translator; Giovanni Aurispa (1376–1459), a humanist most famous for bringing numerous manuscripts of the Greek classics to Italy; Giannozzo Manetti (1396–1459), Florentine diplomat, orator and scholar, a student of Greek and Hebrew: see Giannozzo Manetti, *Biographical Writings*, ed. S. U. Baldassarri and R. Bagemihl, ITRL 9 (Cambridge, Mass., 2003).

108. Lodovico II Gonzaga (1414–1478).

109. The Florentine Luca Fancelli, who in 1444 was entrusted by the Gonzaga with the transformation of the old Castello into the Palazzo Ducale.

110. Vergil, *Ecl.* 9.28.

111. Apparently, the synod called by Nicholas II in 1059, though this was actually held at the Lateran.

112. Lodovico I Gonzaga (1267–1360) seized power in 1328: see *ER*, III, 78–9.

113. Gianfrancesco II Gonzaga (1395–1444), made a marquis in 1433. His wife was Paola Malatesta.

114. Horace, *Serm.* 1.5.32.

115. Vittorino da Feltre (1397–1446), a famous humanist schoolmaster who ran the palace school in Mantua from 1423 until his death.

116. Alfonso II, son of Ferrante.

117. Ippolita, one of the most famous woman humanists of the Renaissance, is believed to have composed the speech herself. It is printed together with Pius's reply, in Mansi, II, 192, 194.

Bibliography

EDITIONS

Pii Secundi Pontificis Maximi Commentarii rerum memorabilium quae temporibus suis contigerunt, a R. D. Ioanne Gobellino vicario Bonnensi iam diu compositi, et a R. P. D. Francisco Bandino Picolomineo Archiepiscopo Senensi ex vetusto originali recogniti. Rome: ex Typographia Dominici Basae, 1584. The expurgated text, edited by Cardinal Francesco Bandini, based on *B*.

Pii Secundi Pontificis Maximi commentarii rerum memorabilium quae temporibus suis contigerunt, a R. D. Ioanne Gobellino Vicario Bonnensi iamdiu compositi et a R. P. D. Francisco Bandino Picolomineo Archiepiscopo Senensi ex vetusto originali recogniti, quibus hac editione accedunt Jacobi Picolominei, Cardinalis Papiensis . . . rerum gestarum sui temporis et ad Pii continuationem commentarii luculentissimi . . . eiusdemque epistolae perelegantes. Frankfurt: Officina Aubriana, 1614. Reprint of the 1584 edition, with the continuation by Cardinal Jacopo Ammannati-Piccolomini.

I Commentarii. Enea Silvio Piccolomini Papa Pio II, ed. L. Totaro. Milan: Adelphi, 1984. Critical edition based on *B*.

Pii II Commentarii rerum memorabilium que temporibus suis contingerunt, ed. A. van Heck. Vatican City: Biblioteca Apostolica Vaticana, 1984. Critical edition based on *A*.

Pii Secundi Pontificis Maximi Commentarii, eds. I. Bellus and I. Boronkai. Budapest: Belassi Kiadó, 1993. The latest critical edition, based on *B*.

ENGLISH TRANSLATIONS

The Commentaries of Pius II. Translation by Florence Alden Gragg, with an introduction and historical notes by Leona C. Gabel. *Smith College Studies in History* 22 (1936–7), 25 (1939–40), 30 (1947), 35 (1951), 43 (1957). Based on *A*.

Memoirs of a Renaissance Pope: The Commentaries of Pope Pius II. An Abridge-

ment, trans. F. A. Gragg, ed. L. C. Gabel. New York, 1959; repr. New York, 1962.

Secret Memoirs of a Renaissance Pope: The Commentaries of Aeneas Sylvius Piccolomini, Pius II, trans. F. A. Gragg, ed. Leona C. Gabel. London, 1988; repr. London, 1991.

Travels in Italy: Selections from the Commentarii of Pope Pius II. Edited with an introduction and commentary by Andrew Hutchinson. Bedminster: Bristol Classical, 1988.

SELECTED STUDIES

Abulafia, D. "Ferrante I of Naples, Pope Pius II and the Congress of Mantua (1459)." In *Montjoie: Studies in Crusade History in Honour of Hans Eberhard Mayer*, eds. Jonathan Riley-Smith, Rudolf Hiestand and Benjamin Z. Kedar, pp. 235–49. Aldershot, England, 1997.

Bryer, A. *Council and Comune: The Conciliar Movement and the Fifteenth-Century Heritage*. London, 1979.

Ceserani, R. "Rassegna bibliografica di studi piccolominiani." *Giornale storico della letteratura italiana* 141 (1964): 265–82.

Cochrane, E. *Historians and Historiography in the Italian Renaissance*. Chicago, 1981.

Feinberg, R. "Aeneas Silvius Piccolomini (1405–1464), Pope Pius II, Model of the Early Renaissance: A Select, Annotated Bibliography of English-Language Materials." *Bulletin of Bibliography* 49 (1992): 135–55.

Gaeta, F. *Il primo libro dei* Commentarii *di Pio II*. L'Aquila, 1966.

Helmrath, J. "Pius II und die Türken." In *Europa und die Türken in der Renaissance*, eds. B. Guthmüller and W. Kühlmann, pp. 79–138. Tübingen, 2000.

Ianziti, G. "Storiografia come propaganda: il caso dei 'commentarii' rinascimentali." *Società e storia* 22 (1983): 909–18.

Lacroix, J. "I *Commentarii* di Pio II fra storia e diaristica." In *Pio II e la cultura del suo tempo*, ed. L. R. Secchi Taruga, pp. 133–50. Milan, 1991.

Miglio, M. *Storiografia pontificia del Quattrocento*. Bologna, 1975.

Mitchell, R. J. *The Laurels and the Tiara: Pope Pius II, 1458–1464*. London, 1962.

Paparelli, G. *Enea Silvio Piccolomini. L'umanesimo sul soglio di Pietro*. 2nd ed. Ravenna, 1978.

Partner, P. *The Pope's Men: The Papal Civil Service in the Renaissance*. Oxford, 1990.

Pastor, L. *The History of the Popes from the Close of the Middle Ages*, trans. F. I. Antrobus. London, 1891–.

Picotti, G. B. *La Dieta di Mantova e la politica dei Veneziani*. Venice, 1912; repr. Trent, 1996.

Pozzi, M. "Struttura epica dei *Commentarii*." In *Pio II e la cultura del suo tempo*, ed. L. R. Secchi Taruga, pp. 151–62. Milan, 1991.

Rowe, J. G. "The Tragedy of Aeneas Sylvius Piccolomini." *Church History* 30 (1961): 288–313.

Russell, J. G. *Diplomats at Work: Three Renaissance Studies*. Stroud, England, 1992.

Setton, K. M. *The Papacy and the Levant, 1204–1571*. 4 vols. (see especially vol. II: *The Fifteenth Century*). Philadelphia, 1976–84.

Totaro, L. *Pio II nei suoi Commentarii*. Bologna, 1978.

Voigt, G. *Enea Silvio de' Piccolomini als Papst Pius der Zweite, und sein Zeitalter*. 3 vols. Berlin, 1856–63.

Index